THE VEGETARIAN *Guide to Eating Out*

A GUIDE TO VEGETARIAN DINING IN BRITAIN

Featuring venues to eat, drink and stay with comprehensive vegetarian options

Includes information on places to go and things to do in Britain, including those of particular interest to conservationists, and offers guidelines and suggestions pertinent to a vegetarian diet

By Alison Fife & Michael Cook

PUBLISHER'S NOTE

Working on this guide with Alison Fife and Michael Cook has been what can only be described as an enjoyable and informative experience. The team here at Griffin Publishing, whilst not totally "converted" are certainly more aware of the philosophy and understanding behind the vegetarian requirement.

We are confident that this guide continues to exemplify the high standards that we set ourselves. In broad terms our titles set out not only to be informative but also to give an enjoyable read.

My thanks to all the team for their hard work in producing this title, especially David Williams and Andrew Forsythe whose line illustrations are "second to none". To Hassina Carder for her energies as Project Manager. Her patience is beyond belief. It has been, and continues to be, my privilege to lead this young, energetic and enthusiastic bunch. We all hope that those who read this guide will get as much enjoyment from it as we did in it's production.

Howard Fagan
Griffin Publishing Ltd April 1994

Cover: Photograph courtesy of Aqua Libra, taken from 'The Recipe Year' developed by Champney's Health Resort
Starter: *Aqua Libra Melon & Lime Soup*
Main Course: *Celeriac & Wild Mushroom Terrine*
Dessert: *Poached Peach with Cinnamon Ice Cream*
Recipes: Courtesy of The Stannary, Mary Tavy, Devon

ISBN 1 898790 00 0

First published in 1994 By Griffin Publishing Ltd

Typeset by Griffin Publishing Ltd, Devon. Tel: (0752) 257034
Scanning and filmwork by TYPEstyle, Devon. Tel: (0752) 698668
Printed and bound in Great Britain by BPCC Wheatons Ltd, Devon. Tel: (0392) 74121

FOREWORD

BY NICOLA GRAIMES

Editor of "Vegetarian Living" Magazine

FIRST BITE

When I became a vegetarian twelve years ago, eating out was often a disappointing affair, restricted to restaurants offering a token meat-free dish. More often than not this was a limp looking omelette or uninspiring lasagne. It was always an unexpected pleasure to discover a restaurant or café whose chef had obviously made an effort to offer vegetarians something more exotic or adventurous. Then there was the added problem of soups made with meat stocks, cheese made with animal rennet, and gelatine used in terrines.

Whilst it would be misleading to say dining out is now all plain sailing, the situation has *vastly* improved over the years. In many areas of the country, particularly in larger cities, there are a wealth of restaurants to choose from, whether they be Italian, Indian or British.

This indispensable guide to eating out helps remove the drudgery of finding such places. Whether you're searching for a quick wholesome bite or an elaborate three course extravaganza, "*The Vegetarian Guide to Eating Out*" lists the feasible options.

The latest research carried out by Gallup reveals that over the last three years a staggering 2,000 people every week have become vegetarian. There are now around 2,500,000 adults in the UK who have rejected meat and fish. What's more, fifty per cent of the population have cut down on the amount of meat they eat. It's refreshing to see that many restaurateurs are responding to this rapidly growing trend, rather than seeing vegetarians as inconvenient and cranky!

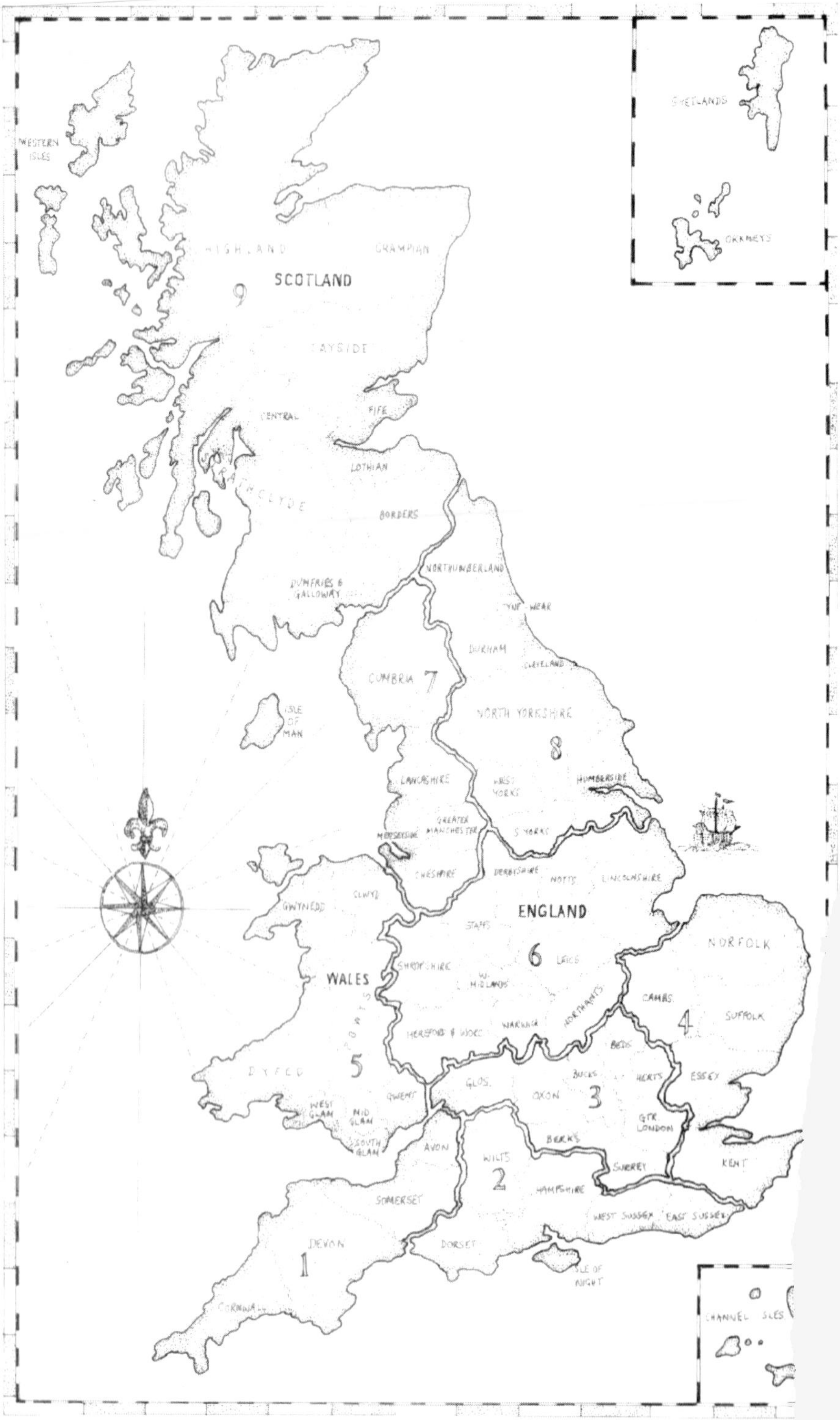
WESTERN ISLES
SHETLANDS
ORKNEYS
HIGHLAND
GRAMPIAN
SCOTLAND
9
TAYSIDE
CENTRAL
FIFE
LOTHIAN
STRATHCLYDE
BORDERS
NORTHUMBERLAND
DUMFRIES & GALLOWAY
TYNE WEAR
DURHAM
CLEVELAND
CUMBRIA 7
ISLE OF MAN
NORTH YORKSHIRE
8
LANCASHIRE
WEST YORKS
HUMBERSIDE
GREATER MANCHESTER
MERSEYSIDE
S YORKS
CHESHIRE
DERBYSHIRE
NOTTS
LINCOLNSHIRE
CLWYD
GWYNEDD
ENGLAND
STAFFS
NORFOLK
6
LEICS
SHROPSHIRE
W. MIDLANDS
WALES
POWYS
CAMBS
SUFFOLK
4
HEREFORD & WORC
WARWICK
NORTHANTS
BEDS
DYFED
5
BUCKS
HERTS
ESSEX
GLOS
OXON
3
GWENT
WEST GLAM
MID GLAM
GTR LONDON
SOUTH GLAM
AVON
BERKS
WILTS
SURREY
KENT
2
HAMPSHIRE
SOMERSET
WEST SUSSEX
EAST SUSSEX
DEVON
DORSET
1
ISLE OF WIGHT
CORNWALL
CHANNEL ISLES

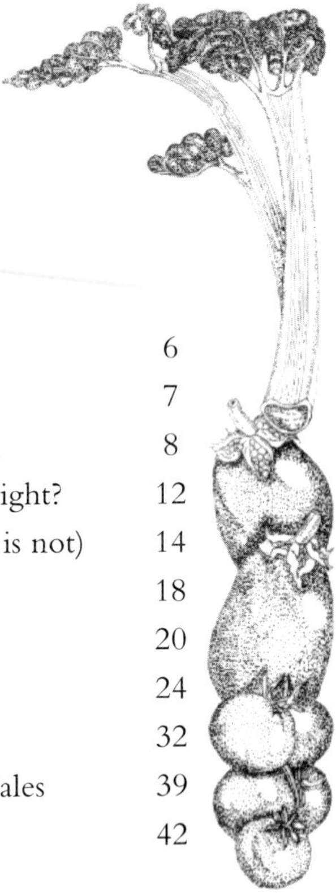

CONTENTS

REGIONAL OPTIONS

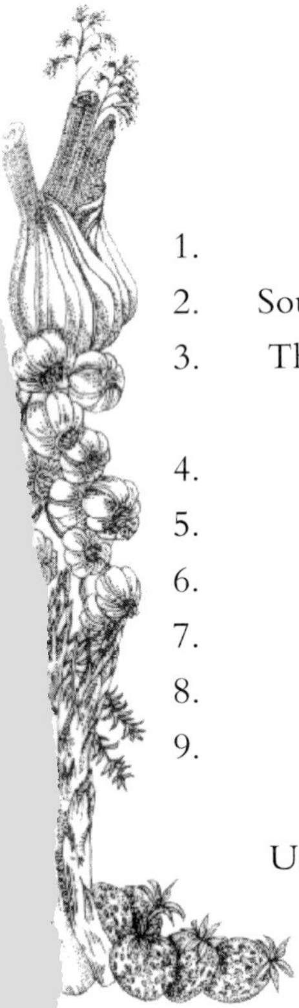

ABOUT THIS BOOK

Alison Fife & Michael Cook of the highly acclaimed vegetarian restaurant, The Stannary in Mary Tavy, Devon, introduce you to this guide

We hope that 'The Vegetarian Guide to Eating Out' will prove to be a valuable source of information for all readers, whether vegetarian or not.

As well as detailed information on a vast array of places to eat, you will find a number of articles on related subjects, general details about each region to assist visitors to the area, lists of useful addresses, a few recipes and some other bits and pieces of information, all of which should add up to an interesting read.

The aim of the guide is to provide as much information as possible on each establishment so that anyone looking for somewhere to eat out can judge which place is best suited to them, in terms not just of food but also ambience and style. There are no subjective reviews or criticisms, the information given being based solely on details provided by proprietors.

Efforts have been made to ensure that proprietors and chefs, most particularly of non-vegetarian establishments, have a full understanding of the requirements of both vegetarian and vegan diets, and that the food they provide really is suitable, at all courses. Where the establishments featured are 100% vegetarian they have been indicated accordingly on the contents page of each chapter.

Inevitably there will be some eating establishments that are providing vegetarian fare but are not included. There are three possible reasons for this, firstly that we simply were not aware of their existence despite careful research, secondly that they did not exist or did not provide vegetarian fare at the time of going to press, and thirdly that having been approached they have decided, for whatever reason, not to be included.

As this guide will be published regularly we would very much like to receive personal views on eating establishments, either those currently included or those not, in order that future editions can reflect the findings of the many individuals using the book.

"NOTHING WITH A FACE"

People come to vegetarianism and veganism from many different angles, their reasons as diverse as medical intolerance, concern for personal health, a dislike of the taste of meat, religious doctrine, a moral objection to farming methods, awareness of environmental damage caused by farming, the waste of the world's resources, or simply an ethical objection to consuming animals.

One simple definition of a vegetarian is that he or she consumes nothing with a face, another way of saying nothing that is, or has come from, a dead animal. This includes all meat, poultry, fish and sea food as well as animal fats and other products made as a result of the death of a creature, such as rennet, cochineal, isinglass, etc. Vegetarians also do not eat eggs other than those produced by hens which are free-range. They do however eat dairy products, provided they have not been treated in any way with animal derivatives, so milk, cheese (made with animal rennet), pure butter, pure yoghurt and so on are acceptable.

Vegans consume nothing at all that comes from an animal, living or dead, so will not eat any dairy products. This also includes honey, because of the supposed exploitation of bees.

Vegetarians and vegans may be travelling in the same direction, so to speak, but not necessarily on the same path.

Avoiding meat and fish itself is relatively easy as all restaurateurs and food producers will know if the main ingredients are suitable, but the difficulty comes with emulsifiers, colourisers, stabilisers and other additives, often not clearly marked, or in any way indicated, on a menu or product label. A more comprehensive list of those suitable and not suitable is given elsewhere in this guide, or can be obtained from the Vegetarian Society's Handbook.

THE RESTAURANT EQUATION

JUST WHAT COULD, OR SHOULD, YOU EXPECT FROM 'THE VEGETARIAN OPTION'

Michael Cook and Alison Fife reflect on the restaurateur's point of view

Having found we couldn't get the sort of meal we wanted anywhere we decided to open a restaurant. Actually the whole thing wasn't anything like that simple, but we mention it to show that before we were restaurateurs we were normal, everyday sort of people who occasionally went out for meals. Now we know the problems from both sides. More importantly, we are well aware from the many friends and acquaintances we've made since we opened this business five years ago, how some other restaurateurs tend to perceive vegetarians.

Every vegetarian would like to be able to walk into any restaurant and get a good and truly vegetarian meal. This is such stuff as dreams are made of. Maybe it will happen one day, but it is certainly a long way off.

In the meantime, and to speed progress, it might be helpful for some of us to think about things from the other side. Does the average restaurateur actually *want* to provide vegetarian meals? Sometimes the vegetarian option is there not to please the vegetarian specifically, but to catch the party reservation that might contain one vegetarian. Of course this is a generalisation and there are seriously good restaurants out there catering well for vegetarians.

Vegetarians are special cases

As vegetarians, all that's different about us is that we don't eat meat or fish so we don't, on the whole, think of ourselves as particularly special cases, but for the vast majority of those providing meals for us we are special. We don't eat the things they want to provide for us. They are providing a particular service for those who want that service, not for people who want something different. Of course they should all provide good vegetarian options, and we should do all we can to persuade them of that, but ultimately the choice of what they provide is theirs. Likewise, we have the choice to eat there or not, and if we don't get what we want then we have gone to the wrong place.

If you are shopping for clothes you know you cannot walk into the first shop and expect them to have exactly what you want, and it is exactly the same with food. After all, you wouldn't go into an Indian restaurant and insist on a

Chinese meal. Different establishments provide different fare, so you might have to shop around for what suits you whether you are vegetarian or not. We can't expect most chefs, who have gone through years of training and working with meat in all its worst aspects, to have much real sympathy for vegetarianism. The best we can hope is that they accept we have a point of view which is different to their's.

It is a fact that vegans and vegetarians *generally* spend less than meat-eaters, so there is less profit for the restaurant. We once had a couple of vegans in The Stannary paying just £2.50 each for a starter and making it last all evening, and they only wanted wine if it was free! (Now you realise why many establishments introduce a minimum charge.) It makes vegetarians and vegans just about as welcome as the tax inspector in most restaurants!

Even in most vegetarian establishments it seems that the majority of customers are not vegetarians. The reasons are probably many, the most important one being that the food is good, other possibilities being that vegetarians are less used to eating out because of the difficulties; vegetarians tend to eat less because they give more consideration to the way they feed themselves; vegetarians tend to be people of a younger generation or in the caring professions and therefore can have a lower disposable income.

Cost or Quality

Perhaps this is why most fully vegetarian 'restaurants' are actually cafes or bistros - whatever they might be called (the word restaurant has come to be used for a very wide range of eating establishments, and really a cafe that is open in the evenings is not a restaurant, but that's another subject). But some vegetarians do want comfort. There is a place for good quality cutlery and crockery, comfortable surroundings, pictures on walls and so on, and for food which is of a particularly high standard, using special ingredients. And quality does cost money.

In most restaurants (across the board that is, not specifically vegetarian) food costs are 30% of the bill, in many it is even less, and this is the way it has to be to cover staff and overheads. In an edition of The Good Food Guide a few years ago the proprietor of a leading country house hotel with a highly rated restaurant, where the average cost of a meal for two was £100, outlined his costs. Their food and drink costs were over 30% of the bill (yes, one person can eat £17 worth of ingredients at one meal) and after staff and basic overheads just £5 was left to go towards the costs of using the building. Luckily for them that cost is really borne by the hotel side of the business or they would not be able to survive. How many people when comparing the costs of eating the same food at home take into consideration the flowers on the table, the laundry costs or petrol to collect supplies?

Of course there are rogues and charlatans out there, but most publicans and restaurateurs are serious honest people doing their utmost to provide a good service. Usually you do get what you pay for, no more and no less.

So whether making comparisons between eating at home or in a restaurant, or in one establishment rather than another, the equation can be a complex one.

But returning specifically to vegetarianism, vegetarian cafe or bistro prices do tend to be the same as in other cafes or bistros, but vegetarian restaurants tend to be cheaper than comparable restaurants, because it is not possible to charge such high prices when comparisons are made not with other normal restaurants, but with other forms of vegetarian establishments. Yet vegetarian restaurants have the same overheads as other restaurants, the same staffing levels, and so on.

How cheap is cheap?

In fact it is something of a misconception that vegetables are necessarily cheaper than meat, and indeed it is not just vegetables that we are talking about, but grains, nuts, seaweeds, dairy products and many other ingredients that are used to create vegetarian dishes. Much can be at least as expensive as meat, some more so, particularly if using organic, fresh, high quality produce. Remember too the herbs and spices often included more profusely in vegetarian dishes; they cost a very great deal more than meat.

Also, vegetarian cheese and free-range eggs are more expensive than normal, and restaurants have to get in stock they would otherwise not buy, often having to use specialist suppliers and not getting their usual bulk discounts.

One of the most important considerations however is not the ingredients but the considerable extra preparation time involved as things are normally created, rather than just bought and grilled or fried with a sauce poured over.

Lower demand, some higher costs and extra time involved together can make vegetarian food more expensive for normal restaurants, not cheaper.

Just how far have we really come?

With the majority of vegetarians being in their teens and early twenties it is strange that vegetarianism is perceived as being stuck in the '60's, long before those people were born. Many people seriously do believe you have to be a hippy, have to have alternative views on almost everything, and have to lead a very basic life, eating only very basic foods. Some people certainly do want this way of life and many of them are vegetarian, but there are also many people who simply don't eat meat or fish but are otherwise unrecognisable.

With growth of interest in eating healthily, prompted to an extent by food scares such as salmonella poisoning and BSE, there are a lot of new recruits to vegetarianism, or at least towards it. Some of these and other would-be vegetarians, particularly the more mature amongst them, can actually be put off by the thought that they will be classed as a part of society they don't feel they belong to. There are also some who are totally vegetarian at home, but not when eating out because they cannot get the sort of meal they want, in the surroundings they want. That indeed is a sad reflection on the majority of restaurants, including the vegetarian ones.

The number of fully vegetarian restaurants in nonspecific restaurant guides is tiny, but there are some, so a handful are showing that vegetarian restaurants can be judged by the same yardstick as other restaurants.

Very occasionally restaurateurs do take advantage of anyone on a 'different' diet, with prices high for no particularly good reason. We know one restaurant which simply put up the price of the vegetarian meal to stop 'meat-eaters' opting for it! Our experience is that the vegetarian option is sometimes more expensive in pubs and 'cheaper' establishments, whereas it tends to be cheaper, or certainly better value for money, in high quality restaurants.

Some of what we have said is certainly in defence of the restaurateur, yet we join wholeheartedly in every effort to encourage better vegetarian food in all pubs, cafes, wine bars and restaurants. Despite the fact that we ourselves run a vegetarian restaurant, we want more places around to be doing good vegetarian food. Everyone is likely to try a vegetarian meal at least once, if that experience is bad they won't try again, but if it is good they will have a vegetarian meal again, so good competition is healthy.

A while ago we went to a restaurant that had a separate vegetarian menu. To our horror we came across a piece of bacon in the main course. None of the desserts were suitable as we knew them all to be brought in and almost every gateau or cheesecake from a supplier has gelatine in it. We were then overcharged. Needless to say, we were not happy. In talking to the owner we discovered that this restaurateur, providing a vegetarian choice on his menu, didn't even know that normal cheese is not vegetarian! Realising afterwards how complicated it was to cater **properly** for vegetarians, that restaurant took the option off their menu. Surely it is better to have no choice than one which is unsuitable?

The answer is only to eat in places known to be doing good food for vegetarians (in whatever price band), with 'The Vegetarian Guide to Eating Out' tucked under your arm.

CAN THE CUSTOMER ALWAYS BE RIGHT?

There are two sides to every story, although it is commonly held that 'the customer is always right', and when straightforward enough most restaurateurs (but definitely not all) aim to work to this principal. But incidents have occurred that have led proprietors to charge, or as a last resort to sue, the customer. There are cases too of customers suing restaurants, but this is less frequent, which must go to prove something or other.

It is important to know that when you make a booking for a room at a hotel or a table at a restaurant, you and the establishment have made a legal contract. It is a fallacy that "a verbal contract is only as good as the paper it is written on", so even though made by phone and not letter, a booking is still a contract. The very last thing anyone wants, or expects, is to end up in court and generally when mistakes or disasters happen - neither restaurateurs nor customers actually being perfect - an apology will probably suffice, or a simple financial settlement will end the matter satisfactorily.

Consideration and common courtesy can save financial and emotional embarrassment, on both sides, and can avoid unnecessary cause for complaint.

Proprietors have chosen the style of food they wish to offer and the decor they feel appropriate. This is their right. If you like pine tables and a relaxed atmosphere make sure the establishment you have chosen fits with these requirements. If it doesn't, book somewhere else instead. The same applies to vegetarian fare - unless advertised as being provided you must ask, or expect to be disappointed. Those who feel all restaurants should provide vegetarian dishes without advance warning are simply being naive.

Having booked a table, it is a matter of common courtesy to arrive at the agreed time, and to be the same number of people as booked. If you know you are going to be delayed, or your party is going to be larger or smaller than anticipated, please do ring. Other people will be eating in the establishment, and the front-of-house and kitchen staff can only serve so many guests at one time, so they really do need to know if their planned timing or seating arrangements are going to be altered. Normally a restaurant will be understanding if, for instance, there is illness or the car has broken down, but if you have a less than satisfactory excuse or you simply fail to turn up the restaurant has the right to charge for loss of profits.

Equally, if you have made a booking for a certain time and number and the restaurant has accepted your booking, they must provide it, or you could charge them for your inconvenience, so it is helpful to keep a record of when you telephoned and to whom you spoke.

A restaurant, being in the business of providing food, must ensure that the food is of satisfactory quality, prepared in hygienic and safe surroundings, and as described on the menu. If, however, a dish is described as hot (in the spicy sense) be warned, your definition of hot may be many degrees cooler than the chef's, as hot in this context is a relative term; but if a dish is described as vegetarian and you find bacon in it, then this is not satisfactory, and you should complain.

You have chosen to eat in this establishment, to experience the cuisine and ability of the chef. If the practice of the house is to do the vegetables al dente, and you ask for yours well boiled, there may be agreement, albeit reluctant, to satisfy the requirement, but don't be surprised if the chef refuses to oblige. Chefs are artists, and have spent years learning to produce food the way they believe it should be, and might well retort: "if you wish to boil your vegetables to death in your own kitchen you may do so, but don't expect me to in mine". A complaint about the way something is prepared or cooked will only be justified if the item is actually cooked wrongly.

A frequent cause of acrimony is the trend to charge for service per se, although serving food is of course an integral part of a restaurant's function, and those that do add a service charge should make this clear on the menu, to be seen before you order. Poor or downright bad service is perhaps the most common cause for complaint and if the service you have received has been incompetent you have every right, at the very least, to withhold the service charge.

However, in the majority of restaurants the price of a meal is inclusive of service and if you feel you have received particularly good attention you may show you appreciation with a tip.

The management makes the rules. If they ask for a certain style of dress, they have the right to stick to that, even if they ask guests to come in swimming custumes (not that they are likely to get much custom). Likewise a restaurant can open and close when it chooses (provided it doesn't contradict their advertised times), can serve the food it chooses, and can refuse admission to whomever it chooses, unless it be on the grounds of race, colour or gender.

It is a good idea if you are planning to go to an unknown restaurant, to ask about things like the dress code when you book.

At the end of the day the last thing a restaurant wants is to sue its guests, and hopefully vice versa. If the restaurateur and the customer each remember the old saying "treat others as you would wish to be treated yourself" everything should run smoothly.

"WHAT'S ON THE MENU?"
OR MORE IMPORTANTLY, WHAT IS NOT?

Things it is useful to know especially in establishments which are not 100% vegetarian

Vegetarians and vegans generally know what is acceptable to their diet and what is not when buying ingredients to make dishes at home, and when buying ready-made products, they can always consult the ingredients list, but when eating out life becomes more complex. Unlike products in a shop, restaurants do not list the ingredients in each dish and although there has been some call for this recently it will almost certainly never happen - to the relief of chefs who, quite naturally, do not want to give away their secrets.

Every effort has been made to ensure that proprietors and chefs of establishments listed in this guide have a full understanding of the requirements of vegetarian and vegan diets, and vegetarians should at all times be able to get a good and truly vegetarian meal from any of them. But, as restaurants change hands, as chefs come and go, or when a junior chef is left in charge of the kitchen, things can possibly go awry.

NO, VEGETARIANS DON'T EAT FISH!

Unbelievably in recent years there have even been a few supposedly wholly vegetarian establishments (just a very tiny percentage) which have used non-vegetarian cheese in some dishes, and there are restaurants using 'vegetarian' in their name which include seafood on the menu. It is advisable therefore not to make assumptions, particularly as there are many establishments with what would appear to be vegetarian-sounding names or philosophies which nevertheless are not, including a number concerned with wholefood, natural and organic foods.

As some people who eat no meat but do eat fish call themselves vegetarians it is not surprising that restaurateurs don't always have a clear understanding of the situation. One restaurant at an historic house has been told by their head office to offer the fish dish to those who ask about the vegetarian option.

Another restaurant told vegetarians that the terrine was a starter suitable for them, but on further enquiry it was found to be bound with gelatine. Another said that they could not possibly make soup (in this instance it was potato and onion) without chicken stock. A survey of food provided in hospitals (this is not strictly relevant to eating out but nevertheless shows up the difficulties which can be faced) stated that vegetarians only cared that there was no meat in the dish and did not care about other animal products, and that some vegetarians do eat fish.

For most vegetarians and vegans the inclusion of animal derivatives in a meal is a great affront to their moral convictions or religious beliefs, and can cause indigestion or even symptoms similar to food poisoning. For a few the effect can be very serious as some are on their diet for medical reasons and can be made seriously ill.

Yet eating out is (or at least should be) a great pleasure in life, as well as being a necessity when travelling, and there are, as this book shows, a great many places where vegetarians can get really good food, be it a snack or dinner. It is to be hoped that the existence of this guide will encourage additional establishments to take the subject seriously and provide truly vegetarian fare, rather than the odd option of a meal without meat (but possibly with fish stocks and so on) just to be able to attract the party of mostly 'normal people' with one vegetarian.

GETTING IN ON THE ACT

Through catering publications, restaurateurs and publicans are constantly being encouraged to bear in mind that with 1 in 14 of the population now vegetarian, on most days there could be several or even dozens of vegetarians visiting their establishment. There are hundreds of ready-made vegetarian meals for them to purchase from a huge array of suppliers. Some of these are good, some are not so good, but they are generally truly vegetarian.

However one frozen food supplier has been known to list everything without meat or fish under a special title of 'Vegetarian Foods', not realising that the cheese made some items unsuitable and caterers were buying the dishes ingood faith and possibly assuring vegetarians that the food was suitable. Another supplier has even been known to tell a restaurateur that gelatine does not always come from an animal source!

Vegetarian ready-made dishes generally come in the form of main courses, and to a lesser extent starters, but only rarely desserts. The majority of eating establishments in this country (but of course not the majority included in this guide) buy-in most of their desserts, whatever they may wish you to believe, and a great many of them contain gelatine or other animal derivatives. Little thought goes into the provision of suitable desserts as it is generally assumed that all desserts are suitable anyway.

THINGS TO LOOK OUT FOR

Even products made on the premises of an establishment with a good understanding of the requirements may not always be suitable: pasta made with non-free-range eggs for instance. Here are a few things to look out for:

Aspic A meat or more generally fish gel likely to be used in savoury dishes which are set, but will most frequently be mentioned on the menu.

Beer See the separate article on the subject of wine as some beers fined in the same way as wine.

Bouillon A type of powdered stock *(q.v.)* used in many dishes to add extra flavouring, which may or may not be vegetarian.

Cheese Cheese may not be mentioned, but things described as 'au gratin', will most likely contain cheese, as will dishes like lasagne. Many farmhouse cheeses are made with a vegetable rennet but most commercial hard cheeses and some soft ones will be made with an animal rennet unless it is specified as being vegetarian. See also 'Parmesan'.

Chocolate Some actual chocolate and many chocolates contain animal fats in one form or another.

Edible fats Can be either animal or vegetable fats.

Eggs Non-free-range eggs could appear in many dishes, such as pancakes, crepes or fritters, in flans, as glazing on pastry, or even in pastry, in sauces such as hollandaise, uncooked egg whites in some sorbets, in some ice creams and true custards, as well as meringue, and of course in the form of soufflés.

Emulsifiers The most common emulsifier likely to be found in restaurants is E471 which may or may not be from an animal source (see 'Additives'). It appears in some ready-made pastry, in many ice creams and a number of other bought-in ingredients and dishes, mainly desserts. Sometimes simply the word 'emulsifier' will appear on a label with no further explanation.

Gelatine Likely to be used in terrines or moulds, many set desserts such as jellies and trifles. Sometimes written without the 'e' on the end of the word, *gelatin* is exactly the same thing. The vegetarian equivalent is agar agar.

Glycerine Used in cake icing and the like, glycerine can be either animal or vegetable.

Junket A pudding made with rennet, which may or may not be vegetarian.

Lard Could be used in pastry, in sponge puddings or for frying.

Margarine Many margarines contain animal fats, so some are not even vegetarian whilst others can be completely vegan.

Mousse The setting of a mousse can be with eggs *(q.v.)* or with gelatine *(q.v.)*, or occasionally just with whipped cream.

Pasta Frequently made with eggs *(q.v.)* and particularly watch out for black pasta which is made with squid ink.

Parmesan Many Italian dishes have parmesan cheese on top, but it is now possible to get a vegetarian parmesan.

Pastry If made on the premises it could contain lard or unsuitable margarine *(q.v.)*, if bought-in it is quite likely to contain the emulsifier E471 which may or may not be from an animal source.

Paté A vegetable paté may not necessarily be vegetarian, possibly containing aspic *(q.v.)*, gelatine *(q.v.)* or eggs *(q.v.)*.

Sauces A sauce based on a vegetable product such as tomato or a dairy product such as cream, may not necessarily be vegetarian.

Soup Even vegetable varieties may not be vegetarian, for instance 'French Onion' is traditionally made with meat stock.

Stock In many restaurants there is a general stock pot, used for soups, sauces and many other dishes, and this is likely to contain meat and/or fish. Stock cubes or bouillon *(q.v.)* are also frequently used and may not be vegetarian.

Suet Used in some sponge puddings, in some pastries and in mince-meat. Vegetarian suet is available.

Whey Often contained in ice creams, artificial creams and ready-made desserts. Whey is milk based, generally a by-product from the manufacture of cheese and may therefore have been tainted by animal rennet.

Wine See separate article on the subject of wines.

Worcester Sauce There is a vegetarian brand available, but the most common brand contains anchovies.

Yoghurt Some brands contain gelatine *(q.v.)*, whey *(q.v.)* or animal fats as well as non-vegetarian colourings. 'Natural' or 'pure' yoghurt is most likely to be acceptable.

ADDITIVES IN FOOD

Those hidden ingredients...

Although they will never appear on the menu, some food in eating establishments could contain animal-based additives, especially if pre-prepared products are used. What's more, alcoholic drinks above 1.2% of volume do not have to have ingredients listed, and neither do chocolate confectionary nor unwrapped breads and cakes, so often establishment's proprietors and chefs can not know the full ingredients themselves.

Rennet too does not have to appear on a label because it is only used in the processing and does not appear as such in the final product. This also applies to finings used mainly for drinks, and to a few other items. Flavourings, if unspecified (and the word 'flavouring' is actually all that is legally required), can be from any source but are frequently not from animals even if a meat flavouring!

In Britain there are 300 or so permitted additives which do have to appear on food labels (by either number or name). An 'E' before a number means that it is an additive approved by the EEC, but there are also many which simply have a number as they are not approved for use throughout Europe.

Due to the introduction of labelling on most shop products and the general awareness of the subject, the inclusion of some additives in some products has reduced significantly. Many, however, are still used, and some are not suitable for a vegetarian diet. The lists that follow give some of the important additives to look out for.

Colourings - E100 to E180

The red colouring **E120** is cochineal (made from scale insects) and is frequently used in desserts and some alcoholic drinks. A colouring which can sometimes be from an animal source (but generally is not) is **E513** (Carbon black), used in some concentrated fruit juices, jams, jellies and liquorice.

Preservatives - E200 to E283

Those which *could* be animal derived are **E203** (Calcium Sorbate) in some yoghurts and margarines; **E213**, (Calcium Benzoate) which, like **E203** can be found in concentrated pineapple juice; **E227** (Calcium Hydrogen Sulphite) used in beers and jams; **E252** (Potassium Nitrate or Saltpetre) mostly used in animal products but also in Dutch cheeses; **E270** (Lactic acid) which is made from milk but could use whey in the processing, is used in a large number of products including margarines, carbonated drinks, confectionary, salad dressings, pickles, tinned vegetables and fruits, jams, cottage cheese and beer; and **E282** (Calcium Propionate) used in dairy and baking products, frozen pizza and processed cheese.

Antioxidants - E300 to E321

The only antioxidant which could possibly be from an animal source is **E302** (Calcium L'Ascorbate).

Emulsifiers, stabilizers and thickeners - E322 to 495

Additives in this range which *could possibly* be from animal sources are: E327, E333, E341a-c, E404, E422 (Glycerol), 430, 431, 432, 433, 434, 435, 436, E470, E471, E472a-e, E473, E474, E475, E476, E477, 478, E481, E482, E483, 491 and 492.

Acids, bases, anti-caking agents, flavour enhancers and sweeteners - 500 to 927

Additives in this range which are *always* from animal sources are the anti-caking agent **542** (edible bone phosphate) not currently known to be used in foods; flavour enhancers **631** (Inosine 5'-[*di*Sodium Phosphate]) which is used in rice snacks, some crisps and otherwise mainly meat products, and **635** (Sodium 5-'ribonucleotide) in potato croquettes and waffles; and **904** (Shellac) made from the lac insect, used in cake decorations, sweets, fizzy orange drink and sugar strands; and the improver **920** (L-Cysteine Hydrochloride) made from hair and feathers used as a flour improver. Others which *could* be from an animal source are **570** (Stearic acid), **572** (Magnesium Stearate), **627** (Guanosine 5'-[*di*Sodium phosphate]), and **901** (Beeswax) which is generally acceptable on a vegetarian diet but not vegan, used as a dilutent in glazes for bakery goods and confectionary.

Other additives

Unnumbered additives from animal sources are Calcium, Mesoinositol, Hexaphosphate, and Spermaceti (Sperm oil); and from a possibly animal source are Butyl Stearate, Calcium Heptonate, Calcium Phytate, Glyceryl Diacetate, Iacetin, Glyceryl Monoacetate, Monoacetin, Glyceryl Triacetate, Triacetin, Glycine, Leucine, and Oxystearin.

SEAWEEDS

"Ah! call us not Weeds, but Flowers of the Sea,
For lovely and gay and bright tinted are we
Our Blush is as bright as the Rose of thy Bowers.
So call us not Weeds, but the Ocean's gay Flowers.

Not nursed like the plants of a Summer Parterre
Where winds are but Sigh of an Evening Air,
Our exquisite fragile and delicate Forms
Are reared by the Oceans, and rocked by the Storms!"

From a Victorian seaweed picture

Seaweeds have been experiencing something of a vogue in recent years - most particularly in restaurants - but still have some way to go before reaching full acceptance and their due status.

All this seems strange to people in some coastal areas, particularly in Wales, where they have been eating seaweeds, whether fashionable or not, for centuries; and possibly even more strange to people from many Asian countries who use seaweeds extensively.

Their recorded use in China goes back to at least the 6th century BC. The ancient Kings of Hawaii cultivated or harvested over 70 varieties of seaweeds, and the Maoris, with a long history of eating seaweeds, sustained themselves on karengo in long marches in the Middle East in the Second World War. The Celts and Vikings certainly made use of seaweeds on their long travels, and the Romans were particularly fond of laver.

If you are one of those people whose initial reaction to the idea of eating seaweeds is something close to disgust, you may be surprised to discover that you have eaten them. They cannot be all that bad if you weren't even aware of it. The standard vegetarian alternative to gelatine, used commercially in hundreds of dishes, is agar agar, a seaweed. Often seaweed extracts are used to hold the head on a glass of beer, or to act as a stabiliser in icecreams and other creamy desserts.

Traditionally seaweeds have simply been collected on the beach, but on our summer visits to the seaside we tend to see rotting seaweeds, covered with flies, smeared with tar and smelling awful. No one would want to eat that, but then, that is not what is eaten, it is only people's perception of seaweed. Another problem for seaweed could be the fact that 'weed' is part of the name. There are those who prefer the term 'sea vegetable', but one accepted definition of a weed is a plant simply growing in the wrong place, so on that basis a rose could be a weed, as could a potato. In the case of seaweed it perhaps refers to the plants dense uncultivated growth and its nuisance value at sea.

Actually seaweeds are now cultivated. They have been for some time in China and Japan where seaweed production is big business (in Japan 300,000 people are employed in the production of nori alone), and more recently in British waters. A seaweed farm consists of ropes impregnated with reproductive spores, attached to a rope or bamboo pole mesh which is anchored to the sea floor.

BUYING AND COOKING SEAWEEDS

In a few coastal areas around Britain, mainly in the west, you will be able to obtain fresh seaweeds at the right time of year but they are not often to be found anywhere else. Luckily they dry well, and most are available this way. Some are also available in jars.

Health food shops are one possible source of supply but oriental shops are generally better (although you may not find the label in English and may not know what you are buying!) . Specialist mail order suppliers are better still as they tend to have a good variety available.

As with any dried food, once you have opened a packet, reseal any unused quantities. Given airtight conditions, seaweeds will keep for a very long time.

Most seaweeds need soaking to reconstitute the original form, but don't try soaking nori (the Japanese name for laver, which is generally the name used for the dried product) which is not dried fronds as such but is actually made in the same way as paper to produce a square sheet.

Other dried seaweeds expand considerably on soaking, although varieties vary, so experiment with a small amount if you are not sure how much you want. First wash it quickly than add clean cold water for soaking, which will take anything from 10 to 30 minutes, depending on the variety. The amount of cooking time, and the method, is different for each seaweed, but you can usually tell from the look and feel just what sort of cooking is needed.

SOME OF THE VARIETIES OF SEAWEED

As most seaweeds are available in their dried form from Japan, it is the Japanese names that are most generally in use, but British names are also shown where appropriate.

Arame — A pretty, delicately flavoured and rather sweet seaweed from Japan which is usually cut into fine strips before drying. It only requires a very quick soaking.

Carragheen — Carragheen, also known as Irish Moss or occasionally as Dorset Moss, is found in abundance all around the Atlantic, and particularly on the coast of Ireland, where it has been used for centuries. During the SecondWorldWar it was eaten extensively in the Channel Islands, much reducing the number of cold and flu epidemics. Originally a reddish purple, it can become bleached whilst drying in the sun. It has good gelling properties and for that reason is often added to soups or stews.

Dulse — A native of the North Atlantic, Dulse has been used as a food for thousands of years, often carried on long marches and sea journeys, where it was noted to reduce the incidence of scurvy. It is gathered in fairly large quantities from around our shoreline in the summer months, and simply dried in the sun and wind. Dried dulse is usually pre-cooked, but fresh Dulse needs several hours of boiling. It is particularly rich in iron and contains high quantities of other minerals.

Hijiki — This is a particularly strongly flavoured seaweed, with long strings that are completely black. It looks particularly good mixed with spaghetti and if it is lightly sauteed tastes good too. As well as in a dried form, Hijiki can be found in jars. Even in the Far East it is not as much used as many of the other seaweeds, but it is prized both for its taste and its nutritional properties.

Kanten *(Agar Agar)* — Agar Agar is usually available in a processed powder or flake form and is used in the same way as gelatine for making jellies and other set dishes. It has very little inherent flavour which means it can be used equally well for sweet or savoury foods.

Kombu *(Kelp)* — In its dried form this seaweed comes from Japan and is sold as Kombu, but fresh in this country it is known as Kelp. It is common all round our coastline, as well as in many parts of the world, particularly on the fringes of the Atlantic. It can be cooked in many ways and either eaten alone or added to dishes as a flavouring, a sweetener and a softening agent, being particularly good with rather tough root vegetables. It also acts as a thickener and the Japanese sauce or stock called 'Dashi' is made from Kombu. It has numerous health benefits and as well as being extensively used for such purposes in the East, is often also to be found as a food supplement in the West.

Nori
(Laver or Sea Lettuce)

Nori is the most commonly available and the most popular of all seaweeds, and an easy one for first-time seaweed eaters. It is the seaweed most likely to be found on restaurant menus, particularly if the type is unspecified. It grows close to the shoreline where river outflows make the water less salty. After harvesting it is ground into small particles and mixed with water to form a slurry which is drained on wire or bamboo racks, like paper. This produces a square shaped sheet, or occasionally you can find it round. It is also available as a condiment in ground form. Unless bought ready-toasted, the sheets will need to be grilled briefly, until they turn a bright green. The nori sheets are traditionally used to form sushi rolls which are common but exquisite foods in Japan. To make them you will need a proper sushi mat.

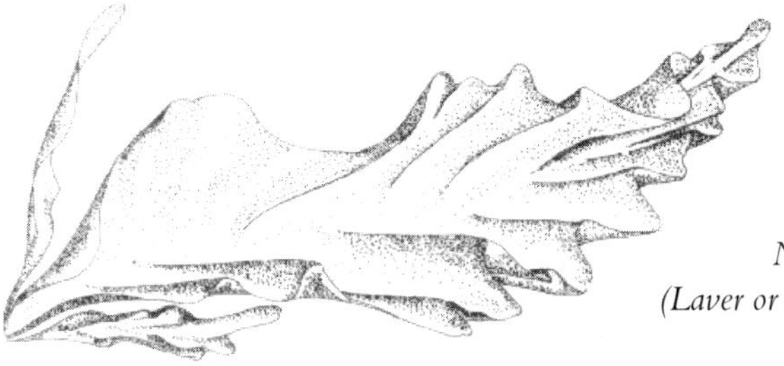

Nori
(Laver or Sea Lettuce)

Laver and Sea Lettuce are exactly the same thing as Nori, Laver being the Welsh name which is occasionally also used in other parts of Britain although it has several local names such as 'Black Butter' in parts of Devon, 'Sloke' in Ireland and 'Slake' in Scotland. Welsh laverbread is a thick purée of the seaweed (generally made from the green form although a purple form is also common) often mixed with and coated in oats and fried as a breakfast dish.

Wakame
(Alaria)

Wakame has a very light taste which makes it good for newcomers to seaweeds, and in Japan it is one of the most popular, added to miso soup, as a salad ingredient or as vegetable. Wakame grows in Japanese waters and Alaria (also known as Wing Kelp or Dabberlocks) which grows around the Atlantic is very similar but not identical. It has most of the same nutritional properties of Kombu.

Seaweeds contain between 10 and 20 times the minerals of land vegetables, supplying calcium, iron, potassium, iodine and magnesium as well as the trace minerals. Vitamins are in abundance too, with A, B, B12, C, D3, E and K. They also contain up to 25% more protein than milk, yet are extremely low in calories, fat and carbohydrates. Seaweeds actually help to dissolve fat and mucous deposits, and remove radioactive and toxic metal pollutants from the body.

MUSHROOMS AND FUNGI

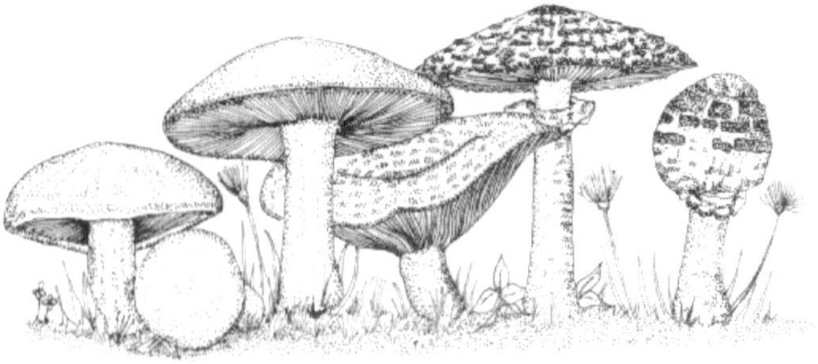

Food from heaven that is very much down to earth

On one hand the word fungus has unfortunate associations, bringing to mind disease, decay and rot. It is an accurate image as, along with bacteria, fungi are responsible for the breakdown of organic rubbish. The fungus family is a large and complex group of *thallophytes* of low organisation, consisting of moulds, mildews, rust, smuts, toadstools, mushrooms, puff balls and the allies of such. But don't be put off.

For cooks and many discerning eaters, the word can conjure up gourmet delights. We all know about mushrooms in their cultivated form at least, but there are other delicious mushrooms and many edible fungi, including delectable truffles.

The Pharoahs believed that mushrooms came from heaven and had magical powers. The Romans held them in high esteem, and Emperor Cladius who conquered southern Britain in the 1st century AD was delighted to find so many varieties growing here; throughout the period from the Middle Ages to the Renaissance they were highly regarded throughout Britain at all social levels; and of course the Chinese have always credited them with health-giving properties.

They are marvellously versatile. They come in a variety of shapes, sizes, colours and tastes and can be cooked in dozens of different ways, or eaten raw. Although superb on their own as an accompanying vegetable alongside a main dish, they can make substantial main dishes themselves, and offer a texture not often found in many other vegetarian foods.

Mushrooms have for a long time been a much used ingredient in vegetarian dishes, and many restaurants are now making use of the more unusual species in order to offer a variety of delicious meals. This is unfortunate only for the very few people who dislike mushrooms, and for those of us who have a yeast intolerance and are unable to eat them.

The part of a mushroom and fungus that is eaten is actually the fruiting body of the plant, which otherwise consists of a fine net of threads growing on and around the plant's food source. Commercially this is a specially prepared compost, but in the wild it will be other plants or the remains of them, often in the form of root structure or newly decaying plant litter as on a forest floor. Fungi cannot produce their own carbohydrates and make use of their host plant for this purpose.

Cultivation of mushrooms started in France and since the time of Louis XIV the main variety cultivated has been the 'Agaricus Bisporus', which now represents 99% of UK commercial production. Whether tiny buttons or large flats, all are actually the same variety at different stages of growth. The demand for mushrooms in this country has doubled over the last 20 years with the commercial production level now at around 111,000 tonnes each year, making mushrooms Britain's most valuable horticultural crop.

There are around 5,000 varieties of wild mushrooms and fungi growing in Europe, with 1,200 of them edible (but not all of them necessarily worth bothering with), but it must be remembered that there are some which are mildly poisonous, and a few which are very poisonous.

Folklore suggests that any fungus that peels, or that is growing in grass, or that does not blacken a silver spoon is an edible variety, but unfortunately it is not as simple as that, and neither is it a case of mushrooms being edible and toadstools not, as many toadstools are perfectly alright. Nor is it good enough to use animals as an indication, as rabbits will eat some which are inedible to us. And you cannot jut avoid those which smell awful, or are brightly coloured, for though bad smell or bright colour can sometimes denote poison, it does not always work that way, for instance the poisonous mushroom appropriately known as the Death Cap is pure white.

Few people are lucky enough to come across fresh truffles in a shop, but they do feature on the menu of some good restaurants, either imported from France and Italy or just occasionally found in this country, most particularly it would seem in Scotland. Experiments are currently taking place; injecting truffle spores into trees to encourage truffle growth (which grow underground on the roots), but so far they are something you find rather than grow intentionally.

Whether you are searching for common or exotic mushrooms, toadstools, other fungi or truffles, going on a foray with someone who really does know what they are looking for is one way to be sure you are not getting something poisonous, and there are often organised events of this sort, generally in October and November, wherever there are suitable fields and woodlands.

Another way of obtaining them, which comes more easily to many people, is to buy them. In recent years some of the more unusual varieties have become reasonably readily available. Supermarkets and greengrocers often sell Oyster, Shiitake and Brown Cap Mushrooms and you may also be lucky enough to find Cepes, Morels or some of the other less common varieties, but if these cannot be found fresh they should easily be available dried. Certain dried mushrooms and fungi can be very satisfactory and only require a little soaking to transform something which appears totally inedible into a very usable vegetable. Drying also opens up a wealth of varieties which would not otherwise be available in this country, so fungi found only in Asia, for example, can now be on the menu in this country.

Some, such as Chinese Straw Mushrooms can be bought in tins, but tinned mushrooms can tend to be very soft, and care has to be taken in using them as even a short amount of cooking can destroy the texture. Truffles are most frequently to be found in jars with oil, which preserves them well.

USING FRESH MUSHROOMS & FUNGI

Mushrooms deteriorate fast, so always buy them as fresh as possible and if there is need to store them first transfer them from any plastic wrapping into an open box or paper bag and keep them in the fridge. Make sure they are kept dry.

They should not (with just a few exceptions) be washed, but just wiped with a damp cloth to remove any dirt. The dirt will most probably be a little compost which is undesirable rather than harmful, and unseen contaminants should not ever be present on commercially grown mushrooms at least. As a general rule, mushrooms should not be peeled. If you need to remove the stalks for stuffing say, do use them in some other dish as they are a good part of the mushroom, with excellent texture.

Many varieties are ideal in salads, particularly tiny button mushrooms and Oyster Mushrooms, and both too are excellent in a stir-fry, but you can also use Browncaps or any other fresh mushroom although some may require slightly longer cooking.

Open Cap Field Mushrooms are very useful for stuffing, and the very large flat varieties are excellent with a stuffing on top, so to speak.

Mushrooms with plenty of texture are most suitable for casseroles and stews.

Adding mushrooms to a dish which is to be baked, such as a pie, requires a little more attention as the extended cooking can cause juices to be extracted leaving watery patches. The way to overcome this is to fry the mushrooms, with just a tiny amount of fat, until all moisture has completely evaporated.

This can take a surprisingly long time, and the resulting quantity is only a fraction of the original, but you nevertheless achieve a superb strong favour which compensates for the lack of volume.

If you have been fortunate enough to come by fresh truffles they will have probably cost you a great deal of money, so treat them with care and avoid wastage.

GROWING YOUR OWN MUSHROOMS

If you happen to have a field or woodland, or even just a garden, you may be growing your own without any effort. A surer way is to buy a mushroom box. Specialist seed merchants and horticultural suppliers now sell these boxes, complete with compost and spores, for growing your own mushrooms. Field Mushrooms, Shiitake and Oyster Mushrooms are generally available.

USING DRIED MUSHROOM AND FUNGI

These will usually come in a packet with soaking instructions, and different varieties do require slightly different treatments. Firstly, bear in mind that they will expand beyond your expectations, so only take out of the packet what you calculate you will need, and keep the rest airtight. Generally, the best method is to pour boiling water over the fungi and after just covering them add about half as much water again. Leave them to stand for 15 to 20 minutes (in most cases it won't matter if they are left somewhat longer). Pour off the water (but you can keep it and use it for stock) and rinse in clean water to wash out any soil particles. You will now be able to follow any recipe for fresh fungi of the same variety. Many of the varieties that come dried have strong flavours, so use them with care to start with.

Naturally, reconstituted dried mushrooms and fungi are not generally good raw, but some varieties can be used, possibly finely shredded, in stir-fries. They are superb for sauces, in casseroles and stews as well as in bakes.

DRYING YOUR OWN MUSHROOMS

With fresh mushrooms available all year round there is no need to dry your own mushrooms now as there was years ago, unless, that is, you have picked a lot of your own and want to keep some for future meals. Freezing, by the way, doesn't work very well for most mushrooms.

The best for drying are the Fairy Ring mushrooms and the Common mushroom, but you can use other types. It is very simple. Remove the stalks if you want to and either thread them onto string using a darning needle, putting a knot between each one, or push them onto a fine wooden (definitely not metal) barbecue skewer, keeping them a little apart from each other so that the air can flow between them. Dry them either hung up in a dry room or airing cupboard, or in an extremely low oven until completely dry. In the past mushroom drying was often done in front of an open fire by spiking the mushrooms onto a twiggy bough, placed in a flower pot, giving the appearance of a strange tree, a little like willow pattern.

SOME OF THE VARIETIES AVAILABLE

Cep The Cep (or Edible Boletus) has a very distinctive, rounded bun shaped cap with a smooth soft brown top, and it has tubes instead of gills underneath, and a short plump stem. The flavour is fairly strong and nutty with a very good texture which is retained in cooking, making it useful for many dishes.

Chanterelle Very pretty, delicate mushroom that is generally pale orange in colour and turned inside-out, showing off the gills. It can be found in the wild or occasionally commercially. Also available dried. It can be eaten raw or in stir-fries, but in longer cooking loses a lot of moisture.

Fairy Ring Champignon This is a small delicate mushroom with a shallow domed cap of pale buff. The stem is a little tough but the cap very pleasant. It was once prized as an ideal mushroom for drying. The rings of lush grass which the mushrooms create from their nutrients after they die down were for centuries believed to be made by dancing fairies.

Field Mushroom This is the common wild variety, found in July to November, from which the cultivated variety is descended.

Giant Puff Ball A very inedible looking object, a white, yellow or brownish sphere or oval, sometimes up to 50cm or more across. It should however only be used when young. Cut it into thick strips and fry, or combine with other fungi.

Horse Mushroom If picking your own, take care; there are two other species which look similar but can cause illness. Many believe however that this is one of the finest of wild mushrooms. It can often be found, as you would expect, in fields with horses (but not exclusively so), in July and August. It tends to be pale and smooth, up to 20cm high and possibly the same for the cap. It should be picked young and used in the same way as cultivated mushrooms with a little longer cooking.

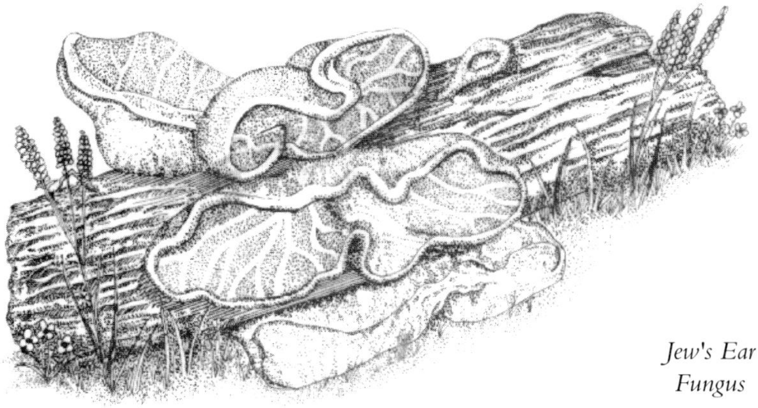

Jew's Ear Fungus

Jew's Ear Fungus The look of this fungus is every bit as bad as you would expect from its name. However it is actually cultivated in China where they regard it as a delicacy. Wash it well and cook for about 50 minutes in milk or stock or as part of a casserole.

Morel A very unusual looking fungus, often almost black although sometimes greyish or brown, with a deep honeycomb texture on the outside of a cone shaped cap. It needs to be washed very well (despite what has been said earlier) because the holes on the surface can collect dirt. It is occasionally available fresh from commercial sources, or can be found in wood clearings. It is also in plentiful supply dried. Excellent with creamy sauces and to give variety of shape and colour to mixed mushroom dishes. Only light cooking is required.

Oyster Mushroom Very delicate mushroom which grows in clumps on the sides of a tree with the gills facing down, giving a one-sided and flat appearance.Usually a soft buff colour, but can also be white, brown, grey or yellow. Ideal raw or just very lightly fried. One of the best.

Parasol This is generally a favourite wild mushroom. It opens from a sphere to almost flat with a tattered appearance. It can be up to 20cm across, and at up to 28cm high it is one of Britian's tallest. The distinctive flavour is useful for a great many dishes, provided it is picked young whilst still tender. It can also be stuffed as the cap is dome-shaped.

Saffron Milk Cap Found mainly under pines in the autumn, this mushroom is funnel-shaped. At first it is orange, becoming grey-green with age. It exudes a milk which is orange at first, and the flesh is pinkish, turning green with age. Use it immediately after picking, coating it in egg and flour and frying or grilling. It is not good baked.

St George's A wild mushroom which is to be found from late April (as the name suggests) to June in wooded clearings. A traditional-looking mushroom that is pale in colour on top and underneath and usually 4cm to 12cm across and about 6cm high. It can be used in the same way as commercial mushrooms but needs just a little more cooking.

Shaggy Cap A common species with a shaggy brown cone which only opens at the base as far as making a bell shape. The flesh is thin and rather watery and the flavour is delicate, it can be used in many ways, including stuffing.

Shiitake An oriental mushroom which is comparatively new to this country fresh, but already very popular, and it is also available dried. It has a thin flat cap, medium-brown, with a slightly rough surface, and a long stem. It can be used much in the same way as the common cultivated mushroom but has a chewier texture.

Tompettes de Morts Translated as 'Horn of Plenty', this is considered to be a great delicacy. It is jet black and somewhat similar in taste to truffles. Sometimes found fresh, imported from France, but most generally dried. Needs a little longer cooking than most varieties.

Wood Blewit One of the most common wild mushrooms (although little used), found during the autumn. It is initially dark brown-violet, getting lighter with age. The taste is similar to Radish. It loses a lot of moisture during cooking, but bearing this in mind it can be used in the same way as cultivated mushrooms.

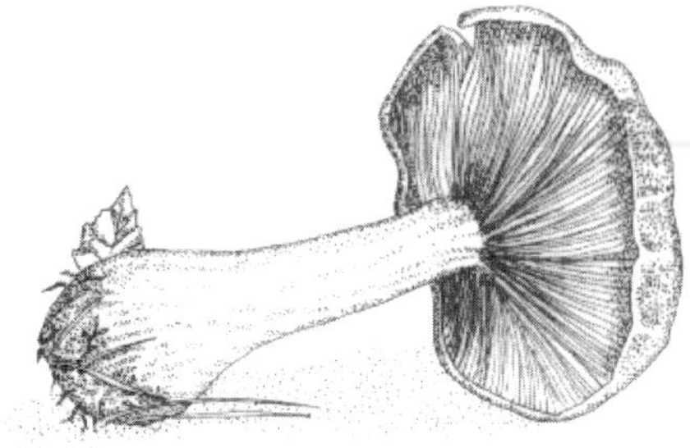

The Wood Blewit

Mushrooms and similar fungi have large amounts of the minerals; potassium, copper, phosphorus and iron, plus good quantities of the vitamins B1, B2, niacin, B12, C and D, and more protein than most other vegetables. They are also high in fibre and low in calories, fat, carbohydrate and salt. The ideal healthy vegetable.

WINE

Michael Cook looks at some of the methods and the mysticism

The history of wine is an amazingly deep and complex subject and to cover it in depth would take an inordinate amount of time and space so I intend to touch on the subject comparatively lightly.

Wine has existed for over 4,000 years, it is not known who first discovered it, but 'vitis vinifera', the species of vine which grows wine-grapes, is believed to have originated in Persia. It was certainly cultivated and drunk in ancient Persia, Egypt and Greece.

As the people of these cultures spread, they not only took their beliefs and ideas but also the vines, and thus it was very little time before the vine had spread from Persia through to Italy, Spain, Germany and eventually to Britain by the Romans. The vine actually managed to conquer more of the then civilised world than any invader, and was often a much more welcome visitor than the people who brought it. Wine lies at the roots of our civilization, it is an integral part of many religions and celebrations, and it should be given its due respect and appreciation.

From the clear white liquid with sharp acidicity and full flower scents, to the deep, dry, wooded reds, all wines are basically grape juice. Every drop of this liquid has been drawn from the ground by the roots of the vine, so the diversity is not only due to the variety of grape but is equally affected by the climate and by the type of soil. The difference between grape juice and wine is the process of fermentation, blending and maturing.

At the final stages of ripening, yeast cells appear on the skins of the grape and cling to it. The process of fermentation is very simple, the yeast cells go to work on the natural sugars and this causes turbulence in the grape juice. Not only is alcohol produced, but large quantities of carbon dioxide, its bubbles keeping the must (broken grapes) on the move. At the same time heat is generated, keeping the must warm, and fermentation continues until the sugar in the must is exhausted (which is what generally happens), or until the yeast cells are asphyxiated by the growing concentration of alcohol being produced. The liquid is no longer a solution of sugar and water, it is now a solution of alcohol in water (this is where we get alc %) with small quantities of acids and oils which give the wine its particular flavour and bouquet. This process is a basic one for the making of all wine, and in general for any other alcoholic drink.

The liquid that is left after fermentation is usually of muddy consistency, due to the dead yeast cells that are either at the bottom of the wine known as the 'leas', or suspended in the wine, and there is also grape debris and possibly a haze due to pectin or proteins in the wine.

VEGETARIAN WINES

In a perfect world the wine would simply be allowed to clear in a process called racking, where the wine is syphoned off the debris that has accumulated at the bottom. Unfortunately this can take a considerable amount of time.

With the pressure today of producing wine at affordable prices many producers are only too keen to find short cuts and many unpleasant and unpalatable ingredients are added to speed up the process of clearing. Unfortunately this makes most of the wine produced today unsuitable for vegetarians, vegans, and those on religious or special diets.

A fining agent is used to attract particles which were floating in the wine (which is different from removing the wine from its deposits). Some of the nasty things used are blood, egg whites, isinglass (sturgeons air bladder), bones, chitins (the shells of crabs and prawns), milk and gelatine. If it is necessary for a wine to be fined - and this has to be up to the producer of the wine who may have financial or climatic restrictions - one would hope he would use bentonite clay, as this product is soil based, and does not infringe any moral, religious, or health convictions.

The practice of fining is used to speed the production of wines for sale, and in general the better quality wines are not fined or filtered in any way. Therefore wines at the cheaper end of the market tend not to be vegetarian. Unfortunately old practises die hard and until more people insist on their wine being produced with the care and respect it deserves we will continue to have finings used in our wine.

ORGANIC WINES

Organic wines are made from grapes which have been grown without the use of synthetic fertilisers, herbicides or insecticides, and with no chemical additives or treatments used in the vinification. Of the 500 chemicals permitted in the protection of the vine and production of wine, 50 are known to be carcinogens, others may cause allergic reactions.

Organic wines tend to have a more distinctive taste and cleaner fruit flavour than wines made with the use of chemicals, but there is no other difference in taste.

There can however be a distinct difference in after effect, and many who normally suffer from headaches or hangovers from drinking wine find no such problems with organic wines. This could be that the allergy is not to the wine but to the the chemicals used, and the lower levels of sulphur dioxide found in organic wine reduce the chances of a reaction particularly for asthmatic or bronchial sufferers. This of course does not apply if you try to drink your own weight in wine at a single sitting!

Organic wines in general tend to be 15% more expensive than equivalent conventional wines, but what has to be kept in mind is the intensive method of farming and lower yields, with higher quality grapes. This levels itself out by the time we get into the price range of Champagne and other more expensive wine.

How do you know the wine you are purchasing is organic? This is now relatively simple, just look for the symbol of an independent organic organisation on the label (for instance: *ce vin est cultivé sans engrais chimiques, sans insecticide,* or *production de l'agriculture biologique,* or *nature et progres*). The Soil Association symbol is now used on both British and imported organic wines, and from any country inspected by the Association.

The quality of organic wines has improved immeasurably over the past few years, and many are winning major awards alongside traditionally produced wines. This is even more astonishing when it is remembered that most organic wine producers are smallholders with small quantities of wine stocks and even smaller budgets.

Yet it does not mean that those of us who are particular about what is put in our wines are any better off as the majority of organic wine is not suitable for vegetarians, vegans, or those on religious or special diets. Many producers who are attempting to produce better quality and cleaner wines, are still stuck with the old and, dare I say, unsatisfactory practice of fining their wines.

This may seem all doom and despondency, but it is not completely so as there are some wine suppliers who are only too willing to help, but do not expect your local off-licence or your local restaurant necessarily to know immediately which of their wines are suitable for you. It takes a great deal of effort and persistence on their part, and this is not made any easier by the fact that a wine that is vegetarian one year, may not be in another.

A rough guide is if you are paying less than £6 in an off-licence or £10 in a restaurant the likelihood is that the wine is not vegetarian.

WINE AREAS

Over the past 20 years more countries have started to export their wines, and more people in this country have been financially able to enjoy them. France and Italy are among the largest producers of wine. The tradition of wine growing in France is very old, and the wide range of red and white wines made in this country has given experience and authority to French winemakers; wines described as 'classic' are predominantly French, simply because they are the wines on which drinkers have formed their standards.

Really this is no longer tenable, as there are many wines coming not only from the old established wine growing areas, but also from the new world that make many French wines look inferior.

All this notwithstanding, some of the finest wines do come from France, and few would dispute that the two finest red table wines in the world are Claret and Burgundy, and that the finest sparkling wine is Champagne.

France is at present the easiest for discovering whether or not the wine you buy is organic or vegetarian.

CHAMPAGNE

Champagne comes from a defined area in the north of France, around the valley of the river Marne and Reims, E'pernay and Ay. It has a proud history, being the wine offered to the Kings of France at their coronation. Although the wines of the Champagne region have been known since at least Roman times (the Romans having built many of the great galleries cut out of the chalky limestone for cellars) they were not fully sparkling until the 18th century.

Napoleon is credited with saying "In victory you deserve Champagne, in defeat you need it".

Such wines are never cheap as the amount of labour and time required is considerable, despite the fact some may not be of outstanding quality. Though all the champagne houses have their own individual procedures, they are quintessentially the same. The wines are made in the usual way, using moderate, or preferably high quality grapes and with the base wine having a high degree of acidity (which is why most quality sparkling wines are white, and from northern vineyards).

The wine is bottled before a second fermentation takes place, and any sediment left in the wine is made to adhere to the cork by turning the bottle on an angle with its neck in a rack. A group of men go round shaking each bottle regularly by the base and giving a slight turn, so progressively the bottle is turned upside down. The wine will stay like this for many years, or until it is required. Then the first cork is removed and with it the sediment.

This is good news for us, as it means very rarely is a fining agent used.

A dosage, or sweetening, according to the type of wine is added, and the final cork is put in the bottle. Many of these processes are now mechanised, but still take considerable time and effort. Fortunately more and more Champagne is being produced by organic methods these days.

WINES OF THE WORLD

Wines are now being produced all over the world, some of a considerably high standard, and new producers are often filtering their wines instead of fining them, and if they need to be fined are using bentonite clay, which is great news for us. As these practices become accepted more widely it is becoming easier for us to discover if the wines are suitable for our consumption.

In Australia, New Zealand and California, it is now relatively easy to find animal-friendly wines. Spain and Italy are improving. The bad news is that some countries are a relative mine field for vegetarians - Germany, South Africa, Chile, Russia, Argentina and Britain, to name a few.

ENGLISH WINE

English wine is wine produced from grapes grown in English vineyards, and not to be confused with British wine which is made from imported concentrate, or grape juice.

Most English wines are white, of German origin and Germanic in style. The German vines Muller Thurgau, Sigerrebe, Reichensteiner, Schonburber, Huxelrebe and the French Madeleine Angevine and Seyval Blanc being the most widely grown varieties. There are one or two red wines being produced which require both a superb site and vine maturity to give good colour and depth to the wines.

Wine production in England is certainly not as young as most people would think and dates back over 2,000 years. The Domesday Book survey of 1086 recorded 83 established vineyards, most owned by the monasteries or the large country estates and feudal barons. There was an increase in the number of vineyards up to the year 1152, when King Henry II married Queen Eleanor of Aquitaine. The Queen's land included the vineyards of Bordeaux, which gave a plentiful supply of what was then the best red wine in the world, and only a short boat trip away. This of course almost killed the English wine trade overnight.

The association lasted for over 300 years, in that time the wines of Bordeaux became the everyday drink of the English who soon had an unquenchable thirst for it. They renamed the pale red wine of Bordeaux and called it Claret. In the 14th century it is estimated that the people of England drank more Claret than is consumed today, not a bad effort when you remember that the population of England was only about two million.

Bordeaux was lost to the English in 1453, a battle best not talked about too deeply as it was one of the few we lost. An apple tree grows on the spot where the last English troops are said to have held the last piece of English Bordeaux, this place is called Castillon.

In 1965 the English Vineyards Association was started and within 10 years it had 200 members; now it has around 400. Not all produce for sale, as many make wine for their own and friends' consumption.

There is no reason why wine grapes should not be grown in this country, the climate is no more unsuitable than in the northern Rhine vineyards of Germany, but generally the vineyards are concentrated in the south of England and in Wales, the northernmost being in Durham. The weather of course can be a problem, but by far the biggest drawback is the birds, they love grapes. For months before the harvest from dawn to dusk the English wine grower has to be in his vineyard keeping watch to prevent the year's work from being gobbled up.

ENGLISH COUNTRY WINES

Country wines in Britain are created from ingredients as diverse as elderflower, elderberry, apple, parsnip, cherry, damson, wild and cultivated flowers, and bark. They are made by fermentation as in traditional winemaking using these other ingredients in place of grapes.

There has always been a great interest in producing country wines, mainly for the maker's own consumption, but some are now being produced commercially.

There are some wine critics who would lampoon English country wines as a second rate product. As a producer of country wines, beers, and liqueurs, I am one of the first to stand up to this snobbish foolery; there are unpalatable and badly made country wines, but this goes equally for some of the grape wine being produced. Country wine that is made with care and consideration, can stand justifiably alongside its contemporaries, and when excellent is a joy to behold, and to drink.

All this said, wine and food with friends is one of the few civilised pleasures left, enjoy both in moderation.

VINEYARDS IN ENGLAND AND WALES

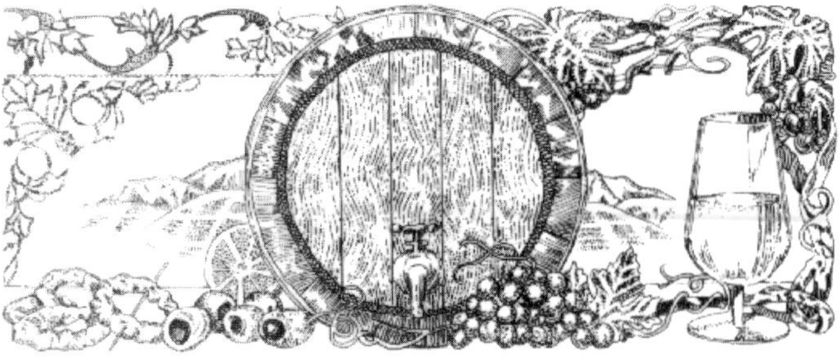

If our information on wine has engendered enthusiasm for vineyards, why not go and see the wine making process for yourself . Those that we have listed are by no means the only vineyards open to the public, but all have their own winery so visitors will be able to see not just the vines but also something of the process of turning grapes into wine.

THE WEST COUNTRY

Bagborough Vineyard
Bagborough Lane, Pylle, Shepton Mallet, Somerset, BA3 4TG. Tel: 0749 831146
7.4 hectares. Vineyard shop. Restaurant.

Clawford Vineyard
Clawton, Holsworthy, Devon, EX22 6PN. Tel: 0409 254177
8.25 hectares. Open summer only.

Loddiswell Vineyard
Loddiswell, Kingsbridge, Devon, TQ7 4EF. Tel: 0548 550221
2.4 hectares. Open summer only. Vineyard shop.

Moorlynch Vineyard
Moorlynch, Bridgwater, Somerset, TA7 9DD. Tel: 0458 210393
6 hectares. Vineyard shop.

Pilton Manor Vineyard
Pilton, Shepton Mallet, Somerset, BA4 4BE. Tel: 0749 890325
9 hectares. Open summer only. Vineyard shop. Restaurant.

Sharpham Vineyard
Sharpham House, Ashprington, Totnes, Devon, TQ9 7UT. Tel: 0803 732203
3 hectares. Open summer only.

SOUTHERN ENGLAND AND THE CHANNEL ISLANDS

Adgestone Vineyard
Upper Road, Adgestone, Sandown, Isle of Wight, PO36 0ES. Tel: 0983 402503
3 hectares. Vineyard shop.

Barnsgate Manor Vineyard
Heron's Ghyll, Uckfield, East Sussex, TN22 4DB. Tel: 0825 713366
5 hectares. Vineyard shop. Restaurant

Barton Manor Vineyard
Whippingham, East Cowes, Isle of Wight, PO32 6LB. Tel: 0983 292835
4.1 hectares. Open summer only. Vineyard shop. Restaurant.

Carr Taylor Vineyard
Yew Tree Farm, Westfield, Hastings, East Sussex, TN35 4SG. Tel: 0424 752501
8.75 hectares. Vineyard shop.

Horton Estate Vineyard
Horton, Wimborne, Dorset, BH21 7JG. Tel: 0258 840258
4.05 hectares. Open summer only at special times. Vineyard shop.

La Mare Vineyard
St Mary, Jersey, Channel Islands. Tel: 0534 81178
2 hectares. Open summer only. Vineyard shop. Restaurant.

Meon Valley Vineyard
Hill Grove, Swanmore, Hampshire, S023 2PZ. Tel: 0489 877435
3.4 hectares. Open all summer, by appointment only. Vineyard shop.

Rock Lodge Vineyard
Scaynes Hill, East Sussex, RH17 7NG. Tel: 0444 831567
5 hectares. Open summer only. Vineyard shop.

Wickham Vineyard
Botley Road, Shedfield, Hampshire, SO3 2HL. Tel: 0329 834042
3.87 hectares. Open at special times by appointment only. Vineyard shop.

THE HOME COUNTIES, THE THAMES VALLEY AND GREATER LONDON

Denbies Vineyard
Bradley Lane, London Road, Dorking, Surrey, RH5 6AA. Tel: 0306 876616
92.6 hectares. Vineyard shop.

Thames Valley Vineyard
Stanlake Park, Twyford, Reading, Berkshire, RG10 0BN. Tel: 0734 340176
10.3 hectares. Open all year, by appoitment. Vineyard shop.

Thorncroft Vineyard
Highlands Farm, Leatherhead, Surrey, KT22 8QE. Tel: 0372 372558
3.5 hectares. Open all summer, by appointment only.

Three Choirs Vineyard
Newent, Gloucestershire, GL18 1LS. Tel: 0531 890 223/555
26.3 hectares. Vineyard shop. Restaurant.

THE SOUTH EAST

Biddenden Vineyard
Little Whatmans, Biddenden, Ashford, Kent, TN27 8DH. Tel: 0580 291726
8.3 hectares. Vineyard shop. Light refreshments.

Bruisyard Vineyard
The Winery, Church Road, Bruisyard, Saxmundham, Suffolk, IP17 2EF. Tel: 0728 75281
4 hectares. Vineyard shop. Restaurant.

Chiddingstone Vineyard
Vexour Farm, Chiddingstone, Edenbridge, Kent, TN8 7BB. Tel: 0892 870277
10 hectares. Open all summer, by appointment only.

Chilford Hundred Vineyard
Chilford Hall, Balsham Road, Linton, Cambridgeshire, CB1 6LE. Tel: 0223 892641
7.4 hectares. Open summer only. Vineyard shop.

Gifford's Hall Vineyard
Hartest, Bury St Edmonds, Suffolk, IP29 4EX. Tel: 0284 830464
5.62 hectares. Open summer only. Vineyard shop.

Lamberhurst Vineyard
Ridge Farm, Lamberhurst, Tunbridge Wells, Kent, TN3 8ER. Tel: 0892 890286
20 hectares. Vineyard shop. Restaurant.

Penshurst Vineyard
Grove Road, Penshurst, Tonbridge, Kent, TN11 8DU. Tel: 0892 870255
5 hectares. Vineyard shop.

Sandhurst Vineyard
Hoads Farm, Sandhurst, Cranbrook, Kent, TN18 5NU. Tel: 0580 850284 and 850296
5.7 hectares. Open summer only. Vineyard shop.

Shawsgate Vineyard
Badingham Road, Framlingham, Suffolk, IP13 9HZ. Tel: 0728 724060
7 hectares. Open summer only. Vineyard shop.

Staple Vineyard
Church Farm, Staple, Canterbury, Kent, CT3 1LN. Tel: 0304 812571
3 hectares. Open summer only. Vineyard shop.

WALES

Llanerch Vineyard
Llanerch Farm, Hensol, Pendoylan, Vale of Glamorgan, Wales, CF7 8JU. Tel: 0443 225877
2.2 hectares. Open summer at special times and by appointment. Vineyard shop.

THE NORTH WEST COUNTIES

Stretton Estates Vineyard
The Estate Office, Carden Park, Malpas, Cheshire. Tel: 0829 250325
4.86 hectares. Open all year, by appointment only. Vineyard shop.

TRADITIONAL CORNMILLS

The surest way to tasty and nutritious baking

One of the arts of good cooking is using the very best of ingredients. This is as much the case for the basics as it is for more exotic products, and flour is therefore no exception.

It is possible to get high quality unadulterated flour in some high street shops, but buying fresh natural stoneground flour direct from a mill is very much the best way. For two centuries or so a refined way of life meant partaking of refined foods. Now it has been realised that such processing removes the most nutritionally important components of the ingredient, as well as much of the taste, and there has been a return to natural products.

With traditional milling the wheat germ and oil are mixed in with the endosperm (white starchy centre) to produce a flour with a flavour and texture that cannot be matched by modern processing. Many mills produce not just wheat flour, but also use rye and other grains to make a variety of products, and use different settings to create varied textures, to suit different recipes and cooking methods. As well as being available from the mills themselves, many have their flour available in local specialist shops or used by local bakers.

Traditional milling is often associated with organic flour, but not all flour produced in this way will be organic. Only flour that is certified by the Soil Association can be sold as organic, so always check for the Soil Association symbol.

The process of milling in these traditional mills is very much the same today as it has been for millenia, the only difference being that our prehistoric ancestors used hand mills whereas the mills listed here are powered by either wind or water. The power from wind sails or waterwheel is transferred through gearing of wood or cast iron to drive the heavy round upper millstone, or runner stone. Grain is fed through a hole in the centre of the runner stone which is turning just above the stationary bedstone, dressed with grooves to assist the grinding. The flour simply emerges from the circumference of the stones. The process is basically simple, although operating a traditional mill is not a straightforward matter, being reliant on wind or water as well as on heavy machinery which has to be kept in perfect working order despite being possibly hundreds of years old.

The list that follows is of mills that are run by members of the **Traditional Cornmillers Guild**. All are fully working mills, and all are open to the public either for tours of the mill or just to buy flour.

THE WEST COUNTRY

Crowdy Mill (water mill)
Harbertonford, Totnes, Devon, TQ9 7HU.
Tel: 0803 732340
Open all year for tours and flour sales. All flour is organic.

Otterton Mill (water mill)
Budleigh Salterton, Devon.
Tel: 0395 68521 or 68031
Open all year as part of craft complex.

SOUTHERN ENGLAND AND THE CHANNEL ISLANDS

Bartley Mill (water mill)
Bells Yew Green, Frant, Sussex, TN3 8BH.
Tel: 0892 890372
Open for tours in the summer and on winter weekends. Farm shop open all year. Most flour is organic.

Cann Mills (water mill)
Shaftesbury, Dorset, SP7 0LB.
Tel: 0747 52475
Open for sales only. All flour is organic.

Luggershall Mill (water mill)
Weald and Downland Open Air Museum, Singleton, Sussex.
Tel: 0243 811348
Open all year as one of the museum exhibits.

THE HOME COUNTIES, THE THAMES VALLEY AND GREATER LONDON

Mapledurham Mill (water mill)
Mapledurham, Reading, Berkshire, RG4 7TR.
Tel: 0734 723350 or 478284
Open for tours during the summer. Open for sales all year.

THE SOUTH EAST

Downfield Windmill
Soham, Ely, Cambridgeshire.
Tel: 0353 720333 or 0533 707625
Open on Sundays for tours. Flour sales on Sundays and some other times. Some flour is organic.

Sarre Mill (windmill)
Canterbury Road, Sarre, Kent, CT7 0JU.
Tel: 0843 47573
Open for tours and flour sales all year. Some organic flour available.

WALES

Bacheldre Watermill
Churchstoke, Montgomery, Powys, Wales, SY15 6TE.
Tel: 0588 620489
Open for flour sales. Some flour is organic.

Felin Crewi (water mill)
Penegoes, Machynlleth, Powys, Wales, SY20 8NH.
Tel: 0654 703113
Open for tours in the summer and Wednesdays. Open all year for flour sales. Some flour is organic.

Melin Maesdulais (water mill)
Porthrhyd, Carmarthen, Dyfed, Wales, SA32 8BT.
Tel: 0267 275472
Open for flour sales. Most flour is organic.

Y Felin (water mill)
St Dogmaels, Dyfed, Wales, SA43 3DY.
Tel: 0239 613999
Open for tours and flour sales all year. Some flour is organic.

CENTRAL ENGLAND

Charlecote Mill (water mill)
Hampton Lucy, Warwickshire, CV35 8BB.
Tel: 0789 842072
Open for tours on Bank Holidays and for flour sales at anytime. Some flour is organic.

Claybrooke Mill (water mill)
Claybrooke Magna, Lutterworth, Leicestershire, LE17 5DB.
Tel: 0455 202443
Tours by appointment. Open daily for flour sales. Some flour is organic.

Maud Foster Mill (windmill)
Willoughby Road, Boston, Lincolnshire, PE21 9EG.
Tel: 0205 352188
Open for tours and flour sales all year. All flour is organic.

Mount Pleasant Windmill
Kirton in Lindsey, Gainsborough, Lincolnshire, DN21 4NH.
Tel: 0652 640177
Open for tours and flour sales all year. All flour is organic.

Wellesbourne Mill (water mill)
Kineton Road, Wellesbourne, Warwickshire, CV35 9HG.
Tel: 0789 470237
Open for tours and flour sales all year.

THE NORTH WEST COUNTIES

The Watermill
Little Salkeld, Penrith, Cumbria, CA10 1NN.
Tel: 0768 81523
Open for tours and flour sales on most weekdays, all year. All flour is organic.

THE NORTH EAST COUNTIES

Crakehall Watermill
Little Crakehall, Bedale, North Yorkshire, DL8 1HU.
Tel: 0677 423240
Open for tours in the summer and all year for flour sales.

SCOTLAND

Golspie Mill (water mill)
Golspie, Sutherland, Scotland, KW10 6RA.
Tel: 0408 633278
Open for tours and flour sales in the middle of summer. Some flour is organic.

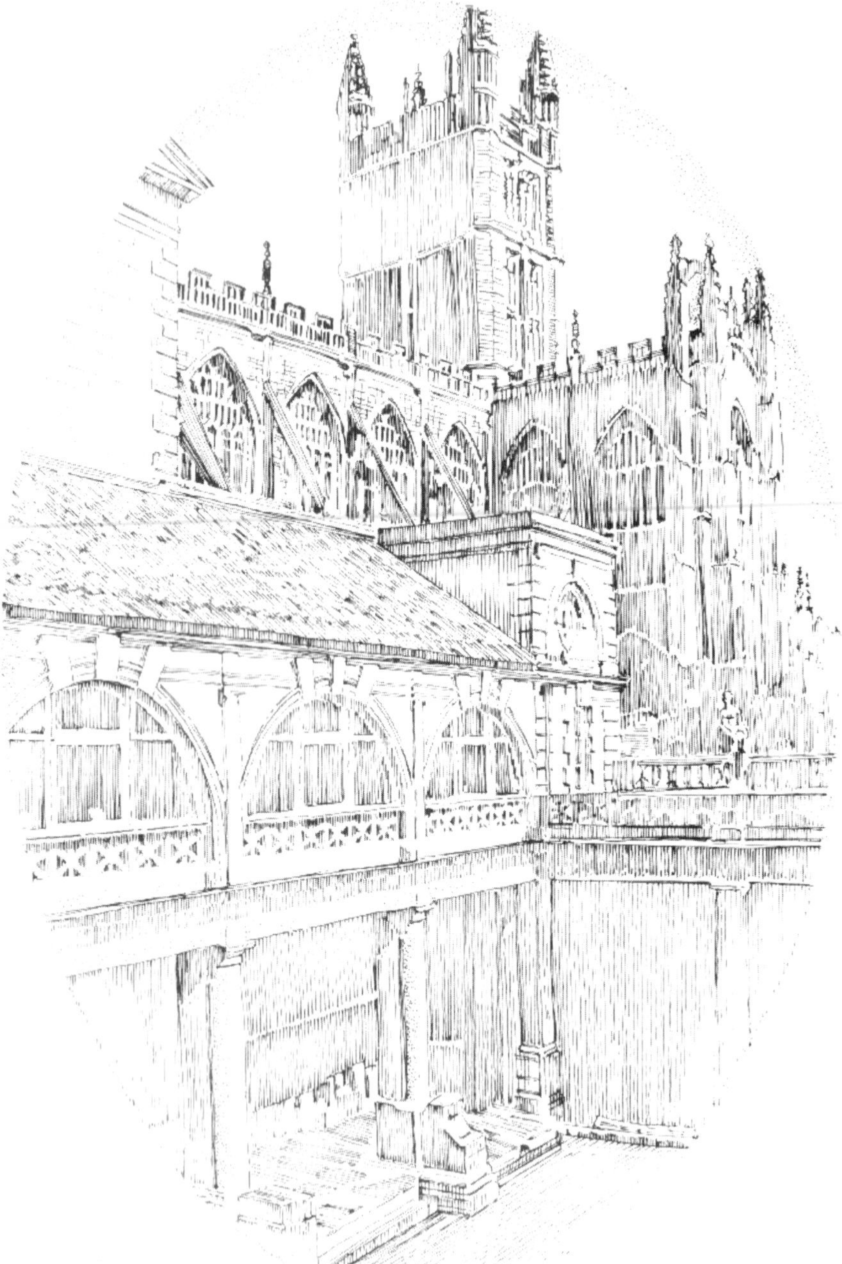

The Roman Baths & Abbey in Bath

Contents

THE WEST COUNTRY

Devon, Cornwall, The Isles of Scilly, Somerset & Avon

Suggested Venues to Dine

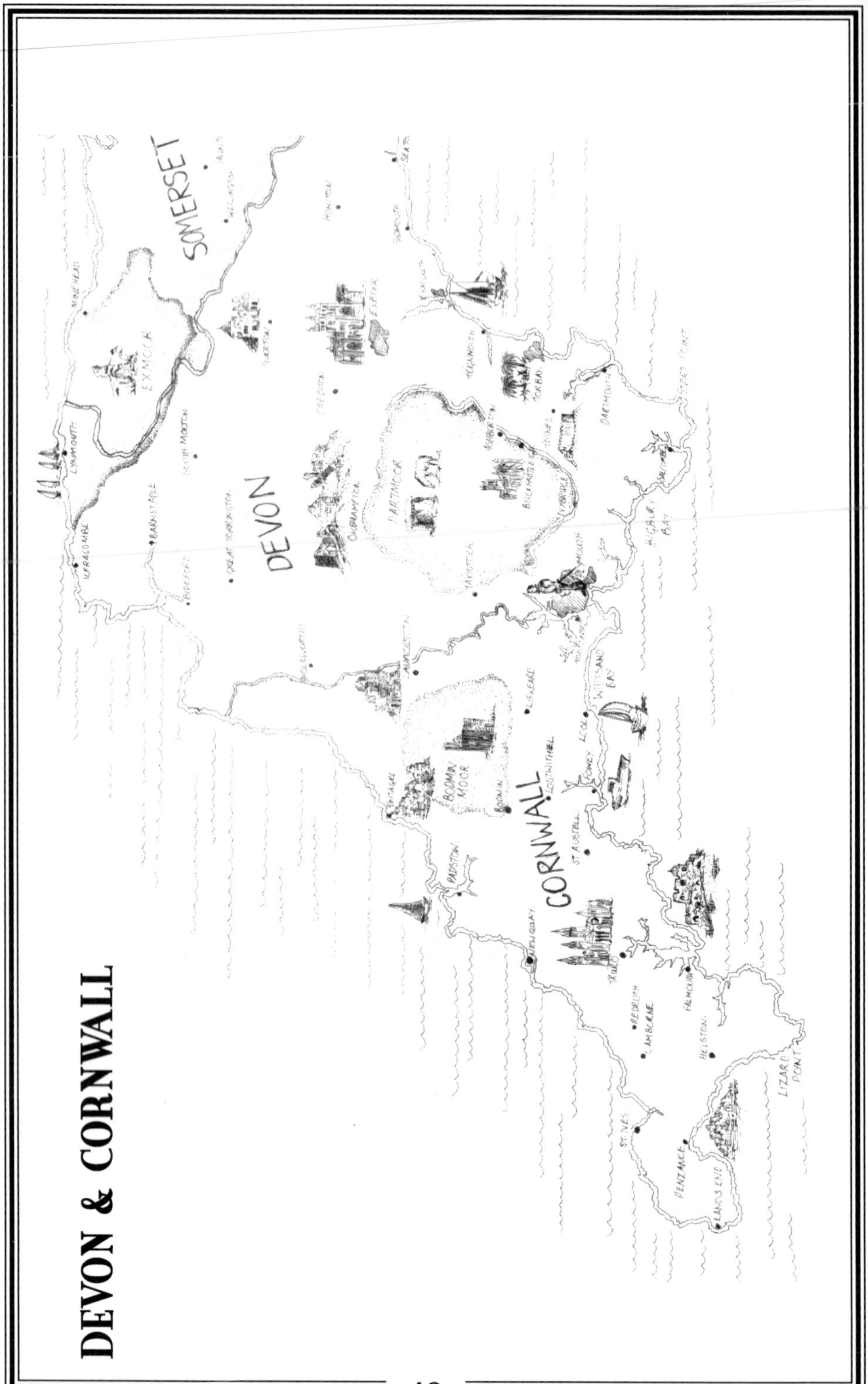
DEVON & CORNWALL
SOMERSET
DEVON
CORNWALL
EXMOOR
DARTMOOR
BODMIN MOOR

SOMERSET & AVON

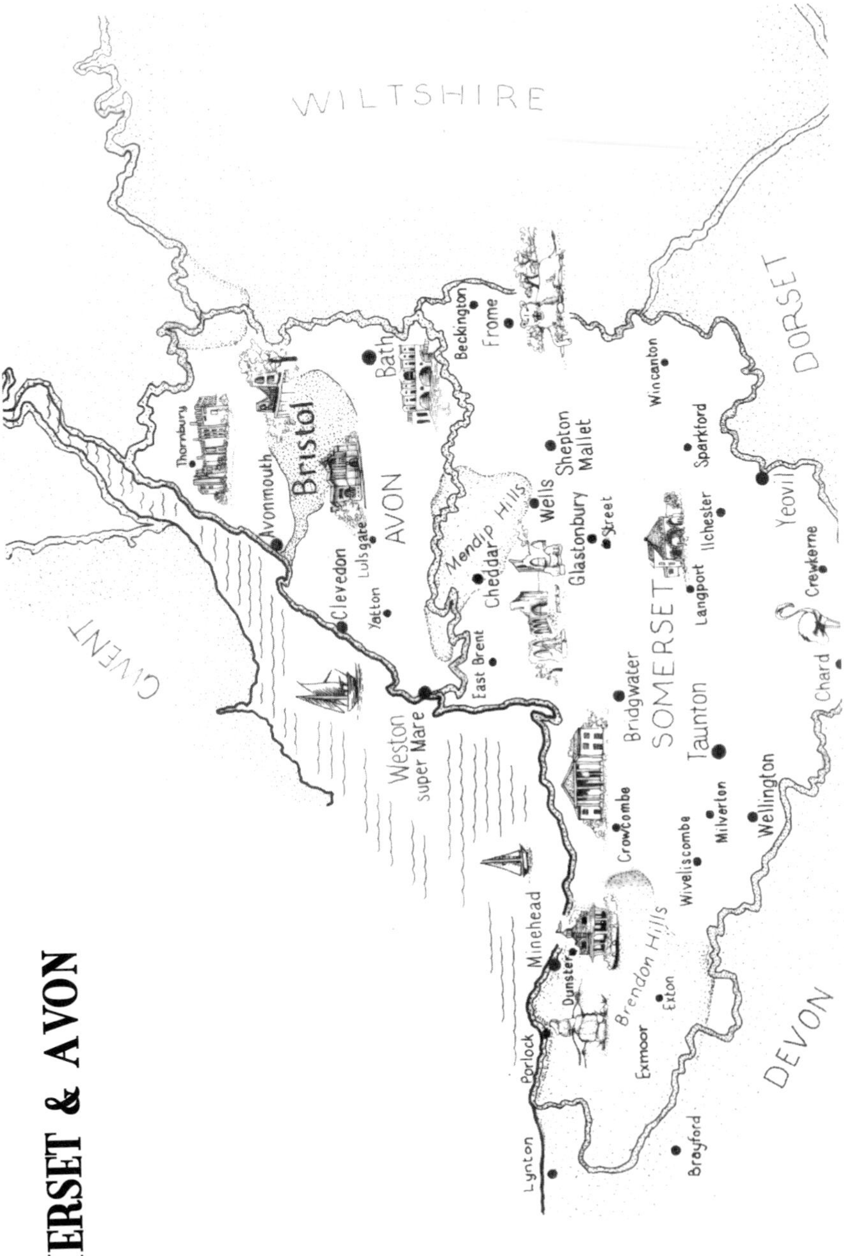

THE WEST COUNTRY

Devon, Cornwall, the Isles of Scilly, Somerset & Avon

Devon and Cornwall are fortunate in having both north and south coasts, facing the varying conditions of the Atlantic and the English Channel, giving a wonderful variety of beaches, coves, cliffs and dunes, almost all of it classified as Heritage Coast. Magnificent views can be found from just about everywhere along the SOUTH WEST COAST PATH which follows the whole of the coastline.

The sea and the rich yet bleak moorlands of Dartmoor and Bodmin Moor as well as Exmoor (which is mainly in Somerset) account largely for the area's great popularity as a holiday destination for those who seek natural rather than man-made attractions. Between the moorlands and the sea are lush cultivated lands benefiting from the warmest average climates in the country.

Dartmoor accounts for one tenth of the whole of Devon, about three hundred square miles, and at its highest points rises to over 2,000 feet. Although often referred to historically as Dartmoor Forest, it is a thinly covered granite outcrop with trees for the most part only to be found in a few woods in some of the river valleys and the lower slopes. Hundreds of hut circles and stone monuments from the Bronze Age and Iron Age are dotted around the Moor, and on a walk you can come across these without any signposts or tourist information boards, turning a walk on Dartmoor into something of an adventure. However walkers should take care on excursions deep into the Moor as the weather can change suddenly with thick mists, and bogs similar to those referred to in 'The Hound of the Baskervilles' really existing.

Exmoor near the north Devon coast is richer in vegetation than Dartmoor and has large herds of Red Deer. Sadly these are hunted and there is also much fox hunting in the area, Devon having the largest number of hunts of any county. This is 'Lorna Doone' country.

Bodmin Moor in Cornwall is smaller and lower than the two Devon moors but has an equally rich diversity of plant and animal life, with ponies and sheep wandering freely and it would seem there is evidence for 'The Beast of Bodmin Moor', possibly a Puma or the like. The eerie bleakness of Bodmin Moor has been made famous by Daphne Du Maurier, her book 'Jamaica Inn' based on real places.

The Cheesewring in the Lynher Valley, Bodmin Moor

Typical of both Dartmoor and Bodmin Moor are the high tors, hard granite outcrops left behind after the retreating ice and erosion.

The toughness of granite accounts also for the ability of the **Isles of Scilly** to withstand the pounding of the seas, miles off the tip of Cornwall. The Isles can be reached via helicopter, plane or boat from southwest Cornwall and the sub-tropical garden on **Tresco** is a wonderful sight in the spring, despite the ravages of storms in recent years. The history of Scilly can be traced at the HERITAGE MUSEUM which includes, appropriately for this archipelago in wild seas, a shipwreck exhibition.

Parts of the far south west of Cornwall appear more like moonscapes than anything you would expect to see on this planet. This is due to the open mine workings of the English China Clays and other producers. Efforts are made to landscape the spoil heaps, but for many years the white hills and white surrounding landscape look quite extraordinary. The history of clay working can be seen at WHEAL MARTYN, close to the centre of the clay mining area at **St Austell.**

Stone is also quarried in the area and at **Beer** in Devon the caverns created by the quarrying are now open to visitors.

Tin mining was a major contributor to the south western economy in the past, as to a lesser extent was silver and arsenic, and hundreds of roofless engine houses can still be seen in both counties, most particularly in west Cornwall. Mines were frequently named after Mine Captain's wives, names like Wheal Charlotte or Wheal Betsy being common here. This is in fact one of only two places in the world where tin is mined underground (even under the sea), and the difficulties of this led to the development by Thomas Newcomen from Dartmouth in 1705 of the 'atmospheric engine', the first practical steam device. Much of the history of mining in the area can be seen at MORWELLHAM QUAY.
Rumour has it that at **Dunchideock** near Exeter there are treacle mines. Visits are restricted, due to the explosive nature of the treacle!

The earliest evidence of man in Britain, dating back some 25,000 years, long before homosapiens, was found in KENT'S CAVERN which is rather incongruously in what is now the resort town of **Torquay**. The mile of limestone caves at **Buckfastleigh** were inhabited not by man but by mammals and have yielded a rich collection of bones and teeth.

"I have no doubt that it is part of the destiny of the human race, in its gradual improvement, to leave off eating animals."

Thoreau

On the far north Cornwall coast, spectacularly clinging to a ragged rock rising out of the sea, are the mystical ruins of TINTAGEL CASTLE. This is strongly believed to have been King Arthur's castle and home also to Merlin. The medieval castle has recently been found to be built on the site of much earlier important habitation, and the site remains an intriguing enigma. The Arthurian legend is attached to many other sites in the region, and high on the Bodmin Moor is the mysterious DOZMARY POOL, said to be bottomless, where the hand reached up to take King Arthur's sword Excalibur.

Castles and forts abound, most particularly around the coast, to ward off invasion. The region also has England's newest castle, CASTLE DROGO on the crest of a gorge at **Drewsteignton**, designed by Edwin Lutyens and completed in 1930 but with a medieval atmosphere. There are also many grand houses, due largely to the wealth earned from the tin mining and shipping.

Most of the important towns and cities in the region, and many of the delightful small villages, lie beside natural harbours and have been associated with some of the earliest trade by sea - both legal and contraband - to within the country and abroad. From these harbours too have gone voyages of discovery. The most famous associations with **Plymouth** are Sir Francis Drake - who, so it is said, was playing bowls on the Hoe at Plymouth when news came of the sighting of the Armada - and the Pilgrim Fathers who sailed from here for America. Francis Drake lived at BUCKLAND ABBEY near **Yelverton** on his return from circumnavigating the world, and there are many other important associations with him in the region. It was also in Devon that Sir Walter Raleigh spent his early life.

The Royal Inn at Horsebridge on the Devon border with Cornwall

Exeter is an attractive and busy city, joined to the sea rather than on it, its quay home to a fine MARITIME MUSEUM.

The Britannia Royal Naval College looks over **Dartmouth** and the Dart estuary (the site for most of the filming of the television series 'The Onedin Line') from where many important voyages have started. This is a very attractive small town, whose extensive history is worth exploring. Boat trips take visitors out to sea, or up the river to Totnes.

The small town of**Totnes** is known as 'the alternative capital' of England. Due initially to the existence of the nearby Dartington Hall Estate which fostered progressive concepts, Totnes has attracted people concerned with conservation issues, with varied forms of healing, with different religious beliefs and with generally alternative lifestyles. It has probably the highest ratio of vegetarians of any part of Britian. In addition, Totnes is a pretty town.

" I do feel that spiritual progress does demand at some stage that we should cease to kill our fellow creatures for the satisfaction of our bodily wants. "

Gandhi

Two miles from Totnes at DARTINGTON HALL you can wander around the landscaped gardens and generally take in the atmosphere of this medieval estate which now houses an array of concerns including a College of Arts, the Schumacher College, and down on the edge of Dartington village the CIDER PRESS CENTRE. The centre includes not only Cranks, but also a contemporary crafts gallery and a miriad of other individual shops all worth a browse. There is also a Dartington Glass shop, but the factory itself is in **Torrington** in North Devon, and is open to the public for factory tours.

Lace is still made in **Honiton**, for which it has been famous since Elizabeth I's reign. Its height of popularity came when Queen Victoria had Honiton Lace for her wedding veil.

If you are visiting Cornwall during the first week of May you can see two local traditions which celebrate the fertility of spring. The **Padstow** Hobby Horse dances through the town on May Day, bringing certainty of husbands and children to the young women, and in **Helston** on 8th May the Furry Dance brings good fortune to the community as the locals dance through not just the streets, but even many of the houses.

Devon and Cornwall have many animal sanctuaries and rare breeds centres. Some visitors may not want to visit the latter because the animals would originally have been bred for meat, but there are certainly a number of good sanctuaries doing a very fine job.

TWIGGY WINKIES FARM near **Newton Abbot** in Devon has many animals which visitors can feed and play with, and is also the home of a Hedgehog Hospital where injured hedgehogs are nursed back to health and released into the wild.

At **Looe** there is a MONKEY SANCTUARY where the woolly monkeys live not in cages but as a wild colony with visitors free to walk among them. The only restraints are where necessary to keep humans out rather than animals in. The Sanctuary was started 25 years ago to provide a stable setting for monkeys rescued from isolated lives in zoos, or as pets, and three generations of monkeys, all native to Cornwall, can now be seen. Their native habitat in the Amazon Rainforest is seriously threatened, and the work of the Sanctuary has been recognised as a conservation triumph. The Sanctuary is now involved in a project to return some of their Woolly Monkeys to the wild in Brazil.

Also 25 years old is the DONKEY SANCTUARY at **Sidmouth** on the south coast of east Devon, it has taken in almost 6,000 donkeys during its existence, many of them previously cruelly treated or abandoned. After a spell in hospital the donkeys are well looked after on the 1,400 acres of farmland where they can lead a life of dignity and comfort. One of their associated charities, The International Donkey Protection Trust, aims to improve the conditions of donkeys and mules throughout the world.

“ *Vegetarianism isn't just about not killing animals, it's about saving the lives of people, of preserving our planet.* ”

Ishia Bennison

Near **Launceston** the TAMAR OTTER PARK AND WILD WOOD gives visitors an opportunity to see native otters in near natural conditions in 20 acres of woodland which is part of a breeding centre aimed at the re-introduction of otters to the wild. The attractive site is also home to three species of deer.

One of the most popular attractions in the region is the NATIONAL SHIRE HORSE CENTRE at **Yealmpton** with parades of the magnificent horses and cart rides.

The BLACKDOWN GOAT CENTRE is a sanctuary as well as a commercial herd of goats producing milk which is turned into yoghurt and cheese (vegetarian), all of which are available in their small shop. The Goat Centre can be found in the village of **Loddiswell** in the lush southern tip of Devon known as the South Hams. The village is also the home of the LODDISWELL VINEYARD which offers tours of the vineyard itself as well as the winery.

With its wines certified as organic, the CHUDLEIGH VINEYARD on its three acre site near **Newton Abbot** offers self-guided tours as well as free wine tasting, and you can also visit the apiary with the bees which are such an important aspect of the successful cropping of the grapes.

Bees can be seen in an even greater number at QUINCE HONEY FARM at **South Molton** in north Devon, the largest honeybee exhibition in the world. To emphasise this, bee colonies can be seen not only in natural situations, but also in an open hive in the form of a globe.

Surrounded by Bronze Age burial mounds, man's place in the world can be seen; by contrast, at GOONHILLY SATELLITE EARTH STATION near Helson on the southwest tip of Cornwall. You can watch and learn as world events are beamed via satellite to the giant dish aerials.

Giant technology is also on view at Britain's first ever WIND FARM near **Delabole** (also famous for its slate) in north Cornwall. Ten machines began harnessing energy from the wind in late 1991 and are now producing enough electricity to power 3,000 households. The three-armed, elegant giants rise 32 metres above the 240 metre hilltop. The turbines are carefully positioned along existing hedgerows, with all cables underground so normal agricultural use of the farm is undisturbed.

Wind harnessing on a more traditional basis is not much in evidence in Devon and Cornwall but with the many rivers running off the moors watermills are many. CROWDY MILL at **Harbertonford** near Totnes is a listed, working water mill producing purely organic flours.

OTTERTON MILL is also a working water mill producing stone-ground flour, with 18th century workings explained for the visitor with a tape/slide sequence and illustrations. The Otterton Mill Centre, which is near **Budleigh Salterton** southeast of Exeter, also houses a cooperative craft shop and workshops and there are lovely riverside walks.

The MUSEUM OF WATER POWER which can be found at **Sticklepath** near Okehampton is a restored waterpowered tool factory, and features the Tarka Trail in the area where 'Tarka the Otter' was written.

Tarka the Otter Country

At **Seaton** an electric tram still runs, in use during the summer by holidaymakers and in winter by birdwatchers.

On a domestic note, there is a curious collection of five round houses which can be seen at **Veryan** near the north Cornwall coast. The oddly shaped houses without corners were built, so it is believed, so that the devil had no north wall by which to enter and no corner in which to hide. Another round house can be found near **Exmouth**, the lovely little grand house A LA RONDE is a tribute to the original owners who decorated the central top section on the inside with shells. There is a house in the Warren in **Polperro** elaborately encrusted with shells on the outside, all found locally on the beach and there is a House of Shells at **Buckfastleigh**.

Built partly of a crude concrete made with sand collected from the beach at **Porthcurno**, and hewn out of the rocks, is the Greek-style MINACK THEATRE, a magical place where open air productions are put on each summer with a backdrop of the sea.

St. Ives is now the proud possessor of its own TATE GALLERY, an airy and elegant modern gallery housing some of the very best recent art. For decades St. Ives has been a magnet for artists, the BARBARA HEPWORTH SCULPTURE GARDEN AND MUSEUM stands as a monument of her work here.

Also around the Cornwall coast are a great many exceptionally fine villages. One such is **Chysauster Ancient Village** dating from the 2nd century and now preserved as a magical view into the past. Devon too can boast special villages such as **Clovelly**, its steep street down to the harbour lined with pretty cottages hung with baskets of flowers, rather full of tourists but mercifully free from traffic. Another is **Appledore** which is a popular beauty spot and the thatched group of cottages at **Buckland-in-the-Moor** are truly picturesque but on Dartmoor the most popular village is undoubtedly **Widecombe-in-the-Moor**, made famous by the tale of 'Uncle Tom Cobbly and All'.

Visitors to Devon and Cornwall are unlikely to leave without having had a 'cream tea' - thick clotted cream with scones and jam - but visitors should also take note of the many small cheese producers making a wonderful array of cheeses, most of them with vegetable rennet.

SOMERSET & AVON

Avon, as a county name, came into being with the 1974 reorganisation, taking in parts of northern Somerset and southern Gloucestershire and incorporating Bristol. It is one of the country's smallest counties, with a mainly urban landscape yet with much beauty from magnificent gorges to elegant buildings and with some rich industrial archeology. Somerset has a different beauty, very much rural in character, its vast open spaces dotted with towns that are comparatively small, but with many large manor houses and with huge stone barns which testify to success in agriculture.

The region as a whole has many truly spectacular sights. One of the most impressive, and well known, being the CLIFTON SUSPENSION BRIDGE built by Isambard Kingdom Brunel and completed in 1864, which crosses the Avon Gorge at a staggering 245 feet above high water level. Brunel's work is much in evidence in this area, often associated with the Great Western Railway which was a feat of elegant engineering. His ship 'Great Britain', the world's first ocean-going, propeller-driven iron ship was built at**Bristol** in 1843 and following restoration after being marooned in the Falklands, is now on display here at the GREAT WESTERN DOCK.

Much of Bristol's prosperity is due to navigation, the Avon estuary just before it reaches the sheltered Bristol Channel acting as a harbour, and a wide river to take cargoes inland. Trade was active from the early days of sail when ships left the port for many parts of the world, bringing back exotic and unusual goods. The medieval woollen trade to Portugal, Spain and Ireland was at the beginning of a long period of importance for fine woollens in the region. More recent industries which have been at the centre of Bristol's success are papermaking, printing, flour milling, tobacco, engineering, chemical processing, and aircraft production. The city's wealth reached out into the surrounding area and can be seen in the status of buildings in many of the towns and villages.

Where the river Avon becomes unnavigable at Bath the KENNET AND AVON CANAL, with its elegant aqueduct and locks, was created to carry goods further inland to the east.

The Kennet & Avon Canal

Bath is a beautiful town, one of the few that even looks good on arrival by train, with classical Georgian terraces harmoniously planned to enhance the Roman buildings. Both major periods of building were due to the huge popularity of the natural spa, the only hot springs in Britain. THE ROMAN BATHS MUSEUM includes the remains of the baths as well as the Temple of Sulis Minerva, in the town they called Aquae Sulis. The town is built for the most part in the attractive Bath Stone, as can be seen to great effect in the elegant ROYAL CRESCENT which was begun in 1767.

Stone is the main building material to be found in most towns and villages in Avon and Somerset, from the yellow Bath Stone in the north, to Blue Lias in the centre and Ham Hill Stone around **Yeovil** in the south. Unusually for the region, the smart town of **Taunton** is mainly of red brick.

The geology of Somerset is very noticeable: the low-lying and flat Somerset Levels in the centre of the county dotted with small round hills, through the middle of it running the Polden Hills, to the north the flat-topped Mendip Hills, to the south-west the Blackdown Hills and to the west the Quantocks beyond which is Exmoor.

> *Never doubt that a small group of thoughtful, committed citizens can change the world, indeed it is the only thing that ever has.*
>
> ***Margaret Mead***

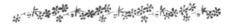

The miles of wet willow-lined Levels are some of the last surviving water meadows in Britain to be left undisturbed by modern farming. Once under the sea, the silt has provided rich soil and peat. Although much has been cut and used in garden composts, where it remains it provides a rare sight of endangered species of flora. Peat is a great preservative and many important finds of Neolithic, Bronze and Iron Age man have been made in the area. Many of the roads that cross this water-logged landscape are on timber Bronze Age causeways and medieval embankments, the suddenly rising hills in the flat landscape once islands in the water. The WILLOWS & WETLANDS VISITOR CENTRE which is at **Stoke St. Gregory** in the Sedgemoor area tells the story of the district and of traditional Somerset basket making from withies.

On the Levels, the fenland isle of **Athelney** is where King Alfred took refuge from the Vikings in the 9th century. Living as an outlaw he was hiding out in the hut of a herdsman's family when the cakes on the open hearth were burned. The wife, not knowing who he was, blamed the King for not keeping an eye on the cooking. Thus came into being the story of Alfred burning the cakes.

Another story relating to food is that of 'Little Jack Horner'. The Abbot of Glastonbury, wishing to placate Henry VIII, sent him a pie containing the deeds of the manor house at **Mells**. The emissary was one Thomas Horner who opened the pie, put in his thumb and pulled out a plum.

In the north of Avon, only just off the M5, at **Tortworth** stands a magnificent chestnut tree, described by the diarist John Evelyn as being from King Stephen's time, and dated on a plaque placed in 1800 as then being 600 years old. This is indeed a 'spreading chestnut tree', its limbs down to the ground and covering a vast area.

Coming down from the Mendips on the M5, BRENT KNOLL can clearly be seen rising from the Levels. Likewise out of the levels, CADBURY HILL with its Iron Age hill fort is considered by some to be Arthur's Camelot. GLASTONBURY TOR is possibly Arthur's Isle of Avalon, now a focal point for many visitors, either for the Glastonbury Festival held on farmland within sight of the Tor, or the nearby GLASTONBURY ABBEY which is the earliest site of Christian faith in England, visited, (so it is believed), by Joseph of Arimathea shortly after the crucifixion. The Abbey Farm houses the SOMERSET RURAL LIFE MUSEUM.

Not far from Brent Knoll, by the pleasant town of **Burnham-on-Sea** is the less than pleasant site of HINCKLEY POINT, the nuclear power station.

The high ground of **Exmoor** to the west (part Somerset and part Devon) has a great variety of birds, rare plants and flowers, shaggy ponies and large herds of deer. This was at one time a royal hunting forest and still today the deer are hunted, but given refuge on land owned by Paul and Linda McCartney for that purpose as well as the sanctuary of land owned by the League Against Cruel Sports. The moorland plateau rises to around 1,700 feet at Dunkery Beacon and terminates with the tallest cliffs in England, overlooking the Bristol Channel, designated as 'Heritage Coast'. Steep wooded combes cut down to the shore and oak trees have grown down the cliffs reaching the pebble beach. Monuments dating back up to ten thousand years include Bronze Age burial mounds and stone circles, Iron Age hillforts, Roman fortlets and medieval castles.

> *"Nothing living should ever be treated with contempt.*
> *Whatever it is that lives, a man, a tree, or a bird,*
> *should be touched gently ...*
> *Civilisation is another word for respect for life."*
>
> ***Elizabeth Goridge***

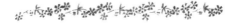

Evidence of early habitation is also to be found elsewhere in the two counties, STANTON DREW CIRCLES AND COVE being possibly the finest Neolithic religious site in the country, consisting of a fascinating assembly of three stone circles, two avenues and a burial chamber. From the nearby hill at **Maesknoll** there are excellent views of the WANSDYKE an old earth wall running from Portishead right to Salisbury Plain in Wiltshire.

The **Quantock Hills** was the first site in England to be designated an 'Area of Outstanding Natural Beauty', its wild, unspoilt heath with deeply cut wooded valleys typifying the landscape. Fox hunting takes place on the Quantock Hills.

The subterranean rivers of the **Mendips** have resulted in wonderful caves, potholes and gorges. A first sight of the spectacular CHEDDAR GORGE and WOOKEY HOLE with the many caves full of magnificent stalactites and stalagmites must have been a wonderful experience for many visitors, now marred by the 1.5 million visitors each year and the introduction of tacky tourist trappings. However, the surrounding scenery of the Gorge is wondrous. It can be seen at its best from the vantage point on the WEST MENDIP WAY, a walk which starts at Wells Cathedral and concludes after 30 breathtaking miles at the Bristol Channel.

Another very attractive walk is the 28 miles LELAND TRAIL following in the footsteps of the 16th century John Leland, starting on the National Trust's Stourhead estate and crossing quiet, southern Somerset countryside to another National Trust Property, Montacute House, and on to the high viewpoint of Ham Hill. The Gardens at STOURHEAD (just in Wiltshire) are best visited in the early summer, but at any time of year the lake surrounded by classical temples and monuments are serenely beautiful. MONTACUTE HOUSE, not far from **Yeovil**, is a fine example of Tudor domestic architecture which, although huge, is on a comfortable scale, set within early Jacobean gardens.

Montacute lies on the route of the Roman FOSSE WAY, one of the Four Royal Roads, running from the south west to Lincolnshire. From this point you can follow the Fosse Way to another of the many fine houses in the region at CRICKET ST THOMAS WILDLIFE PARK, home to many rare and exotic species of animal and bird and recently also to a Heavy Horse Centre. At **Rode** is a 17 acre TROPICAL BIRD GARDEN.

The swans at the BISHOP'S PALACE in **Wells** have learnt to ring a bell when they are ready for lunch. The Palace is within the inner walls of the city which also enclose the Chapter House and Deanery as well as the

CATHEDRAL. With its carved stone figures on the west front the Cathedral is an impressive sight and the inside has strange inverted arches, not part of the original plan but built to give support when the tower foundations began to collapse. Nevertheless they present a memorable and not unattractive feature.

One of England's smallest churches lies hidden in a wooded combe overlooking Bristol Channel at **Culbone**, away from roads and cars. Nearby in a farmhouse Coleridge wrote 'Kubla Khan'.

Coleridge lived at **Stowey** on the Quantocks at the end of the 18th century and his home is now open to the public. Here he wrote 'The Ancient Mariner'. The 'Rock of Ages', immortalised by Augustus Toplady in his hymn, was written at BURRINGTON COMBE on the Mendips.

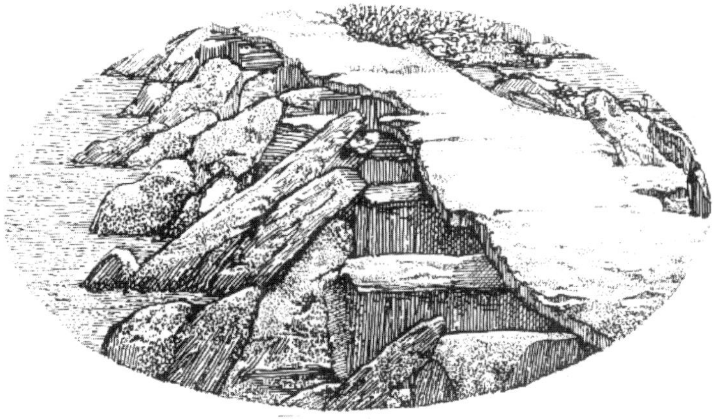

Tarr Steps

Near to **Dulverton** on Exmoor the river Barle is crossed at TARR STEPS with huge, closely fitting stone slabs each weighing up to five tons. The age of the bridge is unknown but it was certainly used by packhorses during the height of the successful cloth trade.

Dunster has an impressive 17th century octagonal market hall by a wide main street, originally used for the sale of locally woven cloth. Here the GALLOX BRIDGE, which again used to carry packhorses, has two ribbed arches, spanning the old mill stream in a picture-book setting. The medieval BUTTER CROSS once stood in the high street but is now some way from the centre.

A very pretty village can be found near Henbury in Avon, **Blaise Hamlet** having been built by the owners of Blaise Castle to beautify the view! There is a museum here with displays of Westcountry rural life.

Throughout Avon and Somerset there are numerous mock ruins and follies, such as ARNO'S CASTLE at **Brislington** built out of slag from a copper smelter; a SHAM CASTLE on Bathwick Hill and BECKFORD'S TOWER with 156 steps to the belvedere with views to Wales, both in **Bath**; and WALTON CASTLE in **Weston in Gordano** near the Gordano services on the M5. At **Barwick** a collection of follies, towers, pinnacles and the like, built to employ out of work glove makers, includes a monument to 'Jack the Treacle Eater' a message runner who kept fit on treacle, and at **Combe Florey** near Taunton a mock church tower was built as a keeper's lodge. In **Midford** just south of Bath is a castle in the shape of the ace of clubs, the card which made the owner's fortune.

In the **Clifton** area of Bristol, Goldney House (now part of the University) has several Gothic fantasies dating from the 18th century, one of which is GOLDNEY GROTTO, a cavern lined with sea shells and a rare quartz known as 'Bristol diamond', a cascade of water and a statue of Neptune. It is only occasionally open to the public during its current restoration. Also in Clifton is the Regency PARAGON, a concave terrace of houses with convex porches and curved doors.

The elegance of **Bath** is home to an eccentric collection of gnomes and royalty memorabilia in a basement garden. People seem compelled to throw money, in thanks for the free displays and thousands of pounds are donated to charity this way.

Not in any way a folly, the church at **Puxton** between Bristol and Weston-super-Mare has a spectacularly leaning tower, the lean greater than that of a certain tower in Italy.

Street was home to Clark's Shoes, but now to THE SHOE MUSEUM showing the history of shoes from Roman times to the present day. Housed in the oldest part of the original Clark's factory, the exhibits include documents and photographs, shoe buckles, fashion plates, hand tools and shoe machinery, as well of course, as shoes. There are also shoe-making demonstrations and 20 factory shops set within this small town made handsome by the Quaker Clark family who landscaped the factory buildings and built a school, a Quaker meeting house and even a temperance inn.

A few miles west of Cheddar Gorge at **Axbridge** is the WHEELWRIGHTS WORKING MUSEUM and GYPSY FOLKLORE COLLECTION where you can see the greatest invention of all time being made, alongside the brightly coloured caravans of the true Romany.

One of the most interesting museums around is the AMERICAN MUSEUM situated within the early 19th century CLAVERTON MANOR near Bath, displaying furniture, paintings and aspects of American domestic life from the 17th to 19th centuries. You certainly don't have to be American to find this museum fascinating.

The Clifton Suspension Bridge, near Bristol

A Domesday cornmill, given by King Athelstan to the Abbot of Bath in 931 AD, is still working today driven by a spectacular watermill and can be seen near Bath. THE PRISTON MILL includes a nature trail and scenic wagon rides.

The history of wine making and drinking can be traced at HARVEY'S WINE MUSEUM in Bristol, with a fine collection of antique drinking glasses, decanters and corkscrews in the unique surroundings of medieval cellars. Somerset is cider-making country and some of the large producers are based here alongside the traditional small orchards and presses. To get a good feel for, as well as a taste of cider, visitors can see its processing at SHEPPY'S FARMHOUSE CIDER at

Bradford-on-Tone or the TAUNTON CIDER MILL at **Norton Fitzwarren** or PERRY'S CIDER MILLS near Ilminster.

Somerset is famous for its Cheddar cheese which is still made here, and throughout the county there are now many farmhouse cheesemakers using a vegetable rennet.

Olive and Peanut Paté

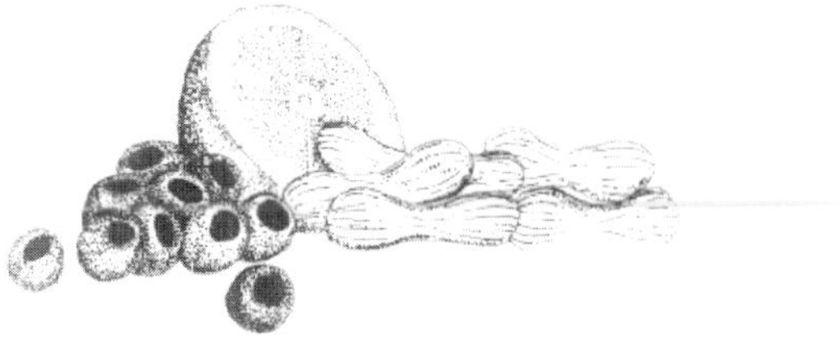

A simple recipe which can nevertheless be impressive. Ideal as a quick and easy starter or snack, with melba toast or French bread, or perhaps in vol-au-vents or pastry cups.

Serves 4 generously

6oz	Green Olives	De-stoned (use olives stuffed with pimento for a different taste and colour)
4oz	Peanut Butter	Crunchy or smooth according to preference
2 Tbs	Olive Oil	
2 Tbs	Lemon Juice	
5 fl oz	Water	exact amount according to preference
some Parsley		(not essential)

Keep back a few olives for decoration, blend the rest of the olives with olive oil, lemon juice and water. Chop most of the parsley. Mix everything together.

Serve at room temperature, decorated with the remaining olives and with peanuts and a sprig of parsley.

Cafe & Restaurant

DEMUTHS

2 North Parade Passage, Bath, Avon, BA1 1NX.
Telephone: (0225) 446059, Facsimile: (0225) 314308

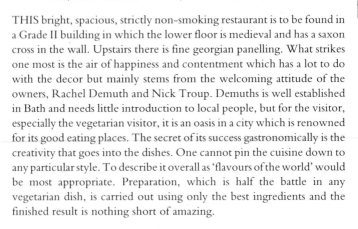

THIS bright, spacious, strictly non-smoking restaurant is to be found in a Grade II building in which the lower floor is medieval and has a saxon cross in the wall. Upstairs there is fine georgian panelling. What strikes one most is the air of happiness and contentment which has a lot to do with the decor but mainly stems from the welcoming attitude of the owners, Rachel Demuth and Nick Troup. Demuths is well established in Bath and needs little introduction to local people, but for the visitor, especially the vegetarian visitor, it is an oasis in a city which is renowned for its good eating places. The secret of its success gastronomically is the creativity that goes into the dishes. One cannot pin the cuisine down to any particular style. To describe it overall as 'flavours of the world' would be most appropriate. Preparation, which is half the battle in any vegetarian dish, is carried out using only the best ingredients and the finished result is nothing short of amazing.

In addition to the main menu there are always daily specials and vegans, diabetics and lacta diets come within the scope of this accomplished establishment. Breakfast, coffee, lunch, tea or dinner at Demuths, with jazz or world music playing in the background, art posters on brightly painted walls, banquettes and potted palms, intimate alcoves, make the occasion memorable. For the sweet tooth there is a fine selection of cakes and puddings, many of them supplied by the award winning Hobbs House Bakery. Demuths is licensed and you will find organic wines on the list. Bottled beers and cider are also available plus a comprehensive range of juices and soft drinks, speciality teas and coffee. Demuths lives up to its reputation and has the added bonus of one of the finest locations in the city with its ground floor windows overlooking Ralph Allen's Townhouse and the towering majesty of Bath Abbey.

Useful Information

OPEN: Mon-Sat: 9am-10pm, Sun: 10am-5pm
CREDIT CARDS: Access/Visa/Mastercard
CHILDREN: As long as parents excercise control over them
LICENSED: Yes
ON THE MENU: Exciting and sometimes amazing vegetarian dishes
DISABLED ACCESS: No
GARDEN: Courtyard with tables
ACCOMMODATION: Not applicable

Wholefood Restaurant

M^c^CREADIES

3 Christmas Steps, Bristol, Avon, BS1 5BS.
Telephone: (0272) 298387

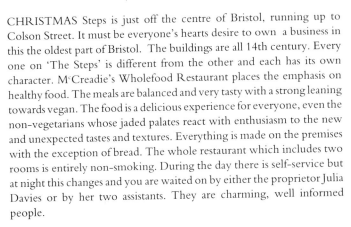

CHRISTMAS Steps is just off the centre of Bristol, running up to Colson Street. It must be everyone's hearts desire to own a business in this the oldest part of Bristol. The buildings are all 14th century. Every one on 'The Steps' is different from the other and each has its own character. McCreadie's Wholefood Restaurant places the emphasis on healthy food. The meals are balanced and very tasty with a strong leaning towards vegan. The food is a delicious experience for everyone, even the non-vegetarians whose jaded palates react with enthusiasm to the new and unexpected tastes and textures. Everything is made on the premises with the exception of bread. The whole restaurant which includes two rooms is entirely non-smoking. During the day there is self-service but at night this changes and you are waited on by either the proprietor Julia Davies or by her two assistants. They are charming, well informed people.

McCreadies has a licence but serves only organic drinks including four wines, two beers and a lager. Ten herbal teas, Five leaf teas, bambu and grubdrinks (Decaffeinated) as well as Cotswold sparkling water are available also seven flavours of fruit juices. The restaurant holds the Heart Beat Award with Bristol City Council and in fact provides the food at the presentation of these awards.

A pretty courtyard garden at the rear is in use in the summer. Sadly, because of the steps McCreadies is unsuitable for wheelchairs.

Useful Information

OPEN: Tues & Wed: 8am-7pm. Thurs-Sat: 8am-10pm. Sun: 11-5pm
CREDIT CARDS: No
CHILDREN: Welcome
LICENSED: Restaurant. Organic drinks
ON THE MENU: Kosher Vegetarian & vegan super food
DISABLED ACCESS: No
GARDEN: Small patio eating area
ACCOMMODATION: Not applicable

Restaurant

MILLWARDS

40 Alfred Place, Kingsdown, Bristol, Avon, BS2 8HD.
Telephone: (0272) 245026

JUST round the corner from the Kingsdown Sports Centre and near the University and main hospitals, Millwards has become a name synonymous with excellent Vegetarian fare. For six years Patricia and John Millward have striven to make their attractive, intimate restaurant in a mid-Victorian building complete with the very high and ornate ceilings of that period, a place on which Vegetarians can rely. That they have succeeded is apparent when you realise that they are former winners of the Vegetarian Restaurant of the Year UK and have an entry in many National and International Food Guides.

You dine at beautifully appointed tables in a totally non-smoking atmosphere with the sound of unobtrusive classical music in the background. The menu is imaginative and highly recommended is 'The Millward's Platter' of two or three courses offering a taste of three dishes at each course. There is a set price for two or three courses. Where dishes are suitable for vegans you will find a V after the entry. Imagine a meal which might be Warm Tabbouleh with Toasted Almonds followed by Aubergine Fritters in a Guinness Batter on a bed of spiced Cous Cous with red peppers and pine kernels. There are also some scrumptious and innovative desserts such as Poppyseed Parfait with Passion Fruit sauce or Millward's brown sugar meringues with ice cream and cream. Delicious.

Millwards is proud of its wine list which features many small growers and also a good selection of half bottles. There is a choice of 70 wines including some from Europe, Mexico, Australia, New Zealand, Chile, USA and England. 12 wines are vegetarian and 15 are organic.

Useful Information

OPEN: Tues-Sat: from 7pm. Closed one week at Christmas, Easter & 2 weeks in October
CREDIT CARDS: Visa/Access
CHILDREN: Welcome
LICENSED: Restaurant

ON THE MENU: Vegetarin with vegan options. Other dishes on request
DISABLED ACCESS: Wheel-chair access but no suitable toilets
GARDEN: No
ACCOMMODATION: N/A

Hotel & Restaurant

PORTHVEAN HOTEL & FRINS RESTAURANT

Churchtown, St Agnes, Cornwall, TR5 0QP.
Telephone: (0872) 552581, Facsimile: (0872) 553773

SITUATED in Churchtown, the centre of St Agnes village, the Porthvean provides all you would expect from a small personally run hotel and much, much more - it is the only restaurant in Cornwall awarded a star from the Vegetarian Good Food Guide. The building itself is old - it was the White Hart over 200 years ago, with parts of the property almost twice that age. Behind the private car park are buildings which are owned by the National Trust. At the front is a small terrace, sunny and sheltered, an ideal point for local events such as the Carnival, Flora Dances and Victorian Street Fayre, or just to sit with a drink and watch the world go by.

Geoff and Frin Robinson own and run this exceptionally nice hotel. Their bedrooms are beautifully appointed to a high standard of decor and comfort. All seven rooms have their own shower, wash-basin and WC together with colour televisions, tea/coffee making facilities, hair dryers and telephones. If the weather is unkind, the well stocked bar has a real log fire to cheer you up and the bedrooms have heaters which you control.

Good food holds pride of place and for vegetarians, 50% of the starters, 50% of the main courses and 100% of the desserts are vegetarian with roughly 20% across the board being suitable for vegans. Very little food is bought ready made other than a paté and some ice cream and sorbets; others are home-made. In the ten years that the Robinsons have been catering for vegetarians they have made sure that every stricture is carefully monitored. For example vegetarian cheese is used for all cooking and gelatine is never used. The menus are always carefully chosen and offer a wide choice of international dishes.

Useful Information

OPEN: All year except Xmas, New year and 3 weeks in January. Dinner 7-9pm
CREDIT CARDS: Visa/ Mastercard/Switch/Connect
CHILDREN: Yes. They must enjoy real food!
LICENSED: Yes. 40 wines from around the world. Some organic & vegetarian
ON THE MENU: Wide range of vegetarian dishes as well as other dishes
DISABLED ACCESS: No wheelchair access or disabled facilities
GARDEN: No, but sunny terrace
ACCOMMODATION: 3 dbl, 2 fmly, 1 sgl, 1 twn. All en-suite

Cafe

GRANARY CAFE

The Devon Guild of Craftsmen, Riverside Mill, Bovey Tracey, TQ13 9AF.
Telephone: (0626) 832223

AN insight into the craftsmanship of the area is superbly displayed at Riverside Mill where The Devon Guild of Craftsmen provide a changing series of exhibitions and a large shop selling some of the finest craft work in the country. Within this attractive Listed Building with its own water wheel is The Granary Cafe, which is an excellent place for anyone to relax and enjoy either a simple cup of freshly brewed coffee or a beautifully cooked and presented meal.

The Granary is not solely vegetarian and does cater for carnivores but at least 50% of the food is vegetarian and when it comes to the delectable desserts, no less than 95%. You are offered a first class choice of cakes, three types of scone and a wide range of main courses, all made on the premises. There is also at least one choice daily of home-made soup with a roll and either butter or Flora, which is a meal in itself. The Granary is open to everyone and there is no need for you to spend time looking at the displays or crafts unless you wish to. Many of the local people pop in regularly for tea or coffee or perhaps a light lunch in order to meet their friends. It is that sort of welcoming place and certainly not expensive. The Granary has a no smoking rule and is self service.

In the summer the courtyard is ablaze with flowers and becomes a very pleasant place in which to sit. The Granary is licensed and although the selection of wines is small, the range has been carefully chosen from French and English wines. There is also lager and organic cider as well as a delicious organic apple juice.

Useful Information

OPEN: 10-5pm. Closed Christmas & New Year Bank Holidays
CREDIT CARDS: Visa/ Access/Mastercard
CHILDREN: Welcome
LICENSED: Yes
ON THE MENU: Good choice for vegetarians. Home-cooked
DISABLED ACCESS: Yes
GARDEN: Courtyard with flowers
ACCOMMODATION: Not applicable

Hotel

COMBE LODGE HOTEL

Chambercombe Park Road, Ilfracombe, Devon, EX34 9QW.
Telephone: (0271) 864518, Facsimile: (0271) 867628

COMBE Lodge Hotel offers you and your family a welcoming, quiet and enjoyable holiday with a difference. They will take you from the hotel to the start of all sorts of wonderful walks and cycle rides and pick you up at the end of the day at a prearranged time. This allows you to explore without the nuisance value of driving. A service for which the hotel has won awards. This small, licensed Victorian property is just on the outskirts of Ilfracombe overlooking the picturesque harbour and sea, and only a 10 minute walk to the shops, theatre, cinema, promenade and harbour. There is a large car park - something very necessary in Ilfracombe.

Some of the bedrooms have their own shower room and toilet, others have a shower within the room, and all have vanity units, shaver points, central heating and tea and coffee making facilities. Some bedrooms enjoy the picturesque view of the harbour and, on a clear day, the Welsh coast in the distance. There are also two public bathrooms and three public toilets. The friendly, cosy bar is somewhere in which you can enjoy a drink, a cup of coffee, an evening snack or try your hand at a game of bar skittles or shove halfpenny. For those who like to sit in the comfort of a lounge and watch television, it is all there for your pleasure.

Combe Lodge is no smoking throughout and has a reputation for good food, and plenty of it, served in their licensed dining-room. The meals are imaginative and typically English with a hint of something special, made up of three courses followed by a good selection of cheese and biscuits, coffee or tea. Most importantly there is a full and interesting vegetarian menu. Wake up to a full English breakfast which will set you up for the day. The hotel is quite happy to comply with any special diets and to make packed lunches on request.

Useful Information

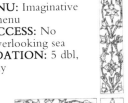

OPEN: All year round
CREDIT CARDS: Access/Visa/Mastercard/Eurocard/Amex
CHILDREN: 10 years and over
LICENSED: Yes
ON THE MENU: Imaginative vegetarian menu
DISABLED ACCESS: No
GARDEN: Overlooking sea
ACCOMMODATION: 5 dbl, 1 Sgl, 3 fmly

Restaurant with Accommodation

THE STANNARY

Mary Tavy, Tavistock, Devon, PL19 9QB.
Telephone: (0822) 810897, Facsimile: (0822) 810898

UNDOUBTEDLY one of the best vegetarian restaurants in the British Isles, The Stannary, is in a charming 16th century and Victorian house, in the quiet Dartmoor village of Mary Tavy, four miles north-east of Tavistock. Set in its own grounds looking out onto the wild, rugged beauty of Dartmoor, this is an elegantly decorated restaurant, Victorian in style and with an impressive collection of antique pottery fruits and vegetables. The talented and likeable owners, Michael Cook and Alison Fife have very strong views on how a restaurant should be run. Their guidelines are based on what they themselves look for when they dine out. Firstly their imaginative and carefully planned menu can not be faulted, secondly the tables are immaculately laid with good silver and sparkling glass. Gentle baroque and classical music plays in the background adding to the sense of tranquillity.

Pre-dinner drinks are taken in the plant-filled orangery and it is here that you first get presented with the menu. Every item is home cooked; nothing is bought in. This is gourmet cuisine, often incorporating exotic and unusual foods such as seaweeds, flowers, wild berries and truffles, in unique creations. The menu attracts many non-vegetarians and with the added blessing of a superb wine list from around the world as well as home-made Stannary country wines, The Stannary deserves every accolade it has had heaped upon it.

The icing on the cake is the accommodation. Here you can stay after dining or for longer if you want to continue enjoying this fabulous food. The rooms have television and there are tea and coffee facilities. It is not inexpensive but the cost includes dinner as well as a delicious breakfast.

Useful Information

OPEN: Generally Tues-Sat from 7pm
CREDIT CARDS: Access/ Visa/Amex
CHILDREN: Over 12 only
LICENSED: Yes. 160 vegetarian wines, many organic
ON THE MENU: Gourmet cuisine
DISABLED ACCESS: No
GARDEN: Yes. 2 acres with views of Dartmoor
ACCOMMODATION: Elegant and comfortable with canopy beds

Restaurant

PLYMOUTH ARTS CENTRE

38 Looe Street, Plymouth, Devon, PL4 OEB.
Telephone: (0752) 660060

THE Plymouth Arts Centre has so much to offer including films that are either not shown in the main cinemas or ones you have missed first time around. There are exhibitions of all kinds, workshops, music, poetry and that boon, a Vegetarian Restaurant. Here in the Arts Centre you can combine a meal and a cinema ticket, enjoy a two course meal or coffee in the restaurant followed by an evening enjoying a film. The combined ticket not only gives you a first class evening out but also saves you money! Children's portions are available. Special nights are occasions to remember, for example it might be Flavours from the Middle East, Food from Gambia or simply Festive Fayre. Whatever the destination the Vegetarian food, music and entertainment will be authentic.

The building dates back to Elizabethan times when it was reputed to be the largest coaching house in England, and has a splendid atmosphere. The Restaurant is surrounded by galleries, the cinema and studios and has a special ambience of its own. It is a peaceful place with no music to disturb one, is partly non-smoking, seats 55 and is self-service. You will find all the food very acceptable and inexpensive. The most expensive dish is a Mushroom Biriani, Dhal and Yoghurt Sauce at less than £3.50. There is a very good Spinach and Courgette Filo Pie, a Spicy Vegetable Crumble a selection of Quiches and many more good things. Bread rolls and some ice cream from Salcombe Dairies are the only ready-made food bought in. The restaurant is licensed and has a small number of wines plus canned lagers, beers and ciders and a variety of country wines.

Useful Information

OPEN: Mon-Sat: 12-2pm Lunch. Evening Tues- Sun: 5-8pm. Light refreshments Tues-Sat: 10-8pm. Mon 10-3pm. Closed Bank Holidays
CREDIT CARDS: None
CHILDREN: Welcome
LICENSED: Restaurant
ON THE MENU: Entirely Vegetarian
DISABLED ACCESS: No. Because the building is so old it is not suitable for wheelchairs although there are toilets for those not so active
GARDEN: No
ACCOMMODATION: N/A

Hotel & Restaurant

HOMESDALE HOTEL & GEMA RESTAURANT

Bayview Road, Woolacombe, North Devon, EX34 7DQ.
Telephone: (0271) 870335

YOU will find this happy, friendly hotel in Woolacombe, on a road owned by the National Trust and looking out over superb seaviews and a picturesque beach. It is the sort of hotel in which people of all ages will find contentment. For those who can take their holiday or short break away from the summer months, Homesdale is a wonderful base in winter or spring. You will be warm, comfortable and well fed and find the countryside and the beaches excellent for walking. Golfers have always found this part of North Devon superb.

Open to non-residents as well as to residents the hotel's Gema Restaurant has a reputation locally for its welcoming atmosphere and imaginative food. This is not a strictly vegetarian hotel, but every effort has been made to ensure that there are enjoyable and varied dishes every day for non-meat eaters and indeed, for anyone on a special diet if prior notice is given. vegetarian cheese is used in cooking, vegetarian jelly is used for desserts and no ready-made food is bought in. For the last ten years Carlos and Teresa Oyarzabal have been catering successfully for vegetarians - and have not lost one yet!

There are some very attractive bedrooms with fourposters at Homesdale. Every room is either en-suite or has a shower and basin. Family rooms have bunk beds for the children and every room has central heating. In the evenings guests and those who are coming to dine in the restaurant, find the cosy bar an excellent place in which to have a drink before a meal. The well stocked bar includes over 100 liquers! The limited but interesting wine list is sensibly priced with the average bottle costing something in the region of £8.

Useful Information

OPEN: All year except February
CREDIT CARDS: All major cards
CHILDREN: Welcome
LICENSED: Yes
ON THE MENU: Interesting English & Continental dishes with a choice for vegetarians
DISABLED ACCESS: Not suitable
GARDEN: Very large
ACCOMMODATION: 2 dbl, fmly, 4 twn, 2 sgl, en-suite or with shower

Restaurant, Cafe & Shop

THE GOAT HOUSE

Bristol Road, (A38), Brent Knoll, Somerset, TA9 4HJ.
Telephone: (0278) 760995, Facsimile: (0278) 760314

SET in rural surroundings, off the M5 at Exit 22, not far from Burnham-on-Sea, Weston-Super-Mare and Bristol, this interesting establishment has several times been featured on TV, the Good Vegetarian Guide and Egon Ronay's 'Baby Comes Too'. One of its attractions is that it is both, restaurant/cafe and shop are built around a courtyard. In the stables you will see varieties of goats and the shop sells goat products including mohair sweaters.

The cafe/restaurant is endowed with much pine giving it a true farmhouse look in which the wood burning stove in winter throws out a wonderful and welcoming heat. Background music which is familiar classical, sometimes classic pop or folk. The eating area is partially non-smoking and one orders a meal from the counter. Everything one eats is prepared and cooked on the premises from natural ingredients to promote healthy eating. The menu is International and whilst not entirely vegetarian there is a high percentage of true vegetarian dishes right across the board. There is a special Goat's Milk Diet. For seven years the owners, Tony and Marjorie Jarvis with the assistance of their chef, have been paying great attention to vegetarian eating and very successfully. The dishes are imaginative, delicious and immensely popular with non-vegetarians as well.

The Goat House is licensed and whilst the number of bins is limited, the wines from France, Germany and Italy are well chosen. None are vegetarian, organic or country.

Useful Information

OPEN: Winter: 8am-6.30pm. Summer: 8am-8pm. Closed 2 days at Christmas
CREDIT CARDS: Visa/ Access
CHILDREN: Welcome
LICENSED: Restaurant
ON THE MENU: International dishes with approx 30% vegetarian
DISABLED ACCESS: Wheelchair access but no suitable toilets
GARDEN: Courtyard
ACCOMMODATION: Not applicable

Restaurant

CRISPINS

26 High Street, Dulverton, Somerset, TA22 9DJ.
Telephone: (0398) 23397

A PENNY Farthing bicycle mounted over the front door is your introduction to this attractive restaurant which was once a row of cottages in the High Street of Dulverton.

Inside there are two rooms. The front and main restaurant is bistro style and seats 22. The centre room has a fine oak fire place and oak beams and seats up to 20. It is used for family groups or small parties. In summer the delightful vine covered garden sets the scene for open-air lunch or candlelit dinner.

Margaret Grimes, who with her husband, Tony owns Crispins, is a talented chef who brings varied, home-cooked dishes to her menu. Some are traditional English but there is also a strong ethnic list chosen from years spent living in the Middle East and India. Crispins has always been attentive to the needs of Vegetarians and today adds a percentage of Vegan options. 55% of the starters are vegetarian and 33% of the main courses. Very little food is bought ready made, just 5% of the starters and 5% of the desserts.

The house wine is Bulgarian, either red or white. The whole list is small but sensibly chosen with wines from Spain, France, Germany and Bulgaria. The average price is less than £8. Somerset Cider Brandy and local Farmhouse Cider are two of the interesting drinks on offer. For anyone wanting to stay in Dulverton, close to the Exmoor National Park, Crispins has a Self Catering Flat.

Useful Information

OPEN: Summer: closed Sun eve, Mon Lunch. Winter: open Tues eve to Sun Lunch. Closed throughout February
CREDIT CARDS: None
CHILDREN: Welcome
LICENSED: Yes

ON THE MENU: High percentage of vegetarian starters, main courses & puddings
DISABLED ACCESS: Yes but no suitable toilets
GARDEN: Yes
ACCOMMODATION: Self-catering flat

Bistro

THE WIFE OF BATH

12 Pierrepont Street, Bath, Avon, BA1 1LA.
Telephone: (0225) 461745

12 PIERREPONT Street is one of Bath's many beautiful buildings. Built about 1760 and designed by John Wood, it is on the site of the old orchard of Bath Abbey. The Wife of Bath is a fine restaurant at the garden level of this Georgian terrace and the owners have kept the cellar ambience with quarry tiled floors and white stone walls. It is a delightful place spread over five rooms - a bar with a room off it, and three inter-linked rooms. Whilst you are enjoying a drink or relishing the delicious food, quiet music plays in the background, sometimes jazz, sometimes pop and sometimes classical.

The menu is not strictly vegetarian but there are always eight snacks, four starters, three main courses and eight desserts which are delicious. The Wife of Bath has been producing vegetarian fare since it opened five years ago and has many regular and devoted followers. The Bistro is licensed but does not have vegetarian or organic wines. The wine list is carefully chosen from countries around the world.

Useful Information

OPEN: 12-2.15pm & 5.30-11pm. Closed Sunday lunch and 3-4 days at Christmas

CREDIT CARDS: Access/Visa/Amex

ON THE MENU: International cuisine. High percentage of vegetarian dishes

DISABLED ACCESS: No

Hotel & Restaurant

THE EDGEMOOR

Haytor Road, Bovey Tracey, Devon, TQ13 9LE.
Telephone: (0626) 832466 , Facsimile: (0626) 834760

THE Edgemoor delights the eye even before you enter its welcoming doors. Inside you will find this elegant, beautifully run house welcomes everyone. The lounge is graced with a 'Minstrels' Gallery' and you are invited to dine in the pretty 'Peach Restaurant' in a relaxing, friendly atmosphere. Smart casual dress is the order of the day as you sit down to dine.

If one were asked to describe the dishes on offer, the term 'Modern English with a French influence' is probably correct in the broadest sense. There are a number of dishes that are suitable for vegetarians for whom the owners, Rod and Pat Day, have been catering for 12 years. The wine list is quite extensive and is chosen from around the world. There are two wines especially for vegans and two that are organic. There are twelve en-suite bedrooms, you will be contented if you stay here with everything possible done for your comfort. Choose to dine here and you will take away a very happy memory.

Useful Information

OPEN: All Year. Lunch: 12.15-1.45pm. Dinner: 7.30-9.30pm. Bar Snacks: 12-2pm & 7-9pm.

CREDIT CARDS: Visa/Access/Diners/Barclaycard

ON THE MENU: High standard of vegetarian dishes included on set price menu which changes monthly

DISABLED ACCESS: Not easy but all toilets on one level

Inn

THE ROYAL INN AND HORSEBRIDGE BREWERY

Horsebridge, Nr. Tavistock, Devon, PL19 8PJ.
Telephone: (0822) 87214

HIDDEN away in delightful countryside near Tavistock, The Royal Inn at Horsebridge is an experience that should not be missed. Originally the pub was used as a nunnery and you will see the Royal Seal set in the doorstep, as you enter the pub's charming and atmospheric interior. It is a welcoming place at any time and super for food. The menu changes with regularity: the bread is freshly baked every day and whilst the dishes are designed for carnivores as well as vegetarians, there are ample choices for anyone who wishes to be strictly vegetarian. You need have no fear of additives and certainly the cheese in cooking is always vegetarian. All the soups are perfect for you and so are the desserts and at least 8 of the main courses as well as 50% of the snacks.

The Woods have been here for 9 years and have catered for vegetarians throughout those years; always successfully. In fact many of their meat eating customers frequently choose the vegetarian dishes. The Royal Inn brews its own beers which are only obtainable here. They also serve a delicious Mulled Wine in winter.

Useful Information

OPEN: 12-2.30pm & 7-11pm. Sundays 10.30pm.
CREDIT CARDS: None taken

ON THE MENU: Home-cooked. Nothing fried. No chips!
DISABLED ACCESS: Yes but no special toilets

Hotel & Restaurant

THE ARUNDELL ARMS

Lifton, Devon, PL16 OAA.
Telephone: (0566) 784666, Facsimile: (0566) 784494

THE Arundell Arms has been one of England's premier fishing hotels for more than half a century and has 20 miles of its own water on the Tamar and four of its tributaries. The hotel, an old coaching inn on a site that dates back to Saxon times, is a part of old England. Warmth and comfort abounds, not only in the sitting room but in the bar with its buzz of talk about the days events, in the bedrooms which have private bathrooms, colour television, direct dial telephones and fresh flowers, and in small, thoughtful things such as the decanter of port placed in the sitting room for guests after dinner.

A leading young English chef, Philip Burgess, prepares traditional English and French dishes with just that little imaginative touch that marks a chef out from his fellows. It is that talent that has allowed him to create so many delicious dishes suitable for vegetarians.

To find it take the A30 and you will find it two miles east of Launceston and the Cornish border in the village of Lifton.

Useful Information

OPEN: Bar: 12-2.30pm & 6.30-9.30pm Rest: 12-2.30pm & 7.30-9.30pm
CREDIT CARDS: Visa/Access/ Diners/Mastercard

ON THE MENU: Superb menu with imaginative dishes for vegetarians
DISABLED ACCESS: Yes, but no special facilities

Hotel

WATERLOO HOUSE HOTEL

Lydiate Lane, Lynton, North Devon, EX35 6AJ.
Telephone: (0598) 53391

WATERLOO House Hotel is a delightful Georgian building found in England's own 'little Switzerland' - a truly beautiful area. It is able to combine the spirit of the early 19th century - in which it has its origins - with all the comforts of modern day. Historically it is one of the oldest, original lodging houses in all of Lynton, its renovations and exquisite decor have created a unique, gracious and warmly welcoming hotel. A log fire is always lit on chilly days.

Most rooms have private en-suite facilities and all are centrally heated, with colour television and beverage making facilities. The elegant dining room features imaginative and tempting menus. The evening meal is a candle lit dinner of four courses, complemented by a varied wine list. Breakfast is in the full English traditional, vegetarian or continental should you prefer. The Waterloo House prides itself on its flexibility and will always prepare special diets and interesting menus to suit vegetarian guests. The hotel has been awarded a RAC Highly Acclaimed, ETB 3 crowns commended and the AA QQQQ Selected Award for high standards of comfort, hospitality & cooking.

Useful Information

OPEN: All year
CREDIT CARDS: None taken

ON THE MENU: Freshly prepared produce. Vegetarian and vegan options always available
DISABLED ACCESS: No.
Bargain breaks available

Guest House

HEATHFIELD HOUSE

Okehampton, Devon, EX20 1EN.
Telephone: (0837) 54211

JANE Seigal owns, and is the talented chef in, this guest house. She runs this country house primarily for people who enjoy the moors as it is situated 800 feet above sea level. Heathfield House literally backs onto the edge of the northern part of the moor, well placed for wonderful walks if you are so inclined, or a drive for miles in the most haunting scenery you will ever see.

Jane has converted a Victorian house into a comfortable home; every bedroom has an exceptionally high standard and all are en-suite. She is a superb cook and housekeeper who specialises in delicious vegetarian dishes. One would think the house and the cooking would take all her time, but not a bit of it. Jane is so well organised that part of staying at Heathfield is walking with her on the moors when she will share with you all her favourite places. This is a non-smoking house and at night everyone tends to sit around after dinner, sipping a glass of wine and chatting over the day's activities.

Useful Information

OPEN: All year
ETB 3 Crown Commended
CREDIT CARDS: Visa/Mastercard

ON THE MENU: Superb range of vegetarian dishes
DISABLED ACCESS: No

Restaurant & Wine Bar

BARRETTS OF PRINCESS STREET

Princess Street, Plymouth, Devon, PL1 2EX.
Telephone: (0752) 221177

TUCKED in just behind Plymouth's Theatre Royal, Barretts of Princess Street is unique in the city. It is a modern 'New York' style wine bar with a restaurant area and in the five years it has been in existence, its ebullient and creative patron, Stephen Barrett, has acquired a reputation, not only for his food, but for his love and knowledge of wine - he is a world renowned expert who writes regularly for leading magazines and travels the world in search of new, exciting wines to add to his list.

His travels have also given him a taste for the foods of the world and this is reflected in his use of ingredients in a manner seldom seen in this part of the country. Firstly he only uses the freshest of products, whether vegetables, meat or fish and secondly you will be offered constantly changing dishes, such as an open Ratouille of Mediterranean vegetables or a Koulibiac of Asparagus. To eat here is a gastronomic experience for vegetarians and carnivores, and to be entertained by Barretts is unforgettable.

Useful Information

OPEN: Mon-Fri: 11am-11pm. Sat: 11-2pm & 7-11pm. Closed Sundays
CREDIT CARDS: Access/Visa/Amex
ON THE MENU: Many excellent choices for vegetarians
DISABLED ACCESS: Yes + toilets

Hotel

LYDGATE HOUSE HOTEL

Postbridge, Devon, PL20 6TJ.
Telephone: (0822) 88209

LOOKING at the charm and elegance of Lydgate House Hotel it is hard to imagine that in the middle of the 17th century it was a squatters' cottage. The main part of the house was built in 1900 as a farmhouse; recently a conservatory has been added and is used as the dining room.

Set in its own thirty six acres with the East Dart River running through, the location is very peaceful. Staying here is much like being part of an informal well-managed house-party. All rooms have their own bathrooms and are furnished in keeping with the house. There is an imaginative but not elaborate menu with influences from India, China, France and Italy. Local and home grown organically produced vegetables are used wherever possible. The menu changes daily and there is a vegetarian dish at every course. Vegans (and other diets) can be catered for with prior notice. Lydgate house is licensed.

Useful Information

OPEN: Dinner is served at 7.30pm. Cream teas served Apr to Oct 3pm - 5.30pm. Closed 3rd Jan - 3rd March
CREDIT CARDS: Access/Visa/Master/Euro
ON THE MENU: Traditional and vegetarian choice from small menu. Reservation required for non-residents
DISABLED ACCESS: Yes but no special toilet facilities

Free House Inn

THE PLUME OF FEATHERS

Princetown, Nr Tavistock, Devon, PL20 6QG.
Telephone: (0822) 890240

THE Plume of Feathers, built in 1785, is Princetown's oldest building, even older than the forbidding Dartmoor Prison which dominates the village. This fascinating, lively pub is a favourite with local people and those who come from miles around to enjoy the hospitality, the beer, the warm welcome and the excellent food.

Everything about the pub is rich in history and atmosphere. Gleaming copper bars, slate floors, original oil lamps, beamed ceilings all enhance the Plume of Feathers. Here you can stay in comfortable bedrooms, campsite or hostel, protected from the wild weather that frequently strikes Dartmoor. On Sunday at lunchtime and occasionally on Friday nights there is live music. It is an excellent base for discovering the majesty of the moor, its flora and fauna. The menu reflects the growing awareness of the needs of vegetarians. There is a more than a satisfactory choice at every course. Home-baked bread rolls, free range eggs and locally grown vegetables reinforce the high standard.

Useful Information

OPEN: Mon-Sat: 11-11pm, Sun: 12-3pm & 7-10.30pm
CREDIT CARDS: Amex/Access/Visa/Eurocard
ON THE MENU: Good choice of vegetarian dishes at every course + snacks
DISABLED ACCESS: Yes + toilets

Restaurant & Coffee Shop

HARBOUR LIGHTS

The River Beach, 3 Queen Street, Teignmouth, Devon, TQ14 8BY.
Telephone: (0626) 779355

BUILT in the 1850's Harbour Lights was once a fisherman's cottage and the restaurant has a definite nautical flavour today with six hand built model ships including Teignmouth's famous Pilot boat 'Storm Siren' much in evidence.

Closed only in January and February, this is somewhere you can get an excellent vegetarian breakfast and equally delicious vegetarian food throughout the day. Some 33% of the main courses are vegetarian and 40% of the snacks, 66% of the starters and 100% of the desserts. Everything is home cooked and whether you are looking for a big meal, a small snack, a cream tea or just a cup of coffee you will be well cared for and at the same time able to enjoy some splendid views over the estuary. Harbour Lights is licensed and also serves some interesting non-alcoholic beverages including hot milk with honey and nutmeg as well as herbal teas and decaffeinated filter coffees.

Useful Information

OPEN: Jun, July, Aug: 9-7pm, Sun-Thurs, 9-9pm Fri & Sat. Other months 9-5pm. Closed Jan and Feb
CREDIT CARDS: None taken
ON THE MENU: Something for everyone including a goodly number of vegetarian dishes
DISABLED ACCESS: No

Hotel

THE CHERRYBROOK HOTEL

Two Bridges, Yelverton, Devon, PL20 6SP.
Telephone: (0822) 88260

SET in the heart of Dartmoor National Park is an old farmhouse built 185 years ago by a friend of the Prince Regent, which is now The Cherrybrook Hotel. In the capable hands of Andy and Margaret Duncan this has become one of the best places to stay for those who want a relaxed atmosphere, the company of people who want to explore the wild, majesty of the moor.

You wake up in the morning ready for the excellent breakfast, collect a packed lunch, if you wish it and set out for your day, returning tired, exhilarated and hungry in the evening, ready for a drink, a good dinner and the fun, banter and chat about the days activities with your fellow guests. Fresh local produce includes a Devon cheeseboard complete with several vegetarian cheeses. On the menu you will find a constant change of vegetarian dishes, traditional English in composition and quite delicious. There are special breaks at excellent prices.

Useful Information

OPEN: All year except Christmas & New Year. Restaurant & cream teas 11-6pm. Dinner 7pm

CREDIT CARDS: None taken

ON THE MENU: 3.5 acres. Tables & benches. Cultivated moor with up to 42 different wild flowers at the last count.

DISABLED ACCESS: Yes + toilets

Inn with Restaurant

THE SEA TROUT

Nr Totnes, Devon, TQ9 6DA.
Telephone: (0803) 762274 , Facsimile: (0803) 762506

This beautiful 16th century inn, once known as The Church House Inn and now as the Sea Trout, is one of the most relaxed and welcoming hostelries in the whole of Devon. To reach it follow the signs to Staverton off the A384 and you will come to it between Totnes and Buckfastleigh. It has become a favourite place in which to stay for many people who not only relish the food, wine and company but know they can rely on well appointed en-suite bedrooms furnished in a country cottage style There is also a garden with a gently playing fountain and a patio.

Recommended by Egon Ronay and having received the RAC commendation for hospitality and the restaurant, one naturally expects high standards, and you will not be disappointed. Whilst there is no specific vegetarian menu there are many dishes that are suitable and the daily blackboard specials always include dishes for vegetarians. An inn to enjoy.

Useful Information

OPEN: 11am-3pm & 6pm-11pm

CREDIT CARDS: Amex/Visa/Access

ON THE MENU: Vegetarian choices on the daily blackboard specials

DISABLED ACCESS: Yes. New disabled toilets by end of 1994

Restaurant

BARRINGTON COURT RESTAURANT

Barrington, Nr Ilminster, Somerset, TA19 ONQ.
Telephone: (0460) 241244

THE National Trust owns the stately Barrington Court, a Tudor Manor House restored in the 1920's by the Lyle family. The beautiful gardens, influenced by Gertrude Jekyll, are laid out in a series of 'rooms'. Since 1992 a restaurant has been added, located in Strode House, built as a stable block adjoining the House in 1670 by the Strode family.

The restaurant is attractive and has glorious views over the garden. Fresh vegetables and fruit grown in the kitchen garden are used in the restaurant which adds to the high standard of the food on offer. The menu is not large but there are always starters, main courses and desserts suitable for vegetarians. The recipes used are traditional English and include delicious home-made scones and cakes. The restaurant is licensed and also has some wonderful apple juice made from apples grown in the orchard.

Useful Information

OPEN: April-September, Sat-Thurs: 11-5.30pm
CREDIT CARDS: Amex/Visa
ON THE MENU: Home-cooked, well chosen vegetarian dishes
DISABLED ACCESS: Yes + toilets. Also batricar for visitors to see the garden

Brighton Pavilion

Contents

SOUTHERN ENGLAND

Dorset, Wiltshire, Hampshire, Sussex and The Channel Islands

Scrambled Egg Sauce

A useful addition to savoury dishes. Egg yolks only are best for colour, taste and texture, but you can use the whole egg if you have no other use (such as meringues) for the whites.

Serves 4

6 Egg Yolks (or 3 whole eggs)
15 fl oz Milk
1oz Cornflour
3 oz Double Cream

Mix the yolks with about one third of the milk and scramble (in a microwave if you have one).

Mix the cornflour, the remaining milk and the cream, and cook through (again a microwave is ideal).

Add the scrambled egg.

SOUTHERN ENGLAND

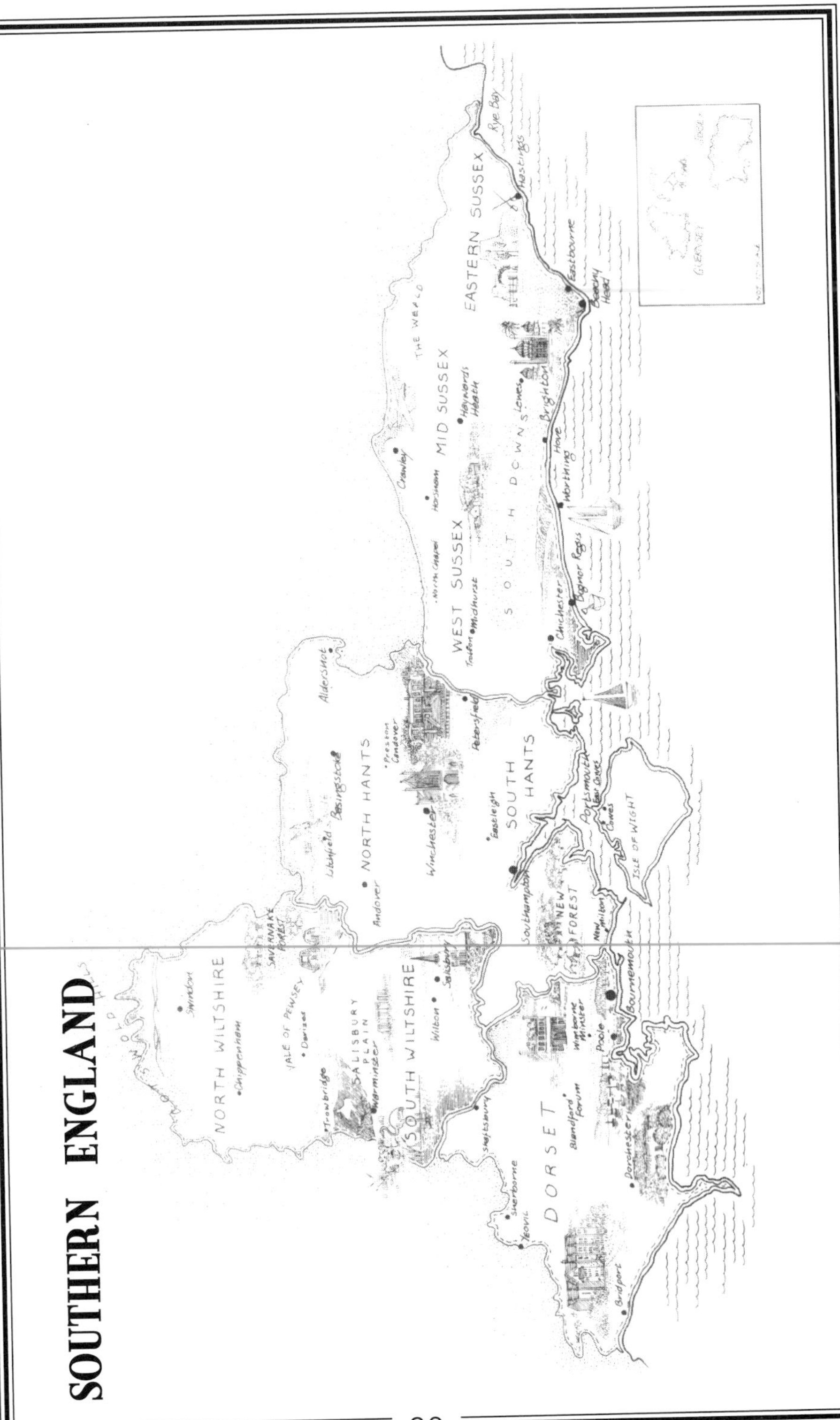

SOUTHERN ENGLAND

Dorset, Wiltshire, Hampshire, Sussex & The Channel Islands

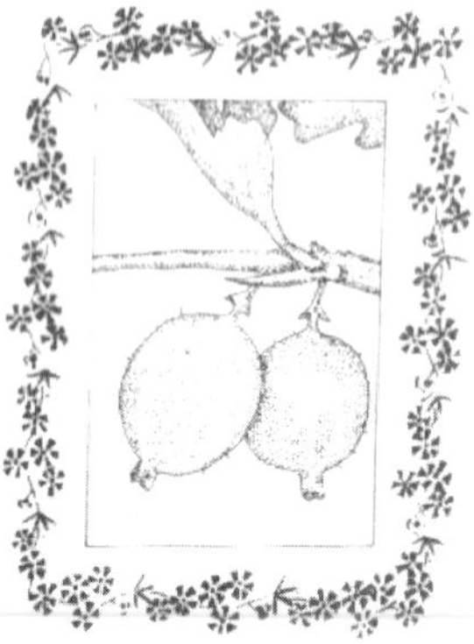

The whole of this region is crammed with history, from the abundant fossils on the Dorset coastline, to the hundreds of stone circles and monuments of early man, the Bronze Age settlements and Iron Age forts, and later sites of events so momentous that they have marked the course of history itself.

The west of this region is more sparsely populated today than the east, and it is here that most, although by no means all, of the early history is to be found.

STONEHENGE in Wiltshire is of course the most famous monument created by early man, something like 5,000 years ago. Yet no less impressive are the AVEBURY STONE CIRCLES, originally part of an enormous prehistoric complex incorporating other standing stones, barrows and tumuli, and the mysterious SILBURY HILL, an extraordinary artificial prehistoric mound, the largest Neolithic construction in Europe, which has absolutely no obvious purpose. As far as explanation of these enigmatic monuments can go, they are interpreted at the AVEBURY MUSEUM.

Like Stonehenge and the lesser-known WOODHENGE near **Durrington**, the majority of monuments can be found on SALISBURY PLAIN, a high undulating area of chalk, often bleak but with pretty villages scattered mainly in the low-lying areas.

The SUSSEX DOWNS were also settled by early man, when the lower surrounding area was too densely forested for the tools and techniques then available. Along the length of the Downs is a string of settlements dating from the Bronze Age and fortified in the Iron Age, including a fine example at **Cissbury** near Worthing.

This region has long been subject to attempts at occupation, both within the country and from across the sea, and fortresses and castles therefore abound: hill forts to keep out the Romans, the Saxon forts to keep out the Normans, the Norman forts to fight back against the Saxons, forts to keep out the French and the Spanish over the centuries, right up to recent times with fortifications to keep out the Germans and their allies in both world wars.

The enormous hill fort at MAIDEN CASTLE near **Dorchester**, is recognised as being the finest Iron Age fort in Britain and was so effective that it was still in use as a fortification, ultimately unsuccessful, against the Roman invasion in AD 43.

Only slightly less impressive is the Iron Age BADBURY RINGS on the Roman road from Old Sarum to Dorchester. Legend has it that King Arthur fought and won his battle against the Saxons, and received his fatal wounds, close to this spot.

Throughout Dorset and Sussex Roman 'civilisation' is much in evidence, many of the current roads being on straight Roman routes, linking important towns and palaces such as FISHBOURNE near **Chichester.**

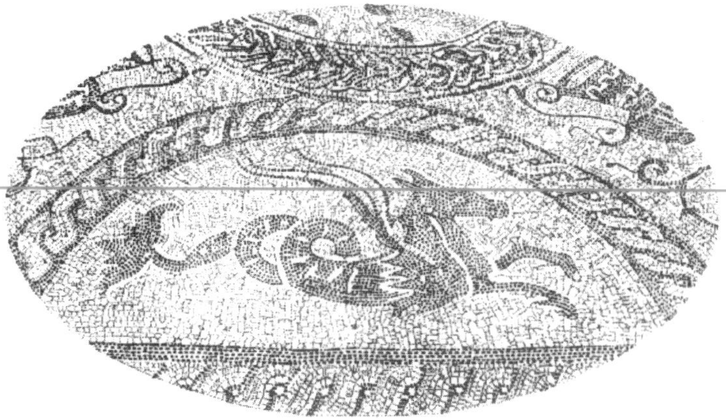

Mosaic panel detail, Fishbourne Roman Palace

Roman walls are also in a good state of preservation at SILCHESTER ROMAN CITY where the almost complete circuit of town walls enclose the site that was the capital *Calleva Atrebatum*. Unusually this site did not continue as a city and the remains are therefore fortunately well defined.

PORTCHESTER CASTLE has the most complete Roman walls in Europe along with an almost perfect Norman keep. Built at the head of **Portsmouth** harbour, it was used as a medieval royal palace and a rallying point for troops, as shown in a lively exhibition that tells the story of the castle, literally, with the use of lifesize figures, as well as interactive displays and even coffin covers you can lift to see some of the Saxon dead!

"The question is not, can they reason? Nor, can they talk. But can they suffer?"

Jeremy Bentham

Today's Hampshire on the other hand owes more to the Saxons and Normans. **Winchester**, created into the capital of Wessex by King Alfred, has a significant number of Saxon properties still to be seen alongside many Norman buildings, including the Cathedral, believed by some to be the most beautiful in Britain.

As everyone knows, William the Conqueror defeated Harold at the Battle of Hastings in 1066 (he actually landed at **Pevensey**), and it is possible to explore this most famous of battle sites as well as to visit BATTLE ABBEY which he founded to atone for the bloodshed. The buildings are well preserved and very impressive.

William brought strong Norman influences to much of the area, initially in Sussex and Hampshire but gradually spreading through the country. Built shortly after the Battle of Hastings, ARUNDEL CASTLE still today has a major presence, commanding the surrounding countryside of West Sussex. The castle grounds have an imposing lake and some lovely trees with walks along the river.

Since the Norman Conquest, the Channel Islands, a part of the Dukedom of Normandy, have retained allegiance to England despite being on the doorstep of France. They are a very individual collection of islands some well populated, some of the smaller ones not, each with its own customs and character.

On the **Isle of Wight** CARISBROOKE CASTLE is a Norman fortress, later used to imprison Charles I before the execution, and now incorporating a museum on the history of the island.

William the Conqueror planted many of the oaks and beeches of THE NEW FOREST in southern Hampshire in 1079, to create a hunting park of about 100 square miles. Sadly the Forest is still much used for deer and fox hunting. It has been a protected landscape since its conception, with a status similar to a National Park and is grazed by some 3,000 ponies along with cattle. It is quite unlike the chalk uplands which typify much of the region, being predominantly a lush, green, dense, forest surrounded by wide heathlands. The story that William demolished dozens of villages in the process of planting is now believed not to be true.

The vernacular buildings at the WEALD AND DOWNLAND OPEN MUSEUM at **Singleton** in West Sussex have all been saved from demolition, drawn from this south east corner. It is one of only two open air museums in the country that actually shows the buildings without interior trappings making it possible to study the techniques and materials used, related to the landscape from which the exhibits come. The 37 exhibits include farms, houses and mills, mainly but not exclusively timber framed.

Weald and Downland Open Museum

An impression of life as it was lived by a wealthy merchant of the medieval period can be gained at the MERCHANTS HOUSE in **Southampton**, faithfully restored and furnished, right down to the availability of fine wines as they were in the shop of the 13th century (although not of that date!). A similar experience can be found in Dorset where the medieval FIDDLEFORD MANOR at **Sturminster Newton** shows more rural life of the period.

Near **Ferndown** which is north of Bournemouth is **Stapehill**, where a one-time Cistercian Abbey amidst lovely gardens now houses a working craft centre and agricultural display. The POWER TO THE LAND exhibition shows rural life from the days of the first plough through the changes brought by the tractor and technology.

The history of the whole world from 4.5 million years ago to the present day can be traced at 'Planet Earth', a small display for such a large subject, part of the GARDEN PARADISE CENTRE at **Newhaven** in East Sussex. Other displays on the same two acre site include a gnome settlement and miniature railway. In the SEVEN SISTERS COUNTRY PARK old Sussex barns have been converted into an interpretive centre with a natural exhibition on 'The Living World'.

"For my part I rather wonder both by what accident and in what state of mind the first man touched his mouth to gore and brought his lips to the flesh of a dead creature."

Plutarch

Chalk dictates much of the topography of the region, great swathes of it designated as 'Areas of Outstanding Natural Beauty'. These include the North Wessex Downs, the largest expanse of chalk downland in southern England; the chalk down of south Dorset, which forms part of the designated area covering half the county; almost all of the Isle of Wight; the Wiltshire Downs adjoining Cranborne Chase; and the historic landscape of the Sussex Downs.

From Winchester in Hampshire the SOUTH DOWNS WAY, Britain's first long-distance Bridleway follows the chalk escarpment for just over 100 miles through West and East Sussex to **Eastbourne**, or an alternative route via **Beachy Head**, with panoramic views over the wooded farmland of the Sussex Weald or to the sea. The Way was almost certainly an important route for Bronze and Iron Age man as can be seen by the scattering of tumuli, hill forts and dykes.

The DORSET COAST PATH is a continuation of the South West Coast Path which having started in Somerset takes in the whole of the Cornwall and Devon coastline. Passing breathtaking cliffs isolated caves and astounding rock formations, the Path takes in the pretty town of **Lyme Regis** with its many fossil exhibitions and shops and The Cobb - the long quay made famous in Jane Austin's 'Persuasion' and in the film 'The French Lieutenant's Woman'.

A little further on the Path reaches GOLDEN CAP which at 626 feet is the highest point on the south coast. At **Abbotsbury**, walkers can rest awhile taking in the beauties of the SUB-TROPICAL GARDENS with its exotic trees, or visiting the famous ABBOTSBURY SWANNERY with its unique 600 year old colony of mute swans, and finding out about local life at the ABBOTSBURY TITHE BARN AND COUNTRY MUSEUM. At this point the path splits, the southern route heading across CHESIL BANK, a 10 mile-long shingle bank, beyond which The Fleet is a haven for a diverse range of plant and bird life, to the peninsula of **Portland Bill**.

The alternative route cuts across land to**Weymouth** and on to DURDLE DOOR, a huge limestone arch, and LULWORTH COVE, a magnificent oyster shaped bowl formed by the waves breaking through hard rock to the softer strata which are beautifully exposed. The nearby STAIR HOLE is another example of this process at an earlier stage. Beyond **Swanage** the coastal path crosses STUDLAND BAY with the chalk pillars of 'Old Harry' (a synonym for the devil) and 'Harry's Wife', through to **Poole** Harbour.

"It is beneficial to one's health not to be carvivorous. The strongest animals, such as the bull, are vegetarians. Look at me. I have ten times as much good health and energy as a meat eater."

George Bernard Shaw

Boats from Poole Harbour take trippers out to **Brownsea Island**, a wildlife sanctuary, home to peacocks and red squirrels.

The **Isle of Wight** is reached by boat from Southampton, reputedly the most expensive stretch of water to cross when cost is compared to distance. In the centre of the island is OSBORNE HOUSE, the seaside home of Queen Victoria, partly designed by Prince Albert. The whole of the coastline is included on the ISLE OF WIGHT COASTAL PATH. At the western tip, the white pinnacles of chalk rising out of the sea are known as The Needles, remnants of a ridge which once linked the island with the mainland. A chairlift takes visitors down to **Alum Bay** where minerals have stained the sand in a kaleidoscope of colour. Above **Freshwater Bay** is TENNYSON DOWN, a favourite spot of the poet who lived at Farringdon House for 30 years. In the first week of August the island is crowded with visitors for Cowes Week. The island has several rare species of flora and fauna.

Several rare species can also be found in the grounds of PARNHAM HOUSE near **Beaminster** in West Dorset, a unique place, a magnificent restored manor house and gardens, a focal point for contemporary furniture with the work and influence of John Makepeace, and close by at HOOKE PARK wonderful natural woodland and a pioneering college exploring radical ways of using wood in a sustainable and effective way. One example of this is their own building within the park using wood as supports in a way that is based on tradition yet is truly innovative. Because Parnham and Hooke Park are primarily working places, opening to the public is on a restricted basis.

The first vineyards in England, since the time of the Romans, were started in Hampshire in the early 1950's and today there are several in the southern counties. The vines grown in this country tend to be Germanic in character, and mainly white as these are the grapes which cope best with our cold damp conditions. Many of the vineyards are open to the public, such as the LYMINGTON VINEYARD in Hampshire. They offer a self-guided tour of their six acres of vines, a slide-show and a wine tasting, and you can also visit their herb garden.

The smallest pub in Britain is to be found at **Godmanstone** in Dorset. THE SMITHS ARMS was a smithy when Charles II stopped to have his horse shod and demanded a drink. As the smith had no licence to dispense ale the King promptly gave him one.

It was Royal influence that created the elegant town of **Brighton** out of 'a poor fishing town', after Dr Russel taught the medicinal value of sea-bathing and the Prince Regent brought the Court to the coastal town to relax. The extraordinary ROYAL PAVILION was built for the Prince Regent after the style of the Moghul palaces of India, and the centre of the town is a glorious array of Regency terraces. A small town worth visiting for its attractiveness and wealth of history is **Lewes** to the north of Brighton, and close by is the world renowned GLYNDEBOURNE OPERA HOUSE. If you want to see an opera during its summer season it is essential to book.

Timing too is important for a visit to ELING TIDE MILL not far from **Southampton**, a working mill and museum, which is the only surviving mill in the world to harness the power of the tide for the regular production of wholemeal flour, as it was centuries ago. Only about five hours of milling is available each tide - ten hours a day, often at inconvenient times. There was a mill on the site by 1086, but the current building is 18th century. The mill is open Wednesday to Saturday throughout the year, but it is a good idea to telephone if you want to be sure you will not miss the tide.Telephone (0703) 869575.

Parnham House near Beaminster

The WILTON WINDMILL, not in the ancient capital of **Wilton** but further north in Wiltshire close to **East Grafton**, is a working windmill where you can see the grain being ground and of course buy your souvenir flour. From the windmill it is a pleasant one mile walk to the CROFTON BEAM ENGINES which are in steam most bank holiday weekends.

Steam engines can be seen at probably the most impressive event of its kind, the GREAT DORSET STEAM FAIR which takes place near **Blandford** around the August Bank Holiday.

Close to Rudyard Kipling's home in **Burwash**, East Sussex, is a restored watermill, with one of the oldest working, water-driven turbines in the world.

The stone used for many of the houses in Bath was taken from a mine which is now the only shaft stone mine open to the public. THE UNDERGROUND QUARRY at **Corsham** is a spectacular labyrinth of tunnels and galleries, and visitors are encouraged to have a go at sawing stone with the 'frig bob'. Also in Wiltshire at **Great Bedwyn** is LLOYD'S STONE MUSEUM, decorated by tombstones, and featuring one tombstone in the shape of an aeroplane with an 11-foot wingspan, tracing the history of carved and worked stone through the ages.

A small museum in the village of **Tolpuddle** in Dorset commemorates the Martyrs and the tree at which they met still stands (with a little help).

The award winning FOX TALBOT MUSEUM OF PHOTOGRAPHY at **Lacock** in Wiltshire shows much of the history of photography.

Close to **Bere Regis** is Lawrence of Arabia's house, CLOUD'S HILL and there is a statue of him in Arabian clothes in the church of St. Martin in **Wareham**. **Steventon** is where Jane Austin spent her early life and wrote several early works, moving later to **Chawton**, also in Hampshire.

Possibly the prettiest town in the region is **Rye** in East Sussex. It has been a magnet to writers and artists for centuries. Henry James lived in the town as did E.F. Benson, and Van Dyck sketched here.

Dorset is Thomas Hardy country, well described - albeit with bogus place names - in all of his novels. His influence has been such that many businesses use Hardy's town names, 'Casterbridge' being a common trade name in Dorchester, the town most frequently featured. His home at nearby **Higher Bockhampton** surrounded by a pretty cottage garden is open to the public, but only by prior arrangement, telephone (0305) 62366. There is a memorial room to him in the COUNTY MUSEUM and a monument in the High Street at Dorchester, but the Hardy Monument at **Portesham** is not to Thomas Hardy but to the Admiral made famous by Nelson's last words.

Dorchester plays host to a unique TUTANKHAMUN EXHIBITION, the only one outside Egypt, the tomb and treasures faithfully recreated in a superb display featuring not just the sights but even the appropriate sounds and smells. From an earlier period, the town houses a DINOSAUR MUSEUM featuring fossils, skeletons and life-size reproductions along with 'hands-on' computerised displays to bring this fascinating world alive.

There is also a DINOSAUR SAFARI at **Bournemouth**, and here too is a recreation of the world famous TERRACOTTA WARRIORS.

In the adjoining town of **Poole** the splendid gardens of COMPTON ACRES are very much worth seeing, with several gardens in one, including a charming Japanese garden and some excellent statuary.

The Heather Dell at Compton Acres

In the far north of this region, the Elizabethan LONGLEAT HOUSE, mansion of the Marquess of Bath, is set in gardens landscaped by Capability Brown, now in part the site of the LIONS OF LONGLEAT SAFARI PARK. Both are major tourist attractions and get very crowded.

STOURHEAD GARDENS at **Stourton** are some of the most important gardens in England, with classical temples set beside huge artificial lakes creating a place of great serenity.

The chalk escarpments to be found throughout the region have for centuries been decorated with figures on the hillsides, cut through the turf. One of the most famous, or infamous, is the CERNE ABBAS GIANT in Dorset, 180ft high, a fertility symbol which women would visit at night, possibly dating from Roman times. THE LONG MAN of **Wilmington** in East Sussex is even larger at 231ft, but probably less old, dating, it is thought, from at least the 7th century. Even less is known of the WESTBURY WHITE HORSE in Wiltshire, which was restored in 1788 to the extent that it was actually turned to face the other way! The many other chalk figures to have been created, some now lost through neglect, include the comparatively new REGIMENTAL BADGES above **Fovant** in Wiltshire, carved by troops on exercises here during the 1st World War.

The 1st World War is remembered at the SANDHAM MEMORIAL CHAPEL built in the 1920's at **Burghclere** near Newbury and movingly decorated with murals by Stanley Spencer of war scenes at Salonica. On the edge of the village is WATERSHIP DOWN, a pretty landscape full of rabbits, as told in the story by Richard Adams.

Selborne, the quiet rural village in east Hampshire, was made famous by the naturalist Gilbert White, a parson, whose house is now a museum and the garden which inspired his writings is now open to the public. In the village main street Gilbert White planted a row of trees to shield him from the sight of slaughter at the butcher's shop.

Finally, visitors to the region are likely to want to make factory tours of two cosmetic companies:

THE BODY SHOP is well known to everyone using their 1,000 shops in 44 countries throughout the world, and at **Littlehampton** in Sussex you can visit their factory and have a good look behind the scenes. The tour includes seeing not only how the products are made but how the company deals with its industrial waste, and information on why they trade with indigenous peoples. It is necessary to book in advance for the tours, telephone (0903) 731500.

A cosmetics factory tour is also available two counties away at **Poole** in Dorset, at COSMETICS TO GO. Their lively weird and wonderful approach to their products and marketing have captured the imagination of many. All their products are, of course, completely cruelty-free and environmentally friendly. Telephone free on (0800) 373366.

Avocado with Roast Walnuts

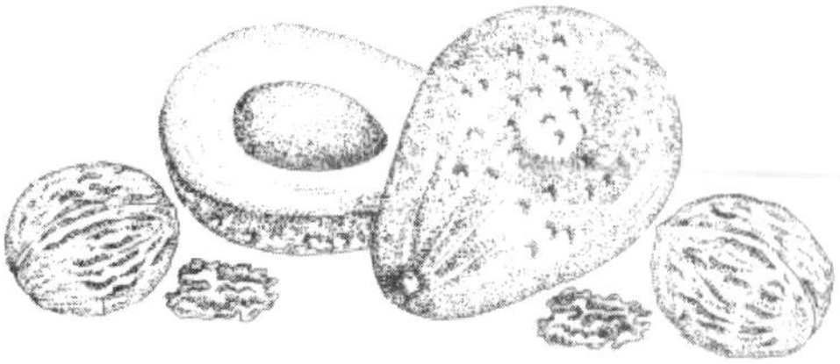

As either a snack, a starter or a main item with salad, this version of guacamole looks and tastes exciting.

Serves 4

2	Avocados	*Use the avocados with hard knobbly skins if available as they are easier to scoop out.*
4 Tbs	Lemon Juice	
4 tsp	Sugar	
2 Tbs	Walnut Oil	
1 tsp	Mint	*(Preferably fresh, but dried is acceptable)*
8 oz	Walnuts	

Keep four good walnut halves and chop the rest reasonably small. Roast the pieces and the whole halves on a baking tray in a reasonably low oven, turning frequently, until dark brown.

Cut the avocados in half lengthways and scoop out the flesh (keeping skins for later). Mix it with everything except the walnuts in a blender, to a smooth cream. Fold in the roast walnut pieces.

Fill each avocado skin, either with a spoon or by piping the mixture in, and place the half walnuts on the top.

Restaurant, Tearoom & Coffee Shop

ESSEX COTTAGE

High Street, Godshill, Isle of Wight, PO38 3HH.
Telephone: (0983) 840232

THIS is a fascinating establishment, parts of which are 900 years old and mentioned in the Doomsday Book. Owned orginally by the Earl of Yarborough and Baron Worley it was used by Queen Victoria, her daughter Princess Beatrice, King Alfonso of Spain and his Queen. It is full of character and decorated unusually with dried flowers and agricultural instruments.

There are three public areas one of which is a bar area and the other two the coffee lounge and the main restaurant. 68 people can be seated comfortably in the restaurant with another 38 in the bar and coffee area, whilst in the summer the pretty garden attracts many more people. Soft harp and flute music plays in the background adding another attribute to an already charming place.

The exciting menu offers dishes from all around the world, many of which are suitable for both vegetarians and vegans. Roy and Christine Dalby are the owners and it is Roy who is the dedicated chef. He is also a vegetarian and in 25 years has collected vegetarian recipes from almost every country in the world. He finds that both carnivores and vegetarians are thrilled with the dishes he creates. Strict attention is paid to the requirements of other diets which are catered for.

Country wines as well as vegetarian ones are on the list. The wide-ranging wine list has been carefully chosen by people who obviously enjoy the grape. The average price is £9 a bottle but there is a very good French Chateau bottled house wine at £1.50 a glass or £7.50 a bottle.

Useful Information

OPEN: 10am-midnight. Full meals: 12-2.30pm & 6.30-10pm. Evenings only: Nov-Feb. Sunday lunch

CREDIT CARDS: Visa/Access/Amex/Diners

CHILDREN: Yes but good behaviour is expected

LICENSED: Yes

ON THE MENU: Exciting vegetarian and vegan dishes from around the world

DISABLED ACCESS: Yes + toilets

GARDEN: Yes & patio

ACCOMMODATION: Not applicable

Restaurant

CORIANDERS

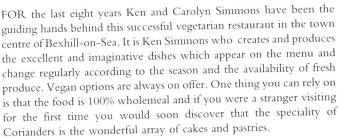

66 Devonshire Road, Bexhill-on-Sea, East Sussex, TN40 1AX.
Telephone: (0424) 220329

FOR the last eight years Ken and Carolyn Simmons have been the guiding hands behind this successful vegetarian restaurant in the town centre of Bexhill-on-Sea. It is Ken Simmons who creates and produces the excellent and imaginative dishes which appear on the menu and change regularly according to the season and the availability of fresh produce. Vegan options are always on offer. One thing you can rely on is that the food is 100% wholemeal and if you were a stranger visiting for the first time you would soon discover that the speciality of Corianders is the wonderful array of cakes and pastries.

There is nothing particularly interesting in the building itself but few would deny that the ambience is just right. It is a warm, cosy and intimate place in spite of the fact that it seats 50 people comfortably. One part of the restaurant is strictly non-smoking and at all times it is self-service.

While the wine list is by no means the priority here it does have some interesting English wines, 50% of which are vegetarian and four are organic. The country wines include damson, redcurrant, elderberry, peach, apple and elderflower. Lager and ales are on sale as well as a German lager. Kaliber is stocked for those who prefer a non-alcoholic tipple.

The Simmons also have self-catering holiday flats on Bexhill Sea front. Anyone staying there will be very comfortable and have the added advantage of a 10% discount on all meals taken at Corianders.

Useful Information

OPEN: 9-5pm daily. Closed Christmas, Easter and Bank Holidays

CREDIT CARDS: None taken

CHILDREN: Welcome

LICENSED: Yes. English wines only

ON THE MENU: 100% wholemeal. Specialises in cakes and pastries

DISABLED ACCESS: Yes plus toilets

GARDEN: No

ACCOMMODATION: Not applicable

Hotel & Restaurant

GRANVILLE HOTEL & TROGS RESTAURANT

124 Kings Road, Brighton, East Sussex, BN1 2FA.
Telephone: (0273) 326302, Facsimile: (0273) 728294

WHETHER you are looking for somewhere special and different to stay or merely for a first class vegetarian meal, the Granville Hotel and Trogs Restaurant are ideal. It is not entirely devoted to vegetarians but every dish that is available to you has nothing that in anyway offends. Everything is cooked on the premises. 47% of the snacks, 70% of the Starters, 25% of the main courses and 100% of the desserts conform totally to vegetarian standards. In addition every wine is organic and two of them are also vegetarian. Even the champagne is organic!

One of the nicest things about this well known and very likeable establishment is that it is somewhere that vegetarians and their non-vegetarian families or friends can relax for an evening in a very attractive restaurant.

The hotel, a Grade II Listed Building, is on the sea front overlooking the sadly derelict West Pier. It is wonderfully central and superbly furnished and decorated. Each of the 24 bedrooms is en-suite and individually designed and themed. Some have four poster beds, some water beds, some rooms have a jacuzzi and there are many rooms with a sea view. You might well ask to stay in the art deco, Noel Coward room, or the Brighton Rock room with its candyfloss pink and white decor. Something which you will either love or hate, is the Black Rock room - all black! It goes without saying that every room has television, tea and coffee facilities and direct dial telephones.

In Trogs Tavern you will find Real Ale that is brewed in the landlords brewery in Brighton. It is a lively, interesting and extremely comfortable place in which to stay and a special pleasure for vegetarians who will find they are particularly well catered for.

Useful Information

OPEN:All year. Light meals & snacks 12-9.30pm. Restaurant: 6.30-9.30pm
CREDIT CARDS: Access/Visa/ Amex/Diners
CHILDREN: Over 5's welcome
LICENSED: Yes

ON THE MENU: A mixture of dishes both vegetarian and non-vegetarian
DISABLED ACCESS: No wheelchair access to toilets
GARDEN: No
ACCOMMODATION: 24 en-suite

Restaurant

CLEMENTS VEGETARIAN RESTAURANT

Rickmans Lane, Plaistow, West Sussex, RH14 ONT.
Telephone: (0403) 871246

UNASHAMEDLY Upmarket, Clements vegetarian restaurant in Rickmans Lane, Plaistow, a small village on the Surrey/Sussex border and 12 miles from Guildford, is one of the best anywhere. Liz and Dave Clement bought an old pub in 1989 and converted it into this stylish and beautifully run establishment. Here you will find a strictly no smoking environment, with an attractive decor, in which every table is laid immaculately. The napkins are crisp linen, the fine glasses sparkle and the soft candlelight enhances the atmosphere.

Listed as one of the top 10 restaurants in the 'Vegetarian Good Food Guide' and runners up in the 1993 National 'Vegetarian Restaurant of the Year' competition, one would expect the food to be outstanding and one is never disappointed. For such an outstanding establishment the prices are realistic. One can lunch well from a main course with salads at around £4.75 and in the evening dine on a menu which includes an aperitif, crudite with dip, three courses and coffee with petit fours for a fully inclusive price of £18.95. If you wish to omit either a starter or a dessert the price reduces to £15.95. Sunday lunch is another outstanding meal - a three course meal for £9.95 and children may eat for half the price. The evening menu changes monthly and the first Wednesday in each month is a £5 off night bringing the price down to £13.95. (Prices are correct at early 1994)

It would be difficult to find such good food anywhere at this price. All the food is freshly prepared on the premises. The 24 choices on the wine list are all organic and vegetarian from France, New Zealand, Australia, England and Germany. The House Wine is Corbiere (Red) and Mauzac (White) priced at £7.95. In summer there are 10 tables in the pretty garden - an additional reason for coming here. A brochure is available, if you ring the restaurant, which includes a copy of the take-away menu and price list.

Useful Information

OPEN: All year. Lunch, Wed-Sun:12.30-3pm (last orders 1.45pm) Eves, Wed-Sat:7-11pm

CREDIT CARDS: Access/Visa

CHILDREN: Welcome at lunchtime. Discouraged in the evening

LICENSED: Yes. All organic & vegetarian wines from around the world

ON THE MENU: International dishes.Everything made on the premises. Outside catering for weddings, etc

DISABLED ACCESS: Yes but no special toilets

GARDEN: Delightful countryside setting

ACCOMMODATION: N/A

Hotel

HOTEL DE FRANCE

St Saviours Road, St Helier, Jersey, Channel Islands, JE2 7LA.
Telephone: (0534) 38990, Facsimile: (0534) 30874

THIS is a hotel that has built its fine reputation over 130 years and for the last 23 years has been in the capable hands of the Parker family. Just five minutes walk from the main centre of St Helier, the Hotel de France has 323 elegantly furnished en-suite bedrooms including 16 suites which are ideal for families. Open all the year round it is the sort of place where one can take a break or a longer holiday at any time of year and have a wonderful time. The main Piazza has a large atrium style glass roof and is filled with a profusion of plants. Throughout the hotel plants and flowers add distinction to the furniture. Soft, easy to listen to classical music provides a background in the lounge and the bar. From time to time there is live entertainment but throughout the year it is the very genuine welcome that makes the Hotel de France such a pleasant place in which to stay.

The needs of vegetarians has become increasingly important to the management and over the last five years an increasing number of non-meat eaters have found the hotel an oasis. Here they can be assured of freshly prepared food which changes daily and always consists of the best local produce available. You will find on the menu that 25% of the snacks and starters, 20% of the main course and 90% of the desserts are always suitable for vegetarians and conform to strict standards. No substitutes are used and only a small percentage of the desserts are bought ready-made. The wine list is a superb selection of wines from Europe and around the world including two Jersey wines. There is no garden but an outdoor pool and sundeck is a firm favourite with residents. There is a full fitness centre, an indoor pool, childrens playground and for those who enjoy nightlife, a nightclub on the site.

Useful Information

OPEN: All year apart from Dec 24-27 inclusive

CREDIT CARDS: All major cards

CHILDREN: Welcome

LICENSED: Full licence. Excellent wine list. Nightclub on site

ON THE MENU: Wide choice for vegetarians

DISABLED ACCESS: Yes, also to toilets

GARDEN: 2 Pools & sundeck, many leisure facilities

ACCOMMODATION: All en-suite. 118 dbles, 38 sgls, 151 twns & 16 suites

Hotel

LES OZOUETS LODGE

Ozouets Road, St Peter Port, Guernsey, Channel Islands, GY1 2UA.
Telephone: (0481) 721288

THIS very pleasant hotel on the outskirts of St Peter Port cares greatly for its guests, those who stay and those who come here to dine. Owned and run by Mr and Mrs Davy who have been here for 14 years, one of their specialities is the genuine approach to the needs of vegetarians. The restaurant which seats 36 easily has an emphasis on fresh fish and seafood of all kinds but for the last five years has made sure that never less than 10% of the dishes on offer at each course are totally vegetarian. Vegetable and fish stocks are used but never meat and occasionally gelatine is an ingredient in a dessert but you will always be aware of this. No ready made food of any kind is bought in. The vegetarian dishes are imaginative and like every other dish mainly French but with a number of English as well.

The wine list offers 50 different bins from France, Germany, Italy, Australia and the USA have been well selected with an average price of £6. None are specifically vegetarian or organic. There is a wide range of spirits, beers and liquors and both non-alcoholic and low alcohol beers are available. The hotel has 14 en-suite bedrooms, one of which is a family room. There are no single rooms. Every room has television, direct dial telephones, hairdryers and tea/coffee making facilities.

Additional attractions at Ozouets Lodge are the very large garden, the heated swimming pool, the grass tennis court, the bowling green and pitch and putt. Children over five years are very welcome but no pets are permitted.

Useful Information

OPEN: March until end of October
CREDIT CARDS: Visa/ MasterEuro/Amex
CHILDREN: Over 5
LICENSED: Yes

ON THE MENU: 10% Vegetarian at all courses specialising in fresh fish & sea-food
DISABLED ACCESS: No
GARDEN: Yes. Swimming pool, tennis courts, bowling green, pitch & putt
ACCOMMODATION: 14 en-suite rooms

Restaurant & Tearoom

CASSANDRAS CUP

Winchester Road, Chawton, Nr Alton, Hampshire, GU34 1SB.
Telephone: (0420) 83144

FOLLOW the signs to Jane Austen's house and there, immediately opposite, is Cassandras Cup, in the picturesque village of Chawton. This is an enchanting tea room with antiques, crafts and gifts as well as offering delicious home-cooked English food which includes a number of dishes expressly for vegetarians, although it has to be admitted they are so tasty that carnivores are frequently tempted. Most of the food is prepared and cooked on the premises but a small percentage of desserts and main courses are bought in.

Cassandras Cup is licensed and has a small but interesting number of European wines as well as the local ropley country wine. Everything is reasonably priced and the standard extremely high, indeed they have been awarded a certificate of excellence. It is a treat to look forward to after a visit to the fascinating home of Jane Austen, one of England's favourite authors.

Useful Information

OPEN: 10.30-5pm (winter 4.30pm). The days and hours are limited from October-March
CREDIT CARDS: None taken
ON THE MENU: Excellent homecooked fare
DISABLED ACCESS: Yes + toilet with a little difficulty

Hotel & Inn

THE CROWN HOTEL & PURE DROP INN

Crown Road, Marnhull, Dorset, DT10 1LN.
Telephone: (0258) 820224

TO discover a pub that dates back to the 12th century and a modern hotel extension added in 1745 take the B3092 from the A30 at East Stour. It is an exciting experience. The Pure Drop Inn is steeped in history and to drink here takes one back in time. The Crown Hotel, in spite of being 250 years younger than the inn, has its own character and its own regular customers as well as the many visitors who come to see the very old and the not quite so old side by side.

The hotel offers bed and breakfast at a very reasonable price and all rooms have a television and tea or coffee making facilties in the room. A function suite is available for weddings and special occasions.

The home-cooked food provides tastes from around the world and is willingly adapted to meet anyone's requirements with prior warning. Whilst there are not a huge range of vegetarian choices on the menu, it nonetheless provides tasty meals or snacks conforming to vegetarian standards.

Useful Information

OPEN: Mon-Sat: 11-2.30pm & 6-11pm
CREDIT CARDS: Visa/Access/ Switch/Connect
ON THE MENU: Good quality, home-cooked, dishes for vegetarians
DISABLED ACCESS: No

Hotel & Restaurant

LANGRISH HOUSE

Langrish, Petersfield, Hampshire, GU32 1RN.
Telephone: (0730) 266941, Facsimile: (0730) 260543

THIS old Manor House house is now a charming hotel with an excellent restaurant. Langrish House dates back in parts to the 1600's and it is in the part which was once the cellar that the owners have created a super, atmospheric restaurant. There have been many additions, some Victorian but the interest stems largely from the house's association with the Civil War. You will find Langrish house three miles from Petersfield off the A272 to Winchester Road and on the road to East Meon.

Set in 13 acres, it lies at the foot of the South Downs and the surrounding countryside has been designated 'An Area of Outstanding Beauty'. The grounds contain many rare and interesting trees and a great variety of wildlife. Traditional French and English cooking with a smattering of exotic dishes including those from India, make up an interesting and ever changing menu. Whilst the restaurant is not exclusively vegetarian you will find that in the last six years it has acquired a reputation for the excellence of its vegetarian and vegan dishes.

Useful Information

OPEN: All year. Closed Christmas & New Year

CREDIT CARDS: Amex/Visa/Access/Diners

ON THE MENU: Excellent and interesting choice for vegetarians, some simple, some exotic

DISABLED ACCESS: No. Restaurant in cellar

Inn with Restaurant

THE BOARS HEAD

Nr Crowborough, East Sussex, TN6 3HD.
Telephone: (0892) 652412 , Facsimile: (0892) 665523

FOR 600 years there has allegedly been an inn on this site although today's Boars Head Inn is a mere relic of the 17th century! It is to be found just off the A26 Crowborough to Tunbridge Wells road, about a mile out of Crowborough. More than worth seeking out, it will reward you with a tremendous atmosphere, a friendly welcome, well kept ale, a good wine list and a reputation for good English fare, plentiful in its portions and deliciously cooked.

In the main it is food for carnivores but Gordon and Jillienne McKenzie have an understanding of the needs of vegetarians, hence considerable thought has gone into the daily dishes which are suitable. The choice is never large but you will always find the dishes on offer attractive. In the summer the garden is an added bonus and the scene of many a pleasurable barbecue when the weather is clement. A no smoking rule operates in eating areas.

Useful Information

OPEN: 11.30-2.30pm & 6-11pm. Sun: 12-3pm & 7-10.30pm

CREDIT CARDS: Visa/Amex

ON THE MENU: Limited but good dishes for vegetarians

DISABLED ACCESS: Yes but no special toilet facilities

Restaurant

STONES

High Street, Avebury, Marlborough, Wiltshire, SN8 1RF.
Telephone: (06723) 514

FOR ten years the likeable partnership of Messrs Howard and Pitts have enjoyed success in their restaurant, Stones, in the small, historical village of Avebury. It stands next to the Great Barn and is, in fact, a beautifully-done conversion of the stable block belonging to the Great Barn. It has a great air of the countryside about it and the philosophy behind the deserved reputation of Stones, is good, fresh, vegetarian food every day. Mainly organic ingredients are used, most of which the owners grow themselves.

Stones is licensed and the wines come mainly from France and Britain. Every wine on the list is either organic or vegetarian. There is a range of organic beers which includes a local ale from 'the wood'. Country wines are also included and so too are organic ciders.

Useful Information

OPEN: March-October: 10-6pm. November-mid December and February-March 10-5pm.
CREDIT CARDS: No
ON THE MENU: Good, fresh vegetarian dishes. Vegan options
DISABLED ACCESS: Reasonable. Suitable toilets

Tearoom

THE VILLAGE HALL TEAROOM

The National Trust, Stourton, Nr Warminster, Wiltshire, BA12 6QD.
Telephone: (0747) 840161

IN 1947 Stourhead was given to the National Trust and since the 1970's people have been able to come here to the Village Hall Tearoom, close to the Spread Eagle Inn and the village church to enjoy some excellent food in a non-smoking atmosphere. Stourhead is famous for its superb landscaped gardens laid out between 1741-1780 and the house which was begun in 1721. It is a magical day out for anyone. It is open from the beginning of April until the end of October every day from 10.30am-5.30pm.

Known for the quality of its snacks and light meals the Village Hall Tearoom offers ploughman lunches, salads, home-made soups, sandwiches and desserts and specialises in a wonderful clotted cream tea and delicious cakes. There is a good selection for vegetarians whether it is a main course, snacks or desserts. The Tearoom has had a Heartbeat Award since 1993.

Useful Information

OPEN: 1st April-31st October, 10.30-5.30pm daily
CREDIT CARDS: Visa/Access/ Amex
ON THE MENU: Choice for vegetarians
DISABLED ACCESS: Yes + toilets

Hotel & Restaurant

HOTEL HOUGUE DU POMMIER

Castel, Guernsey, Channnel Islands, GY5 7FQ.
Telephone: (0481) 56531, Facsimile: (0481) 56260

BUILT in 1712 and once orchards with a farmhouse where the cider was made, Hotel Hougue du Pommier has been a much loved hotel for over 20 years. It has 44 delightful en-suite bedrooms which allow you to enjoy this remarkable place, and all that is fascinating about Guernsey. The restaurant, which is six rooms in one, depicts sections of the old farmhouse, for example part is the bakery, another the parlour. Even if the restaurant did not provide superb food it would still be worth visiting simply because of its charming difference from other establishments.

That it has good food, is well known and is international in its choice of dishes. Not entirely for vegetarians it nonetheless provides four snack dishes, five starters, five main course and four delectable desserts. The ten acres of garden add to the pleasure with a putting green and pitt and putt. Hotel Hougue du Pommier has deservedly won many accolades.

Useful Information

OPEN: All year
CREDIT CARDS: Access/Visa/Amex/Diners/Switch
ON THE MENU: A good number of vegetarian dishes across the board
DISABLED ACCESS: Yes, but no special toilet facilities

St Paul's Cathedral, London

Contents

THE HOME COUNTIES, THE THAMES VALLEY AND GREATER LONDON

Gloucestershire, Oxfordshire, Berkshire, Buckinghamshire, Bedfordshire, Hertfordshire, Surrey, Middlesex and Greater London

Suggested Venues to Dine

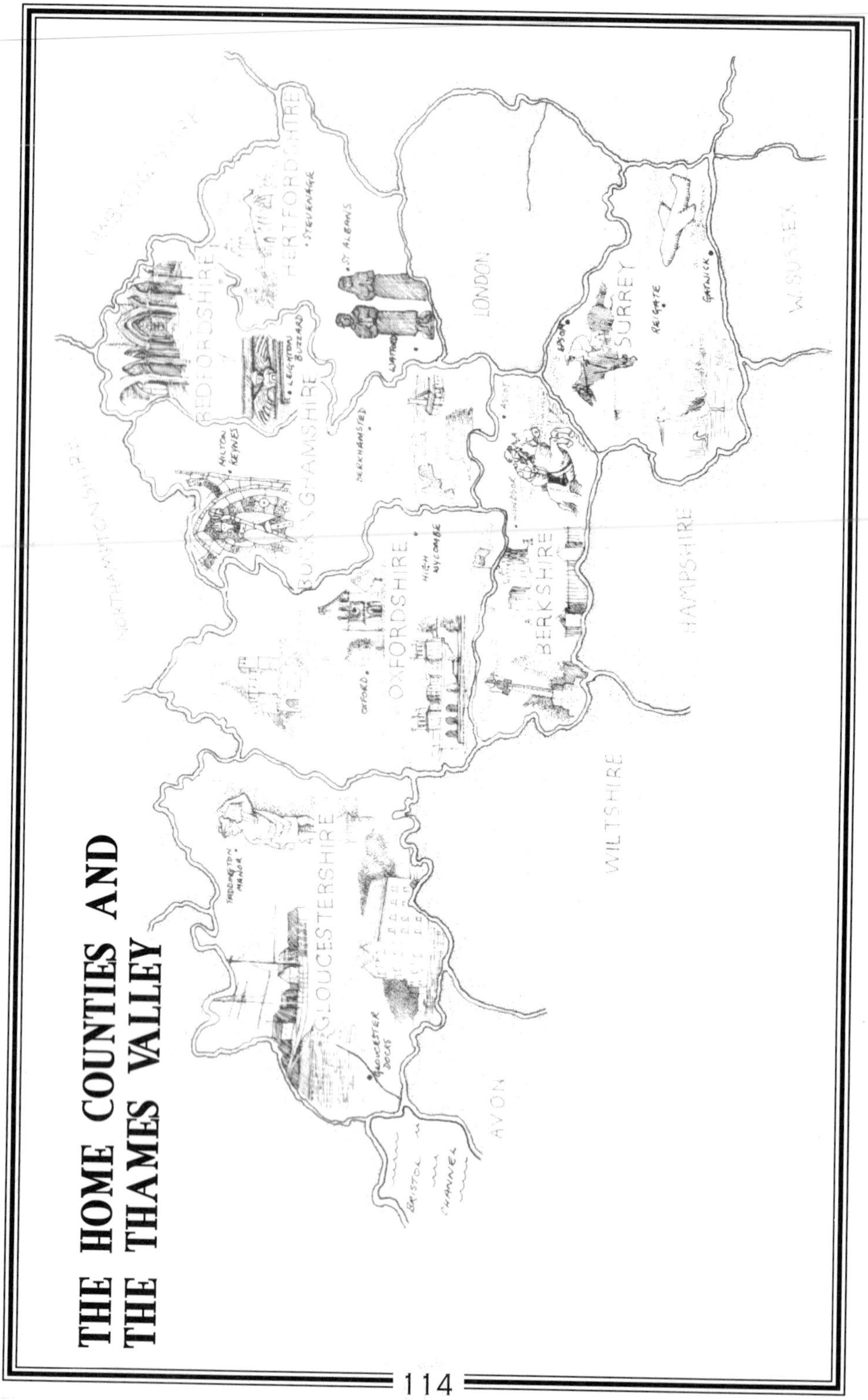
THE HOME COUNTIES AND
THE THAMES VALLEY
NORTHAMPTONSHIRE
BEDFORDSHIRE
HERTFORDSHIRE
BUCKINGHAMSHIRE
OXFORDSHIRE
GLOUCESTERSHIRE
BERKSHIRE
LONDON
SURREY
W. SUSSEX
HAMPSHIRE
WILTSHIRE
AVON
BRISTOL CHANNEL
STEVENAGE
ST ALBANS
WATFORD
LEIGHTON BUZZARD
MILTON KEYNES
BERKHAMSTED
HIGH WYCOMBE
OXFORD
WINDSOR
ASCOT
EPSOM
REIGATE
GATWICK
TADDINGTON MANOR
GLOUCESTER DOCKS

GREATER LONDON

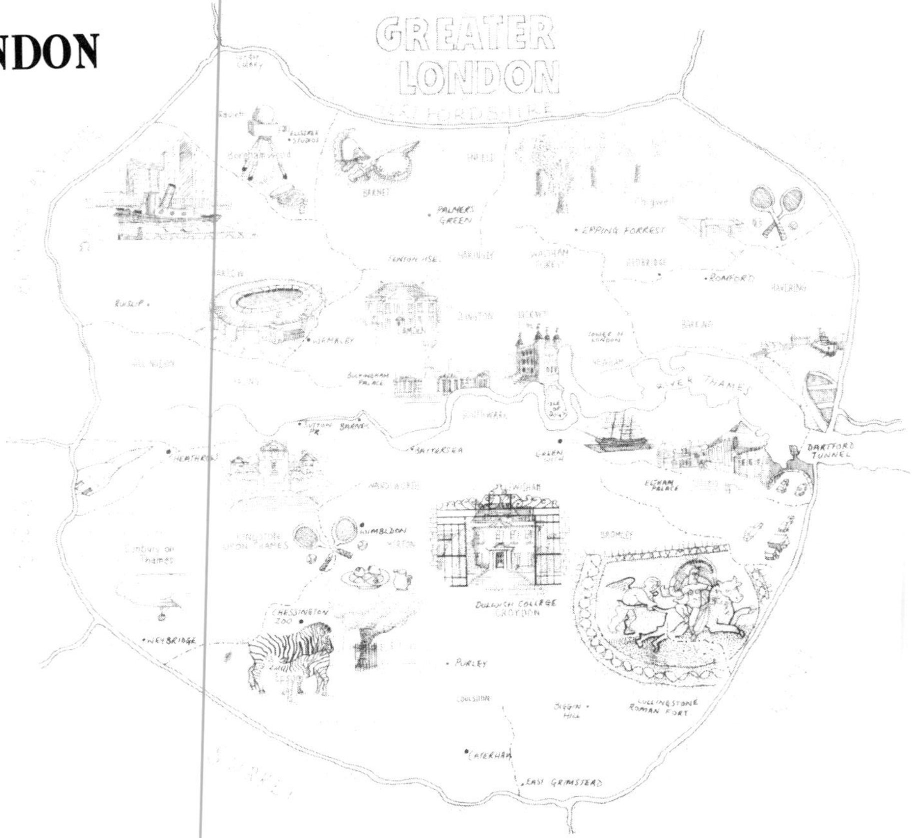

THE HOME COUNTIES, THE THAMES VALLEY AND GREATER LONDON

Gloucestershire, Oxfordshire, Berkshire, Buckinghamshire, Bedfordshire, Hertfordshire, Surrey and Greater London

These counties, from the upper estuary of the Severn to the broad, chalk basin of the lower Thames valley, have all been prosperous, for a variety of reasons, throughout much of this millennium, and therefore have a wealth of fine, large buildings - domestic, church and state - from many periods. These are now mixed in all but the western part of the region with large new estates, and even with new towns which have been a feature of this century as the counties' populations have increased in dramatic stages. The region also contains much natural beauty, the many pretty small woods and valleys dominated by the high points of the Cotswolds, the Malvern Hills, the Chiltern escarpment and the Berkshire Downs, crossed with ancient paths and offering some quite breathtaking views, often across many counties.

Gloucestershire, the western-most and most rural of these counties, offers a diversity of landscape, history and culture; from the timeless, scattered stone villages of the Cotswolds, through the river meadows of the Severn valley to the natural magnificence of the Royal Forest of Dean. There are several Roman relics in the county, the remains of some of the fifty luxury villas that once stood.

Rare species of flora and fauna can be found in the lush undulating tree-lined landscape of the Cotswolds and this 'Area of Outstanding Natural Beauty' also has man-made beauty - even the largest of the farmhouses blending into the landscape due to the mellow local stone used.

THE COTSWOLDS have remained open country because of the suitability of the land for sheep rearing, and the wealth earned from the wool trade as far back as the 15th century. It was the wool merchants who were responsible for the building of the many Cotswold churches which often appear far too ostentatious for the villages they serve. It would seem the predilections of the patrons were frequently given their due, and the superb stained glass windows of the church at **Chipping Campden** include one showing the Eternal Pit into which the damned are being pitchforked - all the damned being women!

Each year in early summer the streets of Chipping Campden are alight with a torch procession, to mark the close of the COTSWOLD OLIMPICKS, founded in 1612 and more recently revived. The extraordinary 'games' include 'Shin Kicking' and 'Pikes & Cudgels'!

Magnificent views on the edge of the Cotswolds are to be seen from **Birdlip** and from **Leckhampton** by the 'Devil's Chimney'.

Devil's Chimney at Leckhampton, an isolated pillar of rock

In contrast to the Cotswolds, the vale of the Severn river is a flat green land, with **Tewkesbury** showing its Tudor origins in the black and white timbered buildings in the centre of town. The town has one other special feature, the Norman TEWKESBURY ABBEY. Here are buried the remains of the Duke of Clarence who, it is said, drowned in a vat of Malmsey wine.

It was in the 12th century that William of Malmesbury wrote 'no county in England has so many or so good vineyards', and the tradition continues with vineyards such as the THREE CHOIRS VINEYARDS near **Newent**, a producer with a particularly high reputation and many awards. Having started with an experimental 1/2 acre it now covers 65 acres with several grape varieties and a potential for over 250,000 bottles annually.

From Tewkesbury the river Severn flows to the county town of **Gloucester**, its several excellent museums including the NATIONAL WATERWAYS MUSEUM at the historic GLOUCESTER DOCKS, both of which are on the riverside walk from Tewkesbury, which then passes the extraordinary SEVEN BORE, a noisy wave from the Bristol Channel that, at high spring tide, can reach seven feet high.

Further still down the river path in the Vale of Berkeley, as the river widens into the Severn estuary, the saltmarshes at **Slimbridge** are famous as THE WILDFOWL AND WETLANDS TRUST CENTRE, founded by Peter Scott. Its 73 acres protect the largest and most diverse collection of wild waterfowl in the world with, in winter, over 2,300 birds of 180 species including swans, ducks, geese and flamingos as well as rare and exotic wildfowl, some of which can be seen from the hides, and some which will feed from your hand. The Centre even includes special facilities for not only the wheelchair-bound but also the blind.

By the opposite bank of the river, close to the Welsh border, the largest holly trees in England are dotted among the oaks and birches of **The Royal Forest of Dean**, one of the few true forests remaining. Some 2,000 miles of woodland paths pass alongside grazing land used by commoners who are referred to, rather oddly as 'Ship-badgers' (perhaps badgerers of sheep?). Many of the hills and dales are actually tips and dips caused by coal and tin mining over the past 2,500 years as can be seen on a journey deep underground at CLEARWELL CAVES AND MINING MUSEUM. The DEAN HERITAGE CENTRE is a museum of forest life, its industrial heritage and natural history, coming up to date with craft workshops. Contemporary art is also on view on the SCULPTURE TRAIL, a circular walk from Beechenhurst, featuring 18 sculptures among the trees.

Trees in a natural but nevertheless man-made setting can be seen at the WESTONBIRT ARBORETUM, regarded as being possibly the finest arboretum in the country. The deciduous trees are particularly beautiful in their autumn colours with the Japanese red maples being quite outstanding. It is also famed for its avenue of tulip trees, just some of the 1,800 trees from many parts of the world, in over 600 acres.

HIDCOTE MANOR GARDEN at **Chipping Campden** is one of the most delightful gardens of England, famous for its rare trees and old roses as well as its open-air Shakespeare performances in the summer. Only a few miles away is KIFTSGATE COURT, another garden worth visiting, and in the centre of the county near **Cirencester** is BARNSLEY GARDEN.

A little to the east, the pretty village of **Bibury** is a true 'chocolate-box' scene with small stone cottages and here too is the COTSWOLD COUNTY MUSEUM at the 17th century Arlington Mill. The CORINIUM MUSEUM at Cirencester tells the story of Roman life in Britain, and the JOHN MOORE COUNTRYSIDE MUSEUM in the Abbey precincts at **Tewkesbury** is on the subject of natural history and nature conservation. The COTSWOLD COUNTRYSIDE COLLECTION on the FOSSE WAY at **Northleach**, once a House of Correction, now houses displays of rural life along with the 'Below Stairs' gallery and special exhibitions each season. On a somewhat smaller scale, the WORLD OF MECHANICAL MUSIC also at Northleach is a museum dedicated to antique clocks, musical boxes, automata and mechanical musical instruments, a special and magical place. Near Gloucester Docks is a MUSEUM OF ADVERTISING. In GLOUCESTER FOLK MUSEUM a roughly carved stone figure holding an animal is said to be of Dick Whittington and his cat. Dick Whittington lived in **Pauntley** before moving to London where he became Mayor, but unlike the story he was in fact born into a wealthy family.

Some of the many, especially pretty, villages and small towns in Gloucestershire include **Bourton-on-the-Hill** with the manor of SEZINCOTE in Hindu-Gothic style which was the inspiration for Brighton Pavilion; **Bourton-on-the-Water** which has a number of small museums and similar attractions; **Stanton**, a single street of pretty houses; **Adlestrop** where King Alfred took refuge when Wessex fell to the Vikings in the 1st century AD; **Lechlade** where three counties meet, a town which has a surprising number of gazebos and summer houses; and **Chalford** with its very narrow and winding lanes.

A village that is not, in most people's eyes, actually pretty but is nevertheless fascinating is **Whiteway**, founded just less than a hundred years ago by a group who left Surrey to live according to the anarchistic principals of Tolstoy. They used no public services, built their own housing and strove for self-sufficiency. Something of this philosophy is still retained by many of the descendants of the original settlers.

For sheer elegance little could surpass **Cheltenham's** Regency terraces and wide tree-lined avenues, an ideal location for the annual festivals of music and literature. This was the birthplace of the composer Gustav Holst and there is a museum dedicated to him. At **Wooton-under-Edge** the church has an organ which was originally in St Martin-in-the-Fields in London and was played by Handel. The CHELTENHAM ART GALLERY AND MUSEUM includes the country's foremost collection of work by William Morris.

Gloucestershire's eastern border along the Cotswolds gives onto Oxfordshire. In the north the county is gentle and undulating, running down to the Thames Valley towards the south and rising in the east towards the Chilterns, with **Oxford** "That sweet city of dreaming spires" in the centre.

The university influences much of life in and around Oxford. The earliest Oxford colleges were founded in the 13th century, and many exceptionally fine and hugely impressive college buildings elegantly dominate the town centre. Most of the college quadrangles are occasionally open to the public as are some of the halls and chapels and other important buildings.

Oxford is a lively place, with many concerts, plays and meetings each evening, and with delightful pubs and restaurants. It can also boast what is, not surprisingly, the only MARMALADE MUSEUM in the world, and there is an enchanting MUSEUM OF DOLL'S HOUSES.

On any fine summer day punts aplenty are to be seen on the Cherwell, whilst not far away the university rowing crews practice for their many challenges, including the University Boat Race. **Henley-on-Thames**, a straight and wide stretch of river is the site each July of the Henley Royal Regatta, and the town itself is not unexceptional although it is overshadowed by the beauty of the surrounding wooded hills.

Henley is the finishing point of THE OXFORDSHIRE WAY which takes walkers on a route linking the Cotswolds and the Chilterns, starting in Bourton-on-the-Water. A walk beside the Thames from Henley to **Goring** is said to be one of the most beautiful walks possible, just one tiny stretch of the newly opened THAMES PATH developed by the Countryside Commission, running from the source of the Thames in Gloucestershire through London to the Thames Barrier.

Oxfordshire has many attractive towns and villages: the village of **Burford** is renowned as one of the most beautiful in Britain, yet the county can also offer contenders such as **Great Tew**, **Ewelme**, **East Hendred**, **Adderbury**; **Dorchester**, a cathedral city from 634 to 707 AD; **Cornwell** rebuilt in the 1930's by the eccentric Clough Williams of Portmerion fame; and **Uffington**, well described in 'Tom Brown's Schooldays'.

William Morris, the designer, printer and poet, was a fascinating character who drew much of his inspiration from the area around his home of KELMSCOTT MANOR which now acts as a testament to his brilliance.

" For as long as man continues to be the ruthless destroyer of lower living beings, he will never know health or peace. For as long as men massacre animals, they will kill each other. Indeed, he who sows the seeds of murder and pain cannot reap joy and love. "

Pythagoras

Abingdon, once the County Town of Berkshire, offers a wealth of wonderful buildings from the medieval period onwards, and **Faringdon** too is an elegant town with fine architecture. The notable FARRINGDON HOUSE gardens are occasionally open, and here you can see doves, their feathers stained in bright colours! The town of **Witney** bears witness to its success in the wool trade, having long been famous for blankets. At **Hook Norton** the BREWERY is the source of some highly regarded real ale, the Victorian building itself being an odd mixture of all sorts of random materials.

This is MORRIS DANCING country, **Bampton** Morris being one of the most important traditions, their dances often now performed in other places, but the Bampton men will insist that no other can be genuine. Folk tradition is also associated with **Banbury** as reflected in the verse "Ride-a-cock horse to Banbury Cross". The original cross was destroyed by the Puritans in 1602, the replacement being a Victorian monument.

A strong puff through the hole of THE BLOWING STONE - which originally stood on the Ridgeway but is now to be found at

Kingston Lisle - produces a note which, tradition has it, Alfred the Great used to gather his chiefs in a fight against the Danes. Alfred was born in **Wantage** and the town is worth a visit for the museum which shows much of the history of the area.

Oxfordshire's Bronze Age stone circle, the ROLLRIGHT STONES or King's Men, is next in importance only to Stonehenge and Avebury, set in a superb situation with fine views over Warwickshire.

The CHILTERNS, dividing Oxfordshire and Buckinghamshire, with their centuries old beechwoods were the home at one time of hundreds of 'bodgers', wood turners making chair legs with manual lathes, and whittlers of clothes pegs. The area is one of astounding beauty, the mainly small buildings a mixture of brick with knapped flints. Where the Chilterns meet the Berkshire Downs and the river has created the GORING GAP through the chalk, the ancient ICKNIELD WAY and RIDGEWAY come together.

The Ridgeway runs along the Berkshire Downs (now in Oxfordshire) heading towards Stonehenge and Avebury although the ancient road pre-dates the great monuments. Being away from modern roads, the Ridgeway provides for peaceful walking or horse riding, with extensive open views. Towards the west of its Oxfordshire section the Ridgeway passes by the WHITE HORSE OF UFFINGTON, nearly 40 feet high, cut through the turf into the chalk. If you leave a horse and a coin in the nearby WAYLAND SMITH'S CAVE, rumour has it that by morning the horse will have been shod. Here too is DRAGON HILL, said to be where St George slayed the dragon.

Many find the otherwise breathtaking views of the Berkshire Downs very much ruined by the dominance of the HARWELL ATOMIC RESEARCH ESTABLISHMENT which can be seen from miles around.

Over the Berkshire Downs from Oxfordshire is the Royal County of Berkshire itself, now a small county with, sadly, much of its Iron Age and Roman history obscured by recent development.

The coming of the railway brought great numbers of people to live in this pleasant yet convenient land and more recently the M4 corridor has seen the creation of Britain's own 'Silicon Valley' as companies involved in modern technology have moved in, along with the workers required to staff them.

It is however still possible to find quiet leafy lanes and open countryside away from the main towns.

The CHILDE-BEALE WILDLIFE PARK at **Basildon** has a huge number of animals - ponies, peacocks and deer being just a few of them - all roaming free in attractive scenery.

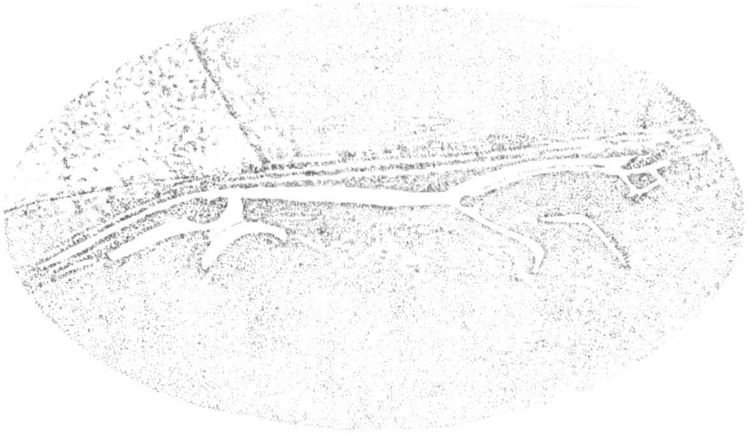

The White Horse of Uffington, probably about 1,000 years old

Beautiful landscapes can be found along the banks of the river Thames and the Kennet and Avon Canel, the southernmost canal in Britain. The best way to see this scenery is in slow motion from the water and THE KENNET HORSE BOAT CO. offers trips by colourfully painted barges, complete with traditionally bedecked shire horses.

Most of the route of the Thames now forms the county's north-eastern boundary, passing by **Sonning, Wargrave, Hurley** and **Cookham** where the scenery is particularly breathtaking. Here it was that Kenneth Grahame took his inspiration for 'The Wind in the Willows', and here too Stanley Spencer lived and painted. Many of his works are of local scenes and can be seen in the STANLEY SPENCER GALLERY. Brunel's railway bridge at **Maidenhead** was the setting of Turner's painting 'Rain, Steam and Speed'.

Mary Mitford lived in **Swallowfield** and her book 'Our Village' gives a beautiful description of the area 150 years ago. Jane Austen went to school in the Abbey Gatehouse in **Reading,** and it was in this town that the imprisoned Oscar Wilde wrote 'De Profundis' as well as 'The Ballad of Reading Goal'.

Reading today has one of the country's particularly unusual museums, DOUGLAS ELECTRIC CLOCKS, a collection of 70 or so mainly pre-1930 battery-driven electric clocks collected from around the world, including an unique grandfather clock which never needs rewinding, powered by the earth. Entrance is by appointment only (0734) 345192.

Farm animals consume over 80% of the world's available water supplies.

Down the River Kennet from Reading is the pretty village of **Aldermaston**, its claim to fame being that it was here that the William Pear was developed, and its claim to notoriety being that it is home to the ATOMIC WEAPONS RESEARCH ESTABLISHMENT.

Each year on 4th June the most famous school in England, ETON COLLEGE just north of Windsor, celebrates its founding by Henry IV in 1440, with a firework display on the river.

Also in June is Ascot Week when royalty, the gentry and celebrities as well as other race goers, many of them in huge and flamboyant hats, attend the meetings at ASCOT RACECOURSE. Race horses being exercised are often to be seen on the Downs around **East Ilsley**.

At **Windsor** the tower of WINDSOR CASTLE dominates the view, a home to the royal family since the 11th century. Following the serious fire in 1993 there is less of the Castle to be seen although this in itself is attracting additional visitors! The town is infused with a royal theme, such as the recently opened CROWN JEWELS OF THE WORLD exhibition consisting of facsimiles of crowns, tiaras, orbs and state jewels from 12 countries.

Near to Windsor is another of the county's somewhat strange and intriguing collections, the MUSEUM OF ANCIENT WIRELESS (owned by a quasi-vegetarian) which includes some very unusual wireless sets as well as disc gramophones, phonographs and wire recorders, and much more than that: the owner and curator, Captain Maurice Sheddon

(Royal Signals, Retired) is the inventor of heated clothing which is on display, and the garden has wind generators to power the clothes. Viewing is strictly by appointment (0753) 542242.

Over the Thames from Windsor and beyond the town of **Slough**, Berkshire joins the tall narrow county of Buckinghamshire on its short southern boundary. At this point Buckinghamshire is low and leafy, rising sharply further north to the Chilterns with its thick beechwoods, then further north still becoming a land of streams and marshes.

A prehistoric boundary known as GRIM'S DITCH runs across the Chilterns near to **Great Hampden** and nearby are two crosses cut through the turf into the chalk. Not as exciting as the White Horse of Uffingham yet nevertheless intriguing.

The Chilterns is renowned for its many footpaths and there are walks both long and short, but rarely strenuous, that can take advantage of the scenery, giving just occasional glimpses through the trees of distant views. The NORTH BUCKS WAY starting near **Wendover** on the Chilterns escarpment takes walkers down to **Wolverton** in the Vale of Aylesbury. On the North Bucks Way can be found the QUAINTON RAILWAY CENTRE with trains in steam on the last Sunday of each month.

The ancient trees of **Burnham Beeches** east of **Maidenhead** form a beautiful area which was bought for the people by the City of London in 1879. At one time this area was also home to Romany gypsies, now long gone.

It takes twice as much water to produce one day's food for a meat eater as it does for a vegetarian.

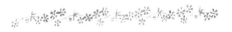

Along the Thames, Buckinghamshire has some attractive towns such as **Marlow** which is particularly beautiful. This was the home of the poet Percy B. Shelley and Mary Shelley of 'Frankenstein' fame.

The poet William Cowper spent the second half of his life in **Olney** where the COWPER MUSEUM celebrates his works, including 'Amazing Grace' which was written here.

Stoke Poges' church is where Thomas Gray wrote his 'Elegy Written in a Country Churchyard' and at **Beaconsfield** lived G.K. Chesterton and Enid Blyton who it is believed was inspired by the BEKONSCOT MODEL VILLAGE with tiny houses spread over a large garden. Milton lived at **Chalfont St Giles** when he fled London to escape the plague and in addition to a small museum his cottage is now open to visitors.

Near Beaconsfield the small town of **Jordans** was home to William Penn the founder of Pennsylvania and he is buried at the small 17th century QUAKER MEETING HOUSE. The MAYFLOWER BARN, also open to the public, incorporates beams taken from the Mayflower after the Pilgrim Fathers sailed to America in 1620.

HUGHENDEN MANOR near **High Wycombe** was the home of Benjamin Disraeli and the house still contains much of his furniture and other belongings. The Prime Minister of current days has a country residence southwest of Wendover, a Tudor house known as CHEQUERS, presented to the nation for just this purpose during World War I.

Another important house in the area is MENTMORE TOWERS which is currently the Great Britain seat of the World Government of the Age of Enlightenment.

From pretty, small villages such as **Hambleden** to modern towns like **Milton Keynes**, Buckinghamshire has absorbed a large increase in population in the latter part of this century, yet outside these conurbations retains its character as a rural area.

However, Bedfordshire to the northeast is very much more rural, one of the smallest counties in England and a land of small charms with little of natural spectacle, but much to enjoy. The Chilterns which we first mentioned in Oxfordshire and which crossed through Buckinghamshire continue their dominance of the landscape in north Bedfordshire, described by John Bunyan as 'the Delectable Mountains'. Elsewhere the chalk gives way to clays and then to sands and gravels in a gently undulating landscape. This diversity accounts for a diversity in agriculture too, with some highly productive arable land and a particular emphasis on market gardening around the town of **Biggleswade**.

THE SWISS GARDEN near Biggleswade is a beautifully restored 19th century garden with fine trees. An intricate French garden features in a park that was laid out in the 18th century and partly re-landscaped by Capability Brown around WREST PARK HOUSE at **Silsoe**, modelled on the French chateaux style. The history of gardening through the ages can be seen here in a setting which includes some splendid water features.

The remains of the 17th century HOUGHTON HOUSE near **Amptill** include some magnificent features attributed to Inigo Jones, and is believed to have been the inspiration for 'House Beautiful' in John Bunyan's 'Pilgrim's Progress'. Bunyan was born in **Elstow**, marked by a granite block alone in a field, and he later lived in **Bedford** as one is reminded by the statue of him in the High Street, close to the gaol where he was imprisoned for nonconformist preachings. BUNYAN'S COTTAGE, the MOOT HALL in Elstow and the BUNYAN MEETING HOUSE in Bedford contain many of his artefacts.

The Chinese Dairy at Woburn

Judging by its huge popularity, no visit to Bedfordshire would be complete without a tour around the splendid WOBURN ABBEY and its stately parklands, complete with wild animals, boat trips, art galleries and shops.

Hertfordshire, along with the extinct county of Middlesex, made up the Northern Home Counties and it is here that the mix of grand country houses and new towns is in greatest contrast - or greatest harmony depending on your viewpoint. **Letchworth** was the first of the new 'Garden Cities', created as early as 1903 in a bid to bring better housing to ordinary people. Its FIRST GARDEN CITY MUSEUM tells the story of the somewhat radical social ideals which were held by those who originally created the town as well as those who lived here. **Welwyn Garden City** followed in 1920 and several other new towns, often around old town or village centres, sprung up in the post-war period of the 1950's.

Despite this recent development, many of Hertfordshire's Roman associations are still in evidence, including the ROMAN WALL built in around 200 AD to enclose the city of Verulamium, once the third largest town in Britain, now **St Albans**. The importance of this site to the Romans was the comparatively easy crossing of the countryside on routes to the north, and the county's Roman roads include Akeman Street and Watling Street, and no doubt they also made use of the ancient Ickneild Way.

The first major programme of placing milestones in Britian took place on the road between Cambridge and the village of **Barkway** and two very fine examples dating from the mid-eighteenth century can still be seen in the village. Other stones seen by the roadside in and around the county are known as 'puddingstones', a natural conglomerate of flints and silica which resembles bread pudding. They are said to have magical powers and to ward off evil spirts.

The origins, and the date, of the ROYSTON CAVE are quite unknown. Having been discovered by workmen in the 18th century, it now sits most oddly down a steep passage off a busy street in the middle of **Royston**. A man-made cave, or more precisely a GROTTO was created by a wealthy Quaker in the town of **Ware**, incorporating decorative stones and patterns of exotic shells. Having taken ten years to build, the 'Fairy Hall' gradually started to fall into decay only another ten years or so later and is only now being restored. It is open very occasionally and anyone wanting to view it should contact the East Herts District Council.

Of particular interest in this county for vegetarians will be SHAW'S CORNER at **Ayot St Lawrence**. Sir George Bernard Shaw, playwright and critic, vegetarian and humanist, lived here for the second half of his long and active life. His vegetarian ideals were based on both moral and health grounds, proclaiming that "Animals are our fellow creatures. I feel a strong sense of kinship with them". The house has been kept exactly as it was at the time of his death in 1950.

The many houses on a truly grand scale include HATFIELD HOUSE originally home to the Bishops of Ely and later to Henry VIII's children and other members of the Royal family, BROCKET HALL which was the home of Lord Melbourne and Lady Caroline Lamb, MOOR PARK the historic home of Cardinal Wolsey later transformed into a Palladian mansion and now a golf club, BASING HOUSE home of William Penn founder of Pennsylvania and SALISBURY HALL a 17th century manor remodelled in 1668 by Charles II for Nell Gwynn.

Sadly others have fared less well, such as the Castle at **Bishop's Stortford** now just a mound, and another earthworks with just a little masonry which was the Castle at Berkhamsted, presented by William the Conqueror to his brother, later visited by Thomas à Becket, Chaucer and three of Henry VIII's wives, and involuntarily visited, for a long term, by King John of France. Another was Ware Park which originally housed the 'Great Bed of Ware' mentioned by Shakespeare in his plays, now in the Victoria & Albert Museum.

Near Ware at **Amwell** is one of the most unexpected of museums in Britain, a LAMP-POST MUSEUM.

Similarly bordering on the outer suburbs of London, the county of Surrey has a very high population, much of it in large villages or small towns, and all of it spread out in pleasant green surroundings.

The well known geographical feature of the HOGS BACK is a part of the North Downs and other high points such as Leith Hill with its view of 13 counties, and Box Hill offer outstanding panoramic views. On the high point of **Chatley Heath** stands a tower which was part of the communication system, sending messages from London to Portsmouth in less than one minute in the days before telegraph.

Box Hill overlooks some of the prettiest of scenery along the River Mole. Despite its rather unpoetic name it is probably the river most written about in poetry, by Spencer, Milton, Pope and others, and the riverside village of **Brockham** is said to have given the name 'brock' to the badger, many of which used to live here.

The riverside meadows of **Runnymede** are famous as being the site of King John's signing of (actually fixing his seal to) the Magna Carta in 1215. The memorial buildings at Runnymede were designed by Sir Edwin Lutyens.

Architecture from the early part of this century can also be seen to great effect at **Whiteley**, built according to the will of William Whiteley who left one million pounds for the creation of this retirement village for staff of Whiteley's Department Store.

Surrey contains other fine recent buildings such as the YVONNE ARNAUD THEATRE in **Guildford** as well as GUILDFORD CATHEDRAL, started in 1936 but not consecrated until 1962 due to the intervening war. With its position high on Stag Hill on the edge of the town it makes a magnificent spectacle.

There are many splendid woods in Surrey and there are arboreta at **Winkworth** and as part of the OLD KILN AGRICULTURAL MUSEUM at **Tilford**.

Loseley Park

Surrey also has several special gardens, the most important of which is WISLEY GARDENS, for over 80 years the show gardens of the Royal Horticultural Society and a source of inspiration for all kinds of gardeners. There are features at their best at each time of year; the Alpine Meadow in spring, the rhododendron-clad Battleston Hill in early summer, and for winter the Orchid House with its naturalistic 'rainforest' setting. Wisley is full of fascinating shapes, textures, sounds and smells, and the special garden for disabled people enables all those with a handicap to take full advantage from them all. There are occasional guided walks and the RHS also runs a series of courses, some of them on aspects of gardening, others on flower arranging or botanical painting. The Information Centre is reputed to sell the most extensive range of horticultural and botanical books in the world, and the range of plants for sale is staggering with something like 8,500 varieties, many of them far from common-or-garden.

Peppermint used to be an important crop in **Banstead**. The watercress beds at **Abinger Hammer**, fed by underground springs are one of the claims to minor fame for the village, and its history as a centre for the iron industry is another. The iron working made use of a hammer mill (hence the name) driven by the stream.

LOSELEY PARK between **Godalming** and Guildford is a splendid Elizabethan house, the home of the More-Molyneux family from the 16th century to the present day. The family farms 1,400 acres around the house, and it is here that Loseley ice cream and yoghurt is made. All Loseley dairy products are free from artificial additives and they also grow organic crops. However the farm tour shows little of the dairy aspect and does incorporate other farm animals.

One of the most interesting of the many towns in Surrey is **Farnham**, an attractive small market town with elegant Georgian housing and with some interesting literary associations including Sir Walter Scott, Swift and William Cobbett (who described the beauty spot of Hindhead as "the most villainous spot God ever made"). There are several historic houses open to the public in and around the town.

Mystery surrounds SHALFORD MILL, an early 18th century water mill which was in full use until 1914 when it fell into some disrepair. It was acquired by the 'Ferguson's Gang' some years later and after restoration was given to the National Trust. The 'Gang' members used code names such as 'Bill Stickers' and none of their identities has ever been known.

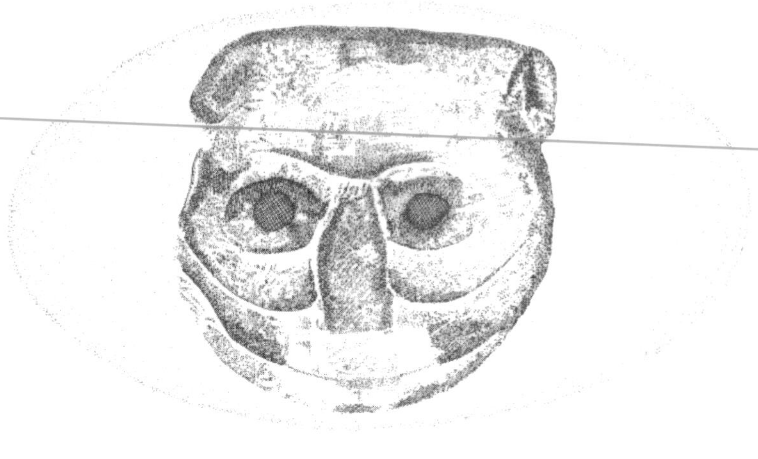

The Cheshire Cat?

Ending on a happy and smiling note, **Cranleigh** Church is believed to hold the inspiration for Lewis Carroll's Cheshire Cat, a grinning cat head carved on the transept arch.

GREATER LONDON

There is so much to see and do in London, it has been so well documented and written about in so many publications that to embark on a general description is unnecessary.

Of course London not only has many excellent vegetarian restaurants, but also many well known vegetarian personalities. One important figure is to be found greeting visitors in the main hallway of the NATURAL HISTORY MUSEUM. 'Dippy', otherwise known as the Diplodocus, Britain's best loved dinosaur, is - or at least was - a vegetarian. Despite dinosaurs' fearsome reputations, this 26 metre giant was purely a herbivore.

THE MUSEUM OF MANKIND also has information on early, (but not that early), vegetarians, and more evidence seems to be available to support man's early origins as at least mainly a vegetarian.

In fact London is crammed with excellent museums, most of them in **South Kensington**, and no visitor should miss the splendid VICTORIA AND ALBERT MUSEUM.

On BUTLER'S WHARF is Britain's first TEA AND COFFEE MUSEUM, featuring hundreds of different coffee grinders and machines, over 1,000 teapots, teabags, prints, photographs, maps and drawings documenting the history of tea and coffee drinking over the past 350 years. There are even tea bushes growing in the museum!

Visitors to **Greenwich's** FAN MUSEUM are introduced to fans and their history through displays which also show their making and the materials used. There are some exquisite examples of 18th and 19th century fans in an elegant Georgian setting, in this, the first and only museum dedicated to the art and craft of fan making.

Just a few of the other exceptional museums around London are the BANK OF ENGLAND MUSEUM with the history of the bank, displays of gold and banknotes; the DESIGN MUSEUM in the Docklands which has collections of well designed, mass production items along with a series of special exhibitions; DICKENS' HOUSE MUSEUM where he lived: FLORENCE NIGHTINGALE MUSEUM telling the story of her life and work; the FREUD MUSEUM in Sigmund Freud's last home; The GUINNESS WORLD OF RECORDS with lifesize models and electronic displays to show the biggest, fastest, etc. KEW BRIDGE STEAM MUSEUM with its unique collection of impressive, working, steam pumping engines; and the LONDON DIAMOND CENTRE where you can see diamonds being cut and polished.

An extraordinary museum, if you can call it a museum, is to be found at 18 FOLGATE STREET in the heart of what was the Huguenot rag trade district of **Spitalfields**. The house is opened a few times a week by the owner who lives there as the house was when it was built in the 18th century, perfect in every detail of decor and, of course with only candle and gas power. However, those intending to visit are requested to 'telephone' for details!

The underground CABINET WAR ROOMS features a Transatlantic Telephone Room and another 20 historic rooms which were operational during the 2nd World War. Very closeby in HORSEGUARD'S PARADE, and also underground is HENRY VIII'S WINE CELLAR which can only be seen by appointment, on a Saturday afternoon.

At **Wimbledon** is what must surely be the only LAWN TENNIS MUSEUM in the world. It is open during the Wimbledon Tennis season to ticket holders.

Also at Wimbledon, as part of the POLKA CHILDREN'S THEATRE, is a toy and puppet exhibition. In Scala Street in central London, POLLOCK'S TOY MUSEUM displays not just Pollock's card cut-out theatres but puppets, dolls' houses, dolls and teddies of the past. The LONDON TOY AND MODEL MUSEUM covers a similar subject, in Craven Hill in **Bayswater**. Somewhat different, but on the theme of puppets, is the SPITTING IMAGE RUBBERWORKS in **Covent Garden**.

Also in Covent Garden, displays of work on an environmental theme are often held at the LONDON ECOLOGY CENTRE, founded on World Environment Day in 1985. The Centre's focus is the Information Service for the general public, a forum for environmental organisations and a single point of contact for the channelling of enquires and queries. Its 'London Sustainable Development Network' collects information on examples of good environmental practice which it then publicises to those interested.

The offices of the Bat Conversation Trust and the Environmental Film Festival are also within the Centre, as is a Meditation Centre.

Covent Garden is an exciting development of mainly shops, cafes and small museums, several of them quite specialised and unique, mixed with street entertainment and an electric atmosphere, in what was the old fruit and vegetable market. No longer are there flower girls to be found under the portico of St Paul's church, but although the area has changed considerably since those days it has retained its lively spirit.

Tower Bridge

A short walk from Covent Garden via the Aldwych brings you to **Fleet Street**, another part of London now much changed. For centuries until just recently Fleet Street was the home of all important national newspapers, now some have moved, mainly to the **Docklands**. The other association with this area, that of the legal profession, continues. Although different, the charm of the old pubs and the alleys persists, with much of its history on view, such as the PEPYS EXHIBITION within the PRINCE HENRY'S ROOM, and the WIG AND PEN where lawyers and journalists have traditionally met, but Sweeney Todd's Barber Shop and the Pie Shop on the other side of St Dunstan's Church are no longer there. In the Strand, TWININGS tea shop is said to be the longest established shop on its original site and also claims to be the narrowest. The names of the streets and alleys sum up something of their past history, with Wine Office Court and Old Cheshire Cheese.

The area of **Bloomsbury** gave its name to the 'Bloomsbury Group' who frequented the many bookshops and publishers' offices. At

UNIVERSITY COLLEGE at the top of Gower Street you can actually see the preserved body of the founder, the vegetarian Jeremy Bentham, who wrote of animals "The question is not, can they reason? Nor, can they talk? But can they suffer?" Around the corner in Euston Road the WELLCOME INSTITUTE displays pharmacy shop fronts from several countries.

In **Westminster** the pretty COLLEGE GARDEN with its LITTLE CLOISTER is only occasionally open to the public. It is said to be the oldest garden of its type in England.

An aerial view of London will show that much of it is covered in green. Not only are there large numbers of private gardens but there are hundreds of public gardens and parks right up to the size of RICHMOND PARK, which with deer roaming wild, really does seem to be a bit of the countryside within London.

The ancient walled CHELSEA PHYSIC GARDEN, just along from the Chelsea Royal Hospital with its red-coated pensioners, was only the second botanical garden to be opened in Britain. It is a serene and beautiful place. It was the seed of a cotton plant taken from here that resulted in America's successful cotton industry.

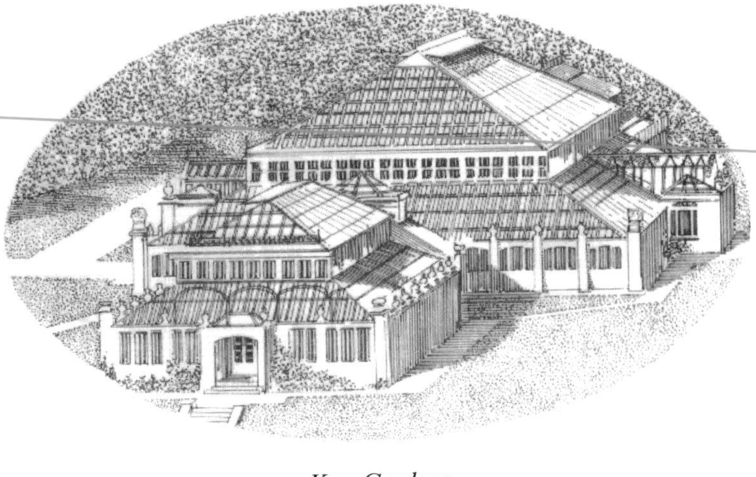

Kew Gardens

The most famous London garden is undoubtedly KEW GARDENS, and indeed it is accepted as being the finest botanic garden and plant research centre in the world, aimed at creating a better future for our planet. It consists of 300 acres of magnificent tranquil gardens alongside the Thames in west London, with 6 acres under glass from the exquisite Victorian Palm House to the stunning new Princess of Wales Conservatory. There are buildings too, including KEW PALACE and QUEEN CHARLOTTE'S COTTAGE. One of the most unusual features is the Pagoda, completed in 1762 as a surprise for Princess Augusta, the Dowager Princess of Wales, who had founded the Gardens only a few years earlier. The ten storey octagonal structure reaches a height of 50 metres, and was at the time the most accurate imitation of a Chinese building in Europe (although to be accurate it should have had an odd number of storeys). Vistas through the Garden enable the Pagoda to be seen in superb settings. The 18th century Kew Gardens was just a tiny portion of that seen today, having the Richmond estate added to it early in the 19th century, with some areas coming more recently into cultivation.

The vegetarian foods market has grown by more than 500% in the past five years and caterers now spend around £10 million a year just on meat-free burgers, sausages and grills. In 1992 the vegetarian food market as a whole was calculated to be worth £11.1 billion.

In addition to the nine exceptional glass houses, the dozen other buildings, the many special garden features and the wonderful parkland of the three arboreta, work goes on behind the scenes to preserve endangered plant species and to conserve habitats. The 44,000 different types of plants at Kew represent one in six of known species (it is believed that there are many plant species still undiscovered and work too continues in this direction), with 13 species extinct in the wild and 1,000 threatened. The botanists at Kew now have some 6 million preserved specimens which through their research could be found to contain important medicines, fuels or food.

Another very important although less well known garden is in **Enfield**. The National Gardening Centre at CAPEL MANOR is actually not just a garden but a College for the study of landscape and garden maintenance and management, a Countryside Centre predominantly used by schools, and it incorporates 'Which? Magazine's' demonstration garden. The gardens extend over 25 acres and illustrate many different designs, styles and periods, from formal images to habitats for attracting wildlife.

In the centre of London, next to Lambeth Palace, is the MUSEUM OF GARDEN HISTORY, run by the Tradescant Trust. The Trust was founded less than 20 years ago to save the historic church of St Mary at Lambeth from demolition. There they established the Museum of Garden History as a centre for plant display, lectures and exhibitions. The Tradescants, father and son, were royal gardeners in the 17th century and brought back from their frequent travels many of the plants which we now know, making them still today possibly the best known name in plant collecting. The plants were propagated in their famous 60 acre garden in Lambeth. Development of the garden is ongoing, with some exciting plans for the future.

Mushroom, Pine Kernel, Asparagus and Walnut Cream Cheese Roll

From Aroma's innovative Sandwich Menu

Sautéed Wild Mushrooms, Toasted Pine Kernels, Oak Leaf Lettuce, Asparagus and Walnut Cream Cheese on Sun-dried Tomato Ciabatta Bread

½ lb	Wild Mushrooms
2oz	Butter
2oz	Toasted Pine Kernels
Several large leaves	Oak Leaf Lettuce
4oz (6 spears)	Fresh Asparagus
4oz	Cream Cheese
2oz	Crushed Walnuts
	Sun-dried Tomato Ciabatta

Sauté the washed mushrooms with butter in a frying pan with a little salt and freshly ground pepper (and garlic if you wish).

Put the pine kernels into a hot oven for about 8 minutes, or until slightly brown. Wash the lettuce leaves and leave to dry. Cook the Asparagus in salted boiling water for 2 minutes (or until cooked but yet very firm). Immediately place under running cold water.

Mix crushed walnuts thoroughly with cream cheese. Cut the Ciabatta loaf in half lengthways and spread both sides with the walnut cream cheese.

Place the sautéed mushrooms on Ciabatta, then sprinkle with the toasted pine kernels. Place the cooked asparagus on top and then add the lettuce.

Close sandwich and cut into three.

Hotel

THE OLD MANSE

Victoria Street, Bourton-on-the-Water, Gloucestershire, GL54 2BX.
Telephone: (0451) 820082, Facsimile: (0451) 810381

BUILT in 1748 in a period of wealth for all the settlements of the Cotswold hills, the family owned and run Old Manse in Bourton-on-the-Water is now a delightful hotel with 12 well furnished en-suite bedrooms. Bourton is one of the most famous of the Cotswold villages and is frequently called 'Little Venice' because of the many picturesque low bridges spanning the wide and shallow River Windrush which flows past, only a few feet from the porch of The old Manse on its leisurely way to the Thames. The whole village has houses which are solidly built and honeyed with the famous limestone.

The Old Manse was the home of the Reverend Benjamin Beddome, the village's Baptist pastor. He was renowned for his biblical knowledge and as a prolific hymn writer. In recent years a modern wing has been added to the hotel. It too is built in traditional Cotswold stone and sits in harmony with its older parts.

The spacious 60 seater restaurant is elegantly decorated and furnished and offers excellent food, using fresh local produce wherever possible. Any special dish of your personal choice will always gladly be prepared by the Chef so that even if you prefer something other than the many super vegetarian dishes on the menu, a meal to your taste is readily available.

The menu changes daily in the restaurant and in the bar there are specials each day. The delicious home-made soups are almost always vegetable based and with fresh granary bread become a meal in their own right.

Useful Information

OPEN: Bar, Mon-Sat: 11am-11pm, Sun: 12-3pm & 7-10.30pm.
Restaurant, Mon-Sat: 6-9pm, Sun: 12-2.30pm & 7-10.30pm
CREDIT CARDS: Access/Visa/Amex/Diners
CHILDREN: Welcome
LICENSED: Yes
ON THE MENU: High percentage of vegetarian dishes across the board
DISABLED ACCESS: Yes + suitable toilet
GARDEN: Small garden
ACCOMMODATION: 9 dbl, 3 twn. Beddome room has a king size four poster

Restaurant

VERONICA'S RESTAURANT

3 Hereford Road, Bayswater, London, W2 4AB.
Telephone: (071) 229 5079, Facsimile: (071) 221 1210

IN the last 11 years this charming establishment has won awards consistently and has always maintained a very high standard. It has also kept a slight Edwardian and Victorian air, in keeping with the age of the building. It is an early Edwardian Stucco fronted terrace building facing the green and leafy Leinster Square. Before World War I it was a fishmongers and the restaurant still retains the wide open sashed window and marvellous mosaics outside. You can sit outside on the terrace overlooking the square in summer. The restaurant itself is in two sections. The elegant front part is high ceilinged and mirrored, and the back is a pretty Victorian kitchen, softly lit by candles at night. Playing in the background is an eclectic mixture of classical and early English music. A truly delightful place in which to eat.

The menu is traditional British both historical and regional. Early English food was particularly healthy and following such recipes is one of the reasons why Veronica's has received so many accolades including nominations for being a 'healthy' restaurant. Naturally vegetarian options are part of a balanced menu and so a large percentage of the dishes at every course are entirely suitable for vegetarians. Everything is prepared and cooked on the premises including their own home-baked bread. Excellent value fixed price menus are always available, as well as the a la carte menu.

The wide ranging wine list with wines from around the world including Britain, has eight vegetarian wines, 16 organic and four country wines - elderflower, gooseberry, raspberry and tayberry. There is even an organic brandy. This is a restaurant which must please vegetarians.

Useful Information

OPEN: Mon-Fri: Lunch 12-3pm, Mon-Sat: Dinner: 7-midnight. Closed Sun, & Sat lunchtime, Bank Holidays & Public Holidays
CREDIT CARDS: All major cards
CHILDREN: Welcome
LICENSED: Full licence
ON THE MENU: Many excellent vegetarian dishes at every course
DISABLED ACCESS: Yes but no special toilets
GARDEN: No, but terrace at front overlooking garden square
ACCOMMODATION: No

Restaurant

DOWNTOWN SULEMAN'S

1 Cathedral Street, London, SE1 1YB.
Telephone: (071) 407 0337

DOWNTOWN Suleman's, a short walk over London Bridge from the City (Monument Station) and three minutes from London Bridge Station, is an experience one should not miss. Set in a Listed Building which belongs to Southwark Heritage, it is housed in the basement with a decor which is both striking, modern but of the past with its stained glass, painted brick walls and wooden flooring; a happy combination. Here you can feast on a menu which is described as 'Continental Cuisine with a Twist'. Not entirely vegetarian it nonetheless offers four starters, three main courses and five desserts which conform entirely to vegetarian requirements and there are vegan options as well as dishes for other diets on request. The only substitute used is Tofu and none of the desserts have gelatine. The cheese used in cooking is always vegetarian.

In addition to the standard menu which has all sorts of exciting dishes, there are Daily Specials and in the evenings the menu produces a Thai Feast - for two or more people which includes a number of dishes totally suitable for vegetarians. This is a delightful restaurant in which to eat; a happy place with a cheerful, smiling staff who are always willing to be of assistance.

The wine list does not offer organic or vegetarian wines but does have a distinctive selection of red and white wines from France, Germany, Alsace and the New World and a first class house wine 'Domaine Desibremont'. Every night is live jazz night which simply adds to the already splendid atmosphere of Downtown Sulemans. This restaurant is fun and at the same time fully understanding of the needs of the ever growing number of vegetarians.

Useful Information

OPEN: Lunch, Mon-Fri: 12-2.45pm. Dinner,Tues-Fri: 5.30-10.30pm.(Tues-Fri: Late Night Jazz)
CREDIT CARDS: Amex/Visa/Access
CHILDREN: Welcome
LICENSED: Yes, but no organic or vegetarian wines
ON THE MENU: International cuisine. High percentage of vegetarian dishes
DISABLED ACCESS: No
GARDEN: No
ACCOMMODATION: Not applicable

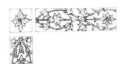

Cafe & Coffee Shop

AROMA

36a St Martin's Lane, London, WC2N 4ET.
Telephone: (071) 836 5110, Facsimile: (071) 240 3507

AROMA offers something that the West End has needed for years. It has brought a blast of brightness to the world of coffee and sandwiches. There are six branches and each, although alike, is refreshingly different from the norm with a curious mixture of outrageous charm and determination. The other five branches are all in central London and are at:

168 Picadilly, Tel: (071) 495 6995
381 Oxford Street in the West One Centre, Tel:(071) 495 6945
273 Regent Street, Tel (071) 495 4911
1b Dean Street, Tel: (071) 287 1633
135 Bishopsgate, Unit 2, Broadgate Centre, Tel: (071) 374 2774

The colour schemes are stunning and go against any preconceived ideas one might have of a coffeeshop. To add to this the astonishing sound of African music which in itself somehow seems entirely right in any branch of Aroma and a spaciousness created out of a small space; the whole goes against any tradition and works quite perfectly.

The coffee is wonderful, the sandwiches extraordinary with an eclectic choice which will suit any palate, any diet and almost any pocket. Aroma is a place of enjoyment both in its surroundings and food but it is much more than that. Their idea of service is quite un-English, not in the least servile or ostentatious but you have no doubt that the staff both know their jobs and are delighted to work for the company. The owner, Michael Zur-Szpiro is a visionary, one who motivates and inspires everyone around him. Aroma is not just a chain of six cafes but a service which encompasses the requirements of businesses who have functions for which catering with a difference is required. Whether it is food for a breakfast meeting, lunch or dinner, a cocktail reception or a 'working tea' - something that foreign visitors love - Aroma will provide everything from food to equipment. Take away is also available. One can only hope that more Aroma establishments will open throughout the country and one does not have to visit or work in London to enjoy them.

Useful Information

OPEN: 8am-11pm
CREDIT CARDS: All major cards
CHILDREN: Welcome
LICENSED: No

ON THE MENU: Wide range of sandwiches, pastries etc, including special vegetarian food
DISABLED ACCESS: Yes but no special toilets
GARDEN: No
ACCOMMODATION: Not applicable

Bistro/Restaurant

CAFE ROUGE

200 Putney Bridge Road, London, SW15 2NA.
Telephone: (071) 2872554 for info on all branches

WE have chosen to write about Cafe Rouge in Putney Bridge Road but the atmosphere of this one, which is typically French, is pertinent to all the group's establishments right across London.

You will find Cafe Rouge in Hampstead, Fulham, Richmond, Knightsbridge, Chelsea, Portobello, Putney, Highgate, James Street, Kensington, Wimbledon, in the City at Tooley Street, in Whiteleys at Bayswater, Fetter Lane, Maida Vale, and Frith Street so all of them are situated in central and convenient places. They are fun, friendly, relaxed and informal with soft music in the background which encourages conversation rather than detracts. Sometimes you may find jazz bands or a pianist playing in some of the branches. Naturally each one has some characteristics of its own but you cannot mistake the essentially Gallic approach in the decor and even the smell! Good coffee, freshly baked bread and the tantalising aroma of good cooking. They really remind one of happy days in Montmartre.

The menu is quintessentially French Bistro. Nothing is bought in and everything is made on the premises including the desserts. A high percentage of dishes are suitable for vegetarians and all the desserts are totally vegetarian. Every day there is a Plat du Jours which will most probably be French Regional cooking. The wines are chosen to complement the food and come entirely from France; four of them are vegetarian and four organic. The house wine is excellent and reasonably priced.

For information or the whereabouts of any of the Pelican Group's excellent restaurants please ring Charlotte on 071 287 2554.

Useful Information

OPEN: 10-11pm
CREDIT CARDS: Amex/ Visa/Access/Switch
CHILDREN: Welcome
LICENSED: Yes
ON THE MENU: Good regional French cooking. Vegetarian options
DISABLED ACCESS: Yes but not always suitable toilets
GARDEN: Only at Highgate, Kensington & City branches
ACCOMMODATION: Not applicable

Cafe

CANADIAN MUFFIN CO

5 King Street, Covent Garden, London, WC2E 8HN.
Telephone: (071) 379 1525

JUST off Covent Garden Piazza and overlooking St Paul's Church, the Canadian Muffin Co is an interesting and unusual cafe owned and run by a friendly couple, David and Frances Blunden. It is an ideal stop for a snack and a beverage whilst exploring Covent Garden with its world renowned market, shopping and street entertainment.

For the last three years they have been delighting their customers with unique Canadian 'muffins', all vegetarian - although some of the savoury varieties are made with non-vegetarian cheese.

The smell of freshly cooked muffins will tantalise your tastebuds as you walk inside. You are given a choice of over 25 sweet or savoury, always wholesome and nutritious oatbran muffins which are baked on the premises daily, using only natural ingredients. On a hot day why not try a frozen yoghurt, each individually made with natural live yoghurt and fresh fruit and totally delicious - there are over 80 flavours on offer! It is doubtful whether you would find anywhere in London offering such a variety.

Whilst the Canadian Muffin Co is not licensed it does have an excellent assortment of hot beverages including speciality coffees, superb cappuccinos, espresso, mocha, amandine, latte, cafe au lait, frothy hot chocolate and delicious steamed almond milk as well as a wide range of cold drinks with natural fruit flavourings.

You will find them featured in Egon Ronay's 'Just a Bite' guide in 1992, 1993 and again in 1994 - as well as being commended with write-ups in Time Out and the BBC Holiday Guide.

Useful Information

OPEN: Mon-Fri: 8-7.30pm, Sat: 9-7.30pm, Sun: 10-6.30pm
CREDIT CARDS: None taken
CHILDREN: Welcome
LICENSED: No
ON THE MENU: Muffins of all flavours
DISABLED ACCESS: Yes, but no special toilets
GARDEN: No
ACCOMMODATION: No

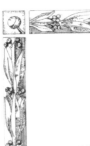

Restaurant, Cafe & Take-Away

FOOD FOR THOUGHT

31 Neal Street, Covent Garden, London, WC2H 9PA.
Telephone: (071) 836 9072, Facsimile: (071) 379 1249

FOOD For Thought is a fun place, full of atmosphere and a wonderfully varied clientele. It is easy to find, just a two minutes walk from Covent Garden. The 18th century Listed Building was once a banana warehouse and the intimate eating alcoves were once used for ripening the fruit. It is ideal for the specialist shoppers who revel in Covent Garden, and a great haunt of those who like to eat before going to the theatre. The staff are efficient and friendly and the interesting and varied clientele certainly adds to the whole refreshing ambience of Food For Thought. Another regular talking point is the eclectic exhibitions of artwork.

The fact that the owners have given thought to their food is quite obvious. Everything is prepared fresh daily on the premises using only quality ingredients, no additives and the minimum of processing to ensure maximum nutritional value. Certainly no freezing or microwaving!

The objective has been to achieve a menu of the world. For 20 years people have been coming to Food For Thought and judging from their comments the claim to be 'Simply the Best' is not without foundation!

Food for Thought has no drinks licence but they welcome customers to 'bring their own' - no charge is made for corkage. For those who are not drinkers there is a range of non-alcoholic drinks from barleycup to a full range of herbal teas. This restaurant is a delightful experience.

Useful Information

OPEN: Mon-Sat: 9.30-8pm, Sun: 10.30-4.30pm. Closed Christmas & New Year
CREDIT CARDS: No
CHILDREN: Welcome
LICENSED: No but welcome to bring your own
ON THE MENU: All fresh produce. Menu changes twice daily
DISABLED ACCESS: No but willing to assist
GARDEN: Street seating in summer
ACCOMMODATION: Not applicable

Brasserie

LA BRASSERIE

272 Brompton Road, Knightsbridge, London, SW3.
Telephone: (071) 584 1668

THIS renowned and long established Brasserie opposite the end of Walton Street, close to the Michelin Building and South Kensington tube station, is a big, typically French Brasserie, so authentic that you may well feel you are in Paris instead of London. This is endorsed by the pleasant sound of French or Jazz music in the background, the crisp, cleanliness and that indefinable aroma that is the hallmark of a good French eaterie. The French always make every meal an occasion and whilst the service is fast if need be, no one is ever rushed. You are encouraged to sit over a meal for as long as you wish.

You will be offered a whole range of old-fashioned, traditional French Brasserie food, not entirely vegetarian by any means but with 30% snacks, 30% starters, 20% main courses and 70% desserts all conforming strictly to vegetarian principles you will not be limited in your choice. It is the very authenticity of the menu that makes La Brasserie such an excellent place in which to enjoy a lengthy meal or the simplicity of fresh croissants and freshly ground coffee at breakfast time.

Wine is as important to the French as food. Every one of the 45 bins on the list comes from the 'Mother Country'. It is a formidable selection. Not cheap - the average price of a bottle of wine is £14.50 - but every sip is value for money. If you enjoy Cognac, Calvados and Armagnac you will find a perfect finish to your meal.

Useful Information

OPEN: Mon-Sat: 8am-midnight. Sundays & Bank Holidays: 10am-11.30pm. Closed Christmas Day
CREDIT CARDS: Access/Barclaycard/Diners/Amex
CHILDREN: Welcome
LICENSED: Full
ON THE MENU: Authentic, old fashioned, traditional French Brasserie
DISABLED ACCESS: No
GARDEN: Not applicable
ACCOMMODATION: Not applicable

Hotel with Brasserie and Public House

ROYAL TRAFALGAR THISTLE HOTEL

Whitcomb Street, London, WC2H 7HG.
Telephone: (071) 930 4477, Facsimile: (071) 925 2149

THIS busy hotel which stands between Trafalgar Square and Leicester Square behind the National Gallery is a modern building with excellent, well-appointed bedrooms, the Battle of Trafalgar pub and a Brassiere designed in the style of 19th century Paris. It is all charming, friendly and well worth seeking out.

Come to the Royal Trafalgar Thistle to stay and you will find yourself in the heart of London. Every room is en-suite and has television, direct dial telephones, trouser press, hair dryer and that blessing to travellers, tea and coffee making facilities. For anyone wanting to enjoy a weekend break in the capital, there is a special rate.

The Brasserie is busy every day but it is restful and the service excellent. The menu is full of exciting dishes and many of them suitable for vegetarians. For example you could start with a warm goats cheese salad with black olives and walnuts, followed by Tagliatelle Carbonara, spinach pasta with a sauce of mushrooms, seasonal vegetables, Parmesan cheese and cream, topped with toasted pine nuts. Every day additional dishes are featured on the blackboard and many are suitable for vegetarians. Sensibly, you will find the menu marked with a capital 'V' denoting that the ingredients are essentially vegetarian.

The wine list, although not specifically vegetarian, has some interesting choices from around the world and the extensive cocktail list offers both alcoholic and non-alcoholic exotic drinks.

Useful Information

OPEN: 7am-11pm. Closed at Christmas
CREDIT CARDS: All major cards
CHILDREN: Welcome
LICENSED: Full licence
ON THE MENU: Brasserie type food with wide vegetarian choice
DISABLED ACCESS: No
GARDEN: Terrace dining area
ACCOMMODATION: 24 dbl, 36 sgl, 48 twn, all en-suite

Restaurant

GREENHOUSE VEGETARIAN RESTAURANT

16 Chenies Street, London, WC1E 7EX.
Telephone: (071) 637 8038

FOR ten years Julie & Angela Haslam with Derek Jeppesen have been flying the flag for good vegetarian eating in The Greenhouse Vegetarian Restaurant, just off Tottenham Court road - the nearest tube is Goodge Street, two minutes away. They have created this popular and likeable establishment in the basement of an old drill hall. At lunchtime it is a busy, bustling restaurant coping with people who come from far and wide to sample the hundreds of different dishes from around the world that appear on the ever changing menu. At night it takes on a totally different personality and becomes quietly relaxed allowing one time to take in the contemporary art exhibits on display and the gentle, unobtrusive music mainly classical and jazz. The Greenhouse is strictly non-smoking and does not have a licence.

Derek Jeppesen is the chef and with the encouragement and enthusiasm of his partners he has collected recipes avidly, making him the possessor of one of the biggest repertoires in the vegetarian catering world. His secret lies not only in presentation but in the imaginative use of the ingredients with which he concocts his dishes. It is not just a job to him but an art form. Here you can have a snack, a light meal or a full meal and if time is of the essence there is a take-away service.

The only food bought in is the bread which comes from a local bakery, the cheese is mostly vegetarian but sometimes other cheese is in use. Only vegetable stocks are used and there are no substitutes of any kind. All the desserts are home-made and suitable both for vegetarians and vegans. You will find the menu contains several options that are suitable for vegans.

Useful Information

OPEN: Mon: 10-7pm. Tues-Fri: 10-10pm. Sat: 12-8.30pm. Closed Christmas, New year and Easter weekend
CREDIT CARDS: None taken
CHILDREN: Welcome
LICENSED: No
ON THE MENU: Ever changing menu featuring hundreds of different vegetarian dishes
DISABLED ACCESS: No, not for wheelchairs
GARDEN: No
ACCOMMODATION: Not applicable

Vegetarian Health Food Restaurant

NUTHOUSE

26 Kingly Street, Oxford Circus, London, W1R 5LB.
Telephone: (071) 437 9471, Facsimile: (081) 691 9366

IN a capital city renowned for the variety and excellence of its restaurants it has to be somewhere very special to stand out. This is the reason that the Nuthouse Vegetarian Health Food Restaurant has become so popular over the years. It has been established since 1969 and in the same skilled, creative hands since 1979. You will find it in Kingly Street just two minutes from Oxford Circus tube station or three minutes from Piccadilly. There are two rooms devoted to the first class cuisine, it is self-service and partly no smoking. People come here knowing that they will enjoy the food, find the prices sensible and, if needs be, the service speedy.

One cannot pin down the range of dishes to any one culture or region. There is a large selection of vegetarian food with vegan options. It is definitely imaginative and many of the dishes on offer are unique to the Nuthouse. People come here expecting to find their time-honoured favourites on the menu and they are not disappointed.

Wine is always enjoyable with a meal. No one could call the wine list here vast but the limited choice comes from England, Italy and France and is extremely reasonable. Less than £5 a bottle on the whole. For non-drinkers there are some unusual and refreshing drinks. The Nuthouse is a relaxed informal place in which to eat and will please carnivores as well as vegetarians when they realise how tasty and exciting the menu is.

Useful Information

OPEN: Mon-Fri: 10.30-7pm, Sat: 11.30-6.30pm
CREDIT CARDS: None taken
CHILDREN: Welcome
LICENSED: Yes
ON THE MENU: Imaginative unique dishes for vegetarians and vegans
DISABLED ACCESS: No
GARDEN: No
ACCOMMODATION: Not applicable

Indian Restaurant

CHUTNEY POT

399 Honeypot Lane, Stanmore, Middlesex, HA7 1AR.
Telephone: (081) 381 2230

IT is only one year since The Chutney Pot opened its doors but it has taken no time at all for local people to realise that its arrival has raised the standard of Indian food available in the area. It is a place that has an aura of the east about it but at the same time is warmly welcoming and a pleasurable place to be. You will find it at the junction of Marsh Lane and Honeypot Lane close to Cannon's Park Station.

Whilst the Chutney Pot caters for all tastes in Indian food it does have a wide choice of vegetarian dishes with all sorts of different and exciting combinations. The owner, Mr Pillai, has been catering for vegetarians for over 20 years and there is little he does not know about the stringent requirements of the diet. You will never find meat stocks or gelatine for example. Every dish created in this kitchen comes to your table served by charming, courteous staff, gentle Indian music plays in the background and you are encouraged to relax and enjoy the tastes of the Orient as they are placed before you.

Wines are always a matter of taste and here the range is limited and none are either vegetarian or organic. In the main they are from France, Spain and Germany and the most expensive bottle is about £14. There is a good house wine also at a reasonable price.

Whilst you are here do enquire about the occasional special vegetarian nights with live music which are always very popular and really allow the chefs to show off their skills.

Useful Information

OPEN: 12-3pm & 6-11.30pm daily
CREDIT CARDS: Visa/ Mastercard/Amex/Diners/ Switch
CHILDREN: Welcome
LICENSED: Yes
ON THE MENU: Good choice, Indian vegetarian dishes
DISABLED ACCESS: Not for wheelchairs but suitable toilets
GARDEN: No
ACCOMMODATION: Not applicable

Indian Vegetarian Restaurant

MANDEER

21 Hanway Place, off Tottenham Court Road, London, W1P 9DG.
Telephone: (071) 323 0660

MANDEER is the oldest of London's Indian vegetarian restaurants. It has been showered justifiably with accolades, the most recent being Vegetarian Living's 'Ethnic Restaurant of the Year 1993'. You will find it two minutes from Tottenham Court Road tube station, just behind the Virgin Megastore. You go downstairs to a basement area into a place of enchantment, reminiscent of an Indian temple, it is low-lit and very atmospheric. Classical Indian music playing in the background heightens the sense of the Orient. Occasionally the music is live with classical concert.

The menu is made up of Gujarati, Punjabi and South Indian dishes, all created on the premises by the talented chefs under the watchful eyes of Mr and Mrs Patel, the proprietors. Every ingredient is traditional and no compromises are made. Each dish is freshly cooked and comes to the table with all the artistry of true Indian cuisine. The smiling, attentive staff make you feel that their whole reason for being there is to ensure your pleasure. In addition to the many vegetarian dishes on the menu, there are a number of vegan options and Mandeer caters for those on a jain diet - in other words no onion or garlic.

Wine complements any meal and with the emphasis on wines from France and Germany at sensible prices, there is an excellent organic chateau des hautes combes house wine. Indian and organic beers are available as well as the usual run of spirits, sherry, liquors and exotic fruit juices. Mandeer is a wonderful culinary experience.

Useful Information

OPEN: Lunch: 12-3pm.
Dinner: 5.30-10pm
CREDIT CARDS: Visa/ Mastercard/Amex/Diners
CHILDREN: Welcome
LICENSED: Yes

ON THE MENU: Exclusively vegetarian, Gujurati, Punjabi & South Indian
DISABLED ACCESS: No. Restaurant in basement
GARDEN: No
ACCOMMODATION: Not applicable

Inn & Restaurant

THE MAYTIME INN

Asthall, Burford, Oxfordshire, OX18 4HW.
Telephone: (0993) 822068

NESTLING alongside the peaceful River Windrush, the Maytime Inn is as charming as its name. A name incidentally which combines the names of the owners, May and Tim, who in the twenty years that they have been in residence have established a reputation for hospitality, warmth, good food and drink and that special ingredient, a keen sense of humour. The building is well over two hundred years old, has the original beams and a flagstone floor which gleams with the patina of age. The unusual galleried bar is surrounded by four restaurants in an open plan. In each of them there are covers for 25 and one is strictly non-smoking. The additional bonus offered by the Maytime is the opportunity to stay in one of the delightfully furnished en-suite bedrooms, each equipped with television, a beverage tray and several other modern amenities.

The menu has a wide range of choice, very much European in flavour. Everything is home-cooked and wherever possible local produce is used. Whilst the food is not exclusively vegetarian there are always five starters and five main courses available as well as all the desserts. Every day the 'Specials Board' also has at least one vegetarian dish. Children are very welcome and a special menu is there for their delectation. The large patio in summer is the ideal place to enjoy a drink or a meal.

Tim has a love of wine and although the wine list is small it has been chosen from the best and most interesting wines around the world. Regulars to The Maytime will know that 'Tim's Wine Basket' holds special wines which are offered at the very reasonable price of £9.95 a bottle. The Maytime Inn is a find, somewhere to remember and in a wonderful position just three miles from Burford.

Useful Information

OPEN: Mon-Sat: 11-3pm & 6-11pm (food 10pm), Sun: 12-3pm & 7-10pm

CREDIT CARDS: All major cards except Diners

CHILDREN: Welcome. Special menu

LICENSED: Yes

ON THE MENU: Always five starters, main courses and desserts for vegetarians

DISABLED ACCESS: Not for wheelchairs. One bedroom

GARDEN: Large patio seating 60

ACCOMMODATION: six en-suite bedrooms

Vegetarian Brasserie & Tearoom

FROG ISLAND BRASSERIE

Hatch Marsh, Abinger Hammer, Nr Guildford, Surrey, RH5 6SA.
Telephone: (0306) 731463

THIS is an exciting vegetarian brasserie situated in between Abinger and Gonshall on the A25. It is the Ideal spot for those who enjoy rural walks and a spot of sightseeing. Equally pleasurable for those who enjoy its rustic, homely charm. The moment you enter this one hundred year old building you sense the warmth of its atmosphere and acquire an awareness that this is essentially a happy establishment. From a mundane point of view there is no doubt that the strictly non-smoking rule is an added bonus.

The owners have the ability to produce an ever changing menu which constantly surprises. They will tell you that many of the dishes on offer are there at the suggestion or request of regular customers, of whom there are many.

One menu might offer carrot and coriander soup, spiced basmati baskets, cheesy almond croquettes or courgette and feta triangles followed by parsnip and peanut loaf, country ale pie or calzone with a creamy Spinach, leek and mushroom filling. The next week there would be a total change. The desserts are always delicious and very tempting. There is a set price for two or three courses.

Frog Island Brasserie is licensed but the wine list is minuscule and all five on offer from France and Italy are either organic or vegetarian. In the summer months the small garden is used for eating out and has seven tables. It is lovely on a warm day. The service is good yet quietly and unobtrusively efficient.

Useful Information

OPEN: Mon-Sat: 10-4pm, Sun: 10-5pm. Thurs, Fri, Sat eve: 7pm onwards
CREDIT CARDS: None taken
CHILDREN: Welcome
LICENSED: Yes
ON THE MENU: Wide range of delicious vegetarian dishes. Vegan options
DISABLED ACCESS: Yes + toilets
GARDEN: Small with tables and chairs in summer
ACCOMMODATION: Not applicable

Wine Bar & Bistro

SEVENS

7 The Borough, Farnham, Surrey, GU9 7NA.
Telephone: (0252) 715345

IN the centre of the town, Sevens wine bar and bistro, is one of the great meeting places for local people and is steadily gaining custom from more and more visitors who come to Farnham either on business or purely for pleasure. One could say that it is entirely because it is such an attractive place in a black and white beamed building which has withstood the test of time for 250 years, but that would be only a small part of the story. Here is an establishment which is run with the easy informality that only total professionalism can bring about. The service is friendly and yet unobtrusive, the decor is charming and everywhere there is a sense of spaciousness without losing anything of its intimate atmosphere. In the summer the pretty walled courtyard provides a colourful, floral setting for those who drink or eat outside. Inside the benefit of an efficient air conditioning system keeps the air fresh. There are areas which are entirely non-smoking. At lunchtime self-service applies for food but at night, in the less frenetic surroundings, cheerful waitress service is available. Sevens is somewhere in which you can spend a relaxed evening or be in and out quite quickly if the demands of the day dictates it.

The food is all home-cooked with a selection of traditional and speciality dishes. It is excellent value for money and for vegetarians offers the opportunity to enjoy the pleasure that Sevens provides as well as being offered some excellent vegetarian dishes right across the board. The menu is changed every two weeks. The wines are superb in quality, come from around the world and are sensibly priced. A bottle of the very good house wine costs approximately £7.50.

Useful Information

OPEN: Mon-Fri: 9.30-11pm, Sat: 9.30-3pm & 6.30-11pm. Closed Sundays & Bank Holidays

CREDIT CARDS: Mastercard/ Visa

CHILDREN: Welcome to eat

LICENSED: Yes

ON THE MENU: Home-cooked, traditional. Good selection for vegetarians at every course

DISABLED ACCESS: Yes but no suitable toilets

GARDEN: Walled garden

ACCOMMODATION: Not applicable

Inn & Restaurant

THE KNIFE & CLEAVER

Houghton Conquest, Bedford, Bedfordshire, MK45 3LA.
Telephone: (0234) 740387, Facsimile: (0234) 740900

SITUATED five miles south of Bedford about one mile from the A6 turn-off this 500 year old hostelry is an atmospheric, brick built inn which has been sympathetically extended by the erection of a Victorian-style conservatory restaurant. This leads on to a flowery terrace where you can eat alfresco on sunny days by the fountain. The award-winning restaurant serves affordably priced vegetarian dishes using all fresh ingredients of the highest quality. The unusual and innovative menu changes on the first of every month but always includes home-made vegetable soups and other vegetarian starters as well as two vegetarian main courses.

The dark Jacobean panelling in the bar is said to come from nearby Houghton House - "House Beautiful" in Bunyan's 'Pilgrims Progress' and here more informal meals are served accompanied by hand pumped real ales or a choice from over 20 wines by the glass. There are nine en-suite bedrooms in the quiet orchard garden.

Useful Information

OPEN: 12-2.30pm & 7-10pm. Closed Sunday nights
CREDIT CARDS: Visa/Access/Amex/Diners

ON THE MENU: Interesting dishes with vegetarian fare across the board
DISABLED ACCESS: Yes + suitable toilets

Restaurant & Art Centre

OSCARS

South Hill Park, Art Centre, Bracknell, Berkshire, RB12 7PA.
Telephone: (0344) 59031, Facsimile: (0344) 411427

SOUTH Hill Park has been an important part of the life of Bracknell since it was built in 1760 by William Watts for his retirement. He did not live to enjoy it for very long but over the years many people have benefited from it, including the BBC who were the occupants from 1953 into the early 1960's. It became an arts centre in 1973 and since then has expanded, adding the Wilde Theatre, a new Art Gallery, Dance and Bar extension and of course, Oscars, a pleasing, friendly restaurant which is a welcoming place to spend an evening dining or in conjunction with a visit to the theatre, cinema or the gallery.

Chef proprietor Mark Bridges provides interesting food at sensible prices and always has a selection of dishes suitable for vegetarians at every course. Couscous or Bean Bourgignone are two favourites of the appreciative regular clientele. Seasonal and private supper parties are a particular speciality with an abundance of interesting vegetarian food. The grounds are attractive with a large lake, trees and lawns. Oscars is licensed.

Useful Information

OPEN: 6.15-9.15pm last orders. Closed 2 weeks Aug/Sept & also from Dec 24th
CREDIT CARDS: Visa/Mastercard

ON THE MENU: Several interesting dishes for vegetarian amidst a varied menu
DISABLED ACCESS: Yes

Licensed Restaurant & Tea Rooms

BO-PEEP TEA ROOMS

Riverside, Bourton-on-the-Water, Gloucestershire, GL54 2DP.
Telephone: (0451) 822005

THERE can be few prettier places in England in which to have tea or a meal than the Bo-Peep Tearooms and Restaurant at the side of the River Windrush in the village of Bourton-on-the-Water known as 'Little Venice'. The Bo-Peep, in parts, dates from the 17th century, and the whole has an olde worlde feel about it with Cotswold stone-walling and antique wood panelling. There are two sections to the restaurant, one of which is totally non-smoking, gentle classical music plays in the background and the whole atmosphere is relaxing.

There is a large range of delicious food and drink to suit every kind of diet and special attention is given to vegetarians. The Bo-Peep is one of only 10 'tea places' in Britain to receive the Tea Council's 'Award of Excellence' for both 1992 and 1993. There is a choice of 40 teas, mainly leaf.

Useful Information

OPEN: Summer: approx 10-6pm (9pm peak months), winter: 10.30-5pm. Phone to check for winter weekdays.
CREDIT CARDS: Visa/Mastercard/Amex/Diners
ON THE MENU: Wide choice. Good vegetarian fare
DISABLED ACCESS: Yes, good access

Restaurant & Cafe

DOWN TO EARTH

11 The Forum, Eastgate Shopping Centre, Gloucester, Gloucestershire, GL1 1NX.
Telephone: (0452) 305832

YOU may need to ask for directions in order to find this very pleasant vegetarian restaurant and cafe. If you ask for Eastgate Market you will then find the entrance to Down to Earth inside the Market. The owners describe it as the restaurant with a view, having a large bay window overlooking the 13th century Greyfriars Abbey ruins.

The interior of their premises is welcoming and comfortable. Open six days a week the menu is full of interesting and tasty vegetarian dishes with vegan options. On Wednesdays there is a special low calorie day. 90% of the food on offer is fresh daily and if you are a lover of good coffee, this is the place for you. Down to Earth lives up to its name and has realistic prices. It is also licensed. Vegans are catered for and children are welcome.

Useful Information

OPEN: Mon-Fri: 9am-4.30pm. Sat: 9am-5pm
CREDIT CARDS: None taken
ON THE MENU: Tasty inexpensive, exclusively for vegetarians & vegans
DISABLED ACCESS: No. There are six steps to get in

Wine Bar & Restaurant

FUNGUS MUNGUS

264 Battersea Park Road, London, SW11 3PB.
Telephone: (071) 924 5578

FUNGUS Mungus probably has the most interesting and remarkable ambience anywhere south of the river. To get there follow the Thames to the Peace Pagoda or more mundanely catch the 45a bus! If you are not careful you will get so carried away by contemplating the four to five hundred objects of interest and art that are just about everywhere and heightened by the use of lights and music, that you will forget to order a meal or a drink! From time to time there is the addition of live music to add to this fantastic atmosphere.

The ever changing menu is exclusively vegetarian with vegan options and the dishes come from around the world. Everything is beautifully presented and always substantial. There are always four starters and four main courses and lots of combination meals with Indonesian platters, desert platters or the aptly named 'Tripping to Thailand'. There is a limited wine list and a pretty enclosed courtyard. Always in the top three vegetarian restaurants in London, Fungus Mungus must be experienced.

Useful Information

OPEN: Lunch: 12-3pm. Evenings: 6-12 midnight. Weekends: 12-12pm - please book at weekends
CREDIT CARDS: None taken

ON THE MENU: Beautifully presented vegetarian meals from around the world with vegan options
DISABLED ACCESS: Yes

Vegetarian Take-away

FUTURES!

8 Botolph Alley, London, EC3R 8DR.
Telephone: (071) 623 4529, Facsimilie: (071) 621 9508

BOTOLPH Alley is close to the Monument , and Futures! is a stylish vegetarian take-away which attracts as many carnivores as vegetarians because of the excellence of its food. It is open for breakfast and at lunch time and is closed in the evenings and on Saturday and Sundays. It is a remarkable place which has a daily changing lunch menu which it faxes out over night to over 200 City companies and has a unique breakfast menu. Food is prepared and sold the same day. It is fresh, of a high quality, varied and tasty. It is the only take-away listed in Hardens restaurant guide and feeds over 500 people daily, necessitating a staff of 16. Over one third of the business is running deliveries into offices in the City.

If you enquire how many covers there are you will be told one stool and a shelf! This is not a place in which to eat but somewhere to acquire a delicious meal, which you can eat whilst you take a look at London's many attractions.

Useful Information

OPEN: Mon-Fri: Breakfast 7.30-10am, Lunch: 11.30-3pm
CREDIT CARDS: None taken

ON THE MENU: Wide range, freshly prepared food
DISABLED ACCESS: No

Restaurant

KRAMPS CRÊPERIE

6 Kenway Road, Earls Court, London, SW5 ORR.
Telephone: (071) 244 8759

THIS is an exciting crêperie with a decidedly French rustic appearance. Somewhere you can eat well and enjoy a good glass of wine at a sensible price. The general bon homie is added to by the mainly traditional jazz that plays in the background, never intrusive but enough to prevent there ever being a silence. This is the sort of place that is open all day and no one minds if you just drop in for a cup of tea or coffee and seize the opportunity to read one of the thoughtfully provided daily newspapers.

The main course crêpes are made from organic buckwheat and wholemeal flour. At least 50% of the main course crêpes are strictly vegetarian and you will find that 75% of the snacks, 50% of the starters and every dessert conforms. For seven years Paul Vernoit has been not only the owner but the chef. He has many regular customers and a growing number of visitors who return whenever they are in London.

Useful Information

OPEN: 7 days, 12-11pm. Closed over Christmas
CREDIT CARDS: Access/Visa

ON THE MENU: Excellent crêpes with vegetarian fillings
DISABLED ACCESS: No

Cafe & Wholefood Store

BENNETT AND LUCK

54 Islington Park Street, Islington, London, NW1.
Telephone: (071) 226 3422

THIS is a pleasant cafe serving light meals and snacks, within a well stocked wholefood store and natural health centre in which you can buy a wide range of organic products, with many herbal and homeopathic remedies.

Eastablished for seven years, Ben and Penny Bennett have made a great impact on the locality. They are well known for the quality of the products and produce that they sell and this extends to the flavoursome food. Here you will find hot soup served every day except in summer when you might find a delicious cold concoction on offer. There are a range of tempting salads, lasagne, quiches and other snacks as well as very good Capuccino and many herbal teas. Bennett & Luck are licensed but for taking-away only. They sell organic and country wines including a particularly good gooseberry as well as organic Champagne, beer and cider. Everywhere is strictly non-smoking.

Useful Information

OPEN: 9-6pm weekdays. Shop until 7pm Mon-Fri & 6pm Sat.
CREDIT CARDS: Visa/Access

ON THE MENU: Snacks and light meals for vegetarians. Vegan options
DISABLED ACCESS: Yes. No suitable toilets

Restaurant

LA LA PIZZA

138 London Road, Kingston Upon Thames, Surrey, KT2 6QL.
Telephone: (081) 546 4888

FOR over 11 years Luigi Abbro has run La La Pizza with as great an understanding of the needs of vegetarians as his carnivorous clients. There are some 32 different pizzas on the menu and at least 30% of these are vegetarian. Everything is freshly prepared and served by a smiling and friendly staff.

The Pizzeria is a late Victorian building which is situated on a corner site on the main entry road into Kingston. The internal decor largely consists of natural wood, with the main wall devoted to a facsimile of the Pont du Gard, the imposing Roman aqueduct in Provence. The aqueduct theme is carried out in the staff shirts and aprons, and the Aqueduct Pizza is one of the most popular. La La Pizza is licensed and has a large selection of Italian, French, German and Spanish wines. Good food, good surroundings and a very happy atmosphere make this a good place to be.

Useful Information

OPEN: 5.30-11.30pm. Closed Christmas Day and New Years Day
CREDIT CARDS: All major cards except Diners and Amex
ON THE MENU: Wide range, freshly prepared pizzas, starters & desserts
DISABLED ACCESS: Yes + toilets

Restaurant

THE HARBOUR TANDOORI

53 Coldharbour Lane, Hayes, Middlesex, UB3 3EE.
Telephone: (081) 561 4134

WHILST the Harbour Tandoori is housed in a comparatively new building, the owner, Mr Uddin, has skilfully and attractively used traditional English Olde Worlde style decor for the interior of his very pleasant restaurant. You will find The Harbour Tandoori near the High Street, and it has the advantage of having plenty of free parking outside. The cuisine is Indian, in Nepalese style, with a wonderful selection of exotic dishes which are also available at a 15% discount to take away.

There are many vegetarian dishes including a Dall Samba made of mixed vegetables and lentils, and Niramishi, a special mixture of dry vegetables. In addition there are a number of vegetable side dishes. Tandoori Breads are one of the specialities of this well ordered establishment - who can resist the aromatic Peswari Nan with almond and sultanas? If you have never tried Indian Ice Cream, this is your opportunity. It is creamy and delicious. The Harbour Tandoori is licensed.

Useful Information

OPEN: 12-3pm & 6-midnight daily
CREDIT CARDS: All major cards plus Luncheon Vouchers
ON THE MENU: Indian cuisine in the Nepalese style. Vegetarian options
DISABLED ACCESS: Yes

Cafe & Lifestyle Centre

NUTTERS HEALTHY LIFESTYLE CENTRE

10 New Street, Chipping Norton, Oxfordshire, OX7 5LJ
Telephone: (0608) 641995

WHOLESOME home-made food which includes chunky vegetable soup, jacket potatoes and savoury or sweet crêpes is the trade mark of Nutters Healthy Lifestyle Centre in the heart of Chipping Norton. It is a popular haunt and deservedly so maintaining a very high standard of food and presentation at sensible prices. Nothing is bought in and virtually every dish is either vegetarian or vegan with just 20% of the main courses devoted to other diets.

Food is not the whole story here. Nutters has a Lifestyle Centre with rebounding, massage, a floatation pool, a solarium and a steam room which is quite likely to persuade you to spend a whole day in this unique centre for relaxation and stress relief. There is a small garden with a pretty walled patio and tables and chairs, wonderful for a summers day.

Useful Information

OPEN: Tues-Sat: 9-6pm. Closed Christmas Day & Boxing Day
CREDIT CARDS: None taken
ON THE MENU: Wholesome home-made food
DISABLED ACCESS: No

Public House

WILLIAM IV PUBLIC HOUSE

Little Common Lane, Bletchingley, Nr Redhill, Surrey, RH1 4QG.
Telephone: (0883) 743278

THIS is a pub that is the epitome of the traditional hostelry at the turn of the century. Recommended by Les Routiers, it has a warm, friendly snug bar, a comfortable lounge bar and a cosy dining room at the rear, decorated and hung with interesting pictures and bric-a-brac. It has been a welcoming watering hole for people in Bletchingley for the last 150 years and it is doubtful if it has even been better run than today.

The menu offers a high proportion of vegetarian dishes across the board. You will find it varied and extensive emphasising quality cooking. People come here for the pubs hospitality but also because they know that the food is generous in its portions and sensibly priced. If you do not wish to eat in the dining room then the bar meals are first class. Every day blackboard specials tempt regulars with the tasty dishes on offer.

Useful Information

OPEN: 11-3pm & 6-11pm. Sun: 12-3pm & 7-10.30pm. Food: 12-2 & 7-9pm. Sun: 12-1.45pm & 7-9pm
CREDIT CARDS: Visa/Mastercard/Eurocard/Access
ON THE MENU: Good vegetarian dishes across the board
DISABLED ACCESS: Yes but no suitable toilets

Restaurant

SIXTIES RESTAURANT

New Zealand Avenue, Walton-on-Thames, Surrey, KT12 1QB.
Telephone: (0932) 221685

THIS well run restaurant has been known for the excellence of its food for over 12 years and in the last five years has added to that by producing interesting, imaginative and tasty dishes for vegetarians at every course. Today you will find 40% of the starters, 20% of the main courses and 60% of the desserts all come within the requirements of the vegetarian diet. The menu is International and has specials from around the world which change daily.

You will find the decor attractive and relaxing, the welcome genuine and the service both friendly and efficient. It is not the sort of place for those in shirt sleeves, rather more smart casual dress is the order of the day. Children over the age of 10 are permitted. The wines are well chosen to complement the dishes on the menu, and they are sensibly priced.

Useful Information

OPEN: Open 12-2.30pm & 6.30-10.15pm. Closed the week after Xmas

CREDIT CARDS: All except Amex & Diners

ON THE MENU: International with excellent choices for vegetarians

DISABLED ACCESS: Yes, also suitable toilets

The Pantiles in Winter
- an early 18th century pedestrian precinct at Tunbridge Wells

Contents

THE SOUTH EAST

Kent, Essex, Suffolk, Norfolk and Cambridgeshire

Suggested Venues to Dine

KENT AND ESSEX

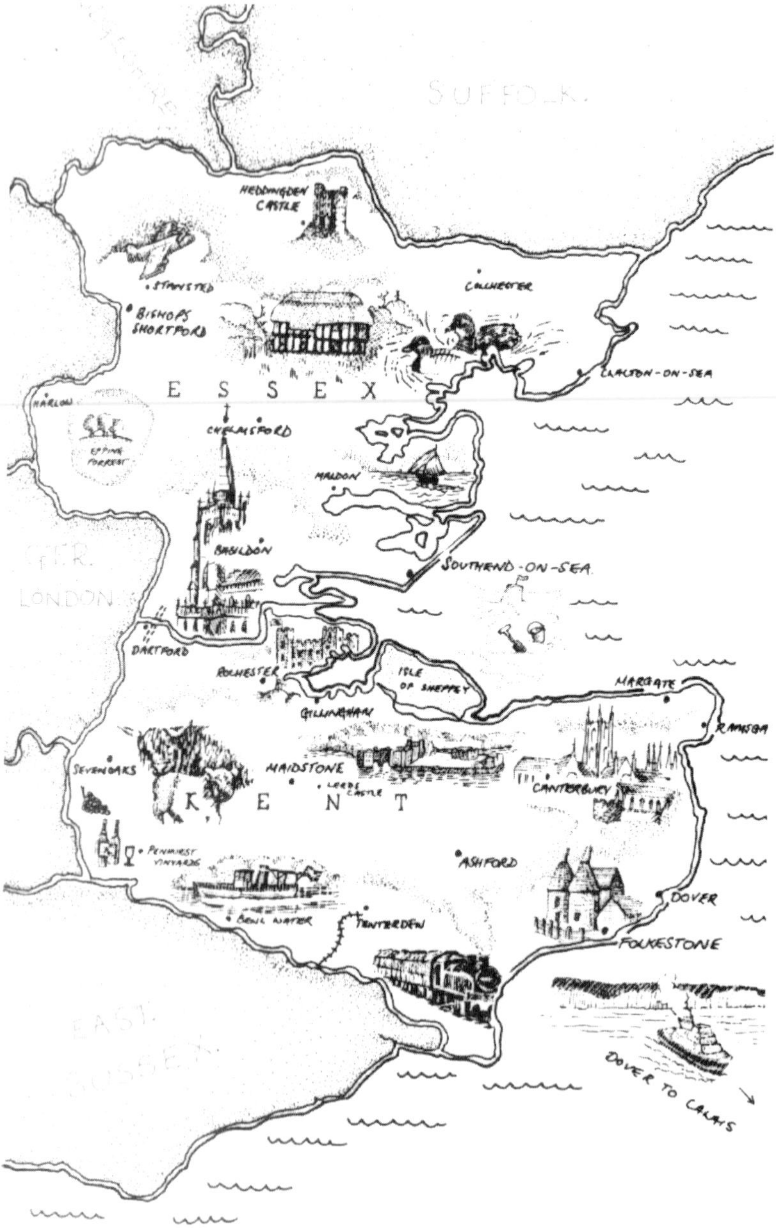

EAST ANGLIA

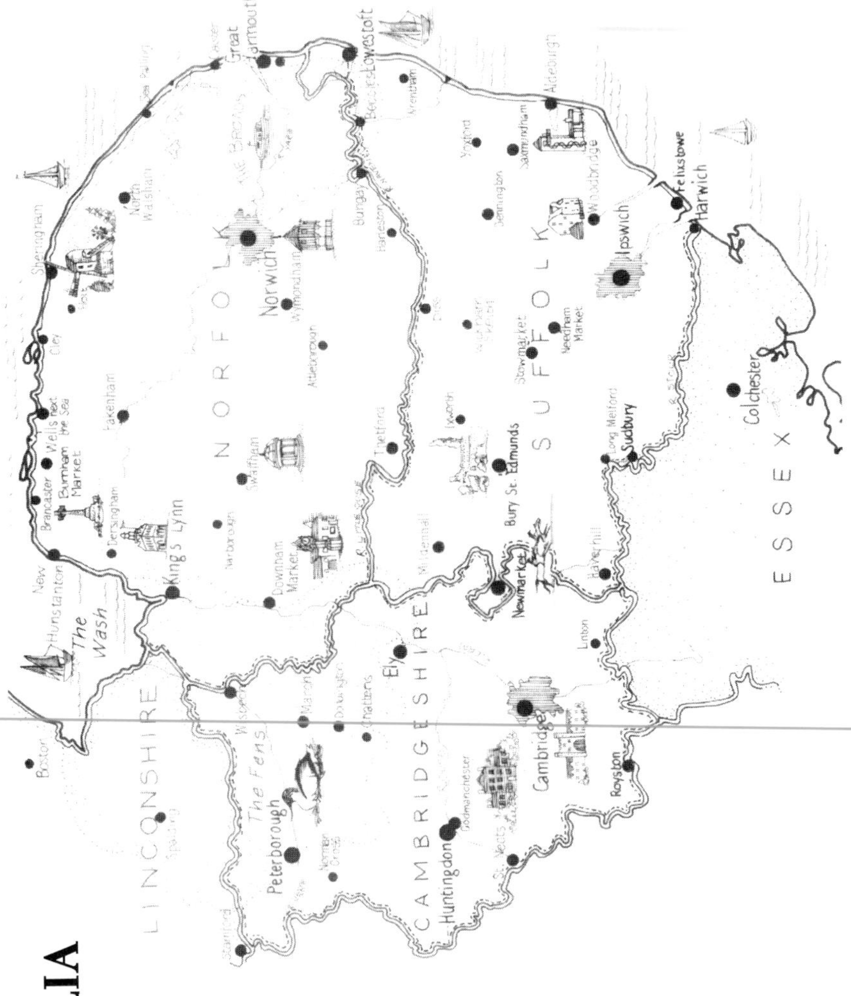
NORFOLK
SUFFOLK
CAMBRIDGESHIRE
LINCONSHIRE
ESSEX
The Wash
The Fens
Boston
Spalding
Stamford
Peterborough
Huntingdon
St. Neots
Godmanchester
Cambridge
Royston
Linton
Ely
Chatteris
Wisbech
March
Newmarket
Mildenhall
Haverhill
Bury St. Edmunds
Long Melford
Sudbury
Colchester
Stowmarket
Needham Market
Ipswich
Woodbridge
Felixstowe
Harwich
Aldeburgh
Saxmundham
Yoxford
Bungay
Beccles
Lowestoft
Great Yarmouth
Norwich
Wymondham
Attleborough
Thetford
Swaffham
Downham Market
King's Lynn
Dersingham
Burnham Market
Wells next the Sea
Brancaster
New Hunstanton
Fakenham
Cley
Holt
Sheringham
North Walsham
Diss

THE SOUTH EAST

Kent, Essex, Suffolk, Norfolk & Cambridgeshire

Kent has long been known as the 'Garden of England' and the rich soils continue to provide abundant crops. The view of Kent as a county of hop fields dotted with oast houses is certainly an accurate one in certain parts, although a great many of the oast houses have now been converted to dwellings.

The largest collection of oast houses in the world, dating from the Victorian era, are to be found at the WHITBREAD HOP FARM which is near **Paddock Wood**. You won't actually see beer being produced, but you can see THE HOP STORY EXHIBITION as well as the WHITBREAD SHIRE HORSE CENTRE and many other attractions.

As well as hop gardens, orchards feature frequently in this fertile landscape in the area known as 'The Weald' which actually covers about half of the county's total area in the south west. Further to the north and east is the North Downs, a high chalk ridge which ends as the White Cliffs of Dover, possibly the best known British landscape, seen from ship and from air by many thousands of visitors each year. The highest point is known as Shakespeare's Cliff, having featured in 'King Lear'.

Very different landscapes can be found in some coastal districts, such as the pretty meadows of the **Isle of Sheppey** in the north and next to it the **Isle of Grain** with the country's largest heronry, and **Romney Marsh** in the south, where the flat open marshes appear sumptuous in the bright summer light but truly desolate by winter. The Marsh was created by the Romans who constructed the Rhee Wall to claim the land from the sea. Although the sea is actually retreating, the small town of Old Romney once on the coast now stands well inland and even **New Romney** further out is now dislocated. In the centre of the marsh stands St Thomas Becket Church, with no village or even hamlet nearby.

Several other communities in Kent have gradually become more distant from the sea, such as **Sandwich** once a Cinque Port and now almost two miles from the coast. Although not necessarily as close to the water as they once were, an amazingly large number of castles and other fortified buildings can be seen around the coastal area, built because Kent, being the closest part of Britain to foreign soil, has been subject to many invasions, and attempted invasions, over thousands of years.

Kent can also show signs of very much earlier occupation with flints found from the Old Stone Age and dwellings from around 6,000 BC. KIT'S COTY HOUSE and LITTLE KIT'S COTY HOUSE, taken from the Celtic for 'tomb in the woods' are two Neolithic burial chambers near **Aylesford**. It was in what is now Kent that the Romans first arrived, and later the Angles, the Saxons and the Jutes all came to these shores. **Dover** is now the busiest of the ferry ports with frequent trips to Calais, which can actually be seen on clear days. Increases to the 'friendly' invasion via the long planned Channel Tunnel are now becoming a reality.

One particularly rare Roman structure is the lighthouse, or 'pharos', which stands within DOVER CASTLE, overlooking the White Cliffs. The castle reflects much of the county's history in one, being a mixture of many dates with its history in the Iron Age and the current buildings being part Roman, part Saxon and extensively Norman, with some later additions. Actually additions is possibly the wrong word to use for the most recent alterations to Dover Castle: tunnels were excavated within the White Cliffs to counter the threat of invasion by Napoleon, and during the Second World War these became a secret operational centre. It was from here that the evacuation from Dunkirk was masterminded.

The expected Napoleonic invasion was also responsible for the construction of artillery towers such as the DYMCHURCH MARTELLO TOWER which formed a chain of strongholds around the coast.

The whole of the Kent coastline, many of the castles and several other historic sites are included on the SAXON SHORE WAY, a 143 mile walk, which links in the middle at **Dover** with the NORTH DOWNS WAY, following the crest of the North Downs and in places incorporating the PILGRIMS' WAY linking **Canterbury** with Winchester in Hampshire. The Pilgrim's Way is actually far older than the name would imply, and was probably first used by the Neolithic peoples.

The first railway to take passengers on a regular basis, operated between **Whitstable** and Canterbury, but survived only a short while, being overtaken by horse drawn carriage!

Canterbury is one of the most visited towns in Britain, and most visitors are making their way, as millions have done over thousands of years to CANTERBURY CATHEDRAL, seat of the Archbishop, Primate of All England. On conversion to Christianity King Ethelbert granted land for the building of the cathedral which was founded by St Augustine in the 6th century, although it was not until after the murder of Thomas à Becket in 1170 that the cathedral gained particular importance. Pilgrims over the centuries have often taken away with them some souvenir of their visit to Canterbury. Commercial souvenirs are not new and hundreds of years ago one of the possible tokens was a small bell. It was from this item that the flower, the 'Canterbury Bell', was named.

Just outside the city walls, the church of St Martin is older still than the cathedral, and is possibly the oldest surviving church in Britain that is still in use today.

On the northern slope of the North Downs the attractive village of **Chilham** is often somewhat overlooked as crowds make their way to CHILHAM CASTLE, a large manor house built by Inigo Jones in 1616, and now with many attractions for tourists, the most spectacular of which are the authentic jousting displays.

Also featuring work by Inigo Jones is COBHAM HALL now a school but open to visitors at times during the holidays. The village of **Cobham** is known to readers of 'The Pickwick Papers' and both here and in Rochester are buildings as well as relics relating to Charles Dickens. THE DICKENS CENTRE in **Rochester** shows much of his life and times, and just outside the town Dickens' home GAD'S HILL PLACE is occasionally open although, as at Cobham, it is now a school. Rochester holds a Dickens Festival in May or June each year.

The novelist and poet Vita Sackville-West and her husband Sir Harold Nicholson lived at the 15-16th century SISSINGHURST CASTLE and created renowned gardens there, which can be visited throughout the summer. The nearby SISSINGHURST PLACE GARDENS are also very attractive.

Not far from Sissinghurst, close to the town of **Tenterden** is SMALLHYTHE PLACE where the actress Ellen Terry spent the last years of her life. It is now a small but interesting museum not just to her but to life on the stage in general and to her fellow actors and actresses.

Smallhythe Place, former home of Ellen Terry, now a museum

Between Sissinghurst, and Tenterden is the pretty village of **Biddenden** with rows of weavers cottages. The church has a stained glass window in memory of 12th century Siamese twins, and their memory also lasts today with the Biddenden Dole, biscuits stamped with an impression of the sisters, paid for by a legacy from them and distributed to the poor. A similar contribution is made to the poor at **Harrietsham**, but the offering here is of bread.

Other exceptionally attractive villages in Kent include **Groombridge** with small cottages and the manor house which was the home of the 17th century diarist John Evelyn, **Goudhurst** with views of orchards and hop fields, and **Appledore** overlooking Romney Marsh.

The village of **Chiddingstone** is also a pretty one, with charming cottages, grand houses and grouped oast houses, and it can claim too a 'chiding stone' used, at one time but fortunately no longer, for the indictment of scolding wives. At **Fordwich**, once the port of Canterbury, is a crane used for dipping nagging wives into the river! Rather more daunting, HEVER CASTLE has a torture chamber.

West along the coast from Romney Marsh the shingle beach of **Dungeness**, a favourite spot for many migratory birds, is overlooked by a huge nuclear power station as well as a modern lighthouse and a fog horn with 60 loudspeakers. Once a beauty spot, but sadly no longer.

The condition of 'black bile' might sound like something to do with nuclear radiation or perhaps tar picked up from the beach, but was actually the term used for what we now refer to as melancholia, and the cure - 20 pints (at one go) of the waters from the spa at **Tunbridge Wells**. The water is freely, if rather unceremoniously available from a spring in THE PANTILES, a truly elegant row of shops in the centre of the town dating from the town's period of high fashionability in the mid 18th century.

Kent and Essex share a few common features: both border on London and indeed include metropolitan areas on those fringes; both are on the banks of the Thames estuary; and both face, although only in part as far as Kent is concerned, the east coast. From northern Kent you see southern Essex, yet with the Thames as a wide barrier between them, only comparatively recently breached by the Dartford Tunnel, the two counties have little of similarity between them.

Essex is popular as a boating area, its coast with many river estuaries, natural ports and its several sizeable lakes bringing visitors out of London at the weekend; the beaches of sand, shingle and pebble also making it a popular holiday area. This resulted in some very attractive Victorian beach huts which can still be seen, but has also resulted in mile after mile of caravan parks, the flat landscape keeping them almost always in view along the coast.

The indigenous housing is quite different. One of the features which has governed the building style of Essex is the shortage of appropriate stone, resulting in buildings either in brick, sometimes with flint added and often with weatherboarding, or commonly either totally in wood or half-timbered. Many of the beautiful half-timbered buildings of the 15th and 16th century, with mellowed silvery oak rather than sharp black and white, as well as a number that are more recent, have thick plaster surfaces decorated with elaborate patterns and pictures in high relief, known as 'pargeting'. These give a unique feel to the county.

Essex's historic importance stems from the decision by the Romans to make **Colchester** their capital. Consequently there are many Roman remains to be seen, some of them collected together in a museum in the CASTLE KEEP, a Norman building on Roman foundations, the largest keep anywhere in the country. Colchester was however an important place long before this, and the BLUEBOTTLE GROVE EARTHWORKS are part of the defence of the town, some 12 miles square, dating from the Iron Age.

Further back still, this land was roamed by elephants, mammoths and elks, and the waters where land now exists were inhabited by turtles, sharks and whales, with fossils having been found, sometimes in quite exceptionally large numbers.

There is much evidence of a high and wealthy population in Essex in the medieval era, PRIOR'S HALL BARN at **Widdington** and COGGESHALL GRANGE BARN near **Coggeshall** being very fine examples of aisled barns from this time, two of many situated in the north west of the county.

At the time those barns were bearing witness to wealth from grain, the manufacture of cloth was an equally important industry to Essex. An associated industry turned **Saffron Walden** into a thriving town of the medieval period, the wealth earned from the crocus plant which gives saffron dye. 'Pargeting' can be seen at its zenith in Saffron Walden on the Old Sun Inn.

Paycockes in West Street, Coggeshall

Coggeshall too was an important clothing town in the middle ages and although not much beauty remains, PAYCOCKES is a fine merchants house dating from about 1500, with rich panelling and wood carving in the interior, plus a lace display and a pretty garden.

Cloth remained an important industry to the county, and the 16th century saw the imigration of many Flemish weavers, followed later by Huguenots. One such as Samuel Courtauld who set up a silk mill in 1816 and later in that century was employing over three thousand people. Wealth from the mill was responsible for much civic pride and much civic building around **Braintree**.

Whilst many concerned with healthy eating choose organic vegetables and fruit, organic fertilisers may include bone meal, hoof and horn, fish meal, blood and of course cattle or poultry manure!

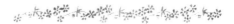

Essex remains a relatively prosperous county, due to the encroachment of London. The London underground reaches into Essex as far as **Epping**, EPPING FOREST being popular as 'a little bit of country' on the edge of the city, its 6,000 acres, the remaining part of a larger forest, being a very pretty place although hardly true countryside. Elizabeth I's hunting lodge is now put to better use as an exhibition of the Forest's history. Epping is the start of the ESSEX WAY, taking walkers through farmland to Constable country in the 'Area of Outstanding Natural Beauty' at **Dedham Vale**, and on to the port of **Harwich** at the mouth of the River Stour.

Close to the banks of the mouth of the Stour near **Manningtree**, pony rides are one way of seeing the 25 acres of MISTLEY PLACE PARK, home to rescued animals and birds. Many of them have been saved from slaughter or the torture of battery conditions, and others were simply unwanted pets, all now given a more natural way of life.

Mistley Place Park encompasses the site believed by historians to be where the self-styled Witchfinder General of the 17th century carried out his gruesome tasks.

Also here is the HEAVY HORSE CENTRE where Suffolk Punches and other horses can be seen in demonstrations of ploughing.

The MUSEUM OF THE WORKING HORSE is by the village of **Finchingfield**, considered by many as the perfect village, possibly the most photographed in Britain, has its pretty cottages grouped around the village pond.

The nearby village of **Hempstead** (not to be confused with the village of the same name in Kent) is where Dick Turpin was born, his parents owned the inn, now the Rose and Crown. Renowned as a highwayman, Turpin was also a cattle and horse thief as well as a house burglar. The story that to fool his pursuers he once shod his horse with the shoes facing backwards, is in fact true. Hempstead was also home to Charles I's physician who discovered the circulation of the blood in 1628.

Another 'first' for the county was the regular series of radio broadcasts made from **Writtle** on the outskirts of **Chelmsford** by engineers for the Marconi company. Chelmsford was another of the important towns during the Roman occupation, and is now a busy county town.

Essex has much recent development including the new town of **Basildon** built in the 1950's, encompassing seven ancient parishes close to the Thames Estuary and not far out of London. Consideration was given to its residents-to-be and to visitors, from the early stages of planning, and the centre of town with its traffic free square, lively market area, statues and fountains all enhance the pleasure of life.

4oz of baked beans contain almost the same amount of protein as a 4oz portion of chicken and considerably less fat (1.6gms from the beans compared with 14gms from the chicken).

The Thames was, in less settled times, a natural and obvious route for invasion, reaching into the country's capital, and was therefore well fortified as can be seen at TILBURY FORT. From here Elizabeth I made her review of the Spanish Armada in the late 16th century, but the building now seen, a large and no doubt impressive deterent, dates from the 17th century with improvements and additions made to its defences over the following two centuries, all of which are well demonstrated in an exhibition on the site.

Buildings of past times have as everywhere been lost due to the ravages of time and progress, but Essex has also lost a lot of properties to the ever rising sea level, or more correctly, to the ever sinking land. From the time when the Romans were here two thousand years ago, the coastal land has sunk some dozen feet or so, and being flat, this means that the sea is several miles inland from its point then. Whole villages have disappeared under water, and the threat continues. There is currently controversy over whether or not defences against the sea should be taken, and if so whether soft defences (flood plains) are preferable and indeed more effective than hard defences (concrete or stone).

The flat land around the coast is the richest area in Britain for the delicious samphire, often called poor man's asparagus although many prefer its crisper texture.

Another food from Essex is jam, for near the Georgian town of **Witham** is the Tiptree factory.

EAST ANGLIA

The three counties which make up the region of East Anglia share a common topography, all basically being flat lands. In addition all have excellent soil for agriculture, and all have many areas that are important for our native plant, animal and bird life. Even today the region is sparsely populated, and almost completely without motorways as it is not actually on the way to anywhere.

Cambridgeshire is a county of two extremes: in the south are the chalk downs with their gentle hills and crops of corn, barley and rye, topped with beech and majestic elms; but to the north the countryside could hardly be more different, the treeless prairie of endless fens and the dark lonely landscape with its cutting winds and endless horizons. Much of it was at one time no more than a continuation of the Wash, but over many years of dedicated work by the inhabitants more than 2,000 square miles have been reclaimed. Today it has some of the richest, yet bleakest, terrain in England.

In the centre of the Cambridgeshire fens **Ely** was at one time an island, and is still referred to as the Isle of Ely. Its Norman Cathedral is exceptionally beautiful, dominating the flat landscape for miles around.

The last of the old fens, still undrained, is WICKEN FEN, a truly natural environment of dense reed-beds, sallow-bushes and sedge jungles, a habitat that is home to many rare butterflies and moths. It is fortunate indeed that nearly all of Wicken Fen is now owned by the National Trust, meaning that not only is this eerie landscape in secure hands for future generations, but also that there is still a place for the indigenous wildlife to breed and prosper.

The Bridge of Sighs in Cambridge

There is no need to explain the delights of the City of **Cambridge** with its truly splendid college buildings and lively atmosphere that the university engenders, but Cambridge has a great deal more to offer. The FITZWILLIAM MUSEUM is one of the principal collections of fine and applied arts in Britain, and also for the art lover is KETTLE'S YARD off Castle Hill. There is also the COUNTRY FOLK MUSEUM at the foot of Castle Hill and the BOTANIC GARDENS with its Chronological Bed showing the diversity of plants introduced over the centuries, and there is much more of interest in this pleasant city which although quite large is on a small market town scale.

If there is one man to be remembered from Cambridge it would have to be Thomas Hobson who, in the 17th century kept horses for hire and ran a carrier's business. He cared about his animals, so he would only hire his horses out in rotation; if customers objected he would reply "this or none", and that's where the proverb came: 'Hobson's choice - this or none'. Today of course shortened as many old proverbs are to just 'Hobson's Choice'.

Earthworks often indicate a deserted village, and this is indeed the case at **Little Gidding**, but this is not an Iron Age or medieval village, but just a 17th century one. It was built as a religious community for followers of the influential Nicholas Ferrar, but the Puritan movement only a few years later was the beginning of the end for the village.

Another village was lost, but later found. **Manea** is so isolated in the fens that it was missed when the Domesday Book was written. For a while in the 19th century there was a thriving colony here, a workers' cooperative with the motto 'Each for All'.

Holywell has what is claimed to be the oldest pub in England called YE OLDE FERRYBOAT INN, which like all old pubs has its fair share of gory history - just outside one of the bars is purported to be the grave of one Juliet Yewsley who committed suicide more than 900 years ago, all because of her love for a wood-cutter, and on the anniversary of her death the ghost of this unrequited lover floats down river.

Suffolk can boast what is probably the best example of man's ingenuity in dealing with the elements. On one side belts of conifers are planted to hold the soil together and stop it being blown away by the winds, and on the other side marram-grass is planted to stop the soil being washed away by the sea. There is a constant battle against the forces of nature here, and at one time or another almost every conceivable material has been used from concrete to marram to help limit the damage done by erosion. Yet again this is an area where the government's rethinking on protection of our coastlines may have dramatic effects on the shape of our seashore.

The county has contrasting soils, sandy heaths along the coast and fertile water-retentive clay in the middle regions called 'High Suffolk', an area created by the hand of man and dependant on the ditches and land drains to carry off the winter rains. 80 years ago windmills were a common feature on every ridge of higher ground as you would expect in a county of corn, but they are no longer common although some have been preserved for prosperity, and some are still working. Fine examples are to be found at SAXTEAD GREEN near **Framlingham** and at THORPNESS HOUSE.

This is an agricultural region, almost flat, and with a great deal of charm. It is known for its thatched, timbered houses and pleasant, narrow, winding byways, a county best seen from the seat of a bicycle or on two feet, to appreciate to the full the peace and tranquillity it has to offer.

The willow-fringed river Stour at **Dedham Vale**, as it passes FLATFORD MILL is depicted in a great many of John Constable's most famous paintings and will be a familiar sight to many, as indeed will be much of the area around **East Bergholt** on the Essex border where he was born. The mill is not open to the public but adjacent to it is BRIDGE COTTAGE which houses an interesting display on Constable and his works. Another artist, Sir Alfred Munnings, lived at Dedham and his home and studio, CASTLE HOUSE, is open during the summer months.

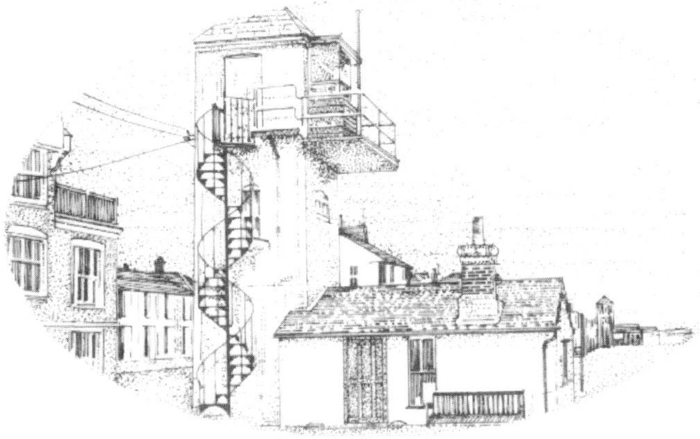

The Watch Tower at Aldeburgh

Another spot well known to lovers of the arts is **Aldeburgh**, where Sir Benjamin Britten lived and where the famous ALDEBURGH FESTIVAL takes place each year. Nearby at Snape THE MALTINGS is another venue for concerts and a memorial to Benjamin Britten.

Thorpeness, houses probably the strangest holiday camp ever envisaged, built in true Victorian style in 1910. The Victorians loved to elaborate and disguise anything mundane or utilitarian, and around the country there are numerous examples, but none as extraordinary as THORPENESS HOLIDAY VILLAGE. The resort was aimed at the better-off holiday maker, mixing the comfort of home with a certain amount of whimsy. In their early brochures it described itself as the 'Home of Peter Pan' and even the islands in the local lake didn't escape, with names of Barry characters and concrete crocodiles. This is a place for the seeker of genuine curiosities, none better than 'House in The Clouds', which is really a water tower, but what an example. The whole of the structure clad by weather boarding and given a pitched roof, to give the impression of a five-storied house, and house it is, at least in part as the lower part is inhabited and the upper part surrounding the tank remains a fraud, even if it does look like there are curtains in the windows increasing in size as you ascend - a reversal of normal building techniques. Many suggestions have been put forward as to why this tower was built, some say it was part of a larger house which no longer exists, another equally feasible theory being that it was as a private study for Lord Freston's daughter. Whatever the reason we are fortunate to have such a handsome building surviving in the landscape.

80% of food poisoning is linked to meat and fish, most of the rest to dairy products.

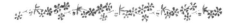

There has always been a dispute over which is the oldest prospect tower in the country, but FRESTON TOWER built by the Latimer family in 1549 which stands to the south of the river Orwell, usually claims this honour. Freston Tower is certainly unusual with its six stories and its windows increasing in size as you ascend - a reversal of normal building techniques. Many suggestions have been put forward as to why this tower was built, some say it was part of a larger house which no longer exists, another equally feasible theory being that it was built as a private study for Lord Freston's daughter. Whatever the reason we are fortunate to have such a handsome building surviving in the landscape.

At **Rendlesham**, 3 miles southeast of Wickham Market, stands the most unusual and possibly the most over-the-top gate house in the country. It is a definite must for those who love the gothic, romantic style of buildings. It does seem a great shame that the gate house is now superfluous, as the hall is no longer in existence, the gate house now standing guard over the flat acres of an airfield. Yet it is an absolutely extraordinary folly, architecturally it resembles a miniature cathedral, but hexagonal in shape, with flying buttresses and pinnacles and with a structure in the middle very much like a belfry, it also has tracery windows and castellations. If only such consideration were given to some of the buildings today.

A very splendid gabled Tudor gazebo survives at MELFORD HALL in **Long Melford**. The gazebo, a forerunner to our modern summer house, first became popular in Tudor times giving the well-to-do a semi-fortified lookout post, where the occupants could sit in comfort and security and keep an eye on their estate, and on their estate workers to make sure they were working and not having too much fun.

The maze at SOMERLEYTON HOUSE is charming and based on curves. It is not especially complex, with tantalising glimpses of the little pagoda's roof in the centre of the maze. However at 400 yards it may take longer to get to the pagoda than anticipated.

At Angel Corner on Angel Hill in **Bury St Edmunds** there is a Queen Anne house with possibly the finest clock collection in the country, all the clocks in excellent condition and in working order. The collection spans five centuries, and the best 'time' to experience them is at noon when the cacophony of chimes seems to pervade every corner of the house.

There is a flint-built parish church at **Clare** with its 13th century tower in the centre of this prosperous village, but Clare is better known for its fine examples of 'pargeting', the art of ornamental plasterwork or the application of moulded plaster to the outside of buildings. There is the date 1473 on the work of THE ANCIENT HOUSE, and it has floral designs on the gable ends and walls.

Every day a staggering 1,648,351 animals are killed in this country for food.

Dunwich Heath is one of the last unspoilt places along this stretch of coast. There is unrestricted access and at the south end of the heath there are observation hides overlooking the MINSMERE BIRD RESERVE. This is another area where the sea has its way and even the heath with its 60 feet cliffs shows strong signs that the sea is winning. It is a shame that today this area's primary claim to fame is the SIZEWELL NUCLEAR POWER STATION.

Ipswich must surely have one of the finest parks of a provincial town, in the grounds of CHRISTCHURCH MANSION. The mansion was built of red brick in 1548 and has an unusual array of grasses and ponds with splendid shrubs and flower borders as well as colourful waterfowl, fitting together to give a really beautiful overall impression.

It is said that Charles II had little regard for the county of Norfolk, and considered that it was only fit to be dug up to make roads for the rest of England! One wonders if he ever visited the county. It is a broad bright place, its green marshes and fir forests, and its fields of barley and purple heather moorlands having given birth to the Norwich School, one of the greatest schools of English landscape painters.

The Norfolk Broads are an extremely popular area, and at certain times of the year are too popular by far, becoming an overcrowded and noisy place best kept away from. But in the spring, autumn and winter the Broads revert to their old secretive beauty of water, marshes and windmills. This area has over 5,000 acres of water and many miles of rivers, and is a haven for some of the rarest birds in England, bringing people from all over the country to see the rare bearded tits, or the equally rare waders and ducks. In spring there is the added bonus of the colourful display given by the wild flowers as they emerge from their slumbers, from orchids to kingcups, meadowsweet to waterlilies, a paradise for botanists.

There are many thatched cottages, and even a thatched church in Norfolk, largely due to the reeds which grow here, considered to be the finest anywhere.

Norwich is a very historic city, and around the Cathedral and Castle many of the streets are pleasantly pedestrianized. There is a plethora of fine houses and museums to see, among them STRANGER'S HALL and the BRIDEWELL, as well as the art galleries which are a must as many house works by the Norwich School of Painters. The Cathedral itself with its 315 feet spire is impressive, the nave, south transept and apse being some of the most notable examples of Norman work in England.

Many of the city's medieval churches still survive, although several of them are now put to other uses. The best street for a medieval atmosphere is ELM HILL where there are many important houses: THE MUSIC HOUSE, ST ANDREW'S HALL and BLACKFRIAR'S HALL to name just a few; if time is short, most worth seeing is the 15th century GUILDHALL with its flint and flushwork representative of the style of its period in this area.

Another magnificent GUILDHALL is to be found in the busy town of **King's Lynn**, alongside some other excellent Tudor and Georgian properties, although outside the centre much of the town is less attractive.

Morston, is another one of these delightful flint villages on the coast, and is a good place to set off for BLAKENEY POINT. It is a hard 4 mile walk on pebbles to reach the point, but a boat ride can be taken from Morston Quay. This area is best known for its seal colony that lives on the sand banks off the coast. There are observation hides an a wooden walkway circling the dunes and accessible to the disabled.

Spiced Lemon Strawberries

Summer strawberries have more flavour, but this is a useful recipe for imported strawberries out of season. Very impressive for Christmas as an alternative light dessert. Oranges can be used instead of lemons for a sweeter dessert.

Serve with shortbread and scented cream (cream with rosewater and icing sugar added then whipped).

Serves 4-6

2 lb	Strawberries
3	Lemons *(unwaxed preferably)*
1 Tbs	Cinnamon
1 Tbs	Mixed Spice
	Sugar

Hull and wash the strawberries. With a zester or grater take off long strands of the lemon rind. Squeeze the lemon juice. Thoroughly mix the juice and the spices, adding sugar to taste, or even more spice if wanted. Gently coat the strawberries in the spiced juice and chill for at least 30 minutes to allow the flavours to mingle. Cover with the lemon rind to serve

Restaurant

HOBBS PAVILION

Park Terrace, Cambridge, Cambridgeshire, CB1 1JH.
Telephone: (0223) 67480

THIS unusual venue is literally housed in a cricket pavilion. It stands just to the south of the historic centre of Cambridge, overlooking Parker's Piece, a large green, and behind the University Arms Hotel. Built in 1930, the whole is still used as a cricket pavilion with Hobbs using the central refreshment area. The Pavilion was built in honour of the famous, Cambridge born batsman, Sir Jack Hobbs (1882-1963). The high ceilinged main room of the restaurant looks out through French windows to Parker's Piece, one mile round the perimeter, where cricket is played in summer.

The food is not entirely vegetarian but there is always one starter and nine main courses plus every dessert suitable - in which there is no danger of finding any ingredient that will offend. No substitutes are used, the cheese, apart from Stilton, is entirely vegetarian and only the wholemeal bread is bought in. You will find the main courses centre on a variation of savoury pancakes served with salads. The major speciality of Hobbs is the superb ice cream and the sculptured dessert pancakes. For 15 years Stephen and Susan Hill have run Hobbs and they have served vegetarian food ever since day one, so they are well versed in what is required.

The wine list is not vast but it is well chosen with bins from France, Italy, sometimes Spain and Australia. There is always one good lager and what can be more delicious on a hot day than freshly squeezed lime, grapefruit and lemon juice? When asked about a dress code we were told that the only restriction is a bare torso which is sometimes a summertime problem!

Useful Information

OPEN: 12-2.15pm last orders & 7-9.45pm last orders. Closed Sun and Mon, also mid Aug to mid-Sept, Christmas, New year
CREDIT CARDS: None taken
CHILDREN: Welcome
LICENSED: Yes. Good wine list

ON THE MENU: Specialises in superb savoury pancakes, salads, icecream & sculptured dessert pancakes
DISABLED ACCESS: No
GARDEN: Vast area of grass
ACCOMMODATION: Not applicable

Public House & Restaurant

DUKE OF YORK

Southend Road, South Green, Billericay, Essex, CM11 2PR.
Telephone: (0277) 651403

FOR almost 10 years the White family have made the Duke of York in Southend Road, one of the most welcoming and popular venues in Billericay. You will find it on the A129 Billericay to Wickford Road about one mile from Billericay High Street. Built round about the turn of the 19th century, it is a good solid building as warm in winter as it is cool in summer. One of the nicest things about the pub is its total lack of gaming machines and juke boxes. It is a place where soft music plays in the background encouraging the art of conversation rather than detracting from it. The whole of the Duke of York is furnished in a comfortable olde worlde style, especially the Tudor style restaurant which is a delightful place in which to dine.

The wide ranging menu, which is a la carte, is mainly French and English in its cuisine. Every day you will find specials, all home-cooked and many of them are especially for vegetarians. Vegan recipes are produced on request. Nothing is bought in and in the last five years the White's have been very aware of the need to provide good, interesting vegetarian dishes. For those not wanting to eat in the restaurant, bar meals and snacks at reasonable prices are also available. If you wish, from Monday to Friday, you may eat your bar meal in the restaurant for about 40p per head extra. On Sunday there are traditional Roasts and specials on the menu.

Anyone with a taste for wine and malt whisky will revel in the vast selection available at the Duke of York. There are some 120 wines from almost every wine producing country in the world and there are no less than 100 malt whiskies collected over the years. At the bar you will find that the malts and the range of liquers and brandies are frequently topics for discussion. This is a very enjoyable pub for many reasons. The Duke of York has just been awarded Les Routiers Corps d'Elite award for an outstanding wine list and it is well-deserved.

Useful Information

OPEN: Restaurant: Mon-Fri 12-2pm & 7-10pm, Sat: 7-10pm. Bar food similar times except Sat 12-2pm & Sun: 12-2.30pm
CREDIT CARDS: Access/Visa/Diners
CHILDREN: Welcome
LICENSED: Yes
ON THE MENU: Good range of vegetarian dishes. Vegan on request
DISABLED ACCESS: Yes but no special toilets
GARDEN: Small patio
ACCOMMODATION: Not applicable

Restaurant

CHIVES OF WESTGATE

12 Cuthbert Road, Westgate-on-Sea, Kent, CT8 8NR.
Tel: (0843) 835138 Catering: (0227) 769180, Fax: (0843) 835138

THIS restful and relaxing restaurant is in the heart of Westgate on Sea, in the six years of its existence Chives has gained an enviable reputation for its cuisine, drawing its customers both locally and from many miles around. It is housed in a Victorian doubled fronted building with the original leaded lights. You will find it light and airy, decorated and furnished in pastel and deep tone greens with lots of plants including a giant yukka. Music plays softly in the background, on the first Friday of the month the music is live from either a soloist or a duo covering a whole range from jazz to blues to folk to classical.

Here you may find yourself enjoying Finnish, English and dishes from around the world. It is not strictly vegetarian but 65% of the snacks, 50% of the starters, 30% of the main courses and 100% of the desserts are vegetarian and some have vegan options. Whatever you choose will be interesting and diverse in influence and ingredients. The fixed price yet flexible menu makes sure the customer knows exactly what the cost is. Gelazone and not gelatine is used in the desserts, Tofu is utilised at Chives, and Whirl, a butter substitute is used as well as margarine, all stocks are vegetable. Every dish is prepared using the freshest ingredients, no convenience foods are used.

Chives is licensed and has both organic and vegetarian wines from France, Italy, Australia, Germany, Bulgaria and Finland. The house wine is Bacon D'Arignac' The average spend on a bottle of wine is £8.50. For those who enjoy beer, the rare Finnish 'Lapin Kulta' brewed exclusively by women in the Arctic is something different to try. Nominated as the Vegetarian Restaurant of the Year a few years ago by Vegetarian Magazine, Chives also offers a full vegetarian/vegan Outside catering service.

Useful Information

OPEN: Mon-Sat: 6.30-10.30pm. Lunch: booking only. Closed two weeks in January
CREDIT CARDS: Access/Visa/Amex
CHILDREN: Welcome
LICENSED: Yes
ON THE MENU: Worldwide menu, largely vegetarian
DISABLED ACCESS: Yes
GARDEN: No
ACCOMMODATION: Not applicable

Restaurant

ARUNDEL HOUSE HOTEL

53 Chesterton Road, Cambridge, Cambridgeshire, CB4 3AN.
Telephone: (0223) 67701, Facsimile: (0223) 67721

THE Arundel House Hotel occupies one of the finest sites in the City of Cambridge overlooking the River Cam and Jesus Green. This elegant, privately owned, 105 bedroom hotel is only a short walk from the city centre and the wealth of fascinating architecture for which Cambridge is famous.

The hotel is well known for the friendly, welcoming atmosphere of its bar and restaurant and has achieved a reputation for providing some of the best food in the area, all freshly prepared in its scrupulously clean, award winning kitchens. The recent refurbishment of the restaurant makes it one of the most attractive places to eat in Cambridge and yet it is not expensive. For vegetarians, it is not only a delightful place to stay but it also offers a superb range of delicious and imaginative, mouth watering dishes on a specially created vegetarian menu.

The hotel also has excellent facilities for conferences, seminars & weddings and with its friendly, efficient staff & ample car parking it forms a perfect base for your visit to Cambridge.

Useful Information

OPEN: All year every day except for Xmas & Boxing Day. Restaurant: 12.15-1.45pm & 6-9.30pm (last orders)

CREDIT CARDS: Visa/Access/ Amex/Diners Club

ON THE MENU: Wide choice for vegetarians at all meals

DISABLED ACCESS: Bar and restaurant designed for wheelchair access. Bedrooms not ideally suited

Inn & Restaurant

THE THREE HILLS INN

Bartlow, Cambridge, Cambridgeshire, CB1 6PW.
Telephone: (0223) 891259

TWELVE miles south of Cambridge in the village of Bartlow is the very attractive, 15th century pub, The Three Hills Inn. It is full of character with a fine old fireplace and the original oak beams still insitu.

It is family run by the Dixons with their daughter Marie in charge of the kitchen. Here she cooks all manner of different dishes from recipes she has acquired, many of them from the Mediterranean as well as India and the Far East. This capable lady always has at least seven vegetarian main courses available daily accompanied by two or more starters and some desserts. Gelatine is used occasionally and so too is non vegetarian cheese in the cooking. The wine list is drawn mainly from Europe and is sensibly priced. The pretty walled garden is popular in summer. Children under 14 are not permitted. The Three Hills Inn is recommended by Egon Ronay, Les Routiers and the Healthfood Guide.

Useful Information

OPEN: Mon-Sat: 11.30-2.30pm & 6.30-11pm. Sun: 12-3pm & 7-10.30pm

CREDIT CARDS: Access/Visa/ Mastercard

ON THE MENU: Good home-cooked, interesting dishes for vegetarians

DISABLED ACCESS: Yes. No special toilets

Restaurant

MARTHA'S VINEYARD

18 High Street, Nayland, Colchester, Essex, CO6 4JF.
Telephone: (0206) 262888

This is an award winning restaurant. Christopher Warren and Larkin Rogers (who is the chef) started Martha's four years ago. It has a super atmosphere and a casual, relaxed ambience.

Christopher and Larkin have always been keen supporters of good healthy food of all persuasions and they strive to ensure that vegetarians and carnivores alike can enjoy thoughtfully prepared, attractive, imaginative and flavourful dishes. Most of the vegetables used are organically grown, as is the flour, and the cheese used in vegetarian dishes does not contain animal rennet. Vegans and other diets can be catered for given prior notice.

Here you have around about 45 wines from which to choose - none of which is specifically organic or vegetarian. The bottles come from around the world and will please any lover of the grape.

Useful Information

OPEN: Tues-Sat: 7.30-9.30pm. Closed 2 weeks in winter and 2 weeks in summer
CREDIT CARDS: Visa/Access
ON THE MENU: A choice of vegetarian dishes from the menu
DISABLED ACCESS: Yes. No special toilets

Hotel & Restaurant

THE MULBERRY ROOM & THE ROSLIN HOTEL

10-12 Thorpe Esplanade, Thorpe Bay, Essex, SS1 3BG.
Telephone: (0702) 586375, Facsimile: (0702) 586663

TO find this interesting hotel you should head towards 'Southend Seafront' and once there turn away from Southend to Shoebury where you will find the Roslin, the last hotel on the left hand side - a large pink building. The restaurant seats 50 comfortably and once at your table you will be offered a wide ranging menu although most of it will not be for vegetarians. What is strictly vegetarian are the dishes that have been perfected over the last 10 years by the resident owners who have owned this stylish hotel for 40 years.

The wine list has been carefully and selectively chosen with wines from around the world, none of which are wildly expensive. Staying in the comfortable bedrooms assures a goods night sleep. Every room is en-suite and each has television, hair dryers, direct dial telephones and tea and coffee facilities.

Useful Information

OPEN: All year
CREDIT CARDS: All major cards
ON THE MENU: A well chosen, vegetarian menu
DISABLED ACCESS: Yes + suitable toilets

Restaurant with Bed & Breakfast

THE TANNER OF WINGHAM

44 High Street, Wingham, Canterbury, Kent, CT3 1AB.
Telephone: (0227) 720532

THE pretty village of Wingham is home to an interesting and enjoyable establishment with strong leanings in favour of vegetarians. Here you can both eat in the restaurant and spend the night in comfortable, well appointed bedrooms knowing that after a good night's sleep, a super breakfast will await you. Midway between Canterbury and Sandwich on the A257, The Tanner of Wingham is a Grade II Listed Building dated 1620 but it is known to have existed in the late 1500's. It is a house, full of nooks and crannies and unexpected finds - the ladies loo is in the inglenook fireplace!

There is an air of peace and tranquillity about The Tanner. Everything seems not to be hurried, yet the service is excellent. At night there is a wide choice of dishes with at least eight main courses suitable for vegetarians. Some of the desserts do contain gelatine but there are many that do not. On Sundays, a first class lunch is served for which it is advisable to book.

Useful Information

OPEN: Afternoon Tea: 2.30-4.30pm. Eves: 7-9pm. Sun lunch: 12.30pm - 1.30pm

CREDIT CARDS: Access/Visa

ON THE MENU: Varied. Good selection for vegetarians. Function Room & Outside-Catering facilities

DISABLED ACCESS: Yes, but no special toilets

Inn & Restaurant

THE RINGLESTONE INN

Ringlestone Road, Harrietsham, Kent, ME17 1NX.
Telephone: (0622) 859900, Facsimile: (0622) 859966

BUILT in 1533 as a Monk's Hospice, The Ringlestone Inn became an ale house in 1615 and today still has the original brick and flint walls and floors, oak beams, inglenooks and centuries old English oak furniture which adds to the enchantment of the whole place. The Inn is described as an' unspoilt medieval lamplit tavern'. An old oak sideboard proclaims 'A ryghte joyouse and welcome greetynge to ye all' and this has become the logo of the inn.

It is friendly, welcoming and without petty restrictions. You may order whatever you like and sit wherever you like, either in the candlelit dining room or by a roaring log fire in one of the cosy bars. Every dish is prepared and cooked to order so vegetarians can feel confident about the ingredients of the exciting, tasty and varied dishes amongst which is a Vegetable Pie, one of the home-made cooked to order pies that are a Ringlestone speciality. Traditional Country Wines based upon ancient recipes are another delight here.

Useful Information

OPEN: Bar: 12-3pm, meals: 12-2pm. Evening: 6.30-11pm, meals 7-9pm. Closed Xmas Day

CREDIT CARDS: Amex/Diners/ Visa/Master/Switch

ON THE MENU: Wide range of home-cooked fare with special dishes for vegetarians

DISABLED ACCESS: Yes, no special toilets

Fast Food Grill Restaurant

BURGHER MASTER

29 Abbeygate Street, Bury St Edmunds, Suffolk, IP33 1UN.
Telephone: (0284) 752941

VERY easy to find, this modern business is housed in a building which is 500 years old and we are told that the main structure dates back 1,000 years. It is believed to be listed in the Domesday Book. It is only 500 yards from the award winning Abbey Gardens, the Norman Tower and Abbey ruins.

Everything on the menu is cooked to order and is nicely presented. You will find that 40% of the menu is entirely suitable for vegetarians although it should be pointed out that they do not profess to use vegetarian cheese, except in one of the grills. It is a very friendly, welcoming coffee shop and restaurant, the service is very quick and efficient, the portions generous and the prices sensible. The coffee is specially roast and ground and is always fresh. There is no liquor licence. The wide variety of grills, snacks and burgers are very popular with local people who use it regularly. There is also an excellent variety of fresh chilled salads which change weekly. Visitors see it as an oasis after exploring Bury St Edmunds, one of the original Magna Carta towns. Coach parties welcome.

Useful Information

OPEN: Mon-Thurs, 8am-7pm, Fri: 8am - 9pm, Sat: 8.45-9pm, Sundays 11am-5pm in Winter and in Summer 10am-6pm

CREDIT CARDS: Visa/Mastercard/ Switch, Diners

ON THE MENU: Wide range of grills & snacks & desserts suitable for vegetarians plus cold & hot drinks

DISABLED ACCESS: Difficult, but can be accommodated

Bistro Restaurant

THE SINGING CHEF

200 St Helen's Street, Ipswich, Suffolk, IP4 2LH.
Telephone: (0473) 255236

IT goes without saying that the vegetarian food is delicious and observes even the most stringent rules but The Singing Chef is much more. To understand this wonderful establishment, one needs to know a bit about the background of the owners. The Singing Chef, Ken Toye and his wife Cynthia, came from France in 1960 to create 'Singing Chef I' in London. They presented regional French dishes, many of them vegetarian, observed in French families of the French countryside. Raymond Postage wrote in the 'Good Food Guide', "Ken's food is Frencher than the French, and he sings like an angel". Yes, songs as important as food- well almost! This current establishment is the Singing Chef 3 where the front room is the bistro and the back room the restaurant.

Wherever you choose to be you will be served with vegetarian variations of French regional dishes. No use is made of the freezer, the dishes are simple and the ingredients fresh. The wine list aims to give experience of the main grape varieties - and succeeds.

Useful Information

OPEN: Tues-Sat: 7-11pm. Lunches by appointment plus Mon dinner

CREDIT CARDS: Visa/Access

ON THE MENU: French regional vegetarian variations

DISABLED ACCESS: Yes + toilets

Powis Castle

Contents

WALES

Gwent, the Glamorgans, Dyfed, Powys, Gwynedd and Clwyd

Suggested Venues to Dine

Italian Stuffed Loaf

Serve hot either as a lunch or supper snack, or cold on a picnic. Ideally buy or make a specifically Italian loaf, but ordinary bread will do too, preferably a round flattish loaf. For authenticity the bread should be white, but you can use wholemeal or granary, or a speciality bread, if preferred. The suggested filling can be substituted with many variations on the theme.

Serves 4

1 large	Loaf	
1 tin	Plum Tomatoes	
2 medium	Onions	
2	Peppers, 1 red, 1 green	
Bunch	Basil or Tarragon	(fresh is definitely best)
	Olive Oil	
6oz	Cheddar Cheese	

Cut the top off the loaf, about ¼ from the top and scoop out the centre leaving a wall about 1cm thick. In a processor if you have one or by hand if you haven't, make the loose bread into crumbs. Separate the tomatoes from their juice and chop them. To the crumbs add as much tomato juice as is needed to soak them, mix well. Chop the onions and peppers and fry them lightly in olive oil. Add the herbs and continue to cook whilst adding the tomatoes and the bread/juice. The mixture should be reasonably stiff, but if it seems too dry add more tomato juice.

Fill the hollowed loaf with the vegetable mixture and place the top back on. Wrap in aluminium foil and bake in a medium oven for 20 minutes. Remove the foil, brush the lower part of the loaf with olive oil and cover the top with grated cheese. Bake again until the cheese is browning. Serve immediately or when cold.

WALES

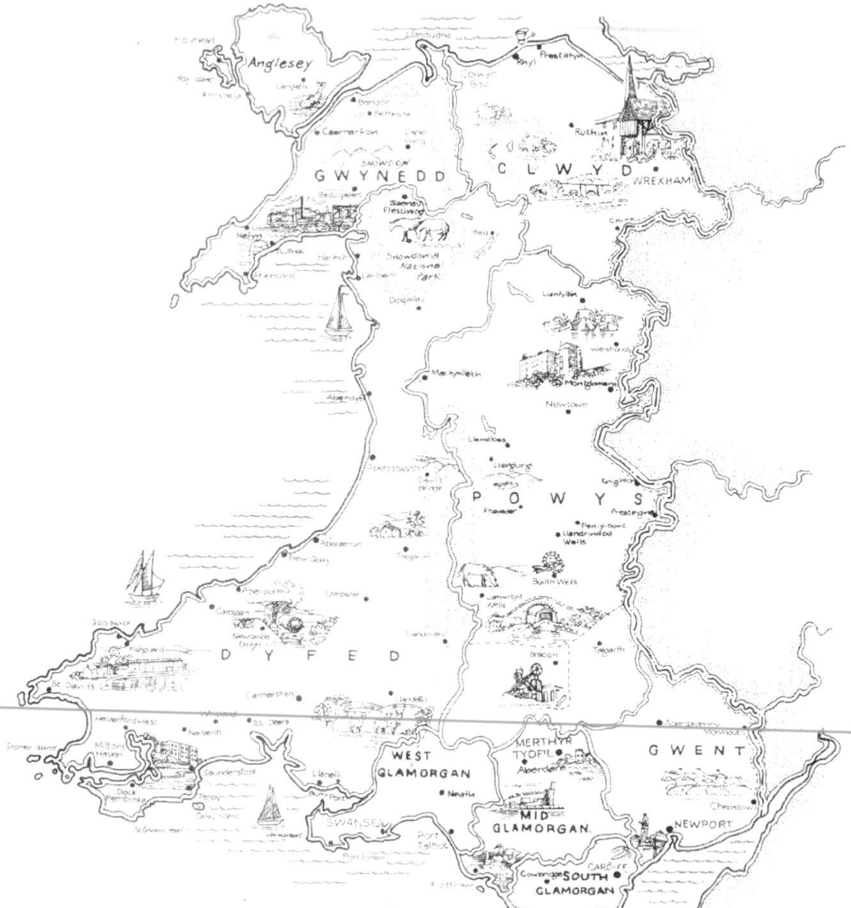
Anglesey
Bangor
Caernarfon
GWYNEDD
Rhyl
Prestatyn
Ruthin
CLWYD
WREXHAM
Snowdonia National Park
Machynlleth
Montgomery
Newtown
POWYS
Builth Wells
Brecon
DYFED
Carmarthen
Haverfordwest
Saundersfoot
Llanelli
SWANSEA
WEST GLAMORGAN
Neath
MERTHYR TYDFIL
Aberdare
MID GLAMORGAN
GWENT
Chepstow
NEWPORT
CARDIFF
SOUTH GLAMORGAN
Barry

WALES

Gwent, the Glamorgans, Dyfed, Powys, Gwynedd and Clwyd

Crossing from England into Wales, in a very short time you notice a country of different speech and different historical and cultural traditions; this is a Principality with deep-rooted national pride, which is vigorously defended.

Possibly one of the best examples of Welsh tradition is the Eisteddfod, the celebration of song and poetry in the Welsh language, which dates back to the Middle Ages and has remained an annual event. Welsh people from all over the world attend, from as far afield as the Welsh colony around Trelew in Patagonia. There is no one centre for the Eisteddfod and the venue is changed each year.

The southern corner overlooking the Bristol Channel, around **Swansea**, **Cardiff** and **Newport**, is densely populated, with much heavy industry, but throughout the rest of Wales there are no very large towns and very little commercialism. What there is in abundance, is scenic natural beauty: three large National Parks, four important 'Areas of Outstanding Natural Beauty', rare flora and fauna, impressive mountains and pretty valleys, lakes, exquisite river scenery and some quite wonderful coastline, much of it designated Heritage Coast.

The SNOWDONIA NATIONAL PARK is the largest National Park in Wales, with a landscape of deep valleys and rugged mountains formed by the glaciers of the Ice Age, giving lakes, rivers and splendid waterfalls which are legendary. The main feature is SNOWDON itself, the highest mountain in England and Wales at 3,560 feet. The long sloping ridges to the peak and the steep drops between them give the climber great scope. Many of the woods and forests reach down the sharp valleys and add a much needed softness to the area.

As always in an area of such diverse terrain, there is a great variety of plants and wildlife. The coastal areas are a particular treat with wide sandy bays and sweeping dunes, and the estuaries are teeming with wading birds of all kinds.

There are Neolithic stone circles above **Penmaenmawr** and Bronze Age burial chambers at **Capel Garmon**. The old Roman road Sarn Helen can be traced running through the Park, and medieval Wales is brought dramatically to life with the castles at **Dolwyddelan** and **Castell-y-Bere**; The Edwardian HARLECH CASTLE gives access to the wild, western mountain area. From the not too distant past you can see the remains and marks that the slate industry has left on the Park, not all bad; the narrow gauge railways are always popular with the tourists. The Park covers an area of 827 square miles and the whole region is a stronghold of Welsh language and tradition.

Harlech Castle

The BRECON BEACONS NATIONAL PARK is an area covering some 522 square miles, with the wild BLACK MOUNTAINS in the west and the old Norman hunting grounds of FFOREST FAWR. The broad USK VALLEY in the north separates the Brecons from the Black Mountains, and in the south the different landscape of millstone grit and limestone has spectacular waterfalls and caves.

The Brecon Beacons contain many remains of castles and hillforts such as GARN GOGH at **Bethlehem**. In the winter months this area can be a foreboding and desolate place with the terrain stretching on for as far as the eye can see. At these times of year walkers should be prepared for extremes of weathers.

The PEMBROKESHIRE COAST NATIONAL PARK has over 100 miles of rugged coastline with broad bays and numerous islands, and is very popular with the sailing fraternity. Further inland are the tree-lined creeks and open moorland of the PRESELI MOUNTAINS. The mild climate means that wild flowers flourish in abundance here and the area is famous for its seal and bird colonies. At **Brynberian** the PENTRE IFAN CROMLECH, just north of the village, is the most impressive prehistoric monument in Wales, four vertical tapering stones hold a capstone, estimated to weigh around 17tons, balanced delicately on their points. There are other ancient monuments as well as the reconstructed Iron Age hillfort of CASTELL HENLLYS, and early Christian relics are to be found throughout the Park.

In Welsh legend this part of Wales is referred to as the 'Land of Magic and Enchantment' and certainly seems to have something for everyone.

In most fast food chains lard is used for the buns that all burgers (including vegetable burgers) go into. Many also fry their chips in beef fat.

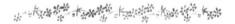

Situated halfway between the Pembrokeshire National Park and the Brecon Beacons and on the far south coast, the 73 square miles of the **Gower Peninsula** in West Glamorgan was, in 1956, the very first area in Britain to be designated an 'Area of Outstanding Natural Beauty', chosen not only because of its classic coastline and outstanding natural environment but also as a last outpost of unspoilt beauty in this otherwise industrial heartland.

Gower's scenery is rich and varied, ranging from saltmarshes and fragile dunes to the rocky drama of one of Britain's finest limestone coasts. The commons that lie inland dominate the landscape eventually merging into wooded valleys and traditional small fields.

The wild **Llyn Peninsula** in Gwynedd, most of it an 'Area of Outstanding Natural Beauty', is edged around its 60 square miles on the north and west coast by rocky coves and sheer cliffs and on the southeast by picture-postcard bays. Next to the bay of **Porth Neigwl** or 'Hell's Mouth', so called because of its treacherous tides, the sheer black cliffs of

MYNYDD MAWR, described as the 'Land's End of Wales', overlook the holy **Bardsey Island**. Inland the volcanic peaks of Yr Eifl abruptly give way to neat countryside with narrow lanes and hedged fields.

At the top of the Llyn Peninsula lies **Anglesey**, an island but linked to the mainland near **Bangor** by the Menai Bridge. Around the dunes of **Aberffraw Bay** and the high HOLYHEAD MOUNTAIN, bird and plant life is plentiful. Further east **Great Orme's Head**, with the town of **Llandudno** the largest resort in Wales, rises spectacularly, with exposed fossils from the tropical sea that this area once was. From here are superb views of the mountains of Snowdonia.

To the east again, the CLWYDIAN RANGE above **Deeside** and the **Vale of Clwyd** is the fourth 'Area of Outstanding Natural Beauty'. It consists of a 20 mile ridge of limestone crags and heather, giving a dramatic contrast to the green pastures below.

Geese taking flight at the Wildfowl & Wetlands Centre at Llanelli

Everywhere there is much to commend Wales to the visitor. The WILDFOWL AND WETLANDS CENTRE, 2 miles east of **Llanelli** just above the Gower, is Wales' premier estuary for wildfowl and waders; it has a visitor centre and many observation points. In 1993 it received Wales' 'Green Award' from the Tourist Board.

CASTLE NARROWBOATS at **Gilwern** in Gwent is another Green Award winner, its canal boat hire business located on the original wharf from where the MONMOUTH AND BRECON CANAL was started 200 years ago. The canal is within the Brecon Beacons National Park, passing through some of its most beautiful and environmentally sensitive areas. In 1982 the first Monmouth and Brecon electric narrowboat was introduced, there are now four of them, one a 40 seater passenger boat. These boats have proved very popular due to their environmentally friendly characteristics - with no exhaust fumes and very little noise, the canal and surrounding environment is hardly disturbed and the re-charging stations have been very carefully sited. Companies intending to operate boats within 'Sites of Special Scientific Interest' are being very much encouraged to use only electric boats, a clear signal as to future trends and legislation.

Listeria infects 12% of pre-cooked, ready to eat poultry, 16% of salami type sausages and 50% of raw pork sausages.

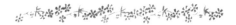

Nestling among historic remains at AVERDULAIS FALLS near **Neath** in West Glamorgan is a unique hydro-electric scheme, which is open to the public. The new TURBINE HOUSE provides access to the top of the falls and visitors are able to see Britain's largest electricity generating water wheel.

The STACKPOLE WALLED GARDEN SENSE CENTRE in **Stackpole** near Pembroke, was opened in 1979 to provide unparalleled accommodation and facilities for the disabled visitor. The object of the sensory garden is to create a place where the primary senses can be stimulated in a therapeutic manner: through sound, based on the concept of outdoor musical instruments; sight, using optical illusions; scent in the form of a raised garden for the blind; and through all of them the sense of touch. It is believed that such a centre on this scale is unique in the UK.

Of great importance to those with a concern for the environment is the CENTRE FOR ALTERNATIVE TECHNOLOGY at **Machynlleth** in Powys. It is unique in Europe. The Centre was started in 1974 on an abandoned slate quarry and after many years of hard and dedicated work there is now a seven acre display circuit (on a 40 acre site) open to the public. They have been experimenting with and demonstrating ways in which individuals, families and small communities can have a sustainable, whole and ecologically sound way of life. It has only been in the last few years that governments and consumers have started to look seriously for more environmentally friendly ways of producing the power needed for sustaining our modern day way of life. The number of visitors who find their way to CAT is continually on the increase, and with over 100,000 visitors each year there is no doubt the message is getting through.

The Centre is proving that a comfortable, varied, but in many ways rather ordinary lifestyle can be carried on with a fraction of the resources normally considered necessary, and in general with much lower environmental impact. Obviously this is not achieved without care, organisation and above all efficiency in the matching of resources to their uses.

At the Centre you can spend a very interesting and enlightening day. On arrival you can choose either to walk to the upper station by the main 250m track or by the woodland walk, or better still you can get to the upper station by a unique piece of environmental engineering, the centre's water-powered cliff railway, one of the steepest such railways in Britain, which operates on the principle of 'water-balancing'; with the two carriages connected via a winding-drum at the top, water is run into a tank beneath the upper carriage until it is just heavier than the lower carriage plus its passengers, then the parking brakes are released and gravity does the rest.

Some battery egg producers add food colourings to chicken feed in order to make the egg yolks a darker yellow. One of these is a substance called Canthaxanthin (E161g) which is known to cause crystals to form in the back of the eye.

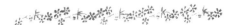

At the upper station, displays are arranged in a more-or-less circular route, and range from organic gardening through hydro and solar power onto composting and recycling and much more. The centre also holds courses on subjects as diverse as birdwatching, alternative sewage systems, wind power, and vegetarian cookery.

The area all around **Machynlleth** along the Dyfi Valley has much to offer the visitor. There are nature reserves, forest trails and a heritage trail, a pony-trekking centre, enigmatic stone circles, magnificent water falls and lakes, an organic vegetable garden, a wind farm, a craft centre and a railway museum. There is also the steam, narrow gauge TAL-Y-LLYN RAILWAY running from near**Abergynolwyn** through Snowdonia National Park to the coast at **Tywyn**.

Not far from here is **Craig-yr-Aderyn**, otherwise known as 'Bird Rock', created when the sea receeded with the silting up of the Dysynni, leaving the rock stranded four miles inland. It is a strange oddity with its craggy cliffs soaring over 700 feet above the fertile meadows of the Dysynni Valley. Cormorants still nest here, not seeming to care about the extra distance to go for lunch.

North from this valley rises the CADER IDRIS mountain range, beyond which is Snowdonia. As Snowdonia joins the Llyn Peninsula around **Porthmadog** is the small town of **Tremadog**. In 1888 T.E. Lawrence, better known as Lawrence of Arabia, was born here as shown on a plaque on the house which is on the south side of town, now the Centre for Christian Mountaineering which opens its doors to all faiths who wish to participate in its environmental, climbing and adventure courses. The town also has connections with the poet Shelley who incurred the anger of the locals by his belief that sheep were in general unhappy and ill, which led him to put them out of their misery without first making sure that they were not incurable.

Very close by is **Portmeirion**, by any standard a very 'different' place. Often referred to as 'Little Italy', it was built in 1920 by Clough Williams-Ellis who moved to Dyfed to reproduce his idea, supposedly using Portofina as a template. With its peculiar architectural style Portmeirion has succeeded in creating a place of lightness and beauty with an air of tranquillity. Critics who prefer a more serious architectural style would say that the diversity of buildings and the air of unreality make this place too much like a fairyland, but Portmeirion is one man's attempt at capturing a certain ambience and culture, built with love and with no intension of creating a theme park.

Those of us old enough to remember the television series 'The Prisoner' will recognise Portmeirion as the place where the programmes were made. 'Blithe Spirit' by Noel Coward is said to have been written during his stay here. Portmeirion is unique, probably best described as a surreal village, a bold statement. You may love it or loth it, but you couldn't dispute it was worth the visit.

Portmeirion

More conventional buildings are to be found at the WELSH FOLK MUSEUM at **St Fagan** near Cardiff. Over 20 buildings from all over Wales have been brought together on a 20 acre site to form an open air museum. There are various types of farmhouses and agricultural buildings, a Unitarian chapel, woollen mill, smithy and toll house. These are important collections of Welsh social history, supplemented by displays of costumes, material culture, agriculture and vehicles to work the land, some in the reconstructed houses others in a special museum.

St Fagan also gives the visitor a good idea of the social and cultural life in Wales over the past couple of hundred years through regular demonstrations by craftsmen, such as smithying and wood turning, dyeing and weaving. The museum also sells traditional Welsh bedspreads. To find out what it was like to be a successful merchant in the 15th century, visitors can walk around the TUDOR MERCHANT'S HOUSE in **Tenby.** To find out, on the other hand, what it was like to be a gold miner in the 1930's, visitors can now explore the DOLAUCOTHI GOLD MINES near **Lampeter** which were first exploited by the Romans some 2,000 years ago. Welsh gold has been used for many important items for the Royal Family for centuries.

Three and a half miles east of **Llangollen** stands PONTCYSLLTE AQUEDUCT, the longest aqueduct in Britain at 1007 feet long and 127 feet high, built by Thomas Telford and completed in 1805. The stupendous structure has 19 sets of arches, and is still in use, although more now by holiday cruisers than by the commercial barges for which it was built. In a former warehouse is an exhibition on the subject of the part canals have played in Britain's history.

Halfway between Llandeilo and Ammanford and well off the main road near the hamlet of **Trapp** is CARREG CENNEN CASTLE. The medieval masonry may be unkempt and ruinous but it sits defiantly and breathtakingly on top of a sheer-sided limestone cliff overlooking the forbidding Black Mountains. Well worth the effort is the walled passageway, hewn out of the side of the cliff leading to a cave beneath the castle itself, unearthed here were a number of prehistoric skeletons.

Llantrisant in Mid Glamorgan was the home of Dr William Price, a preacher who in his time was considered something of a revolutionary with strong views on subjects such as vegetarianism, politics, nudism and sex, and he was not averse to preaching about them. In the 1800's even thinking about these issues could make you extremely unpopular. A statue of this unusual character with his fox-skin head-dress stands, appropriately, in Llantrisant's BULL RING.

Knighton is the only town that stands on top of Offa's Dyke. King Offa of Mercia in the 8th century had the earth works constructed as the first official border between England and Wales. The OFFA'S DYKE CENTRE is able to give information on the 170 mile footpath which follows as nearly as possible the line of the Dyke, running close to the border with England.

Savoury Pineapple Pancakes

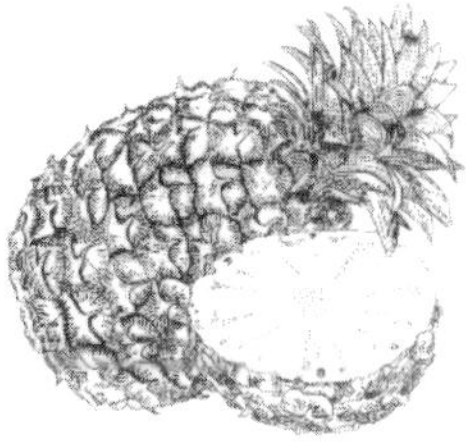

Once you have mastered the cooking of pancakes it is easy to create delicious dishes with a variety of fillings. This is just one suggestion. Also try it with dried apricots. Serve with a crunchy vegetable and fruit salad

Serves Four

PANCAKES:	
4oz	*Wholemeal plain flour*
1	*Egg*
10 fl oz	*Milk*
1 oz	*Mixed herbs*
FILLING:	
10 oz	*Natural Greek Yoghurt*
4 Tbs	*Tomato Purée*
4 Tbs	*Smooth Mustard*
2 oz	*Cous Cous*
2 tins	*Pineapple Rings (or 1 rings and 1 pieces)*
	use pineapple in juice rather than syrup if obtainable

Blend or whisk the pancake ingredients. Leave to stand for 30 minutes. Preheat a smallish frying pan (ideally nonstick with gently sloping sides) on a hot (but not too hot) ring. For each pancake coat the pan with a little oil or margarine and ladle in enough batter to coat the bottom of the pan evenly when swirled around. When the under side is cooked the pancake should become loose in the pan. Turn the pancake over and cook until browning in patches. This mixture should make eight pancakes if not too thick. Pile the pancakes on a plate until needed (they can even be frozen for later use if wanted).

Set two of the pineapple rings aside, break up the remaining pineapple and mix it with the other filling ingredients, using a little of the pineapple juice to make a soft dropping mixture (the cous cous will stiffen it as it cooks). Spread each pancake with the mixture and either make into one pile (which overcomes the problems of not having exactly 8 pancakes) or roll each one to make individual portions. Place them in a covered ovenproof dish and bake for 15-20 minutes. At the same time place the pineapple halves in an uncovered ovenproof dish with some butter or margarine and turn them occasionally so that they are nicely browned. Use them to decorate the pancakes when serving.

Broccoli and Chestnut Soup

Cauliflower can be used instead of broccoli, but although the taste may be no less pleasing the colour certainly will be. For the broccoli version, the addition of a little spinach further enhances the colour.

Serves 4

1 head	Broccoli	(or bunch of smaller pieces)
1 tin	Chestnut Purée	(unsweetened)
2 oz	Spinach - optional	(frozen is acceptable)
¼ pt	Double Cream	(or soya milk with less of the water)
1 Tbs	Grainy Mustard	
Salt & Pepper		
Water		

Cut the very tops of the broccoli into small florets, and trim the stalks as they are also used in this recipe. Roughly chop the stalks and place them in shallow water below a steamer containing the florets. Steam the florets lightly and boil the stalks until soft. Blanch the spinach if using fresh, or defrost frozen spinach. Blend the stalks and the spinach with the cooking water to reduce it all to a fine pulp.

Blend in the chestnut purée, cream and seasonings, and transfer the mixture to a saucepan. As the soup heats up add the broccoli florets and as much water as wanted to create either a thin or thick soup.

Public House & Restaurant

Y DAFARN NEWYDD

Mountain Street, Rhosllannerchrugog, Wrexham, Clwyd, LL1 4BT.
Telephone: (0978) 840471, Facsimile: (0978) 840471

THE quiet village of Rhosllannerchrugog, has a typically Welsh public house. The sort of place that gives you a feeling of stability as well as a warm welcome. You will find it going south west off the A483. Turn right at the memorial at Johnstown Road and a mile further on you turn left into Mountain Street. Sue and Geoff Hodgkinson have been licensees for 25 years, sixteen of which they have been the landlords at Y Dafarn Newydd. Throughout their years in this pub they have served vegetarian food amongst the other dishes which all tend to be 'A Taste of Wales'. Sue is a good cook and has an instinctive knowledge of what will please her customers. She has also won recognition in the 'Heartbeat of Wales' awards.

On the menu you will discover that very little food is bought in ready made; pate, pickled herrings, apple pies and chocolate fudge cake seem to be the extent. Sue promises that 40% of her dishes, across the board from snacks to desserts, are entirely suitable for vegetarians and whilst some are especially for vegans, prior warning will ensure an appropriate menu is prepared. There are a number of very tasty Indian derived recipes. Dragon Butties are a popular snack - pitta bread filled with hot mince - soya mince is the vegetarian version if requested.

The big garden is in great demand during the warmer months and in the winter, pool and quiz games entertain visitors and locals. Music plays gently in the background and occasionally the evenings are enlivened with a disco. There is no restriction on children and the access for wheelchairs is easy. This is a value for money pub without any pretensions.

Useful Information

OPEN: Mon: 6.30-11pm, Tues-Sat: 12-3pm & 6.30-11pm, Sun: 12-3pm & 7-10.30pm
CREDIT CARDS: None taken
CHILDREN: Welcome
LICENSED: Yes
ON THE MENU: 40% vegetarian in every course plus some vegan dishes
DISABLED ACCESS: Yes. Toilets available but no special fittings
GARDEN: Large
ACCOMMODATION: None

Restaurant

WAVERLEY RESTAURANT

23 Lammas Street, Camarthen, Dyfed, SA31 3AL.
Telephone: (0267) 236430

THIS interesting restaurant is housed in a building that is believed to be 17th century. You will find it along Lammas Street going west, just past the Crimean War Memorial. The rooms are large, airy and the whole atmosphere is relaxing. It is quite an experience to eat here. Most of the dishes are created especially for the Waverley. For example Barley and Vegetable Madras or Caribbean style vegetables. The menu is exclusively vegetarian with vegan options but special diets are available for those who need organic foods or a gluten free diet. On the whole everything is cooked on the premises but up to 10% of the main courses may be bought in to be finished as necessary.

At lunch time you will find this busy restaurant with 45 covers, offering both light and full meals from a table d'hote menu and take-aways are also available. The Waverley is licensed and carries 13 different wines from France, Italy, Australia and Britain. None of these are vegetarian but six are organic. There are seven country wines as well as cider and premium lager. Hot drinks include barley cup and dandelion coffee.

Each month there is a wonderful gourmet evening, usually on the last Saturday. The menu is well and imaginatively planned including perhaps Borsch with Mushroom Pierozki - a Persian style barley casserole perhaps followed by a selection of freshly home-made desserts. These are evenings to savour and bookings are taken in advance.

One should not forget that the Waverley also has a health food shop attached to it from which you can purchase a whole range of delicacies as well as practical necessities.

Useful Information

OPEN: Mon-Sat: 9-5pm. Gourmet evenings 7.30 till late

CREDIT CARDS: Visa/ Access

CHILDREN: Welcome

LICENSED: Yes

ON THE MENU: Interesting dishes specially created for the Waverly

DISABLED ACCESS: Yes but no toilets

GARDEN: No

ACCOMMODATION: Not applicable

Country House With Restaurant for Guests

CNAPAN COUNTRY HOUSE AND RESTAURANT

East Street, Newport, Dyfed, Wales, SA42 0SY.
Telephone: (0239) 820575

TO understand what a magical place Cnapan is, you need first to meet Eluned Lloyd and her husband John, who run it with their daughter and son-in-law. It is spacious and comfortable with five beautifully furnished en-suite bedrooms for those in residence, and a restaurant with 38 covers. Eluned Lloyd is a talented chef who finds her ingredients where others would fail to look. You will frequently see her making tracks for the seashore, carrying new bin sacks. Ask her what she is doing and she will tell you she is off to get the ingredients for your dinner from her 'secret garden'! Go with her, and where the tide reaches the rocks she will stop and start gathering armfuls of green leaves - or that is what it will look like to you. Not so, this is young wild spinach, which produces the most wonderful flavour and beyond that, she will point out mint and wild fennel which seems to throw off the tingling smell of aniseed. It is this love of natural foods that makes her such a wonderful cook.

Cnapan is Welsh for a game played with a ball up until Elizabethan times and Eluned finds herself using ingredients which would have been available then. As people did not have supermarkets, they would use what they could gather around them! Eluned uses young hawthorn leaves, wild garlic stems, nettles, elderberry flowers, salt-washed stems of samphire - a great delicacy. She will tell you she is never quite sure what dishes she is going to make but is famous for her pies! For 10 years the family have run Cnapan with increasing and deserved success. They have received accolades from Which, Michelin, Ackerman, Egon Ronay and the Welsh Tourist Board. Eluned has appeared on television and is a frequent contributor to vegetarian recipe books. Cnapan is a rare treat.

Useful Information

OPEN: 6 days a week from Apr-Oct inclusive, & closed Tues. From Nov-Mar open weekends only. Closed Feb

CREDIT CARDS: Access/ Visa

CHILDREN: Welcome

LICENSED: Yes. Fine wine list, some organic & vegetarian

ON THE MENU: Imaginative home cooking based around local ingridients

DISABLED ACCESS: Yes

GARDEN: Secluded, sunny, table and chairs

ACCOMMODATION: 3 twins, 1 double room, 1 family. All en-suite

Restaurant & Take-Away

HERBS COOKSHOP

30 Mount Street, Bangor, Gwynedd, LL57 1BQ.
Telephone: (0248) 351249

PAM Marchant has been the successful proprietor of Herbs Cookshop since the day it opened ten years ago. It has a mixture of purposes but throughout it is devoted to the cause of vegetarian living at its highest standard. The Cookshop offers an extensive variety of tasty, wholesome food to take-away. From salads and soups to filling main meals, all the food is freshly home-made and suitable for vegetarians (there is always a vegan alternative on the menu). Also on offer are a range of refreshing drinks from organic coca-cola to pink lemonade. The only problem you might encounter is *which* delicious pizza, quiche or pie to try next! If you are lunching out in town, Herbs makes a healthy change from your usual take-away.

For those who like to eat in style, you should try Herbs homely restaurant, where a meal costs as little as £1.50 as we write in November 1993. On a cold day a delicious bowl of hot home-made soup in front of the fire is a meal in itself, and the variety of hot and cold dishes will leave you spoilt for choice. It is possible to book the restaurant in the evenings for parties of eight persons or over.

Herbs also has a first class catering service. If you require food for a business lunch, party or special occasion, then the value is excellent with a price of anything from £3.50 to £7 per head. It is wonderful to be able to relax and let Herbs handle the occasion for you, quietly and efficiently. Food is prepared to allow for those who are meat eaters if it is requested. Herbs is well known for the service it provides for special occasions such as weddings. It is not surprising that Herbs has received recognition from the Vegetarian Travel Guide, Vegetarian Good Food, Sara Browns Best of Vegetarian Britain and Taste Magazine.

Useful Information

OPEN:, 10-3pm Mon-Sat: Evenings by appointment. Closed Bank Holidays
CREDIT CARDS: None taken
CHILDREN: Welcome
LICENSED: No - Bring your own
ON THE MENU: Fresh, home-made, interesting
DISABLED ACCESS: Not wheelchairs
GARDEN: No
ACCOMMODATION: Not applicable

Guest House

GRAIANFRYN

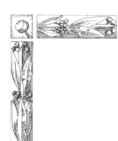

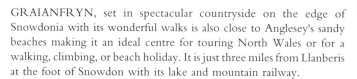

Penisarwaun, Caernarfon, Gwynedd, LL55 3NH.
Telephone: (0286) 871007

GRAIANFRYN, set in spectacular countryside on the edge of Snowdonia with its wonderful walks is also close to Anglesey's sandy beaches making it an ideal centre for touring North Wales or for a walking, climbing, or beach holiday. It is just three miles from Llanberis at the foot of Snowdon with its lake and mountain railway.

Amongst the many tourist attractions within close proximity to Graianfryn are the castles of Caernarfon, Beaumaris and Conwy, narrow-gauge railways (including Ffestiniog railway), Portmeirion and Bodnant Gardens. Road communications to North Wales have been greatly improved making it easily accessible from England and there is a railway station at Bangor.

The early Victorian ex-farmhouse is beautifully furnished throughout with beams, original fireplaces, log-burning stove, antique furniture etc and offers luxurious accommodation. Catering is to a high standard and is exclusively vegetarian and wholefood. The dishes are imaginative and created on the premises using healthy and fresh ingredients (organic and from the garden where possible). Specialities include home-made bread, ice-creams and tempting desserts and cakes.

The evening meal is served by candlelight in the romantic setting of the pretty and intimate dining room. Vegans and special diets are well catered for. The house is strictly non smoking. A brochure is available from Christine Slater at the above address. As all meals are freshly prepared please telephone in advance.

Useful Information

OPEN: All year, please give advance notice of arrival

CREDIT CARDS: None taken

CHILDREN: Welcome to share parents' rooms

LICENSED: No. Please bring own wine

ON THE MENU: All wholefood vegetarian. Vegans & special diets with advanced notice

DISABLED ACCESS: No

GARDEN: Patio with picnic benches. Herb, fruit and vegetable garden

ACCOMMODATION: For 6 adults. Children may share parents room

Farmhouse

PENTRE BACH

Llwyngwril, Nr Dolgellau, Gwynedd, LL37 2JU.
Telephone: (0341) 250294, Facsimile: (0341) 250885

DOWN a 250 yard private drive from this pretty costal village, Pentre Bach has a well-signed entrance, 40 yards south of the stone bridge. It is a delightful home, centrally heated throughout and has the atmosphere of a warm, welcoming country house, with stripped pine and antiques, together with some fine pictures and hangings from abroad. Parts date back to before 1770 but it was extensively rebuilt in 1868 and completely restored by the present owners. It is still blessed with the original fireplaces and window shutters and stands 600 yards from the sea.

At Pentre Bach, Nick and Margaret Smyth, the owners, cater to suit individual guests. All the dishes, which one would describe as 'light wholefood with modern classical tendencies', are home prepared and cooked with their own ingredients wherever possible. They grow their own fruit, vegetables and herbs organically in the walled garden. Eggs are from Pentre Bach's own free range hens. You will find exciting Welsh specialities on the menu. A set menu is offered with fruit juice and 3 courses plus coffee and petit fours, with choices at each stage. If however, guests do not want the whole meal, deductions are made. The house is not licensed.

There are three en-suite rooms, two double and one twin bedded, each with its own television, easy chairs and hot drinks tray. Bed, breakfast and an evening meal are on offer, and a packed lunch is available. The grounds are a pleasure to be in, with ponds, shrubs, lawn, and a ha ha, to ensure uninterrupted views to the sea. Most days, guests can choose their own breakfast time; so far, the earliest and latest have been 4am & 4pm! Two hours notice is requested for dinner. French, Spanish, some German and a little Welsh are spoken. Vegetarians and vegans will find this an excellent place in which to stay. Pentre Bach is strictly non-smoking.

Useful Information

OPEN: To suit guests
Smoking is banned.
Awarded 3 Crowns & Highly Commended

CREDIT CARDS: Mastercard/Visa

CHILDREN: Welcome

LICENSED: No

ON THE MENU: Excellent, home-prepared wholefood

DISABLED ACCESS: No

GARDEN: Acres of attractive grounds. Uninterrupted sea views

ACCOMMODATION: Two doubles, 1 twin, all en-suite

Hotel

TREMEIFION VEGETARIAN COUNTRY HOTEL

Talsarnau, Nr Harlech, Gwynedd, LL47 6UH.
Telephone: (0766) 770491

TREMEIFION Vegetarian Country Hotel is at Talsarnau on the A496 between Maentwrog and Harlech. You take the road to Soar and approximately 300 metres on the left is Tremeifion. The hotel has spectacular views across the estuary towards Portmeirion and the Llyn Peninsula. The glorious countryside surrounds Tremeifion with woodland, valleys, hills, mountains, lakes and rivers all waiting to be explored. The ancient town of Harlech has five miles of wide and safe, sandy beaches with extensive and interesting sand dunes. If you have a passion for steam trains then the 'Great Little Trains of Wales' will keep you contented. There are slate mines, copper mines, castles, yachting, golf, bird watching, pony trekking and horse riding, and, for a photographer it is a rare opportunity. Last and by no means least is famous Portmeirion with its fascinating Italianate village - home of 'The Prisoner' and seven and a half acres of wonderful woods and gardens.

The hotel's aim, apart from providing their guests with such a wonderful base from which to explore, is to make everyone feel relaxed and comfortable. There is a choice of five comfortable bedrooms, three of which are en-suite and all have tea and coffee making facilities, hair dryers and radio clocks. For breakfast there is a variety of cereals, including a special, Tremeifion muesli, home baked rolls and speciality breads, fruit and a cooked meal. In the evening, a candlelit dinner with two choices for each course, accompanied by good wines from France, Italy and Australia, all of which are vegetarian and organic. There are organic beers and lagers. liquors, spirits and several soft drinks. The menu is strictly vegetarian with vegan options, although other diets can be catered for with prior notice. No meat or fish is ever included. Tofu and Sosmix is used and the only food bought ready made is the after dinner mints! The aim is to give a wide range of healthy balanced meals. Desserts are usually fruit based although there are some indulgences. Welsh vegetarian cheeses are also on offer.

Useful Information

OPEN: All year with exception of Jan 94.Bargain weekend breaks Oct-Jun inclusive

CREDIT CARDS: None taken

CHILDREN: Welcome. Dogs allowed

LICENSED: Full On Licence

ON THE MENU: Wide range of healthy balanced meals. Open non-residents, booking essential

DISABLED ACCESS: No wheelchair access

GARDEN: 3 acres of wood-land and open land with seating

ACCOMMODATION: 3dbl en-suite, 1 twn and 1 fmly, h&c. No smoking throughout the hotel

Cafe

GREAT OAK CAFE

12 Great Oak Street, Llanidloes, Powys, SY18 6BU.
Telephone: (0686) 413211

LLANIDLOES is an attractive market town just seven miles from the source of the River Severn. 300 yards from the old Market Hall in the centre of the town is the Great Oak Cafe in Comptons Yard, part of the Comptons Yard Trust, a registered charity, set up in 1982 to provide facilities of social benefit to the people of the Llanidloes area. The Great Oak Cafe is run in the most efficient and pleasant manner by a workers' co-operative. It has been in business since 1982 and during that time gathered a very good reputation which brings customers from miles around. It is a relaxed, informal establishment where you may linger as long as you wish. It is quite small with roughly 28 covers, self service and partly no smoking. Sometimes you may find yourselves being entertained by live folk music. Whilst dogs are strictly taboo, children are genuinely welcome and a high chair is available. You may look askance at the very old Gaggia coffee machine but it cannot be beaten for the excellence of the coffee it makes.

The cuisine is entirely vegetarian with vegan options and the only things purchased ready made are the rolls and bread which come from the local baker. You will find the cafe serves a good range of light meals and snacks, all at very reasonable prices. One of the cafe's specialities is a wide range of herb teas which allow you to experiment. Whilst the cafe is licensed they do not always have wine in stock.

On a warm day it is very pleasant to sit and have your meal or a cup of tea in the courtyard which is mainly cobbled and is arranged with plants and tables. It is a safe area for children's play. Before or after your meal you may care to take a look at the various studios that make up the complex. Since opening in February 1988, Studio 13 has been used for all sorts of workshops at all age levels. There have been meetings on Third World issues, education for our children and Holistic health care, also exhibitions of work by artists and crafts people.

Useful Information

OPEN: Mon-Sat: 10-4pm. ClosedChristmas Eve to New Years Day inclusive
CREDIT CARDS: None taken
CHILDREN: Welcome
LICENSED: Yes
ON THE MENU: Exclusively vegetarian with vegan options
DISABLED ACCESS: Yes, but no special toilets
GARDEN: Courtyard with tables
ACCOMMODATION: Not applicable

Tearoom and Coffee Shop

OLD STATION COFFEE SHOP

Dinas Mawddwy, Machynlleth, Powys, SY20 9LS.
Telephone: (0650) 531 338

THE Old Station Coffee Shop is in a beautiful spot on the side of the River Dyfi with a packhorse bridge dating back to the beginning of the 17th century directly opposite. To find it on the A470 go one mile north of Mallwyd Roundabout junction A458 road from Welshpool. Do not go to Machynlleth, that is the postal address and merely confuses. The coffee shop was built as a railway station in 1868 to take slate from the quarry to the main Shrewsbury to Aberystwyth line. It has been non-operational since 1951 and the coffee shop came into being in 1971. For the last ten years it has been in the capable hands of Eileen Minter, a warm hearted lady who produces delicious, buffet style food. Do not even consider lighting a cigarette inside this charming place; it is definitely taboo.

Eileen is famous for her home-cooking and in particular for cheese scones which are freshly baked every morning and available from 10.30am. The Welsh tea bread bara brith is another of her specialities. You will find a large display of tempting salads and always a choice of home-made soups, some of which conform entirely to vegetarian standards. Taking a percentage overall of the dishes suitable for vegetarians it would stand at 75%. Occasionally meat stocks are used and the cheese is not vegetarian. Eileen or her staff will always confirm the ingredients used in any of her home-cooked dishes.

The Old Station Coffee Shop is licensed, and has a very small selection of wines, cider, pale ale and lagers and 'cerist' a mineral water from the Dyfi valley. In summer you can sit outside and enjoy the glorious view. The coffee shop is quite blase about the number of mentions and awards it receives from reputable guides. Eileen believes in people deciding for themselves.

Useful Information

OPEN: March-early Nov: 7 days; 9.30-5pm. Closed late Nov to end of Feb
CREDIT CARDS: None taken
CHILDREN: Welcome if well behaved
LICENSED: Yes
ON THE MENU: Home-cooked, buffet style food
DISABLED ACCESS: Yes + toilets
GARDEN: Tables with benches. Lovely view
ACCOMMODATION: Not applicable

Restaurant

PEPPERS RESTAURANT

Puzzle Square, Welshpool, Powys, SY21 7LE.
Telephone: (0938) 555146

PEPPERS has grown in stature as a restaurant which provides as much good vegetarian food as it does for meat eaters. The philosophy behind the running of this attractive, light, airy establishment was accentuated by Wendy Waldron and Judith Ward who became the energetic and perceptive owners some two years ago. They took stock of Peppers which had been in being for some six years and decided it had much they liked, but even more that they could improve upon. The regular clientele who have discovered this quiet oasis, in a secluded square to be found off many of the alleys that lead from the main street of Welshpool, will tell you that they come here as much for the ambience as the excellent food. Peppers is not large, it has 32 covers added to in the summer months when you can sit outside and enjoy a meal while knowing your children and animals are safe in a traffic free area.

The criteria for any good eaterie has to be home-cooked food using as much as possible of both local produce and ingredients. This is very much so here. You will find that everything is made on the premises and covers a wide range from snacks, which are 75% vegetarian to light meals where 50% of the starters are vegetarian and both the main courses and desserts on offer are 50% vegetarian. There is a wide variety of pies and quiches, also jacket potatoes with numerous fillings and hot dishes of the day. The cheese, onion and potato pie is a by-word for many a mile. There are few people who do not rave about the excellence of the home-made scones and cakes.

Whilst there is a very limited wine list, there are a number of delicious and unusual specialist teas including many herbal varieties.

Useful Information

OPEN: Mon-Sat: 8am-5pm. Sun: 10-5pm. Closed Autumn/Winter Sundays & Christmas and New Year

CREDIT CARDS: None taken

CHILDREN: Welcome

LICENSED: Restaurant. Limited list

ON THE MENU: A mixture of vegetarian and meat dishes. All home-cooked

DISABLED ACCESS: Yes but no special toilets

GARDEN: No, but secluded square

ACCOMMODATION: Not applicable

Wine Bar & Bistro

JODIES BAR AND BISTRO

Telford Road, Menai Bridge, Anglesey, LL5 9DT.
Telephone: (0248) 714864

SITUATED at the Anglesey end of the Menai Suspension Bridge, Jodies Bar and Bistro is a popular haunt for regulars and visitors who find this one time bridge building foreman's cottage, a welcome, friendly place. Its newest attribute is a wonderful conservatory which allows you to sip an excellent glass of wine whilst looking out over the majesty of the Menai Straits. There are three attractive restaurant rooms and two rooms entirely devoted to drinking.

You will find the award winning cuisine unusual and refreshingly original, certainly deserving of the Egon Ronay 1993 'Just a Bite' accolade. A large percentage of the dishes on offer are suitable for vegetarians. Everything is cooked freshly on the premises without additives, eggs are free-range and stocks are vegetable. The wine list is equally as good and at sensible prices. Who could resist home-made mulled wine in winter in front of a roaring log fire and the cool, refreshing taste of freshly made lemonade in the garden on a summer's day.

Useful Information

OPEN: Lunch: 12-2pm. Eve: 6-11pm. Closed Christmas Day & new Year's Day

CREDIT CARDS: None taken

ON THE MENU: Refreshingly original. Vegetarian choices

DISABLED ACCESS: Yes but no special toilet facilities

Vegetarian Guest House

STREDDERS

Park Crescent, Llandrindod Wells, Powys, Wales, LD1 6AB.
Telephone: (0597) 822186

Stredders was established early in 1986 with the specific aim of providing accommodation of a high standard for vegetarians and vegans. Being vegetarians, the owners Mike and Sian Redwick-Jones, are only too aware of the problems they face when in need of 'watering and feeding' and they set out to provide an alternative to cheese omelettes, vegetarian lasagne and salads! Stredders is the only vegetarian guest house in the area.

Open all the year Stredders occupies a spacious Victorian family house. All rooms have every modern convenience. There is a guests' lounge with colour TV, video recorder with a large library of tapes, stereo system, lots of books and an open fire. Mike and Sian offer a laundry service and packed, or more formal, lunches. They are licensed and carry an extensive range of organically produced vegetarian wines from France and Germany. Stredders is ideally situated for touring the breathtaking scenery of mid Wales. There is plenty of opportunity for cycling, bird-watching, horse-riding, golfing, tennis, bowls, badminton, volleyball and squash.

Useful Information

OPEN: All year

CREDIT CARDS: None

ON THE MENU: Totally vegetarian or vegan. No smoking

DISABLED ACCESS: No

The Sundial at St Lawrence's Church, Eyam

Contents

CENTRAL ENGLAND

***The Heart of England* - Hereford & Worcester, Shropshire, Staffordshire, West Midlands and Warwickshire, *The Midshires* - Derbyshire, Leicestershire, Northamptonshire, Nottinghamshire, Lincolnshire and South Humberside**

Suggested Venues to Dine

THE HEART OF ENGLAND

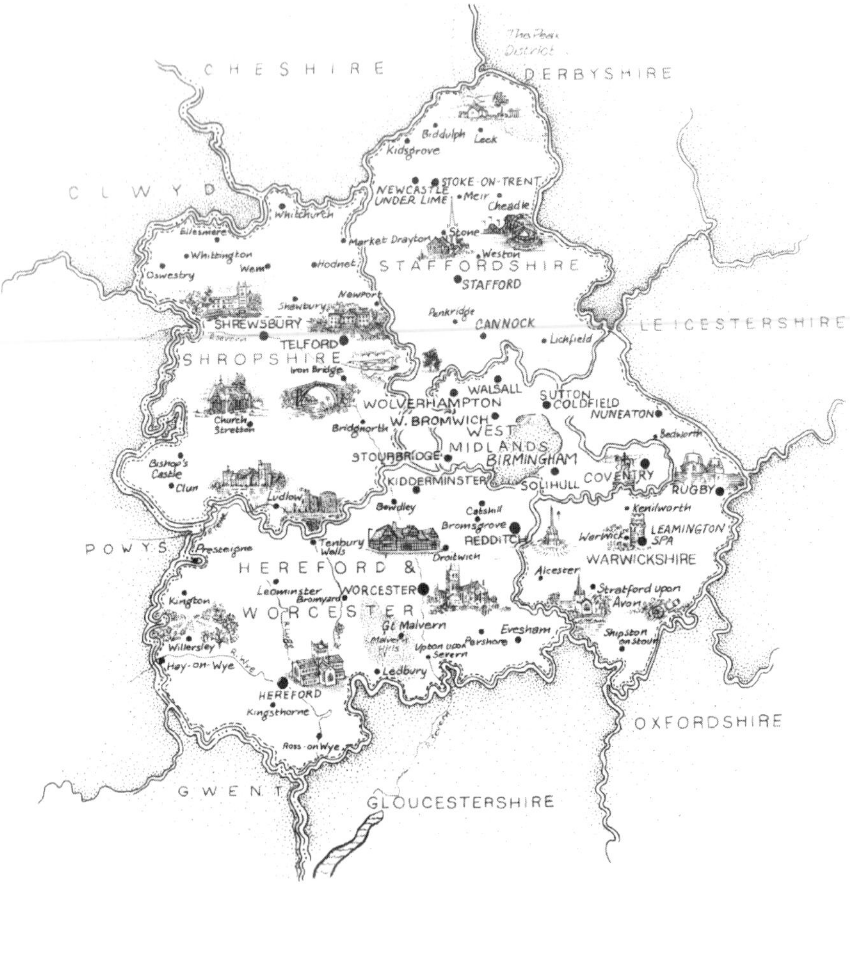

THE MIDSHIRES

CENTRAL ENGLAND

The Heart of England - Hereford & Worcester, Shropshire, Staffordshire, West Midlands and Warwickshire
The Midshires - Derbyshire, Leicestershire, Northamptonshire, Nottinghamshire, Lincolnshire and South Humberside

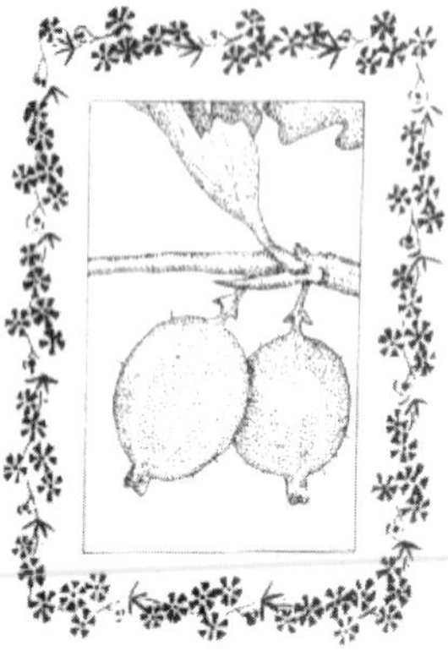

Actually further south than north, and right over to the west of England bordering Wales, this region has nevertheless become known as the 'Heart of England'. Right in the centre, the county of West Midlands is very much an industrial one, and industry has thrived around this core, particularly to the north in Staffordshire, but there are too particularly good farming lands and some, on the whole, very pretty countryside.

The red soil around Hereford in the far south west of the region is rich and well farmed. It is derived from old red sandstone and when the fields are ploughed the contrasting colours of the soil and the green of the trees will leave most people lost for words. This is a stunning district, its numerous rivers and oak woods, its wild daffodils and its superb black and white timbered buildings, giving the impression of a managed landscape. They may not actually farm to beautify the countryside here, but that is what they achieve.

Apple trees, some of them of unknown age, proliferate throughout Hereford & Worcester and cider has always been an important industry here, from the large scale of the Bulmers factory in Hereford, to the small scale of the various farmhouses advertising their wares with signs by the road. At **Much Marcle**, **Putley** and **Lyne Down**, the old fashioned cider farms are opened to visitors and there are several organised cider events each year.

Recently grapes have become almost as commonplace as apples, and there are now many vineyards in this region.

A little to the east across the MALVERN HILLS the county's personality is best personified by its three rivers, the temperamental fast running Teme, the slow running Avon, and the Severn with its numerous tributaries. The areas around these rivers have a distinctive character all their own. This is an area where almost anything can be grown in the black soil but mostly to be seen are orchards and market gardens. The **Vale of Evesham** is famous worldwide for its plums as well as its asparagus, but all around are orchards of cherry and apple and fields of corn and hops, and beside the Teme willows are grown for cricket bats.

Shropshire is divided roughly in half by the longest river in England the Severn. The south of the county is green and lush land, in places wooded, in contrast to the wilder far northwest. In the north the countryside is mainly used for dairy and arable farming in a rich green landscape. The village of **Cressage** is said to be in the running for having the oldest tree in the country, the 'Cressage Oak'. This flat land is suddenly contrasted by LONG MYND towering 1,674 feet above the Shrewsbury to Ludlow road, a bleak heather covered plateau of grit and shale, occupied by wild ponies and lamenting grouse. In the west the hill falls suddenly away taking the full force of the prevailing winds making it a mecca for gliding and hang-gliding enthusiasts. WENLOCK EDGE is well known for its exceptional views, but also for its lime quarries. This region with its limestone core is as much in contrast with the grit of Long Mynd as it is with the glacial rugged gorge at IRONBRIDGE, or the red sandstone of CLEE HILL.

In the far north lie the Shropshire meres, six huge sheets of water which are a paradise for plants and wildlife, naturalists and botanists coming from all over the world to study the area and soak up its beauty.

Warwickshire has many notable castles and churches and some particularly impressive houses and parks, such as PACKINGTON, COUGHTON and COMPTON WYNYATES, the best of which have been landscaped by Capability Brown. Unfortunately nature has created a countryside which, even though productive, is not necessarily spectacular, and no county has more justification for mourning the almost total loss of the elm, once called the 'Warwickshire Weed' as its demise has had its effect on the beauty of this county and has seriously marred the long, straight Fosseway.

No visitor is allowed to forget that Warwickshire is Shakespeare country. Many of the buildings that just might have any connection with Shakespeare or his writing have been 'sympathetically' restored. Alas the tacky side of tourism has not been excluded, and visitors can have a Shakespearian breakfast or even worse a Shakespeare icecream! Another down side of all this is that people from all over the world come to **Stratford-upon-Avon** and at any time of the year the town can be knee deep in tourists. Yet if this can be ignored it is possible to walk the streets and soak in the beauty and serenity of the buildings and imagine what it must have been like to live in those times. SHAKESPEARE'S BIRTHPLACE and the adjoining SHAKESPEARE CENTRE are open all year, as are ANNE HATHAWAY'S COTTAGE and other associated properties. Of course what draws many of the visitors are the performances by the ROYAL SHAKESPEARE COMPANY.

Shakespeare's birth place

Warwick largely dates from the late 18th century, much of it having been rebuilt after a great fire, and thus the town has pleasant architecture and a unique atmosphere.

The county of Staffordshire has probably some of the dullest and most depressing industrial areas in the land, but within a short drive the visitor can get right into the countryside. In the east of the county around **Uttoxeter** there is some of the best dairying countryside in England, and the scenery around **Dovedale** is wild and rugged and has a presence of foreboding, even more so when the black clouds cling to the snarling peaks and ring out their thunder which echoes and groans in the valleys for miles around.

In the north, Staffordshire shares thePEAK DISTRICTwith Derbyshire and this area is a National Park to be explored again and again. In the south is the Cannock Chase, a 16 square-mile area which attracts hoards of local people and visitors. Half this area is afforested with incongruous foreign conifers, but the other half is beautiful, open moorland with natural woods of oak and silver birch. Visitors should be warned that Cannock Chase is immensely popular and it is necessary to walk quite a way to avoid the crowds and to be rewarded with a sight of the wild deer and grouse.

Industrialisation is the word which springs automatically to mind when thinking about the West Midlands, but the county does have rural areas mixed in with its two great cities, its three cathedrals, three universities and many old schools. It is said that Queen Victoria ordered the blinds of the royal train to be lowered so that she could not see the belching chimneys and furnace fires as she passed through the area. Thankfully the area has changed a great deal since her time, and there is now a dignity, both in the Georgian and Victorian buildings and the many modern constructions, be they artistic or utilitarian, along with parks and other amenities built for the enjoyment of the people.

Recent population studies have shown that vegetarians have fewer heart attacks and lower blood cholesterol.

Birmingham is certainly a city which has seen an improvement in its standard of living in recent years, and is now an important centre for the arts. It has quite a lot worth seeing, all well documented in other publications, as are the attractions of **Wolverhampton** and **Coventry**. Due to the many businesses and activities taking place in these conurbations their inhabitants have come from all over the world, giving a great diversity of culture to this area.

Diversity also applies to the region's museums. Often thought of as places to go to on a rainy day, a visit to some of the museums here will not prove a sanctuary from the weather as there are several in the open air.

Close to the new town of **Telford** in Shropshire, is the award-winning and famous IRONBRIDGE GORGE MUSEUM, actually a series of museums along the valley, some three miles long and half a mile wide, where preserved in situ is a complete industrial landscape. Included are factories, mills, railways, blast furnaces and so on, offering the visitor the opportunity to experience first hand the conditions of workers in the 18th and 19th century. It also shows in vivid detail why at this time Britain was the leading industrial nation.

Part of this site, BLISTS HILL OPEN AIR MUSEUM covers 50 acres overlooking **Coalport** and here the buildings have been reconstructed to illustrate social and industrial history. Just a short distance down river is where the fine Coalport China was made. The museum has reopened the old china factory, and the products and processes of china-making occupy the old bottle ovens and workshops. At **Coalbrookdale**, the DARBY IRONWORKS is well worth a visit for those who enjoy their art in metal. The museum boasts a very ornate and magnificent clock tower and houses some outstanding, elaborate Victorian ironworks, quite possibly the best examples in the world.

It is the 'five towns' of Staffordshire, most notably **Stoke-on-Trent** that are at the heart of the pottery industry. No trip to the area is complete without a visit to several of the potteries, and very much worth a visit is the GLADSTONE POTTERY MUSEUM in **Longton**, a Victorian pottery which gives demonstrations of this area's traditional skills.

But Staffordshire's oldest industry is coalmining which dates back over 600 years and there is now a museum at the CHATTERLEY WHITFIELD COLLIERY near **Tunstall**, where visitors are taken 700 feet below ground to view the Holly Lane coal seam.

THE BLACK COUNTRY MUSEUM in **Dudley** has been developed on a canalside site near the entrance to Dudley tunnel; it has shops, a coal mine, a pub and more, and its aim is to reflect the culture of this industrial area.

CHARLECOTE MILL at **Hampton Lucy** in Warwickshire is a beautiful old working watermill on the banks of the River Avon. It opens to the public on certain Sundays and several Bank Holiday weekends, and the visitor can purchase stoneground flour here.

Just to the south of **Bromsgrove** is AVONCROFT MUSEUM OF BUILDINGS, a must for visitors interested in architecture, with its houses, barns, its mill and granary. The aim of the Museum is to preserve and interpret historical building technology in relationship to the landscapes the buildings have come from.

DINMORE MANOR, 6 miles north of **Hereford** up a long idyllic country lane off the road to Leominster, was founded by the Knights of St John of Jerusalem in the 12th century. The west wing has since become a splendid shrine to the arts and crafts movement of William Morris, with fine architecture including a wonderful cloister. There are other surprises in the garden, with a grotto with stained glass palm trees as well as a beautiful hillside garden.

The Counting House at Avoncroft Museum

At **Claverley** in Shropshire is a cottage built for someone very small, it measures only 8 feet by 10 feet and is thatched, it claims (as do others!) to be the smallest house in Britain. Also in Shropshire, at **Tong**, is what must be the most elaborate hen house ever constructed, called the EGYPTIAN AVIARY.

The town of **Ross-on-Wye** is itself a tourist attraction, a very pretty town beautifully situated along the river. There is much to see and to do here but it is also a centre for visiting the surrounding countryside of both Hereford & Worcester and the Cotswolds. On the old Gloucester Road in Ross is the shop and workshop of the candlemakers ALPENHOF DESIGN where you can browse, buy and also talk to the man who makes the candles. The factory supplies buddhist temples and therefore has some 'cruelty-free' candles.

In the bustle of the busy Queens Street in **Wolverhampton** stands the business of tea merchant W.T.M. SNAPE. On entering this establishment the shopper is transformed back to the Dickensian era with its original gas lamps, brass scales, wrought iron fittings and its tea dust and wonderful fragrances; the tea leaves are displayed in a small wooden chest and teas from all over the world are blended and sold, even by the ounce if so desired, just as they have been for generations.

According to the findings of a major programme of research, obesity is related to ***what*** *people eat rather than how much. Adjusted for height, the Chinese consume 20% more calories than Americans - but the latter are 25% fatter.*

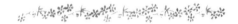

And finally, it is to be hoped that visitors to this region will be making their way to THE NATIONAL CENTRE FOR ORGANIC GARDENING at **Ryton-on-Dunsmore** in Warwickshire, home to the HENRY DOUBLEDAY RESEARCH ASSOCIATION, the leading light in the organic gardening and environmental movement. Its aims are to research, advise, and teach individuals, groups and even local authorities the benefits of growing plants without the aid of chemicals or pesticides. Their Advisory Department receives around 3,000 enquires each year on all aspects of organic growing and pest control and even on 'winter green manures', and they have built up a formidable library of knowledge, respected far and wide. There are always trials of different plants and seeds for the visitor to investigate and for those wishing to start making their own compost Ryton Gardens aim to have every composting bin on the market on show!

Recently they have been putting a lot of time and effort into finding alternatives to peat as a growing medium including recycled materials and organic waste which could also save the countryside from being used as a landfill dump. HDRA has just constructed its own reedbed sewage treatment system - effluent is collected in four large tanks and filtered through various processes before passing through a tank planted with *Phragmites austalis*. The filtered water then runs into their lake, dribbles out slowly through the overflow and sinks into the ground, this is a very efficient system and all the effluent on this site is thus recycled. The HDRA is also involved with work overseas helping likeminded organic groups to come to terms with their individual problems of climate and soil conditions so that the most can be achieved with as little detrimental effect on the environment as possible. Ryton is definitely a place to spend the day.

THE MIDSHIRES

From the high peaks of the Pennines in the north west to the flat flower fields in the east and the undulating farm lands of the south this region is one of mixed terrain. It has always been crossed by major roads, from truly ancient tracks to Roman roads, trunk roads and more recently motorways, resulting in an area rich in history. It is also crossed by hundreds of miles of canal linking the area to important centres of trade, mostly further to the west.

Northamptonshire is often given no more consideration than being somewhere it is necessary to travel through to reach an intended destination. This is the county of 'Spires and Squires': its Saxon churches and its grand country houses, being very fine, although its domestic architecture is generally less impressive. Many of the large country houses are still privately owned and many of them not open to the public or only by appointment.

A column at **Naseby** marks the place where the Parliamentarians beat the Royalists in 1645.

RUSHTON LODGE, in the grounds of Rushton Hall, is one of this country's oddities, a three storey triangular building, built by Sir Thomas Tresham in the late 16th century, when he returned from imprisonment for his religious beliefs.

Variations on the number '3' are everywhere to be seen, the facades decorated with trefoils and triangles in groups of three, three gables to each of the three sides, and so on. He started but never quite completed another property nearby, LYVEDEN NEW BIELD, also full of catholic symbolism.

The land now given to farming covering much of Northamptonshire was at one time the ancient Rockingham Forest, with just a few small areas remaining. There are also industrial areas here, which in the 19th century made much use of the GRAND UNION CANAL. At **Stoke Bruerne** is an interesting WATERWAYS MUSEUM.

The Grand Union Canal continues through Leicestershire via the FOXTON LOCKS, an incredible flight of ten locks which raises the water by 75 feet.

This county is a stronghold of fox hunting. It dates from the days when the area was heavily forested, and although now mostly farm land the hunting continues, with some of the most important hunts in the country. It is even said that the modern landscape "has been moulded for the needs of fox hunting". Leicestershire is said to be the least visited of all counties in England - could there be a connection?

But the county does have things worth seeing. A really pretty building is the market place at **Market Harborough**, actually a school built on stilts.

Over half the world's cereal harvest is fed to livestock being reared for meat.

The small village of **Appleby Parva** has an astonishing school, designed by Sir Christopher Wren as a result of the Lord Mayor of London, who had commissioned Wren to undertake St Paul's Cathedral, asking him then to design a school for the village where he was born. The Great Paul Bell in St Paul's Cathedral was cast at the world famous bell foundry in **Loughborough**.

Not so grand is All Saints Church at **Beeby**, the spire just started but never completed being no more than a stump on top of the tower. One story is that two brothers were building the steeple when one pushed the other off to his death in an argument. In his remorse the remaining brother then threw himself off. Thus the building was left unfinished.

Only a little of **Leicester**'s Roman heritage remains, however, the 30 feet high JEWRY WALLS around the city of *Ratae Coritanorum*, forming one side of the exercise hall of the civic baths, are some of the best in the country.

The town was the home of Joseph Merrick, the Elephant Man, who was shown at freak shows in theatres such as one in Wharf Street which still has its stage although now a shop. The town of **Oakham** was the home of the world's smallest man, Jeffrey Hudson, who was taken up by Elizabeth I and who lived to a good age despite twice being captured by pirates and being sold into slavery.

Beautiful landscaped gardens surround BELVOIR CASTLE, its galleries full of exceptional Dutch and Flemish paintings, its public rooms with fine Gobelin tapestries. The orchards of the estate now produce some high quality fruit cordials.

The county is noted for two cheeses, 'Stilton' which was actually not made in **Stilton** itself, but was eaten here at the Bell Inn, and 'Leicester' which is a pleasant red cheese made in the south of the county.

Just in Derbyshire on the Leicestershire border CHALKE ABBEY is one of the fairly new introductions to the list of National Trust properties to be opened. The huge house in an immense park was hidden from everyone for more than a century, the reclusive family keeping totally to itself, not even allowing any motor vehicles within the grounds.

Another abbey of note in Derbyshire is DALE ABBEY, the largest surviving remnants of a dissolved abbey in Britain. Here too is the smallest church, a part of which is actually a house, and closeby is a cave occupied in the 12th century by a pious baker.

A large corner of Derbyshire is taken up by the PEAK DISTRICT NATIONAL PARK, for the most part a wild, desolate moorland. The outside edge is the Dark Peak of peat, the centre a landscape of undulating limestone with caves, criss-crossed by dry stone walls and deep wooded valleys with delightful unspoilt villages. One such is **Castleton** with spectacular panoramic views over the Peaks and perching high above it PEVERIL CASTLE. The area abounds with spectacular caves and caverns, the show caves at Castleton being some of the best. At **Eldon Holt** is an apparently 'Bottomless Pit'.

The United Kingdom could support a population of 250 million people on a vegan diet.

The elegance of the Peak District town of **Buxton** owes its existence first of all to its spa water and later to the lime industry and to copper. There is an important, international but also low budget opera season here each year. The town is the centre for exploration of the Peak District and has several museums including A NATURAL WORLD EXHIBITION.

Matlock is another spa town, home to the PEAK DISTRICT MINING MUSEUM and many other interesting places worth visiting.

The county has many Neolithic stone circles as well as a wealth of medieval castles and 18th century grand houses. The 'Stonehenge of Derbyshire', more generally known as ARBOR LOW STONE CIRCLE with its giant stones around a sundial, and beside it the slightly later round GIB HILL BARROW are important Neolithic and Bronze Age monuments. Nearby are similar monuments at High Low, Lean Low and Carder Low. Other early monuments include the NINE LADIES STONE CIRCLE and to the north EYAM MOOR TUMULUS AND STONE CIRCLE.

Eyam is also known for being 'the plague village', which in 1666 created its own quarantine to prevent the plague from spreading. The tradition of 'Well Dressing' has associations throughout this region with the plague, the people who were not affected being grateful for the untainted water that their wells supplied. It is however believed that the tradition has even earlier roots. The small town of **Tissington** dresses five wells with flower pictures on Ascension Day each year.

It takes 10 lbs of grain to yeild 1 lb of intensively reared beef and takes 3 lbs to produce 1lb of poultry.

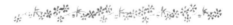

One of the impressive grand houses of the area was the project of the then 71 year old Bess of Hardwick, widow of four husbands. The Elizabethan HARDWICK HALL not far from **Chesterfield** was built to replace an even older house, the ruins of which are still to be seen, and now under the ownership of the National Trust it is one of the country's most popular historic houses. In **Crich** visitors can travel back in time at the TRAM MUSEUM, with over 40 steam, horse-drawn and electric trams making it one of the finest transport museums anywhere.

Derby is an important industrial town: home to ROYAL CROWN DERBY porcelain, which has its own museum; birthplace of the Rolls Royce and with various associations with railway engineering, as can be seen in the INDUSTRIAL MUSEUM.

The restored OLD MILL at **Cromford**, alongside the CROMFORD CANAL, is where Richard Arkwright first used water-power to drive a cotton mill.

In Nottinghamshire industry is also in evidence, nowhere more elegantly than at the PAPPLEWICK PUMPING STATION in **Ravenshead**, set within landscaped gardens. The supporting pillars of the two beam engines are decorated with gilded ibises, water lilies, fishes among reeds, as can also be seen in the stained glass windows. A splendid example of Victorian self-confidence.

The National Tramway Museum at Crich

More famous than anything happening today in Nottinghamshire, and more famous than any positively documented history, is the legend of Robin Hood and his exploits in and around **Sherwood Forest**. There are some known facts which tie into the legend, and much of what is only recorded in the form of a story is likely to be true, but Robin Hood nevertheless remains something of a mysterious character, and perhaps it is best this way. Sherwood Forest once covered a huge area, and although what remains is still reasonably large by today's standard it is not on the large and daunting scale of past centuries. Possibly the best known tree anywhere is the MAJOR OAK, a hollow tree several hundred years old. In the same area of **Edwinstowe** is an interesting forest visitor centre.

NOTTINGHAM CASTLE has been rebuilt a couple of times and now houses a ROBIN HOOD EXHIBITION.

The city of **Nottingham** is well known for Nottingham Lace which is still made today by dozens of companies, and the long history of its production is told in THE LACE CENTRE in Castle Road as well as in the MUSEUM OF COSTUME AND TEXTILES.

Under the city is a honeycomb of ancient caves, some linked by passages, used as dwellings until quite recently. There is even a pub here carved out of the rock, the 'Trip to Jerusalem' which dates from the Crusades.

Eastwood is known as the birthplace of D.H. Lawrence and the family house in Victoria Street is now a museum to him, although he did not live there in adult life. He did however use the town and surrounding area with lightly disguised names in many of his novels, and the local library has a LAWRENCE STUDY ROOM.

Newstead Abbey at Kirkby-in-Ashfield

Nottinghamshire was also home to the Byron family, but Lord Byron and his mother were too poor to move into the huge NEWSTEAD ABBEY at **Kirkby-in-Ashfield** when they first inherited it, and it was sold just a few years later.

The county does of course have farm land as well, and at **Laxton** farming is still carried out according to the traditions of Middle Ages strip farming, regulated by a special court.

The low-lying eastern areas of Lincolnshire, around the fens and dykes of the Wash, are often referred to as 'Holland', and in the early summer are bright with tulips. Consisting of silt and peat the fens were mostly drained in the 17th century, making excellent land for growing flowers in the flat fields. Corn has also been a major crop and windmills have been many, although their uses have sometimes been other than for flour, for instance the grinding of woad or for pumping water from the land. One impressive example, built in 1877, the only windmill with six sails instead of the more usual four, is SIBSEY TRADER WINDMILL a little to the north of **Boston**.

The Bishop's old palace, Lincoln Cathedral

Land that was Lincolnshire has been taken by the sea throughout history, and some startling evidence of this is to be seen at **Huttoft Bank** which was at one time, possibly something like 1,000 years ago, a forest which later succumbed to the peat bog and was preserved beneath clay. Now the sea has washed away the layers to expose the ghosts of former trees which can still be seen at low tide.

Further inland is the area beloved of Tennyson, the **Lincolnshire Wolds**, with open high landscape and peaceful villages tucked in green valleys, an 'Area of Outstanding Natural Beauty'. The Wolds are crossed on their southern crest by the BLUESTONE HEATH ROAD, a prehistoric ridgeway, passing nature reserves and some superb viewpoints, plus the deserted medieval villages of **Calceby** and **Calcethorpe**.

Alfred, Lord Tennyson's home in **Somersby** is not open to the public, but all around the south Wolds are the places which inspired his poetry. A statue to Tennyson can be found beside Lincoln's Minster.

Known as *Lindum Colonia*, **Lincoln** was a retirement town for Roman soldiers and there is much evidence of Roman occupation in the area.

It is said that King John borrowed from a moneylender in Lincoln, AARON THE JEW'S HOUSE also having as a claim to fame the fact that it is believed to be the oldest house in the country, dating from around 1,100. Also in Lincoln is a pretty row of 16th century houses spanning the river Witham.

20 years ago the area to the south of the Humber was part of Lincolnshire, now joined with the area north of the river which was previously the East Riding of Yorkshire, to form the county of Humberside. In South Humberside evidence of our forebears abounds, place names mapping the successive invasions of the Romans, Saxons and Danes. Deserted medieval villages can be found, such as at **Gainsthorpe** which was comparatively recently discovered from the air.

The now ruined Augustinian THORNTON ABBEY to the south of the Humber has a magnificent 3-storey gatehouse with a facade ornamented with finely-carved detail.

Alkborough could be described as an amazing place. There are several mazes to be found here, the largest and original is JULIAN'S BOWER MAZE standing on a high escarpment overlooking the confluence of the Trent and the Humber, a turf maze some 44 feet in diameter, probably cut by monks in the early 13th century. In the church is a replica of it in the floor of the porch. There is also one in a stained glass window and one on a tombstone.

Courgette Filled Courgette Flowers

Courgette flowers can sometimes be bought with tiny courgettes still attached, but better still grow your own. Serve either as a main item with salad, or as an accompaniment at a barbecue, for an outdoor summer lunch.

Serves 4

8	Courgette Flowers
8 baby	Courgettes
4 oz	Wholegrain Rice
4 oz	Pine Kernels
	Fresh Herbs
	Mayonnaise

Cook the rice. Dice and lightly sauté the courgettes. Toast the pine kernals in a moderate oven or under a grill until brown. Chop the herbs. Mix the stuffing ingredients when cold with just enough mayonnaise to hold together. Having ensured the flowers are clear of insects (but do not wash them), fill with the stuffing mixture.

Inn

THE NAGS HEAD

Hilltop, Castle Donington, Derbyshire, DE74 2PR.
Telephone: (0332) 850652

THIS lively, friendly inn is an excellent stopping point. Close to the M1 Junction 24 on the B 6540 through Castle Donington towards Donington Park and there it is at the top of the hill on the left. It has been a hostelry for over a hundred years and inside you will see what a welcoming place it is with its low beamed ceiling and open coal fires which send out a great warmth in winter. It is the sort of inn where locals gather and at the same time has become the haunt of many visitors who have found great enjoyment in the bar or the dining room over the years. There is a small room for darts and bar billiards and every Sunday evening there is live jazz - a popular occasion. The garden is well used in summer and many a good game of Petanque has been played on the Boules Pitch.

Ian Davison and his partner Jennie Ison are the owners. Ian is also the chef and it is his enthusiasm for vegetarian dishes that has ensured an entry in this guide. All the food is prepared and cooked on the premises and mainly to order. Fresh produce is used at all times including vegetables and potatoes. You will never find chips on the menu! Twenty five per cent of the menu is strictly vegetarian and other diets can be catered for with notice. If one had to describe the type or style of cooking it would be difficult. Ian is imaginative and has the sort of rapport with herbs and spices that will always make the food at The Nags Head just a bit different. For those who have a sweet tooth the puddings will appeal particularly.

Marstons Pedigree and Marstons Burton Bitter plus Head Brewers choice are the beers on offer. The wines come from around the world including some from this country. None are specifically organic or vegetarian.

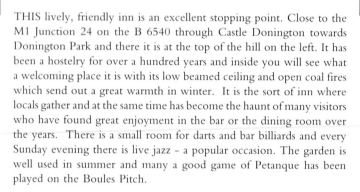

Useful Information

OPEN: Mon-Sat: 11-2.30pm & 6-11pm, Sun: 12-3pm & 7-10.30pm
CREDIT CARDS: Access/ Visa/Switch
CHILDREN: Not in bar. Well behaved in restaurant
LICENSED: Full licence
ON THE MENU: Dishes for vegetarians at every course
DISABLED ACCESS: Yes but no special toilets
GARDEN: Yes, boules pitch
ACCOMMODATION: Not applicable

Inn & Small Restaurant

THE BRIDGE INN

Michaelchurch Escley, Herefordshire, HR2 0JW.
Telephone: (0981) 23646

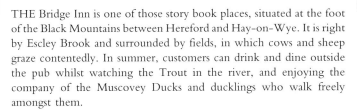

THE Bridge Inn is one of those story book places, situated at the foot of the Black Mountains between Hereford and Hay-on-Wye. It is right by Escley Brook and surrounded by fields, in which cows and sheep graze contentedly. In summer, customers can drink and dine outside the pub whilst watching the Trout in the river, and enjoying the company of the Muscovey Ducks and ducklings who walk freely amongst them.

Some parts of the pub date back to the 14th century. It has been added to over the years but it still has the feel of centuries about it. Once it was used by Drovers who would stop here whilst they were driving their sheep to market in Hereford. Imagine the fun people have on the Sunday of August Bank Holiday weekend when the famous 'Duck Race' takes place. Plastic ducks are released two miles away up river and the winning post is the Bridge Inn. It is all for charity and is a yearly favourite with many people. Another popular occasion on the agenda is the regular pianist that adds cheer at any time of the year.

In the pub there is a lounge, a public bar and a restaurant that seats 22. Jean Draper, the owner, does all the cooking with the help of Rosie her assistant. The menu is mainly English, but it is not unusual to find Indian, Italian or French specials. She uses many of her own recipes all the year round, vegetarian ones in particular. Her 'Leek Croustade' - leeks in sauce with a crunchie topping - is a mega favourite for which people keep coming back. It really is a super pub.

Useful Information

OPEN: 12-2.30pm & 7-11pm
CREDIT CARDS: None taken
CHILDREN: Yes, well behaved
LICENSED: Full Licence
ON THE MENU: Excellent vegetarian recipes cooked by the owner.
DISABLED ACCESS: All one level
GARDEN: Large lawn & patio for eating etc.
ACCOMMODATION: Not applicable

Healthy Fast Food!

OAT CUISINE

47 Broad Street, Ross-on-Wye, Herefordshire, HR9 7DY.
Telephone: (0989) 66271

IF ONE says that 47 Broad Street is 500 years old then the immediate reaction is that it must have low ceilings, oak beams and uneven floors. Sadly one can see no sign of its history but you can take an even bet that the inhabitants of those distant days would not be surprised at the type of food that is available, only the manner in which it is cooked and the speed with which it is served. All the old fashioned, nutritious, non additive foods are available and everything - whether it is a snack, a light meal, a full blown feast or a take-away - is for the vegetarian or the vegan and any one on a gluten free diet. The taste is scrumptious and the calibre of both the presentation and the menu is of the very highest standard.

Little is bought in ready-made other than a very small percentage of main courses and a number of desserts. In every case the content has been checked to ensure that the ingredients used are strictly within the scope of vegetarians. cheese is totally vegetarian, the eggs are free-range, the only substitute used is TVP. There is no license for wines or other alcoholic drinks. However Ame red and white, elderflower cordial and presse, Dorset ginger and Norfolk punch are all readily available.

One of the nicest things about Oat Cusine is the owner, Trevor Rogers and his staff led by the talented chef, Deanne Paganuzzi. They genuinely love their work and care about the people who come to sample the food. A growing reputation is their reward.

Useful Information

OPEN: Mon-Sat: 8.30-6pm, Sun: 11-5pm. Closed on Sundays in Jan-Feb only
CREDIT CARDS: None taken
CHILDREN: Very Welcome
LICENSED: No
ON THE MENU: Good, imaginative fast food, vegetarian
DISABLED ACCESS: Yes. No toilets for wheelchairs
GARDEN: No
ACCOMMODATION: Not applicable

Public House

THE BLACK HORSE INN

94 Main Street, Foxton, Market Harborough, Leicestershire, LE16 YRD.
Telephone: (0858) 84250

IF you like canal side pubs you will thoroughly enjoy the atmospheric Black Horse Inn in Main Street. Full of character, abounding in hospitality, it is a favourite haunt of the locals and many people have discovered it is fun to be here, to listen and sometimes join in, the banter at the bar. David and Jennie Quelch have worked hard to bring The Black Horse to the standard they were looking for. You will find the canal bar full of memorabilia and in the lounge comfortable seats make drinking and eating a pleasure. This is somewhere you can also stay, not in luxury but in attractive bedrooms, with well sprung beds, showers and hand basins as well as a television and that boon to travellers, a beverage tray. Two and a half acres of grounds are in full use during the summer with frequent barbecues when the weather is kind. Children enjoy the freedom of the Play area which has several items to gladden their hearts.

Food is all important and whilst The Black Horse does not cater soley for vegetarians, both David and Jennie have a great understanding of their requirements. You will find well thought out dishes on the menu which are both sustaining and nourishing as well as being very tasty. Such dishes are available whether it is a full meal or a bar snack.

The wine list is extensive and explores both old favourites and some exciting wines of the new world as well as at least three organic wines. None of them are out of reach of ones bank balance and the house wines are especially good value. The Black Horse is there to be discovered and once having done so you too will want to become a regular.

Useful Information

OPEN: Mon-Sat: 11-3pm & 6-11pm. Sun: 12-3pm & 7-10.30pm
CREDIT CARDS: Visa
CHILDREN: Welcome
LICENSED: Yes

ON THE MENU: Good vegetarian dishes at every course
DISABLED ACCESS: Yes with suitable toilets
GARDEN: Two & a half acres. Childrens play area
ACCOMMODATION: Three letting rooms with shower

Wine Bar & Restaurant

MILLERS WINE BAR

Mill Court, Corre Street, Sleaford, Lincolnshire, NG34 7TR.
Telephone: (0529) 413383

IN a building that dates back to 1857 and once was an old coach works, Millers Wine Bar is an attractive place in an unusual setting in Mill Court, quite near to the Tourist Information Bureau in Money's Yard where there is a large car park. It has been many things over the years including a carriage works, a grain store, a convalescent hospital and a little theatre. At one time it was derelict but one of the quirks of bureaucracy gave it a preservation order which was then rescinded and followed by a demolition order. Fortunately, for its present customers, it was rescued and painstakingly rebuilt using the original stonework and timbers.

Inside there is one large bar with an intimate separate restaurant leading to a large garden and patio with tables for use in the summer. It is the most restful place to be, almost an oasis away from the busy world outside. It is used extensively by local people who recognise that it is somewhere they will be well fed at prices that are sensible. The a la carte menu has a high proportion of vegetarian dishes, some 75% of the starters, 50% of the main course and 25% of the desserts.

One very useful factor here is that if you are tied for time you can telephone beforehand and order a meal which will be ready and waiting for you when you arrive. Everything about Millers is designed to please customers - as it should be but is so often not the case. Visitors to Sleaford should put this friendly, efficient and informal place on their list. They will not be disappointed.

Useful Information

OPEN: Bar: Mon-Fri: 11-3pm & 7-11pm, Sat: 7-11pm, Sun: 7.30pm-10.30. Restaurant: Mon-Fri: 12-2pm & 7-midnight, Sat: 7-midnight, Sun: bookings only
CREDIT CARDS: Switch/Visa/Master/Delta/Amex
CHILDREN: Welcome
LICENSED: Full On & Supper
ON THE MENU: Good range of dishes for vegetarians
DISABLED ACCESS: Welcome, stepped entrance
GARDEN: Delightful with plenty of seating
ACCOMMODATION: Not applicable

Bistro

OLIVERS VEGETARIAN BISTRO

33 High Street, Ironbridge, Shropshire, TF8 7AG.
Telephone: (0952) 433086

IF you enquire what is the special secret of success of Olivers, Pete and Paul, the owners, will tell you that they believe good food must be married with caring service in personalised surroundings to achieve maximum client satisfaction. Olivers believes it has the right combination - a fact with which all its regular customers would agree. Here in a 200 year old Grade II Listed building in the heart of Ironbridge Gorge, a World Heritage Site, Olivers has been delighting people for many years. Beneath exposed beams one dines at candlelit tables in a strictly nonsmoking environment. A background of soft music - anything from the sound of a Celtic harp to contemporary Soul makes for relaxed and casual surroundings attracting vegetarians and non-vegetarians alike. You will find the service efficient and friendly and a strictly vegetarian menu that offers around eight choices at each course changing regularly.

Alongside the familiar, recipes on offer, you will also find a variety of unusual dishes but the emphasis is always on providing tasty food without going overboard on spices and certainly eschewing too much salt and saturated fats. All meals are freshly prepared to order using the finest ingredients. France, Germany and Italy provide the wines, most of which are vegetarian and organic. There is an excellent house wine at a sensible price. In addition there is a full range of the usual spirits and popular liquers. A worthy winner of a 'Heartbeat Award' for excellence in fat free options and for a high standard of health and hygiene, Olivers is a must.

Useful Information

OPEN: Tues-Sat eve: 7-11pm, Sat Lunch: 11-3pm, Sun: 11-5pm + Bank Holidays and week-day lunches in season
CREDIT CARDS: Access/Visa /Mastercard (4% surcharge)
CHILDREN: Welcome
LICENSED: Yes organic & vegetarian wines
ON THE MENU: Traditional/ familiar and exciting vegetarian dishes
DISABLED ACCESS: Yes but no special toilet facilities
GARDEN: No
ACCOMMODATION: Not applicable

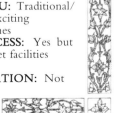

Hotel

THE FEATHERS AT LUDLOW

Bull Ring, Ludlow, Shropshire, SY8 1AA.
Telephone: (0584) 875261, Facsimile: (0584) 876030

OPEN for breakfast, lunch and dinner as well as offering 40 comfortable and well-equipped rooms, each with its own private facilities, The Feathers at Ludlow is somewhere that, once having seen and visited, you will never forget. For three hundred years it has catered and cared for travellers and never better than at the present time. It is famous for its superb 17th century facade and an interior that, although it has been slightly modernised, still has all the nooks and crannies and interest of a 300 year old building.

The Feathers has an unbeatable atmosphere which assails everyone who steps through its old doors. Within, you are treated to an old-fashioned courtesy and service and offered food and drink of a very high standard. Whilst it has a totally relaxed informality, nonetheless gentlemen are requested to wear ties at dinner. The menu caters for every taste but 30% of the snacks and main courses and 20% of the starters and desserts conform entirely to vegetarian requirements and some to vegan. If one had to describe the food, it would probably be correct to say that it is traditional British. The 'Bill of Fare' is very flexible and provides inexpensive as well as luxury food. There is no service charge, no cover charge or minimum charge. You are requested not to smoke in the restaurant.

As one would expect in an establishment of this calibre, the wine list is extensive and the selection covers wines from around the world. The Feathers at Ludlow is wonderful at any time but it would be delightful for weddings and dances and is a much sought after venue for banquets and conferences of all sorts. How good it is, is reflected in the fact that 70% of its business is repeat or personal reccommendation.

Useful Information

OPEN: All Year. 11am-11pm
CREDIT CARDS: Amex/ Visa/Mastercard
CHILDREN: Welcome
LICENSED: Yes
ON THE MENU: Traditional British fare with a good choice for vegetarians
DISABLED ACCESS: Yes
GARDEN: No
ACCOMMODATION: 12 dbl 12 sgl, 12 twins, 4 family, all en-suite

Bistro

LE BISTRO

13 St Johns St, Wirksworth, Derbyshire, DE4 4DR.
Telephone: (0629) 823344

THE happy atmosphere of Le Bistro, a cellar restaurant in a Grade 2 Listed Building, approximately 200 years old, is one of the reasons why it is such a popular venue. Food, of course, has a lot to do with it and the vegetarian influence has brought many people through its welcoming doors. You enter into a reception area which is also the bar and then down a spiral staircase into the attractive restaurant with pine tables, stone and white walls and beamed ceilings. There are 28 covers and it is one of those places where you may stay for as long as you please; no one is going to hassle you.

Based on French cooking, all the dishes are freshly cooked. There are many vegetarian choices across the board with five starters, main courses and desserts. For vegans there is only one main dish. The wine list offers an interesting range of wines from Germany, France, Spain and Portugal, none of them organic or vegetarian.

Useful Information

OPEN: Mon-Sat: 6.30-9.30pm. Closed for 2 weeks holiday & Christmas and New Year's day
CREDIT CARDS: All major cards except switch
ON THE MENU: French regional dishes including vegetarian options
DISABLED ACCESS: Not suitable

Vegetarian Restaurant

BLOSSOMS

17b Cank Street, Leicester, Leicestershire, LE15GX.
Telephone: (0533) 539535

FOR six years Blossoms has produced excellent vegetarian fare to the delight of its many regular customers. Oddly enough there are as many carnivores who come here to eat as there are vegetarians and this is basically because much time and effort has been put into producing a regularly changing menu of interesting dishes. This is a self-service restaurant with a non-smoking area and is ideally situated in Cank Street, close to the hustle and bustle of the city centre.

Everything is prepared on the premises so there is absolutely no danger of non-vegetarian ingredients finding their way into the food. They offer a range of speciality teas and coffees and there is a delicious range of home-made cakes, snacks and pastries served throughout the day. Blossoms is licensed but serves only a good, inexpensive house wine plus cider and lager. You will find a pleasant relaxed atmosphere here. Children are very welcome and its doors are open daily from 10am-4pm.

Useful Information

OPEN: Daily 10-4pm
CREDIT CARDS: None taken
ON THE MENU: A totally vegetarian restaurant with interesting dishes
DISABLED ACCESS: No, the restaurant is upstairs

Indian Restaurant

SHARMILEE

71-73 Belgrave Road, Leicester, LE4 6AS.
Telephone: (0533) 610503, Facsimile: (0533) 681383

THIS is an authentic Indian Restaurant in which not only will you eat a memorable meal, but your surroundings will enhance the food. It is quietly attractive, almost unassuming. In the background gentle Asian/Indian music plays and every now and again there is the pretty tingling sound of bells. The well trained, courteous staff do everything they can to make sure you enjoy your meal.

Every dish is suitable for vegetarians and those in the know always ask the staff for assistance when it comes to selecting a meal from the extensive menu. In so doing they know they will always get the balance right. Belgrave Road, Leicester is famous for its high standards and Sharmilee does nothing to detract from this.

Enjoy your choice of dishes, and with them a bottle or glass of wine at a very reasonable price.

Useful Information

OPEN: Tues-Thurs:12-2.30pm & 6-9pm, Fri-Sun:12-9pm
CREDIT CARDS: Visa/Access/Diners/Amex/Switch
ON THE MENU: Excellent vegetarian Indian dishes
DISABLED ACCESS: Not really but there are suitable toilets

Cafe/Restaurant

THE GREENHOUSE

First Floor, 27/29 Biggin Street, Loughborough, Leicestershire, LE11 1UA.
Telephone: (0509) 262018

YOU will find The Greenhouse above Codd's Bookshop in Biggin Street. It may not be a historic building or have any outstanding features but once inside the welcoming doors of this pleasant restaurant-come-cafe you will find it spacious, airy and attractively decorated. Sizeable green houseplants thrive here and the walls are frequently home to art exhibitions.

Dishes are taken from a worldwide cuisine and adapted according to the season, the availability of produce, customers' preference and the chef's inventiveness. No ready-made dishes are bought in and few substitutes are used other than Tofu. It is 3½ years since Mr Keen started producing vegetarian food and in this time he has made vast improvements to the Greenhouse, a fact liked and respected by the many vegetarians who beat a path to his door. The restaurant is non-smoking. Whether you want a full meal or a light snack or take-away you will be equally well looked after. All the wines from England and Europe are organic and vegetarian.

Useful Information

OPEN: Mon: 12-2pm, Tue-Wed: 11-5pm, Thurs-Sat:10-5pm. Ring for details of evening opening hours
CREDIT CARDS: None taken
ON THE MENU: Totally vegetarian + vegan options. Imaginative dishes
DISABLED ACCESS: No

Free House & Restaurant

THE CHEQUERS

Main Street, Gedney Dyke, Lincolnshire, PE12 OAJ.
Telephone: (0406) 362666

TO find this old 18th century inn with its beamed oak ceilings and boasting some of the finest hanging baskets in Lincolnshire, if you are travelling towards Kings Lynn on the A17 take the B1359 left, which winds into Gedney Dyke. At the post office turn left. It is about 400 yards to the Chequers. (Approx two miles in all).

In the winter the comfortable, separate restaurant is a popular spot but this is equalled in the summer when many regulars know they can enjoy a light meal sitting in the garden amongst a profusion of flowers.

During 1994 a garden room is to be added. Any diet can be coped with given notice but there are always vegetarian dishes. The menu might well be described as eclectic and varied with the accent on seasonal fresh foods and quality ingredients from local suppliers. Some desserts may use gelatine but fresh fruit is always on offer.

Useful Information

OPEN: Bar: 12-2pm & 7-11pm. 6.30pm July & August. Closed Christmas & Boxing Day

CREDIT CARDS: All major cards

ON THE MENU: Very varied. Good vegetarian dishes

DISABLED ACCESS: Yes. No special toilets

Retailers/Takeaway

HIZIKI WHOLEFOOD COLLECTIVE

15 Goosegate, Hockley, Nottingham, NG1 1FE.
Telephone: (0602) 505523

THERE will be few businesses with a higher degree of knowledge on all matters vegetarian and vegan than Hiziki Wholefood Collective. Here all the staff are either vegetarians or vegans and thoroughly enjoy sharing their knowledge with customers. It is in fact an employee owned co-operative and has been so for the last nine years.

It is known far and wide for the level of stock and for the wholefood snacks and cakes etc which are available for anyone wanting to take a meal away. Every day fresh, excitingly filled sandwiches are available as well as the delectable cakes. If you ask them their speciality they will tell you that it is in producing vegan alternatives. The premises are licensed and you can get some very good organic and vegetarian wines as well as a number of country wines including damson, strawberry, blackberry and elderberry as well as many others. There is a small range of organic beers and a limited range of cider.

Useful Information

OPEN: Mon,Tues, Thurs, Fri: 9.30-6pm. Wed & Sat: 9.30-5.30pm

CREDIT CARDS: None taken

ON THE MENU: Good, exciting, sandwiches & cakes etc

DISABLED ACCESS: Yes

Inn

FALCON HOTEL

St Johns Street, Lowtown, Bridgnorth, Shropshire, WV15 6AG.
Telephone: (0746) 763134

AS a 17th Century Coaching House, the Falcon Hotel has for several centuries provided the traveller with the sort of hospitality typical of the best English Rural Inn. Not far from the motorway network (M54 - 15 minutes), it is ideally situated as a base for business trips in the West Midlands area, or for a pleasant family holiday or minibreak in a county renowned for its beautiful countryside which is steeped in Industrial Heritage.

With 15 individually designed bedrooms all with private bathrooms and every modern facility you will be very comfortable With a perfect combination of 17th Century character, and a warm and friendly atmosphere, the bar/restaurant offers the opportunity for a relaxing drink and a wide range of dishes from traditional English to the more unusual from far off countries. Excellent dishes are available for vegetarian and other diets. It is a delightful place to stay.

Useful Information

OPEN: All year
CREDIT CARDS: Amex/Visa/Mastercard
ON THE MENU: English fare with vegetarian options
DISABLED ACCESS: Yes

Restaurant

THE GOODLIFE WHOLEFOOD RESTAURANT

Barracks Passage, Wyle Cop, Shrewsbury, SY1 1AX.
Telephone: (0743) 350455

WITHIN the walls of a finely restored 14th Century building this is the only building in Shrewsbury with its original 'smoke hole' in the roof. Audrey and Fred Weston serve whole and natural foods in this charming restaurant. The menu is derived from fresh vegetables and fruit wherever possible, 100% local Pimhill organic wholemeal flour, free-range eggs, fresh milk, soya, demerara sugar, herbs and spices. These are prepared on the premises and result in various quiches, savoury nut loaves, cheeses, jacket potatoes, salad bowls which include over 20 fruits and vegetables, fruit crumbles, cakes and scones, with soup and several hot dishes served daily. Cakes and pastries are made with soya margerine and soups exclusively vegetable, and therefore suitable for vegans.

A range of teas, filter or decaffeinated coffee, unsweetened natural fruit juices, wine, cider and traditional beer are all selected with the same care. At The Good Life you sit in peace at clean pine tables in a building with a wonderful atmosphere that is in one of the oldest parts of this historic and lovely County town. All of the menu is available to take-away.

Useful Information

OPEN: Mon-Fri: 9.30-3.30pm. Sat: 9.30-4.30pm. Closed Sun, Christmas and all Bank Holidays
CREDIT CARDS: None taken
ON THE MENU: Good, imaginative wholefood
DISABLED ACCESS: Limited for wheelchairs. No special toilets

Restaurant

BRIEF ENCOUNTER

Great Malvern Railway Station, Imperial Road, Great Malvern, WR14 3AT.
Telephone: (0684) 893033

THE Brief Encounter is a charming restaurant in an unlikely place! Here you may dine on delicious vegetarian food in a romantic setting although one has to hope that any romance will have a happier outcome than Noel Coward's original 'Brief Encounter'. You will find it three quarters of a mile from Great Malvern town centre. The station was opened on the 25th May 1860 and has recently been restored to its original splendour and in 1989 won the 'Heritage' award.

Adjoining the restaurant is 'Lady Foley's Tea Room' which serves excellent home-made food catering for those who wish to eat inside or take their food outside on Platform 1. There is always a vegetarian dish of the day. The whole has come about under the inspired ownership of Terry Page and Margaret Baddeley. Everything is cooked on the premises. Whilst the tea room opens daily, Brief Encounter is open only Thursday, Friday and Saturday from 7-11pm.

Useful Information

OPEN: Thurs-Sat: 7-11pm.
Lady Foley's Tea Room: Mon-Sat: 9-6pm. Sun: 3-6pm
CREDIT CARDS: Visa/Access

ON THE MENU: Home-cooked. Vegetarian with vegan options
DISABLED ACCESS: Yes.

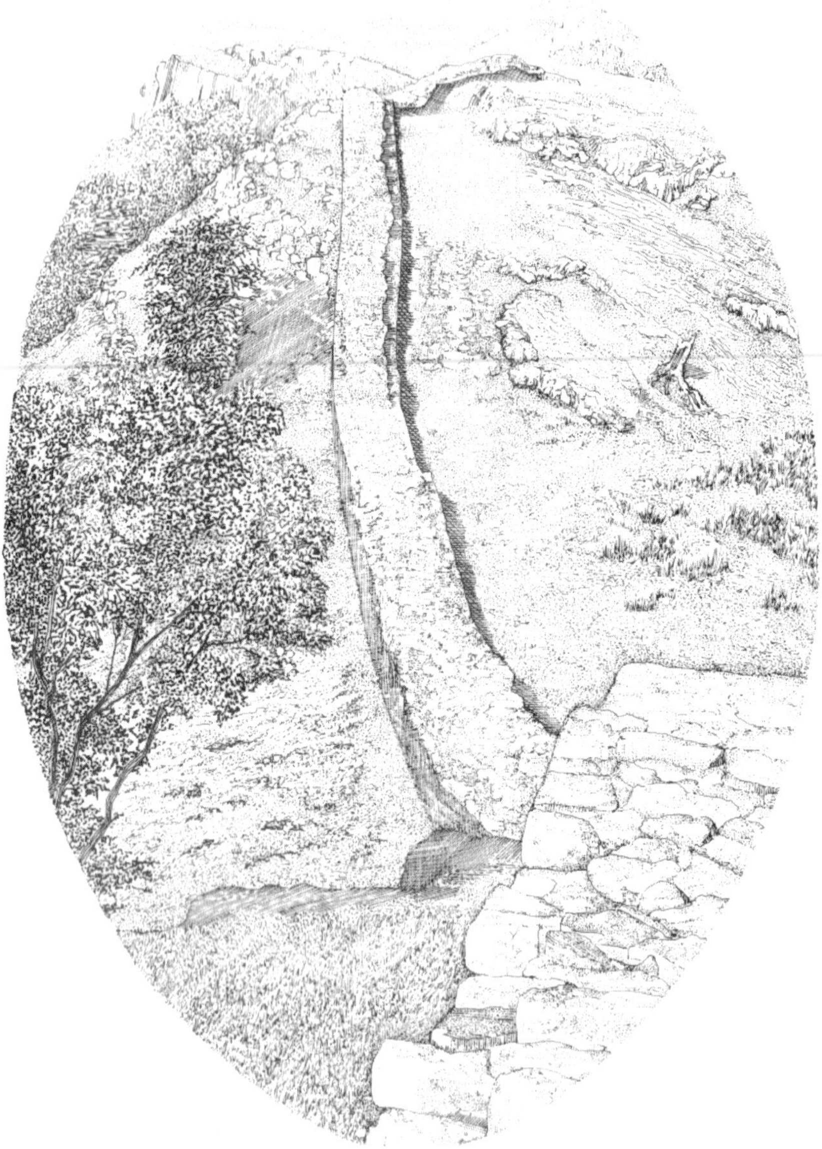

Hadrian's Wall

Contents

THE NORTH WEST COUNTIES

Cheshire, Greater Manchester, Merseyside, Lancashire, Cumbria and the Isle of Man

Suggested Venues to Dine

Sweet & Sour Pasta Sauce

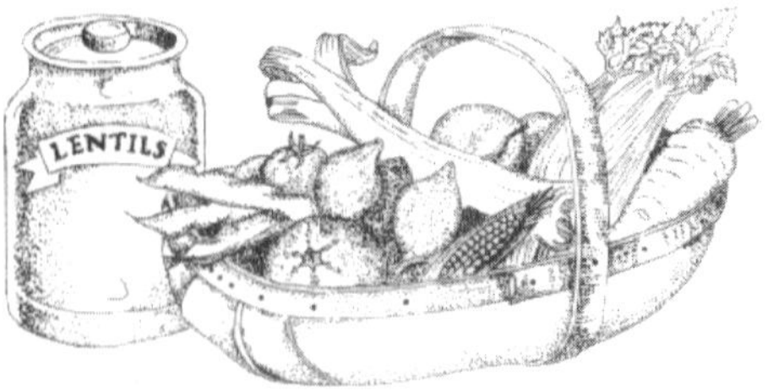

Many different vegetables could be added to the basic sauce to make a light or substantial dish.

Serves 4

8 oz	Lentils
4oz	Crystallised Ginger
5 fl oz	White Wine Vinegar
10 fl oz	Orange Juice
4 Tbs	Lemon Juice
1 Tbs	Mustard Seeds
	Dried Apricots
	Celery
	Baby Sweetcorn Cobs
	Peas
	Carrots

Cook the lentils in just enough water until completely soft. In a processor with a sharp blade blend the ginger to form a smooth paste. Add the cooked lentils, the vinegar, and the orange and lemon juice and blend again until completely smooth.

Cut the vegetables as required into small neat pieces. In a shallow pan fry the mustard seeds until popping then add the vegetables and stir fry until cooked but still crunchy. Add the chopped apricots and the lentil mixture, and heat through.

THE NORTH WEST COUNTIES

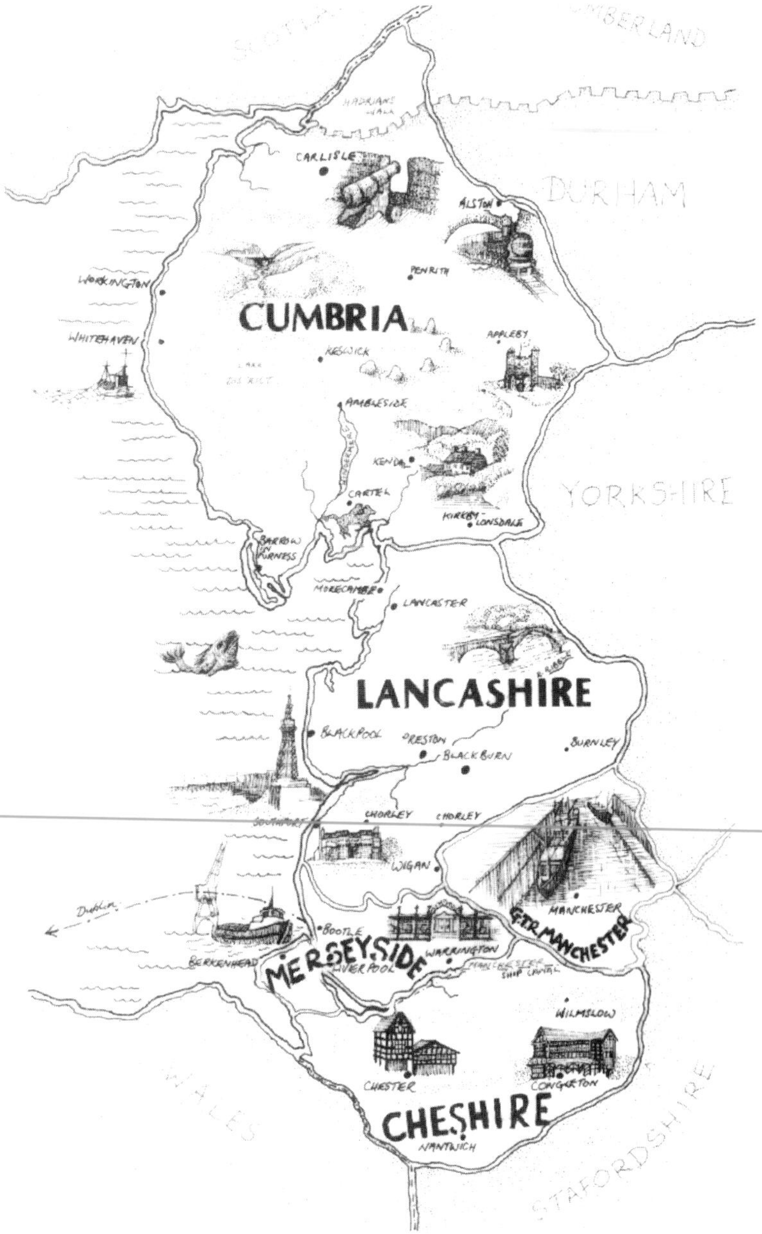

THE NORTH WEST COUNTIES

Cheshire, Greater Manchester, Merseyside, Lancashire, Cumbria and the Isle of Man

This thin band of counties stretches from a border with Wales to a border with Scotland, and includes within its bounds two very important cities, several elegant towns, famous seaside resorts, picturesque villages, the magical Lake District and the fiercely independent Isle of Man.

Surrounding the mainly urban counties of Merseyside and Greater Manchester, parts of Cheshire to the south and Lancashire to the north have to some extent become commuter belts for Liverpool and Manchester. For centuries these areas have benefitted from wealth generated both in the cities and from cotton growing and processing as well as dairy farming, a wealth which can be seen in the quality of much of the domestic building. The intricate black and white designs, which abound in Cheshire, decorate some of what are surely the most attractive buildings to be found anywhere.

The centre and far south of Cheshire are rich farming lands, in part overlaying bands of salt. Unstable, the salt has caused landslips and where it has been mined not far from the surface the land has sometimes collapsed into the void, both features leaving their mark on the landscape, often in the form of meres, and occasionally on buildings which can be found here at strange angles. The story of the salt mining from Roman times is told in the SALT MUSEUM at **Northwich**.

From around the early 16th century **Liverpool** was growing in importance due to the shipping of the local salt, and through this trade came the need for larger vessels turning the port into a major area for ship building. At the height of the British Empire, Liverpool was one of the main trading ports and the town itself became greater and grander, with many impressive buildings.

Manchester's importance grew from the cotton industry, as is evident from its one time colloquial name of 'Cotonopolis'.

Trade from Liverpool and Manchester was much benefitted by a network of canals. The town of **Ellesmere Port** grew up around the MANCHESTER SHIP CANAL in Thomas Telford's canal basin, which now houses THE NATIONAL WATERWAYS MUSEUM, Europe's largest collection of inland boats along with much other memorabilia and information. At**Northwich** is the unique ANDERTON LIFT, water-filled tanks, used to lift and lower boats from the TRENT CANAL to the MERSEY CANAL and vice versa.

The availability of coal and appropriate sand led to the setting up of glass works in and around **St Helens**; an industry continuing to flourish here. The PILKINGTON GLASS MUSEUM is well worth a visit.

A third of the world's population is starving and 15 million children die every year as a result of malnutrition, yet the planet could supply ample food for everyone.

As well as the natural ports and the canals, the coming of the railway was responsible for shaping much of the region, in particular in the area around **Crewe** in Cheshire where many of the important locomotive workshops were sited, **Carnforth** now houses a RAILWAY MUSEUM. The railway also brought visitors, in particular to the seaside villages which became resorts with the popularity of sea bathing, and to the **Lake District** which nevertheless retained a remoteness which is still evident today, largely due now not to any difficulty of travel as such but to the nature of the landscape.

Motorways have ensured that these areas have retained their importance, **Manchester** being at the centre of the most comprehensive network of road and rail.

There has not always been a happy association between workers and officialdom in this region, and one situation led to militant workers being killed and injured at 'Peterloo', an altercation which took place at St Peter's Field in Manchester.

Yet provision of pleasant living conditions for workers has perhaps been given more consideration in parts of this region than elsewhere in

Britain, and the Georgian STYAL MILL and its model workers' village in Cheshire is now a major museum with demonstrations and displays, illustrating the life of the mill workers and the impact of the mill on the area. **Southport**, an elegant resort town in the far northern tip of Merseyside, was one of the first garden cities, laid out with pleasant gardens and wide avenues. **Bromborough Pool** in Merseyside was created by Price's Candle Company, whilst a little later another of the industries which has had great impact, the Lever soap factory, gave rise to the garden city (actually a village) of **Port Sunlight**. The whole village is listed, and includes much worth visiting, including the LEVER ART GALLERY. Nearby **Thornton Heath** was rebuilt as a model village by Lord Leverhulme.

Lord Leverhulme was responsible for the restoration of the 14th century HALL I' TH' WOOD near **Bolton**, the birthplace of Samuel Compton who invented the spinning mule in 1779, which is now a fine museum. Also at Bolton is a TEXTILE MACHINERY MUSEUM and the BOLTON STEAM MUSEUM, both with displays of engineering important to the industry of the area.

There is also a TEXTILE MUSEUM at **Blackburn**, the home of James Hargreaves, inventor of the 'spinning jenny'. **Preston** was the birthplace of Sir Richard Arkwright, inventor of the spinning frame and other devices which sped up the production of the all important cotton cloth.

Preston has the privilege of being Lancashire's administrative capital, although **Lancaster** is still the county town.

Chester, the capital of Cheshire, is a truly beautiful small city, and one that is full of history. As the Roman camp of *Castra* it was strategically important, close to the natural harbours of the Mersey and the Dee and by the route from northern Wales into England. Roman life was not only about defence, and an exceptionally fine amphitheatre can still be seen. The walls which today encircle the ancient city are part Roman and partly date from another important era for Chester, the Medieval period, which was also responsible for the narrow walkways known as the 'Rows' which connect churches, houses and inns. It was the Tudor period which was responsible for most of the traditional black and white framework which epitomises this part of Cheshire. Chester is well served with museums which give the visitor a very good understanding of the history in the area.

The county abounds with grand houses, none grander than LYME HALL near **Stockport**, originally Elizabethan but with impressive later additions and alterations, all of the very highest quality, with exceptional Grinling Gibbons carvings and exquisite furniture, the whole set within an immense park. TATTON PARK is one of the country's most visited of large country houses, but many may want to avoid its Tenants' Hall, built by the 4th Earl of Egerton to house his hunting trophies.

The famous Chester Rows

One of the most famous of the half-timbered houses, frequently drawn, painted and photographed as a depiction of old England, is LITTLE MORETON HALL to the south west of **Congleton**. A grand house, it is nevertheless on a very human scale and has many charms, its bold designs and even bolder angles, its leaded windows, its cobbled courtyard and moat, and its splendid long gallery, all add up to a house that is large yet quaint.

BRAMALL HALL at **Bramhall** in Greater Manchester is considered one of the country's finest 16th century black and white properties, and well worth a visit. Other good examples of black and white timbering are to be found at RUFFORD OLD HALL near **Ormskirk** and the REFECTORY and the OLD HALL in the village of **Gawsworth**. In nearby MAGGOTY'S WOOD is the grave of Maggoty, England's last Jester. Pretty half-timbered buildings are also to be found in the village of **Farndon** with its exceptionally fine 14th century bridge linking England and Wales, and surrounded by strawberry fields. The village of **Great Bedworth** is so pretty that it has frequently featured in films and television programmes.

Lancashire's **Downham** is a picturesque village built for the estate workers at Downham Hall.

Some of the buildings to be found in the ancient market town of **Knutsford** are very different. Built by a wealthy eccentric at the turn of this century, the RUSKIN ROOMS, the GASKELL MEMORIAL TOWER, the KING'S COFFEE HOUSE and others are in more or less Italianate style.

The average supermarket 'Farm Fresh' egg is 8 days old.

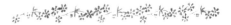

Unusual for a church, the stained glass windows in All Saint's Church at **Daresbury** are based on Tenniel's original drawings for 'Alice in Wonderland', as a memorial to Lewis Carroll, otherwise known as the Rev Charles Dodgson, who was born in this village.

Further to the north, some of the buildings of Lancashire owe most to defence against the Scots and in a later period to the copy-cat inventiveness of the Victorians with their high Gothic style, such as at SCARISBRICK HALL near **Stockport**, which being a school is unfortunately not open to the public.

The Metropolitan County of Merseyside was created in the 1970's to take in the City of **Liverpool** and its surrounding towns and villages, and includes much of the **Wirral Peninsula**, detached from the rest of the county except by boat over the Mersey at **Birkenhead**, and more recently by a total of three tunnels taking rail and road transport. Although a small county it manages to include 30 golf courses, many of them world famous.

Liverpool was created by King John when, in 1207, he offered 2 acres of land to anyone wishing to settle in the area, in order that he could create an army base here to keep Ireland, of which he was Lord, under his control. It was the harbour of the Mersey estuary which made the area ideal for King John, and the harbour which has ever since played a vital role in Liverpool's development. The trio of early 20th century waterfront buildings - the LIVER BUILDING, the CUNARD BUILDING and the PORT OF LIVERPOOL BUILDING - owe their existence to the importance of shipping, of both goods and passengers, from Liverpool. Liverpool is known as the 'City with Two Cathedrals', both of them from this century. Sir Frederick Gibberd's Roman Catholic conical building in concrete incorporating the original crypt designed by Sir Edwin Lutyens excites most of the interest, both pro and anti. Sir Giles Gilbert Scott's Anglican Cathedral, the largest cathedral in Britain, was completed less than twenty years ago, but considerably pre-dates the other from the time of conception.

To many, Liverpool is still most famous as home to the Beatles, and BEATLE CITY takes fans on a trip back down memory lane.

Lancashire's holiday beaches overlooking the Irish Sea are well renowned, the most famous of all being **Blackpool** with its illuminations, but it was **Morecambe** which started the trend, its first illuminations being candles in glass jars.

Much of the south of this region lies on a plain and has little of drama in its landscape, but what hills there are give superb views over surrounding countryside. In the far south of Cheshire on its border with Staffordshire is a suddenly rising hill known as MOW COP, which has seen much history and is now surmounted by an 18th century mock castle ruin.

From Greater Manchester the 1,553 feet peak of BLACKSTONE EDGE looks over into West Yorkshire. The ridge is crossed by an ancient road, possibly built up by the Romans, which has a mysterious groove running down the centre, for what purpose experts have only theories.

Methane is one of the gases causing the Greenhouse effect. According to the 'New Scientist', British cattle are responsible for about 23% of this country's methane emissions.

The high peak of RIVINGTON PIKE is another splendid viewing point, close by the 400 acre LEVER PARK presented to the public by the 1st Lord Leverhulme. From PENDLE HILL by **Clitheroe** is a superb view of the Ribble Valley. This part of Lancashire countryside has long been associated with tales of witchcraft whilst to the north of this plain in the county of Cumbria, which makes up almost half of this north west region, exceptional views are almost commonplace. **The Lake District** has been shaped by the elements, in particular during the Ice Age, to produce sculptured lakes in wondrous valleys surrounded by dramatic hills and mountains. The huge variations in level can be seen to particularly great effect around WASDALE HEAD where Britain's deepest lake, WASTWATER, is set immediately at the foot of Britain's highest mountain, SCAFELL PIKE at 3,210 feet.

The weather still has its part to play in the atmosphere of this area, with the highest average annual rainfall in Britain, and with sometimes fearsome skies that make the human race seem insignificant against such huge forces.

The Lake District can be appreciated fairly well from a car, but is naturally best seen on foot and well away from the few areas that are well populated with holidaymakers. The more remote areas are home to some rare flora and fauna. **Kendal** is at the southern gateway to the Lakes, where many visitors start their tours, making a visit first to LEVENS HALL, an Elizabethan house with an exceptionally fine topiary garden.

Ambleside is another of the excellent centres from which to base a walking holiday, close to LAKE WINDERMERE, England's largest lake with steam boats in operation, and to WANSFELL PIKE and LOUGHRIGG FELL. The village of **Buttermere** is pleasantly situated between the lakes of BUTTERMERE and CRUMMOCK WATER. ULLSWATER is a truly grand lake, bordered by GOWBARROW PARK with its daffodils, depicted in Wordsworth's most famous poem. CONISTON WATER was made famous by Donald Campbell's water speed records. DERWENTWATER is situated close to the particularly pretty and much visited valley of **Borrowdale** with its ancient fort CASTLE CRAG, and within easy access from another of the centres for a walking holiday, **Keswick**. Near Keswick there is an enigmatic ring of 48 standing stones, known as the CASTLERIGG CIRCLE, measuring 100 feet in diameter. Larger still is the stone circle LONG MEG AND HER DAUGHTERS near **Little Salkeld**.

Eskdale is one of the few lakeless valleys, noted for its magnificent waterfalls and its cliff railway and for the spectacular views from the Roman fort at HARDKNOTT PASS.

Many poets have been associated with the Lake District, undoubtedly the most famous being William Wordsworth. Born at **Cockermouth**, he later lived at **Grasmere** and **Rydal**, and is much in evidence around the area, but generally in an informative rather than tacky manner. John Ruskin is another famous name, having lived at Brantwood near **Coniston** for 30 years. The museum here is now dedicated to him and includes many of his artefacts.

Eller Close Vegetarian Guest House at Grasmere

Beatrix Potter's 17th century HILL TOP FARM at **Sawrey** attracts huge numbers of visitors each year.

Sadly much fox hunting and beagling goes on in this county, not seen by summer tourists, but very evident to visitors who choose to escape here in the winter months. There is a tradition of Hound Trails which use a drag rather than a live animal to chase, but this is the least popular of the 'sports'.

Today's Cumbria consists of areas which from time to time have belonged to Scotland, and both Runic and Celtic names show that the ancestry of the area is closely linked with its northern neighbours. In addition to HADRIAN'S WALL there is significant evidence of Roman occupation here. **Penrith**'s ruined castle can testify to some of the later border skirmishes, as can that at **Carlisle**.

But not all of Cumbria is either the Lake District or the nothern lands, and along the flat coast are some lovely towns and villages, with much more pleasant weather, and a great contrast to the drama that is just a short way inland.

Way out into the Irish Sea the 227 square miles of the **Isle of Man** is a law unto itself, literally, an independent kingdom with its own taxation system and currency and its own government. Today the Isle of Man is known primarily as the venue for the TT races and as a holiday destination, and indeed it has plenty to interest the visitor, with a lot of history and with sunny beaches. From the top of the highest mountain, SNAEFELL, there is a view not only of the whole of the island but also, on a clear day, of England, of Scotland and of Wales.

Hotel & Restaurant

ROTHAY MANOR

Rothay Bridge, Ambleside, Cumbria, LA22 OEH.
Telephone: (05394) 33605, Facsimile: (05394) 33607

A VISITOR summed up the character of Rothay Manor -"In theory you should be just like other hotels with high standards. But you're not. You must be doing something different though I can't put my finger on it. I just like it here". A valid statement. There is just that intangible something that makes this 18 bedroom hotel a most pleasurable experience. The rooms are beautifully and individually appointed and have every modern comfort. Three luxury suites are available in the grounds and the Wansfell Suite is ideal for a honeymoon or other special occasion with its canopied double bed and bathroom with double bath. The Loughrigg and Cottage Suites are spacious enough to comfortably house a family group and the Loughrigg Suite has been adapted for disabled guests.

It is not just the accommodation. There are 'Mini Breaks' in the winter. A wonderful traditional four day house party at Christmas. The 'Classics' on Sundays allow you to combine a Sunday Lunch at the Manor with a concert at the Grizedale Theatre. In the restaurant there are special dinners with anything from a Southern Italian Dinner to a Dickens Christmas Dinner or a Brittany Dinner. There are special holidays for those with an interest in a variety of subjects including gardening and music, silver & antiques and the Lake District in Water Colour. Whatever might be your choice it will be a wonderful experience. Add to that superb food from a menu which has a wide choice of vegetarian starters, desserts and a separate vegetarian menu for the main course, together with a wine list that has no less than 150 bins, some of which are organic, not a lot more needs to be said. Rothay Manor deserves a visit.

Useful Information

OPEN: 10.30am-9pm. Closed Jan and first two weeks in Feb
CREDIT CARDS: Amex/ Diners/Visa/Mastercard
CHILDREN: Welcome
LICENSED: Yes
ON THE MENU: Wide choice. Excellent vegetarian fare
DISABLED ACCESS: Yes. Special bedroom adapted
GARDEN: 1 acre. Free use of nearby leisure centre
ACCOMMODATION: 18 bedrooms, all en-suite

Inn & Restaurant

THE ROYAL OAK INN

Bongate, Appleby-In-Westmoorland, Cumbria, CA16 6UN.
Telephone: (07683) 51463, Facsimile: (07683) 52300

VERY old buildings have a special aura and sometimes age does not lend enchantment but this cannot be said of The Royal Oak at Bongate which has gradually been extended since 1200. The newest part is of the 17th century. It has everything one would expect from such a fine establishment. Its years have given it a very special atmosphere and the skill of the owners, Colin and Hilary Cheyne, has ensured that any refurbishment merely enhances and does not take away character. This is particularly noticeable in the charming bedrooms which have been skilfully altered to allow en-suite facilities to be included as well as many other modern attributes like television and a hostess tray.

The inn has a friendly tap room and a snug as well as a lounge and restaurant. There is a private sitting room for residents and a non-smoking dining room for those who prefer it. The wide ranging menu provides dishes to suit everyone and Hilary Cheyne, who is the chef, spends a great deal of time and care making sure that suitable vegetarian dishes, across the board, are available daily. She is a gifted chef and thoroughly enjoys the challenge of making tasty, unusual food for vegetarians. Great care is taken in choosing the ingredients for all the food at the Royal Oak and 'organic' is specified wherever possible.

The Royal Oak is known for its good house wines, of which there are many, as well as for the selection of malt whiskies - over 50 of them! The wines come from around the world and there is usually an organic wine as well as country wines. During the winter they serve a delicious mulled wine.

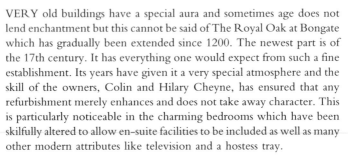

Useful Information

OPEN: Food: weekdays: 12-2pm & 6.30-9pm, Sun: 12-2pm & 7-9pm

CREDIT CARDS: Amex/ Diners/Mastercard/Visa

CHILDREN: Welcome

LICENSED: Yes

ON THE MENU: Dishes from around the world. Not exclusively vegetarian

DISABLED ACCESS: Yes. No special WC, assistance available

GARDEN: Terrace at front of hotel

ACCOMMODATION: 4 dbl, 2 twn, 1 finly, all en-suite. 2 sgls with private facilities

Inn with Rooms

THE DRUNKEN DUCK

Barngates, Ambleside, Cumbria, LA22 0NG.
Telephone: (05394) 36347

YOU may not find The Drunken Duck Inn easy to find so before we go any further let us address that minor problem, for this is somewhere you must not miss. There are dozens of delightful ways to approach the 'Duck'. We will concern ourselves with one of the most direct: Leave the M6 at Exit 36. You are now well within a hours pleasurable drive. Take the A590 towards Newby Bridge and Barrow. Just after Newby Services prepare for rather spiteful corners immediately after which you turn right onto the A592. It is a beautiful scenic drive up the eastern shore of Windermere to the head of the Lake. The road forks at the Waterhead Hotel. Bear left (A593) the lake cruiser pier on your left, past Galava Roman Fort. Left over the Rothay Bridge. In half a mile, at Clappersgate, turn left. A mile through heavily wooded country then take the first obvious, right fork. Less than a mile and you have arrived.

For 400 years The Drunken Duck has cared for travellers - that's a lot of practice. It is a mellow place and the good news is that it is as keen to care for vegetarians as it is for those who prefer other foods - the latter are rapidly growing to love some of the delicious vegetarian dishes available. There is a blackboard menu which has vegetarian options offering dishes that have been perfected over the last 10 years. There are three starters, 15 main courses and eight desserts on offer on this extensive menu. Try the celery, stilton and walnut pasta or the fennel, orange and butterbean bake and you will realise what a treat The Drunken Duck is for vegetarians - or for anybody else for that matter. Stay in the inn where you will be accommodated in one of their well appointed, en-suite rooms and spoilt with a splendid breakfast each morning.

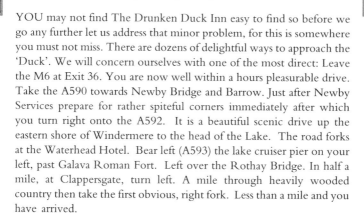

Useful Information

OPEN: 11.30-3pm & 6-11pm
CREDIT CARDS: Visa/Access/Mastercard/Switch
CHILDREN: Welcome
LICENSED: Full licence

ON THE MENU: Wide choice especially for vegetarians
DISABLED ACCESS: Yes
GARDEN: 60 acres. Walking land, own fishing tarn
ACCOMMODATION: 10 en-suite rooms. 2 day stay. Nov-March, Sun-Thurs only

Restaurant

QUINCE & MEDLAR

13 Castlegate, Cockermouth, Cumbria, CA13 9EU.
Telephone: (0900) 823579

RIGHT next to Cockermouth Castle, Quince and Medlar is housed in a tall, elegant and carefully restored georgian building which retains many of its original features. It is run under the caring and capable hands of the owners, Colin and Louisa Le Voi, with Colin creating the super food and Louisa there to welcome you and make sure you have everything you need. The pretty restaurant is candlelit and intimate, with three rooms, one of which is a sitting room where you can relax and enjoy coffee & home-made chocolates after your meal. Wood panelling in the dining room takes one back in time to georgian days and the presence of fresh flowers everywhere brings an awareness of ongoing life

Everyone who comes here enjoys the relaxed atmosphere which is enhanced by the gentle classical music in the background. Children under seven years are not permitted and it is a restaurant where people dress smartly in honour of the meal they know they are going to relish. There is a firm no-smoking rule in the dining room, no-one will rush you over your meal and you will be waited on by people who obviously enjoy what they are doing.

The restaurant is totally vegetarian with vegan options. Everything is home-made including the bread and you will find many of the dishes are original. The wine list includes wines from around the world and of the 37 bins on offer, four are vegetarian, five organic and elderflower with silver birch is the Country wine. In summer Quince and Medlar stock an interesting range of German fruit nectars. This is a restaurant that has been a consistent award winner since 1988 when the Le Voi's acquired the business.

Useful Information

OPEN: Evenings only from 7pm Tues - Sun in Summer, Tues-Sat in Winter. Closed two weeks in Nov and three weeks in Jan/Feb
CREDIT CARDS: Access/Visa
CHILDREN: Not under seven
LICENSED: Restaurant

ON THE MENU: Totally vegetarian with vegan options. Interesting and original dishes. Everything home-baked including bread
DISABLED ACCESS: No
GARDEN: No
ACCOMMODATION: Not applicable

Hotel/Guest House

ELLER CLOSE HOUSE

Grasmere, Cumbria, LA22 9RW.
Telephone: (05394) 35786

THIS charming Victorian house nestles between steep sided fells just above Grasmere with commanding views over the Vale to Silver Howe and Helm Crag. It is just a few minutes walk from Grasmere itself and there are many walks one can take straight from the front door. Eller Close House, which is strictly vegetarian with vegan options, also has a self contained garden cottage flat available for weekly lets or short breaks at a very reasonable price.

The accommodation comprises of two en-suite double rooms, one twin and one family as well as another family room which is not en-suite. All the rooms are attractively furnished with a Victorian style decor and making the very best use of pretty Laura Ashley designs. Each room has television and a generously filled tea and coffee making tray. The charge, as we write in November 1993, starts as low as £13.50 per night for bed and a splendid breakfast. There are special winter bargain breaks for three, five and seven nights. The secluded garden with mature trees, lawns and a mountain stream, has wonderful views of the Vale of Grasmere. Here you can relax and do nothing, or play croquet. Eller Close House caters mainly for bed and breakfast but the occasional evening meals can be arranged. One of the bonuses in staying here is being able to take advantage of the excellent packed lunches. Breakfasts include juice, fresh Swiss muesli, cereals and a delicious cooked selection. The entire house is strictly non-smoking.

It is run by the welcoming, resident owners Nick and Pauline Greathead who never seem to be phased by any request. An excellent choice for any vegetarian - or for anyone in fact.

Useful Information

OPEN: All year
CREDIT CARDS: None taken
CHILDREN: Welcome
LICENSED: Not licenced

ON THE MENU: 1st class vegetarian breakfast. Evening meals on request
DISABLED ACCESS: No
GARDEN: Croquet lawn, Secluded with mature trees and lawns. Mountain stream
ACCOMMODATION: 2 dbls, 1 twn,1 fmly en-suite. 1 fmly not en-suite + Self catering cottage

Hotel & Restaurant

LANCRIGG VEGETARIAN COUNTRY HOUSE HOTEL

Easedale, Grasmere, Cumbria, LA22 9QN.
Telephone: (05394) 35317, Facsimile: (05394) 35058

THIS house which is about 150 years old has had admirers almost since the first stone was laid. It is a house of timeless charm in the serenity of Easedale. There is a total absence of traffic and the peace is broken only by the sound of waterfalls and birdsong. There are acres of private, rare woodland, with paths and streams. It is no wonder that Wordsworth, Tennyson and Coleridge were frequent visitors. It was in Lancrigg Woods that Wordsworth wrote 'The Prelude' and other poems. The famous explorer Sir John Booth-Richardson also lived there. For the last 10 years Lancrigg has gained a reputation as probably the finest vegetarian country house Hotel for hundreds of miles, if not in the British Isles. Individual descriptions are really necessary to describe the bedrooms as no two rooms are the same. Because of the rambling and unusual character of the house which blends a cottage style with that of a country house, some rooms lend themselves to luxurious en-suite accommodation with four poster beds, whirlpool baths and antique furniture. There are three ground floor rooms. All the luxury country house rooms are en-suite. They tend to be the most spacious and peaceful rooms and have individual characteristics and all are named. The en-suite and cottage rooms all have colour television and tea making facilities. The cottage rooms have washbasins. They tend to have a cosy feel enhanced by their individual decor.

The fare is the best of wholefood home-cooking using a wide range of the best fresh and natural ingredients, organic where possible and always free of artificial additives. The cheeses are vegetarian. The evening menu changes daily. All the bread, croissants and cakes are made from organic, stone-ground flour, milled by waterpower. The extensive organic wine cellar is accompanied by unusual beers, aperitifs, brandies and fruit liquors, all organic. Meals are served in the elegant chandelier lit dining room which has superb views across the valley. Lancrigg is a sheer delight.

Useful Information

OPEN: All year, all day, all night
CREDIT CARDS: All major credit cards
CHILDREN: Welcome
LICENSED: Yes
ON THE MENU: The best vegetarian wholefood home-cooking
DISABLED ACCESS: Yes. No special toilets
GARDEN: Acres of beautiful woodland, paths and streams
ACCOMMODATION: 11 dbl, 1 sgl, 2 twn, 2 fmly en-suite, 2 dbl, 1 sgl

Restaurant & Tea Gardens

THE ROWAN TREE

Church Bridge, Grasmere, Cumbria, LA22 9SN.
Telephone: (05394) 35528

BEFORE the present bridge was built over the river Rothay in Grasmere, intrepid travellers to the scenic lake district were required to dismount from their coach and horses to negotiate the ford by St Oswalds Church. At that time an enterprising local woman served them with warm beverages. This continued over the years and by the late 19th century a tea garden was to be found on the site where Victorian visitors were able to sit outside, by the river, and enjoy fine views of the surrounding fells. Food has been served here ever since and the new Rowan Tree now continues this tradition. Since 1989 imaginative and wholesome food and drink have been provided by the Rowan Tree, a small restaurant in the back lanes of Grasmere. Now relocated to this prominent and historic position the aim is to extend the range of good food and drink, served from convivial surroundings in this beautiful corner of England.

This gives you the background of this enchanting haunt which serves exclusively vegetarian food with vegan options and most other special diets if notice is given. No food is bought in ready made and you may have complete faith in every ingredient keeping to the letter of the law of vegetarian eating. Gillian and Barry Calveley have owned the Rowan Tree for five years but have only been in residence in this new and delightful site for less than a year. They have carried their high standards with them and their reputation is second to none. The non-smoking ruling is firmly adhered to both in the restaurant and tea gardens.

For those who enjoy a glass of wine there are 21 choices from six different countries. All are both vegetarian and organic with Rock's elderflower and green gooseberry included. The average cost of a bottle of wine is approximately £8. The Rowan Tree opens daily at 10am and, with a break of one hour between 5pm-6pm, carries on until 9pm. You will find the menu imaginative and covers everything from an all day breakfast to delicious home-made cakes and a special Children's Menu.

Useful Information

OPEN: 10-5pm & 6-9pm 7 days. Closed Christmas , Boxing, New Years Eve and New Year Day
CREDIT CARDS: Visa/ Mastercard
CHILDREN: Welcome. Special menu on request
LICENSED: Yes
ON THE MENU: Exclusively vegetarian with vegan options
DISABLED ACCESS: Yes. Suitable toilets
GARDEN: Patio & Tea Garden
ACCOMMODATION: Not applicable

Hotel & Restaurant

LUPTON TOWER VEGETARIAN COUNTRY HOUSE HOTEL

Lupton, Nr Kirkby, Lonsdale, Via Carnforth, Lancashire, LA6 2PR.
Telephone: (05395) 67400

THIS, very special, delightful 18th century country house lies just two miles from Junction 36 of the M6, towards Kirkby Lonsdale and Skipton on the A65. It is a house of charm, with a gentle faded elegance that makes one believe that one is in a country house rather than a hotel, although every quality of a modern day establishment is there for your use. It serves two main purposes, the first as a hotel with seven beautifully furnished rooms, five of which are en-suite; somewhere where one can stay in a relaxed, contented atmosphere. Every room is equipped with that great boon, a hostess tray for making tea and coffee. It should be pointed out that because of the age of the building there is no access for wheelchairs. The second, and possibly more important purpose, is the excellence of the vegetarian restaurant, which is open to non-residents. Light classical music plays softly in the background, the decor and furnishing is elegant, the linen immaculate, the gentle light of candles illuminates each table and brings sparkle to the fine glasses. It was voted Vegetarian Restaurant of the Year in 1992.

A set five course dinner is served each evening. The dishes are varied and imaginative. Fresh, and wherever possible, organic produce is used to create delicious meals. One of the specialities of this restaurant is the super, home-made organic breads which are both light and delicious. No substitutes are used, no food is bought in ready-made and everyone will find great satisfaction in the meals that are served. The very extensive wine list from Europe and the New World includes four organic and vegetarian wines as well as 10 country wines which include most of the Rocks Country Wine range. The House Wines are French and the average cost of a bottle of wine is £13.00.

Useful Information

OPEN: All year except two weeks in January.
CREDIT CARDS: Welcome
CHILDREN: Access/Visa/Mastercard/Eurocard
LICENSED: Fine wines at sensible prices
ON THE MENU: Imaginative & varied using fresh and where possible, organic produce
DISABLED ACCESS: Not for wheelchairs
GARDEN: Three acres, eating, swings, walks
ACCOMMODATION: 3 dbl, 1 twn, 1 fmly, en-suite, and 1 dbl, 1 twn, H&C

Hotel

THE DERWENTWATER HOTEL

Portinscale, Keswick, Cumbria, CA12 5RE.
Telephone: (07687) 72538, Facsimile: (07687) 71002

THERE are some places that one visits which will always stay in your memory for the very best of reasons and The Derwentwater Hotel is just such a place. It has a wonderful situation, set in 16 acres of naturally beautiful grounds, right on the lakeshore of Derwentwater. It is not enough however just to have a good position. There are many more ingredients that are needed for a hotel to be completely successful. Here you will find attractively appointed bedrooms, all en-suite, and equipped with colour television, trouser press, hairdryer, direct dial telephone and a generously laid out beverage tray. At certain times of the year there are very good value special breaks which are worth enquiring about. In the grounds you will find croquet and a well manicured nine hole putting green. It is a hotel that has earned many accolades including those from Ashley Courtney and the English and Cumbria Tourist Board.

During the day, bar snacks are available as well as lunches and in the evening it is a great pleasure to dine on food that is prepared and cooked by chefs who obviously care deeply about their profession. Whilst carnivores have the lion's share of the menu, vegetarians can count on there always being at least three snacks, one or two starters, five main courses and three desserts from which to choose. The menu is decidedly International and changes constantly. The emphasis is on freshly cooked food using local produce whenever possible. Very little is bought in other than petit fours and a very small percentage of desserts. You are asked to dress in a smart but casual manner at lunchtime and a slightly more formal approach at night when dining. There is no smoking permitted in the dining room before 8.30pm - a great blessing.

Useful Information

OPEN: All year 7.30am-10.30pm
CREDIT CARDS: All major cards
CHILDREN: Welcome
LICENSED: Yes
ON THE MENU: Good choice for vegetarians from an International menu
DISABLED ACCESS: Yes but no special facilities
GARDEN: 16 acres grounds on the shoreside
ACCOMMODATION: 31 dbl, 6 sgl, 30 twn, 3 fmly. All en-suite

Restaurant

GIANTS CAUSEWAY RESTAURANT

Bushmills, Antrim, Northern Ireland, BT57 8SU.
Telephone: (02657) 31582

THE unique volcanic columns which were formed 55 million years ago bring thousands of visitors to The Giants Causeway to enjoy its majesty and the scenic coastline which provides not only superb views but wonderful walks. The Giants Causeway is in the hands of the National Trust who have developed good walkways and access to the pathways.

Walking and sightseeing is guaranteed to produce a thirst and an appetite. With that in mind some ten years ago the National Trust created a very pleasant restaurant which looks out over the Causeway. It is light and airy and seats 90 people with ease. A lot of thought has been given to the sort of people who wish to visit The Giants Causeway. None more so than the easy access for wheelchairs and the specially adapted toilets for the disabled. The Restaurant which is self service is open from March to October every day from 10.30am-6pm.

Snacks and light meals are available at all times. The menu consists of good traditional home-made fare. If you are a lover of good soup try the pea soup which with fresh bread becomes a meal in itself. There are jacket potatoes with a whole variety of fillings, generously filled sandwiches using white or wholemeal bread, some mouthwatering vegetarian quiches, a wide selection of salads, and for those with a sweet tooth, the choice of scones, tray bakes and sweets will be a welcoming sight. The restaurant, which is not licensed, is a member of 'The Taste of Ulster', a scheme run by the Northern Ireland Tourist Board, promoting the use of fresh Ulster produce.

Useful Information

OPEN: March to Ocotber daily 10.30am-6pm. Closed November to February
CREDIT CARDS: Visa/ Access
CHILDREN: Welcome
LICENSED: No
ON THE MENU: Home-cooked snacks & meals, with vegetarian options
DISABLED ACCESS: Yes for wheelchairs & with WC
GARDEN: No, picnic site
ACCOMMODATION: No

Country House Hotel with Restaurant

NANNY BROW COUNTRY HOUSE HOTEL & RESTAURANT

Clappersgate, Ambleside, Cumbria, LA22 9NF.
Telephone: (05394) 32036, Facsimile: (05394) 32450

THIS beautiful country house was designed and built in 1908 by a London architect for his own use. It remained a family home, with only one change of ownership until 1952 when it began its tasteful conversion to the elegant hotel it is now.

One soon becomes accustomed to the comfort and contentment of gracious country house life. The relaxed atmosphere is wonderful. A garden room bar and an intimate, non-smoking dining room in which vegetarians can choose from an international menu completes the picture.

Much loving care and attention has gone into creating pretty, chintzy bedrooms and four poster suites. The five acres of peaceful gardens and woodlands are not only pleasant to stroll in but also have spectacular views across the beautiful Brathay Valley towards Wetherlam, Wrynose Pass and the famous Langdale Pikes.

Useful Information

OPEN: All year round
CREDIT CARDS: All major cards
ON THE MENU: At least 60% of the dishes at every course are suitable for vegetarians
DISABLED ACCESS: Yes + suitable toilets

Bistro

THE MOON

129 Highgate, Kendal, Cumbria, LA9 4EN.
Telephone: (0539) 729254

IT would be very trite to say that people are 'Over the Moon' when they have eaten at this charming, informal bistro, but it is a very fair description. Val Macconnell, the chef proprietor, has that intangible something that makes both herself and The Moon special.

The blackboard menu makes good reading with individual, imaginative and original bistro dishes on offer. The vegetarian side of the menu is most creative and is always changing. Imagine fennel, rice, mozzarella and sweetcorn cabbage dolmas served on lemon and raisin cous cous with tomato, garlic and allspice sauce. Everything is made by Val and nothing is bought in. The Moon's wine list, which is small but well chosen, has two vegetarian wines, two organic and elderflower country wine. The Moon has published two successful cook books and has a monthly 'pudding club' with a great following, and is one of Britain's top ten in the Vegetarian Good Food Guide, It deserves its accolades.

Useful Information

OPEN: Every eve, Sun-Thur: 6-9.30pm. Fri & Sat: 6-10pm. Summer open half an hour later. Closed last two weeks in Jan and first two weeks in Feb
CREDIT CARDS: Visa/Access
ON THE MENU: Imaginative, high standard
DISABLED ACCESS: Yes. No special toilets

Restaurant

ORCHARD HOUSE

Borrowdale Road, Keswick, Cumbria, CA12 5DE.
Telephone: (07687) 72830

HERE we have a charming, part Victorian, part 18th century house offering great comfort and spectacular views. It is in Keswick but away from the melee and just a short stroll from the town and a short walk to the lake. There are nine rooms in all, some with sloping ceilings, curious corners and lots of character. Both residents and non-residents are invited to settle down for an unusual and enjoyable meal in the dining room that overlooks a pretty garden. The food is all home-cooked and wholly vegetarian, the ingredients: fresh, wholesome and in season, locally grown, organic fruit and vegetables.

The daily-changing four course set menus are a blend of the familiar and the unusual, for example Grilled Goats' Cheese Salad, Celeriac Soup, Bulgar Wheat & Nut Rings with Leek, Fennel and Red Pepper Filling, or a fresh Lemon Tart, To complement the food, a wine list that consists exclusively of organic wines and organic beers too.

Useful Information

OPEN: All Year
CREDIT CARDS: None taken
ON THE MENU: Wholly vegetarian, familiar and unusual. Dining room open to non-residents
DISABLED ACCESS: No

Guest House

BEECHMOUNT

Near Sawrey, Hawkshead, Ambleside, Cumbria, LA22 0JZ.
Telephone: (05394) 36356

TWO miles from Hawkshead on the road leading to Lake Windermere car ferry is the large, spacious and delightful Beechmount Guest House, with wonderful views over Lake Esthwaite to the Langdales in the distance. The village of Near Sawrey is where Beatrix Potter lived and wrote her books in the house known as 'Hilltop'.

Open all the year round Beechmount caters predominantly for vegetarians but does permit carnivores for whom they also cater extremely well. This is a small, comfortable, easy going establishment where you will sleep in comfortable beds and come down in the morning to a sumptuous, wholefood breakfast. Richard Siddall the owner, and his wife Sylvia, are vegetarian and vegan respectively and so you may be certain of good food. They make their own, delicious mushroom and lentil burgers which are part of the main course at breakfast. You will find Beechmount an excellent place in which to stay for a break or for a Cumbrian holiday.

Useful Information

OPEN: All year
CREDIT CARDS: None taken
ON THE MENU: Good wholefood
DISABLED ACCESS: No

Restaurant

WOODY'S VEGETARIAN RESTAURANT

5 King Street, Delph, Oldham, Lancashire, OL3 5DL.
Telephone: (0457) 871197, Facsimile: (0457) 820862

WHEN a restaurant has the accolade of being a 'Vegetarian Restaurant of the Year' finalist every year, it has reached an enviable standard and not only for its food but for the ambience and the hospitality. Woody's has style, its tables are beautifully appointed in the classical manner including shimmering cut glasses. Here you can be assured of a wonderful meal in a restaurant which is set in Delph, a conservation area Pennine village.

Music of the right sort always aids the digestion and whilst every evening the gentle sound of classical music provides a backdrop on some evenings this is enhanced by the presence of a gifted classical guitarist. The imaginative menu offers a choice of 10 or 12 starters, main courses and desserts as well as Blackboard Specials. It would be virtually impossible not to find a dish to relish. The wine list includes wines from around the world all of which are organic and most vegetarian. Mike and Liz Wood are your talented hosts.

Useful Information

OPEN: Tues-Sun: 7.30-11pm (last bookings 9.30pm)
CREDIT CARDS: Access/Visa
ON THE MENU: First class choice of imaginative dishes at all courses
DISABLED ACCESS: Yes, but no special toilets

Also from
Griffin Publishing Ltd

an invitation to
THE CATHEDRAL CITIES
of Southern England

" an unusual insight into the life of each Cathedral and City and some interesting places within easy reach "

" written by people with a love of Cathedrals and their Cities "

* 352 pages, hundreds of beautiful illustrations
* Available at most good book shops or directly from Griffin Publishing, 24-26 George Place, Stonehouse, Plymouth, PL1 3NY.
* Priced at £9.95 + £1.95 p&p

The Market Place at Thirsk

Contents

THE NORTH EAST COUNTIES

Yorkshire, Cleveland, North Humberside, Durham, Tyne & Wear and Northumberland

Suggested Venues to Dine

Nuteree

A version of kedgeree. A simple dish (but not quick if you count the time for cooking the rice), suitable either for a light lunch or supper, or more particularly for breakfast. Serve hot on toast or with crusty bread, and accompany with something like sage and apple jelly.

Serves 4

8 oz	Rice (white or wholegrain)
2	Rosehip Teabags
½ tsp	Turmeric
1 lb	Mixed Nuts
1 Tbs	Sage
1 Tbs	Olive Oil
	Water

Using the amount of water required to cook the rice (quantity depends on the cooking method used), pour boiling water onto the teabags and turmeric and leave to stand for 5 minutes. Use the tea to cook the rice.

Chop the nuts so that some of them are well ground, some in large pieces and a few still whole. Into the rice mix the nuts, sage and olive oil and just enough water to allow the whole thing to cook through without sticking and hold lightly together. Top with fresh herbs for serving.

THE NORTH EAST COUNTIES

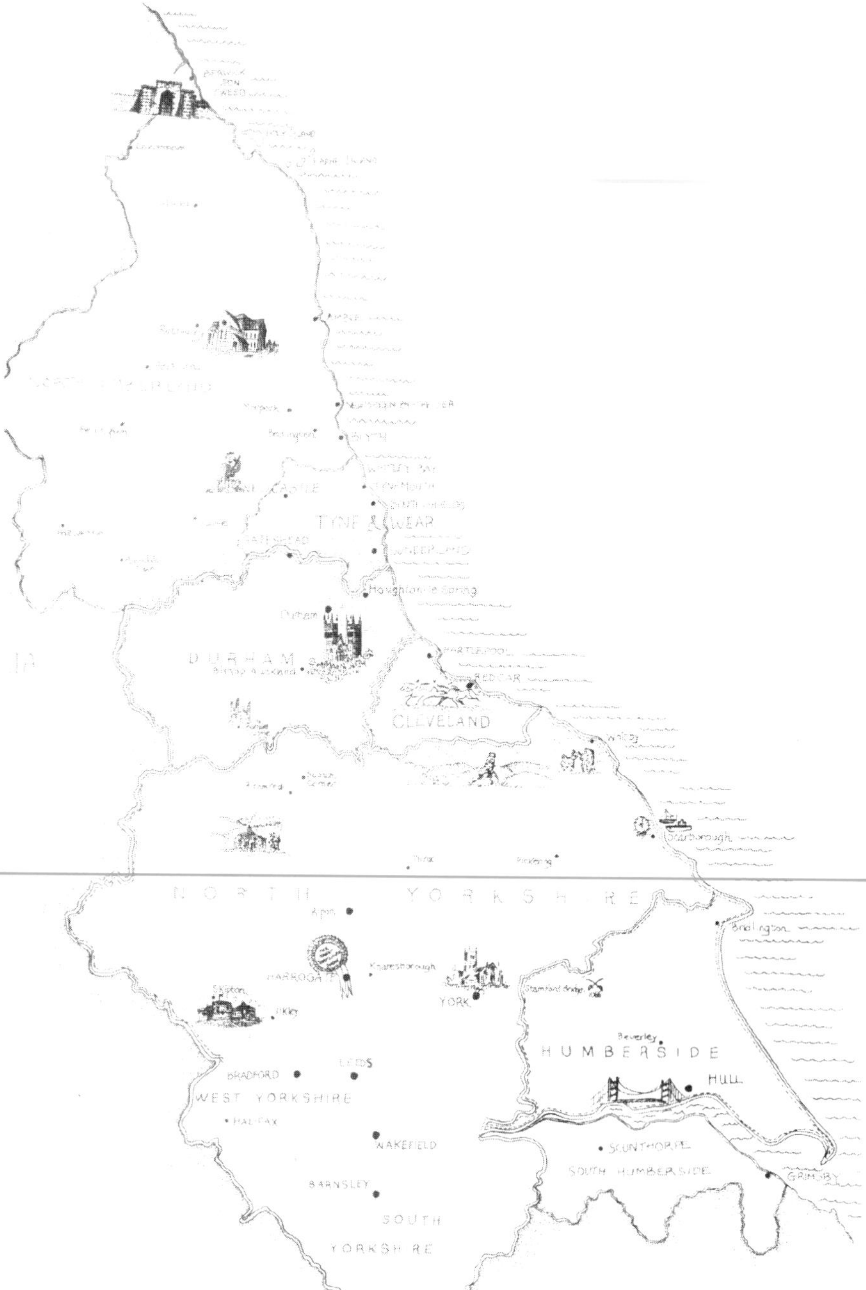

THE NORTH EAST COUNTIES

Yorkshire, Cleveland, North Humberside, Durham, Tyne & Wear, and Northumberland

From the high, sometimes desolate, ground of the moorlands to the wide sweeps of the east coast, from the mellow cottages clustered in small villages to the heavy industry in densely populated conurbations, this region is one of great diversity. The newer industrial areas cannot be described as being in any way attractive and some of the areas are blighted by coalfield scars, yet many of the earlier mill sitings have a unique picturesque quality. A large portion of the region is designated either as National Park or as an 'Area of Outstanding Natural Beauty'. The area's beauty is a very powerful one.

Some of the roughest of the landscape is to be found high on the PENNINE CHAIN, the backbone of England, consisting of hard dark rock that can give a bleakness all its own.

The 256 mile PENNINE WAY, which for much of its distance more or less marks the western boundary of the region, is obviously a favourite with walkers. So much so that it has suffered much from erosion. From the CHEVIOT HILLS and the NORTHUMBERLAND NATIONAL PARK the Way crosses the NORTH PENNINES to the YORKSHIRE DALES with their seemingly never-ending stretches of bracken and rough long grass only interspersed in the autumn with beautiful purple heather, through the CALDER VALLEY where it joins the 50 mile circular CALDERDALE WAY around Brontë country near HARDCASTLE CRAGS VALLEY with its many splendid walks, to the PEAK DISTRICT NATIONAL PARK.

Sadly it is not just the erosion from billions of walking boots that is causing damage here, industrial pollution having already stripped many hill sides.

This area has generally suffered its fair share of invasions and rebellions. It is recorded in the Domesday Book, that land values fell drastically after the Norman Conquest, the North having rebelled against William and much property having been destroyed. The Normans built castles here, ruins of which remain including those at **Pontefract** and **Conisbrough**.

Many say that Yorkshire is still fighting Lancashire in the 'Wars of the Roses', a fierce exchange which took place more than five hundred years ago.

Animals are legally classified as a commodity or chattel, no different from a plastic duck, a porcelain hen or a wooden rocking horse.

In the Civil War of the 17th century the West Ridings of Yorkshire were split, the west for Parliament - the east for the King. In the 18th century the West Ridings were split again, not this time by politics but by religion: John Wesley frequently preached in the western part of the county, which has remained largely nonconformist with numerous small chapels.

When the industrial revolution came, textile operatives took to the streets in revolt, there were riots and even murders, some of the 'Luddites' being tried and hung at YORK CASTLE having been betrayed by one of their own. Close to **Huddersfield** is the TOLSTON MEMORIAL MUSEUM at RAVENSKNOWLE HALL which has an exhibition of looms as well as relics from the Luddite riots.

The many castles, the great abbeys and old parish churches, the fine houses of the nobility and the pretty cottages, and scores of early mill buildings present a wealth of fine architecture. Of special interest are the yeoman clothiers' houses of the 17th century, and the old weavers' cottages, with their long row of windows in the second storey, many of which are still to be found in the hills around **Halifax** and Huddersfield. There are several museums created from erstwhile cottages and mills, showing all the processes of spinning, dyeing, weaving and manufacture involved in making this an important area in the cloth and clothing industry. THE COLOUR MUSEUM at **Bradford** is an award winning display on the subject of light, colour dyeing and textile printing, incorporating some of the latest computer technology. The town's pre-eminence in the wool trade is also detailed in the museum of BRADFORD'S YORKSHIRE.

Due to the abundant iron ore, to coal for power, and to water, the area in the south of this region gained great importance in the steel industry, which also gave rise, more than 600 years ago, to **Sheffield**'s pre-eminence as a manufacturer of cutlery, as shown in the town's INDUSTRIAL MUSEUM.

Industrial success means that the counties of West and South Yorkshire are now heavily populated, with large towns that merge on their fringes, yet moorland does remain on the doorstep of the towns and the grazing of sheep continues, even though the pastures are scant. Here is the town of **Ilkley,** once a spa, best known as a starting point for walks over Ilkley Moor. To the north **Grassington** is a useful centre for exploring WHARFEDALE and should not be missed.

Haworth, a little to the south is an old weaving village that is today a literary shrine to the Brontës. The BRONTË MUSEUM in their home, The Parsonage, contains many artefacts of the Brontë sisters, and even the sofa that Emily died on. At the back a path leads to the moor and the BRONTË FALLS. The steam WORTH VALLEY RAILWAY makes a stop at Haworth.

Holmfirth south of Huddersfield has been made famous by the television series 'Last of the Summer Wine'.

In the centre of **Barnsley** is the 40 acre LOCKE PARK, named after Josepth Locke, at one time an apprentice railway builder to George Stephenson. South of Barnsley the WORSBROUGH MILL MUSEUM has two working corn mills, one 17th century, the other 19th century.

In the west the county of North Yorkshire starts just as the industrial heartland reaches out to the Yorkshire Dales. It is the largest English county, and also has within its boundaries the NORTH YORK MOORS

The scenery of the YORKSHIRE DALES is spectacular; powerful, fast rivers run down the main dales, Swaledale, Wensleydale and Wharfedale, cleaving the Pennines, which rise to over 2,000 feet. Near **Hawes**,

HARDRAW FORCE is the highest single drop waterfall in the country, but this is just one of many spectacular waterfalls in the area.

The south west of the Dales is a potholers paradise, the main centre for which is **Ingleton** below Ingleborough Hill. There is a veritable maze of caves, and being a limestone area this gives rise to magnificent stalactites and stalagmites. The WHITE STAR CAVES which were discovered in 1923 have splendid rock chambers, and there is also GAPING GHYLL HOLE, the largest in Britain.

North York Moors National Park

Clapham and **Craven** too are important centres for potholing, as well as walking and climbing.

MALHAM TARN at **Settle** has a delightful waterfall at JANET'S FOSS, there are also over 90 acres of beautiful countryside below MALHAM COVE. This area and the wetlands surrounding it are of international importance and were designated a National Nature Reserve in 1992. It was at TARN HOUSE, now a field centre, that Charles Kingsley wrote 'The Water Babies'.

Apart from its 'inconvenient' holes, one of the main reasons this area has remained unspoiled is that the water is hard, having come through limestone, which has been a discouragement to industries such as textiles. This has kept the Dales green and sparsely populated. The flora and fauna are similar to many other counties, but with the purple heathers, bilberries and white bolled cotton grass, and in the wilder parts the melancholy cry of the curlew, the acrobatic peewit and the lamenting grouse can make the Dales a mystical, magical and mournful place.

The NORTH YORK MOORS are also limestone. It has been quarried for local buildings, giving them a warm mellow glow, also, as clay is to be found, roof tiles and bricks have been made locally. The houses, churches, abbeys and other buildings constructed of limestone with mellow red pantile roofs are a pleasure to behold. Surrounded by miles of heather and parklands, these are some of the most delightful villages in England.

10 acres of land (that's about 5 football pitches) will support: 61 people on a diet of soya beans, 24 people on a diet of wheat, 10 people on a diet of maize or 2 people on a diet of cattle meat.

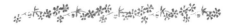

Pickering in North Yorkshire is a market town and tourist centre for the North York Moors and PICKERING VALE. Some beautiful 15th century murals were discovered under a coat of whitewash in the nave of the church here. The NORTH YORKSHIRE MOORS RAILWAY begins here and travels 18 scenic miles over the Moors to **Grosmont**, using both steam and diesel locomotives. It was reopened in 1973 as a private venture after the line had been closed by British Rail eight years earlier.

The Pickering Vale reaches the east coast at the elegant town of **Scarborough** and just to the south **Filey** has a mile long reef which, when the tide is out, is an excellent place to investigate the hundreds of rock pools.

Robin Hood's Bay halfway down the coast of the Moor is a Mecca for artists with its picturesque, narrow streets and tightly packed houses right down to the water, where one would expect to find smugglers around every corner.

The village of **Hutton-le-Hole** is most attractive, with a stream and village green. This is again an area of potholes, and here too is the RYEDALE FOLK MUSEUM set in 18th century farm buildings where they have reconstructed cruck cottages to illustrate country living with its crafts, working practices and superstitions.

At the edge of the village of **Brandsby** which is on the edge of the **Howardian Hills** to the south of the North York Moors is a turf maze called the CITY OF TROY.

At **Ilton**, on MASHEM MOOR west of **Ripon**, there is a convincing imitation of ancient stone circles such as Stonehenge. However the ILTON TEMPLE was made in the 1820's, a whimsical folly. The graves around the village of **Kirkheaton** can be amusing. There is one with a monument in the shape of a beer barrel, the occupant was a well known local 'boozer'.

Away from the Moors, North Yorkshire is softer but no less beautiful: a charming beauty rather than an aggressive one.

York is generally considered the capital of the north and is also a Mecca for tourists, and quite justifiably so. Architectural interest abounds, from YORK MINISTER and the medieval shops in the SHAMBLES, to the NATIONAL RAILWAY MUSEUM, the diversity of places to see seems endless, and this is definitely a place to spend time on foot discovering all the nooks and crannies. You could easily spend a day in the Minster itself. Work started in the year 1220 and took two and a half centuries to complete. There are 125 stained glass windows the best known being the East Window and The Five Sisters which have made the Minster world famous.

Every year the average meat-eating Briton will consume more than his or her own weight in meat products. In a lifetime each will consume over 36 pigs, 36 sheep and 750 poultry birds.

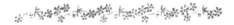

It must be remembered that in 1984 much of the Minster was destroyed by fire, and it now stands in all its glory as an example of excellence, and a testiment to the hard work and dedication of the craftsmen and the people of York.

If you want to experience the history of early York the YORVIK VIKING CENTRE is worth a visit, but do be warned that in high season the queues can be long, so pick your time carefully, and in the meantime visit some of the other exceptionally fine museums or simply stroll around the streets. Even the shops in York are interesting.

All around York are large estates and mansions. CASTLE HOWARD between York and Scarborough is one of the most impressive and was the location of the television serialisation of 'Brideshead Revisited'.

BRAMHAM PARK off the road from York to Leeds is a Queen Anne house restored in 1907 after part of it was destroyed by fire 80 years earlier. The oratory and stable block were designed by James Paine and overlook the lake, with its French gardens where running water is used to great effect.

North from Leeds is the elegant town of **Harrogate**. There is plenty to do and see here. You could go to the ROYAL PUMP ROOM which is now a museum, or try the spa waters, go for a stroll and look at the fine houses and gardens, or visit the art nouveau THEATRE. In August there is a festival of arts and sciences. If the place seems familiar and you are a reader of James Herriot your assumptions will have been correct as this is the place he called 'Brawton'.

Out of Harrogate to the north at **Summerbridge** is the spectacular formation of BRIMHAM ROCKS, 'stacks' of millstone grit carved and eroded by the weather over thousands of years, set in open moorland overlooking **Nidderdale**.

Nearby, FOUNTAINS ABBEY is England's most romantic ruin, and also England's most visited. If approached from the north via STUDELY ROYAL GARDENS, the walk beside landscaped Italian water gardens is a magical prelude to this very special place. The early 12th century Abbey was abandoned in the 16th century, the roof was dismantled and its treasures dispersed, yet it retains a graceful dignity. It acquired its wealth through the wool trade and successful land ownership and was of great size. The Chapel with nine altars and the nave with 11 bays are of particular interest; as now is the architectural gem of a visitor centre, low-lying and unobtrusive in vernacular form yet very evidently modern.

A little to the west, NEWBY HALL is a splendid example of an Adam house set in beautiful gardens, with a tapestry room, Chippendale furniture with Adam's sculpture. There is also a miniature railway in the garden.

Just north of Ripon, NORTON CONYERS is a Jacobean house with a Brontë collection and has an 18th century walled garden still being cultivated, it is thought that this house was used as a model for Thornfield in Charlotte Brontë's 'Jane Eyre'.

The Royal Pump Room Museum, Harrogate

As at Fountains, RIEVAULX ABBEY, yet a little further north, is a truly spectacular sight, huge 12th century monastic ruins set in a deeply wooded valley. An exhibition shows how successfully the Cistercians at Rievaulx ran their many businesses.

Humberside, which takes in the old East Ridings of Yorkshire, has large and imposing industries in and around Hull and the Humber estuary, surrounded by flat pastures. Most of the county is underlayed by a chalk belt, the YORKSHIRE WOLDS rising to over 800 feet, a dry upland with a thin covering of soil and swept by strong winds. It has over the years been reclaimed by the local people and now between August and September field after field of swaying corn stretches into the distance as far as the eye can see.

As the chalk belt reaches the coast it can give spectacular effects, the chalk eroded by the sea into caves, chalk pillars standing defiantly alone against the elements, white cliffed bays and pebble beaches; a visual extravaganza of the forces of nature in action. **Flamborough Head**, a magnificent place for bird watching, is the only place you will find gannets nesting on the mainland.

Further south at **Holderness** the chalk is much lower and covered with alluvial soil left by the ice age. This is now some of the richest land in Britain, the boulder clay of the cliffs hold little sway against the ravages of the sea, and are worn away at an alarming rate of up to 30 yards a year, ending up at Spurn Head, a spit of sand some three miles long. This area of the country is likely to change beyond recognition in the coming years, due to the Government's new thinking on erosion; whether they are right or not, whether we should fortify our coastlines against the sea or allow the sea to reclaim some areas, feelings are running strong. Peoples' views could of course be tempered by how close they live to the problem.

3,850 different additives are currently permitted in food.

HORNSEA MERE is a large freshwater lake less than a mile from the sea and about 12 feet above it, a sanctuary for breeding heron and other birds, try to ignore the people fishing. This area abounds with so called 'country sports', fishing, hunting, and shooting. Perhaps this proves the old adage that there is both a heaven and a hell on earth; possibly it has something to do with which end of the barrel you are looking down?

Northumberland, Durham, Tyne & Wear and Cleveland are the four counties which covered the old Anglo Saxon Northumbria, the Kingdom of Eric Bloodaxe. In the wide Dales sheep are the main inhabitants, but elsewhere the coal industry has left its mark. The WOODHORN COLLIERY MUSEUM at **Ashington** reflects the mining communities' way of life through displays of original colliery buildings and artefacts, along with vivid portrayals by the Ashington Group of Artists. Shipping too has been an important industry and the historic JACKSONS DOCK incorporates HARTLEPOOLS HISTORIC SHIPS along with a history of the ships and the docks.

As large industries creep inevitably inland, most of the coast remains a haven for birdlife, and a delight to the soul.

The old priory on the Holy Island of **Lindisfarne**, the beginning of Celtic Christianity, is well worth a visit, if you remember it is impossible to cross to the island from two hours before until three and an half hours after high tide. The CASTLE was converted into a private house in 1903 by Sir Edwin Lutyens.

Just to the south, the **Farne Islands**, a small group of islands off the coast at **Bamburgh**, are home during the summer months to over 17 species of sea birds: puffins, kittiwakes, eider ducks, guillemots, terns and fulmars just to name a few.

Bamburgh is a seaside village unspoilt by time, clinging beneath a red sandstone fortress jutting out 150 feet above the water. From here you can get a splendid view of the **Farne Islands** and the National Trust bird sanctuary.

South of **South Shields**, around SOUTER LIGHTHOUSE, is a spectacular coastline, an area to walk the open grassland of THE LEAS and look at the famous bird colonies. **Marsden** offers the visitor a descent (by lift) into the bar of an inn excavated from the cliffs, where you can hear and see the congested colonies on MARSDEN ROCK. At the lighthouse you can see the Engine Room, Battery Room, the Light Tower and Fog Signal Station, which were the summit of lighthouse technology in 1871 when it was built.

Inland down the Tyne near **Stocksfield**, wood engraver and naturalist Thomas Bewick, Northumbria's greatest artist, was born at CHERRYBURN which now houses a small exhibition on his life and work. There are occasional demonstrations of wood engraving and printing.

Over 2,000 adults are turning vegetarian every week according to a major survey by Gallup.

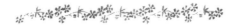

Durham is dominated by its castle and cathedral, the CASTLE is a university and the buildings are a good example of 12th century construction, the best view is from the 18th century PREBEND'S BRIDGE. To get a good view of the CATHEDRAL the best vantage point is from the gardens of St Aidan's College. The cathedral is considered splendid due to the fact that the nave, chancel and transept were built in a single period between the years 1093 to 1140. The two principal additions were Bishop Pudsey's Galilee Chapel in 1170 and in 1230 the Chapel of The Nine Alters. The Monks Dormitory which is attached to the cathedral has some fine Anglo Saxon carvings.

Escomb in Durham has a nearly perfect Anglo Saxon church, and the porch with a sundial over it is reputed to be the oldest in the country. At **Finchale**, on the bend of the river Wear, lies a 13th century priory considered to be the most important remains in the county.

Priors Vegetarian Restaurant & Craft Shop at Barnard Castle

BARNARD CASTLE, near **Bowes** in Durham is a ruin overlooking the river Tees, in the castle is the BOWES MUSEUM, a must for art lovers with its fine collection of decorative arts with paintings, furniture, ceramics and textiles from Britain and western Europe.

Charles Dicken's 'Dotheboys Hall' in 'Nicholas Nickleby', was said to be modelled on the local school at Bowes. Unsuprisingly it closed soon after the book was published!

In the south Durham town of **Darlington** the TEES COTTAGE PUMPING STATION has a good range of motive power machines, and for the railway enthusiast there is a real treat because at the DARLINGTON RAILWAY CENTRE AND MUSEUM Stephenson's 'Locomotion No. 1' and 'The Derwent' are on display. 'Railway mania' hit the north east in the mid 19th century and the area is now very well served with railway museums. At **Wylam** near **Bywell** in Northumberland there is a RAILWAY MUSEUM as well as GEORGE STEPHENSON'S COTTAGE which the National Trust opens to the public.

Hydraulic and hydroelectric machinery is on view at the ARMSTRONG ENERGY CENTRE which has many of such inventions by Lord Armstrong who owned CRAGSIDE HOUSE (the first house in the world to be lit by hydroelectricity) and grounds at **Rothbury** in Northumberland, which were only recently first opened to the public. It is a high and formal Victorian house in grounds which extend to over 1,000 acres, the millions of rhododendrons being of special interest as are the orchard house, Italian garden, terraces, rose loggia and fernery with man-made lakes.

Kielder Water high on the Northumberland National Park is the largest man-made lake in Europe, 7 miles long with over 27 miles of shoreline, and said to be 170 feet deep in places. A place of great popularity for walking and water sports.

At **Chollerford** in Northumberland there have been extensive excavations, exposing a ROMAN BATH HOUSE, with hot, cold and steam baths and changing rooms in a five acre site, as documented in an excellent museum.

HADRIAN'S WALL, most of which is in what is now Northumberland, was built around the year 122 AD and must have been a mammoth undertaking. Built of stone it was ten feet broad and too high to be scaled by one man standing on another man's shoulders, and protected by a ditch. The wall had gateways, a Roman mile apart, called milecastles, and there were watchtowers and 17 fortresses. From one in particular of them, Housesteads, one can get a truly glorious view along the Wall.

The ROMAN FORT of Arabia at **South Shields** features reconstructions along with excavations, marking its importance in the construction and garrisoning of Hadrian's Wall.

Northumbria's history is displayed in a great many excellent museums in the area, possibly none finer than the NORTH OF ENGLAND OPEN AIR MUSEUM at **Beamish** south of Gateshead.

Restaurant

PRIORS

7 The Bank, Barnard Castle, Co Durham, DL12 8PH.
Telephone: (0833) 38141

ADJACENT to the Market Cross near the centre of Barnard Castle, Priors vegetarian restaurant occupies a building that dates from the early 18th century. It has been carefully and lovingly restored keeping its unique charm and exposing many of the original features which make it such an interesting place to be. The restaurant, fronted by a craft shop and gallery, has attractive pine tables on cast iron sewing machine bases, matched by comfortable wooden chairs. From a tiered pine ceiling hangs an abundance of ivy which adds to the relaxing and peaceful surroundings, and to the enjoyment of a meal.

The vegetarian menu provides vegan options and gluten free, sugar free diets are also catered for. The international vegetarian menu, changed daily, is made up of a wide range of tasty and imaginative dishes. Everything is cooked on the premises and the only substitute used is soya-mix. In the eight years that Sonia and Mark Prior have owned this business they have learnt exactly how to please and their customers find that Priors is everything they could wish for. Children have fun with - and also eat heartily from - the "Little Monsters Menu".

On the small but well chosen wine list are some 28 wines from France, Italy, Morocco, New Zealand and England, most of which are organic and all vegetarian. The house wine is rock's elderflower and Guy Bossard's Blanc de Blanc from the Loire Valley, while the red is Domanie des Soulie. Rabenhorst health drinks, Amé, Orchid herbal teas (served chilled), additive free cola and fruit nectars are all available for those who prefer something non-alcoholic. Priors is a restaurant which is the recipient of many, well deserved awards and mentions including the Heart Beat award and one from The Vegetarian Travel Guide.

Useful Information

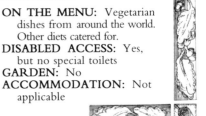

OPEN: Mon-Fri: 10-5pm, Sat: 10-5.30pm Sun: 12-5.30pm. All year
CREDIT CARDS: Access/ Visa/Amex/Diners
CHILDREN: Welcome
LICENSED: Yes. mostly organic and all vegetarian
ON THE MENU: Vegetarian dishes from around the world. Other diets catered for.
DISABLED ACCESS: Yes, but no special toilets
GARDEN: No
ACCOMMODATION: Not applicable

Inn with Rooms & Restaurant

ROYAL OAK HOTEL

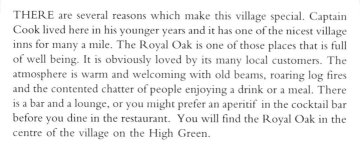

High Green, Great Ayton, Middlesbrough, Cleveland, TS9 6BW.
Telephone: (0642) 722361, Facsimile: (0642) 724047

THERE are several reasons which make this village special. Captain Cook lived here in his younger years and it has one of the nicest village inns for many a mile. The Royal Oak is one of those places that is full of well being. It is obviously loved by its many local customers. The atmosphere is warm and welcoming with old beams, roaring log fires and the contented chatter of people enjoying a drink or a meal. There is a bar and a lounge, or you might prefer an aperitif in the cocktail bar before you dine in the restaurant. You will find the Royal Oak in the centre of the village on the High Green.

The Royal Oak offers small but comfortable bedrooms which are centrally heated and have both television and tea and coffee making facilities. Four of the bedrooms are en-suite and the only single room has its own shower and a separate toilet. People like staying here because it is so friendly and easy going.

The inn stays open all day from Monday to Saturday and on Sundays conforms to normal licensing hours. There are ever changing menus in both the bars and the restaurant. The latter is very popular in the evenings when customers know that they will get a good, tasty meal at sensible prices and with the meal the opportunity of sampling a bottle from the wide range of world wide wines on offer.

One could never describe the Royal Oak as being especially for vegetarians but great care has been taken to ensure that attractive and interesting vegetarian and vegan dishes are always available at each course.

Useful Information

OPEN: Mon-Sat: All day, Sun: 12-2pm & 7-10.30pm
CREDIT CARDS: Visa/ Switch/Mastercard/Diners
CHILDREN: Welcome
LICENSED: Yes
ON THE MENU: Mainly for carnivores but a good choice for vegetarians
DISABLED ACCESS: Yes but no special toilet facilities
GARDEN: No
ACCOMMODATION: 3dbl, 1 twin all en-suite,1 sgl with shower

Inn

THE BAY HORSE INN

Terrington, York, North Yorkshire, YO6 4PP.
Telephone: (0653) 648416

THE village of Terrington can be found from the A64 by taking the turn off to Castle Howard. If you are approaching from York then you follow the signs to Strensall and Sheriff Hutton. Three years ago you would have found The Bay Horse Inn boarded up, yet for 150 years it had served the village well as a watering hole for locals and a welcome stopping place for travellers. The Snowdons saw the pub, liked what they saw and having purchased it, set about restoring it to what a good village inn should be. They have made it warm, friendly and comfortable and patiently collected farming and countryside tools, harnesses etc which are attractive and add to the pleasing atmosphere.

In addition to the three bars and the dining room there is a conservatory which not only adds to the space but provides a very pleasant place in which to sit and eat.

Great thought has been put into the planning of the dishes on the varied menu. Many traditional pub favourites are there but mainly it consists of true country dishes using local and seasonal foods. Talk to Mrs Snowdon and you will discover she is very interested in researching old Yorkshire recipes in amongst which are many devised for vegetarians. In fact there are six snacks, six starters and six main courses as well as several desserts which conform to vegetarian requirements. An excellent Sunday lunch is served at an inclusive price. Wine with your meal is as well chosen as the menu. It is a list full of interest from Europe, South Africa and Australia and offered at reasonable prices; the average for a bottle is £7.

Useful Information

OPEN: Weekdays: 12-3pm & 6.30-11pm. Sun: 12-3pm & 7-10.30pm
CREDIT CARDS: None taken (Cheques only)
CHILDREN: Welcome
LICENSED: Full On
ON THE MENU: Interesting farmhouse recipes. Good range for vegetarians
DISABLED ACCESS: Yes + toilets
GARDEN: Yes
ACCOMMODATION: Not applicable

Restaurant

SALA THAI RESTAURANT

13/17 Shaw Lane, Headingley, Leeds, West Yorkshire, LS6 4DH.
Telephone: (0532) 788400

ORIENTAL 'Joss' shone on the Sala Thai Restaurant when it opened its doors at the beginning of August 1993. It was just at the conclusion of Keith Floyd's Far Eastern trip which excited the palates of anyone who saw his programmes; Thai food became all the rage and the Sala Thai enjoyed immediate success. Its continuing success however has nothing to do with Keith Floyd or any television exposure, it comes from the superb manner in which this delightful restaurant is run.

You will find it in leafy Headingley on the Otley Road as you leave Leeds. Shaw Lane is at the second set of traffic lights in Headingley. The building is some 100 years old and stands in attractive gardens which adds to the romanticism of eating here.

Everything about the restaurant reminds one of Thailand. It is serenely beautiful and quietly gracious. You will be served by Thai women in traditional clothing whose charm is an additional bonus. In the background soft music from their homeland plays and you become lulled into a complete sense of relaxation and well being. It is of no use going to the Sala Thai if you are in a hurry; time is of no importance. In addition to the bewildering range of mouthwatering and intriguing sounding dishes on the ordinary menu which offers a dozen starters and just as many options on each of the beef, chicken, and seafood lists, there is also a complete vegetarian menu with some 10 starters and 11 main courses. The spring rolls stuffed with mixed vegetables, vermicelli, deep fried and served with plum sauce is just one of the starters. Kang matsaman pak as a main course is a superb vegetable curry cooked with coconut milk, potato and peanuts. Wonderful food complemented by a small but interesting European wine list or Thai beer, makes the Sala Thai a restaurant to remember.

Useful Information

OPEN: Mon-Fri: 12-2.30pm, Mon-Sat: 6-11.30pm
CREDIT CARDS: Visa/ Access/Diners/Amex
CHILDREN: Welcome
LICENSED: Yes
ON THE MENU: Mouth-watering Thai food. Special vegetarian menu
DISABLED ACCESS: Yes with suitable toilets
GARDEN: Large, attractive gardens
ACCOMMODATION: Not applicable

Restaurant & Cafe/Bistro

FILBERTS VEGETARIAN RESTAURANT

47 Borough Road, Middlesbrough, Cleveland, TS1 4AF.
Telephone: (0642) 251506, Facsimile: (0642) 251506

FILBERTS is the place to be for vegetarian food in Middlesbrough, with a warm and friendly welcome, and a melange of music adding to the air of relaxation and well-being.

The extensive menu is all home-cooked with fresh produce, organic grown vegetables, wild mushrooms and free-range eggs. Everything is cooked to order. Alison Waldegrave - founder, chef and life-long vegetarian, will happily cook for any special diet, and there are always options for vegans, Gluten-free, and sugar-free diets. Coffees in many blends, espresso (served as in Italy with iced water and a biscuit), cappuccino and filter. The wines are all organic and vegetarian, with numerous country fruit wines, mulled wine by the glass whenever it is cold, and elderflower cordial on warmer days.

In short, the most discerning visitor, whether seeking a comforting drink or a gourmet meal is assured of a pleasing experience at a very reasonable price.

Useful Information

OPEN: Mon-Wed: 10am-7pm. Thurs-Sat: 10am-11pm.
CREDIT CARDS: None taken
ON THE MENU: International vegetarian and vegan dishes
DISABLED ACCESS: Yes, but toilets are upstairs

Cafe/Restaurant

FOUNTAINS ABBEY & STUDLEY ROYAL

The National Trust, Fountains Abbey, Nr Ripon, North Yorkshire, HG4 3DY.
Telephone: (0765) 601003, Facsimile: (0765) 608889

FOUNTAINS Abbey and Studley Royal is a World Heritage Site and the National Trust's most visited property. There will be few who have not heard of it and those who are seeing it for the first time are to be envied. The ruins are romantic and magnificent and the 18th century water gardens breathtaking.

The Restaurant is part of the award-winning new Visitor Centre with good car parking and a National Trust shop. The essentially British menu offers a good range of home-made dishes using Yorkshire suppliers wherever possible. You will find that 50% of the snacks and starters, 33% of the main course and 100% of the desserts have been designed for non-meat eaters. The restaurant is licensed.

Useful Information

OPEN: Summer: 11-6pm. Winter: 11-4pm. Closed Christmas Eve and Christmas Day
CREDIT CARDS: Yes
ON THE MENU: Large number of dishes suitable for vegetarians
DISABLED ACCESS: Yes + facilities

Vegetarian Cafe, Bakery & Wholefood Shop

GILLYGATE WHOLEFOOD BAKERY & MILLERS YARD CAFE

Millers Yard, Gillygate, York, N. Yorkshire, YO3 7EB.
Telephone: (0904) 610676

LESS than two minutes walk from the Tourist Information Centre and just round the corner from York Minster, Gillygate Vegetarian Restaurant with its attached bakery and wholefood shop has become an established favourite of the discerning eater for the last 15 years. The operation is housed in old Georgian stables within a Listed Building in a conservation area and offers outside seating in a pleasant courtyard.

It is simply furnished but very welcoming and offers nutritious and delicious vegetarian food which is freshly prepared every day. The menu is definitely wholefood but has international dishes and changes regularly. The smell of freshly baked bread assails the nose as you walk in. There is no licence and it is non-smoking, but customers are very welcome to bring their own wine.

In the shop a full range of wholefood vegetarian groceries and ecological products are available, together with fresh bread, cakes and savouries.

Useful Information

OPEN: Oct-Mar, Mon-Fri:10-4pm, Sat: 10-4.30pm. April-Sept, Mon-Fri: 10-4.30pm, Sat: 10-5pm. Closed Dec 25th, 26th & Jan1st
CREDIT CARDS: None taken
ON THE MENU: Wholefood, freshly prepared
DISABLED ACCESS: No.
SHOP: Open 9am-5.30pm, Mon-Sat

Tearoom

YORK TEAROOM

The National Trust, 30 Goodramgate, York, North Yorkshire, YO1 2LG.
Telephone: (0904) 659282

AFTER visiting the magnificence of York Minster, the relaxed, informality of the attractive York Tea Room in Goodramgate, a few hundred yards away, is something to enjoy.

Here in a building part of which dates from the 13th century, a split level room is devoted to the tearoom in which you can enjoy everything that is good about traditional Yorkshire and English food. Everything is home-made and vegetarians can be assured that at least 50% of the dishes on offer are entirely suitable. The menu varies daily. The only warning is that non-vegetarian cheese is used in cooking. If you enjoy country wines you will find plum, elderberry, gooseberry, blackberry, parsnip and raisin available as well as a limited number of French and English wines.

York Tea Room shares the building with the National Trust Shop.

Useful Information

OPEN: Summer 9.30-5.30pm. Winter 9.30-5pm
CREDIT CARDS: Yes
ON THE MENU: Traditional home-made fare with vegetarian dishes
DISABLED ACCESS: Yes + toilets

Cafe

J & N's CAFE

620 Attercliffe Road, Sheffield, South Yorkshire, S9 3QS.
Telephone: (0742) 617541, Facsimile: (0742) 422770

ON the outskirts of Sheffield on the Attercliffe Road on the new Supertrain Route, near Meadowhall Shopping Centre, the Sheffield Arena and Don Valley Stadium, and located in the Banners Building - to those in the know, a Sheffield Landmark - J & N's Cafe is a small friendly place with an eccentric and outgoing staff who are fun and at the same time know how to keep their customers happy.

Whilst meat eaters are catered for the needs of vegetarians is a major priority. Every day there is a two course vegetarian special for less than £2! The cafe's home-made Homity pies and Mushroom Stroganoff are especially popular. The source of the ingredients used is local suppliers. All bread products are vegan and some of the snacks. J & N's make all of their main course vegetarian dishes themselves. All the desserts are strictly vegetarian. It is not licensed.

Useful Information

OPEN: Mon-Sat: 8-4pm
CREDIT CARDS: None taken
ON THE MENU: Good inexpensive vegetarian dishes
DISABLED ACCESS: Yes + toilets

Restaurant & Coffee Shop

HEATON'S VEGETARIAN RESTAURANT

11 Northgate, Halifax, West Yorkshire, HX1 1UR.
Telephone: (0422) 350826

YOU will find that the entrance to this inexpensive, pleasant restaurant and coffee shop is through the ground floor of an extensive health food store named 'Food Therapy'. Go up the stairs and you will discover that it is completely therapeutic to eat here in pleasant surroundings.

There are covers for thirty people in a non-smoking environment. The food is exclusively vegetarian with vegan options. Other diets can be catered for including allergies to wheat etc. All the dishes which include soups, quiches, pizzas, savouries and more elaborate daily specials, are prepared on the premises from fresh materials. Heaton's is not licensed but you will find a choice of some thirty different herbal and fruit teas as well as a range of coffees including decaffeinated. This is a cheerful, friendly spot in the centre of this busy town.

Useful Information

OPEN: 9.45am-4-15pm daily. Closed public holidays
CREDIT CARDS: None taken
ON THE MENU: Choice of inexpensive, home-cooked fare
DISABLED ACCESS: No

Restaurant

JAVA RESTAURANT

75 Wharf Street, Sowerby Bridge, Halifax, West Yorkshire, HX6 2AF.
Telephone: (0422) 831654, Facsimile: (0422) 835116

THE Java Restaurant at the Ash Tree is renowned for its fine Indonesian cuisine; the finest in the North of England. From the M62 turn off at Junction 22 or 24 and follow signs for Sowerby Bridge. Once there you will find this delightful establishment right opposite the canal wharf.

Owner Mark Wilson, a caterer and restaurateur by profession, lived in Indonesia for many years before returning to his native Pennines with his Indonesian wife, Enny, in 1981. At the Java Restaurant they serve a very extensive range of vegetarian dishes, and the house speciality is the 'Rijsttafel', a traditional banquet from the colonial days of the Dutch East Indies, consisting of 12 different dishes. The many exotic herbs and spices used are imported from the Indonesian 'Spice islands' and are practically unavailable in Europe. Good at any time, The Java excels with its unique vegetarian Sunday lunch.

Useful Information

OPEN: Every evening: 6.30-11pm. Sunday lunch: 11.30am-3pm

CREDIT CARDS: Visa/Access/Diners/Amex/Switch/Master

ON THE MENU: Wonderful Indonesian vegetarian dishes

DISABLED ACCESS: Yes but no special toilet facilities

Thirlestane Castle

Contents

SCOTLAND

Dumfries & Galloway, Borders, Lothian, Strathclyde, Central, Fife, Tayside, Grampian, Highlands & Islands

Suggested Venues to Dine

Sweetcorn Cream Horns

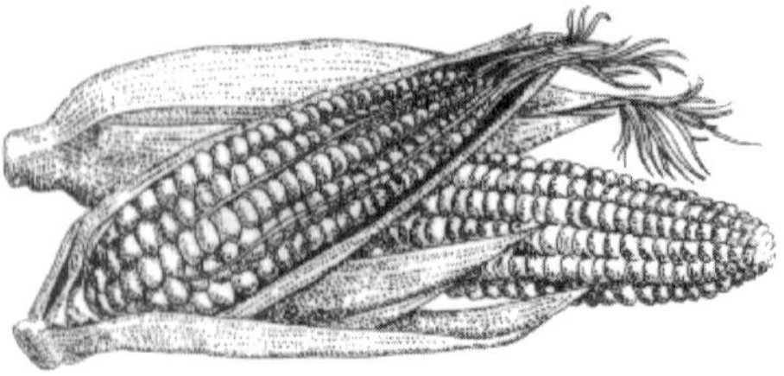

A dish which looks like a dessert but is actually a savoury.

Serves 4

	Puff Pastry
1	Egg
1 lb	Sweetcorn (frozen)
8 oz	Cream Cheese
1 tsp	Rogan Josh Curry Paste
	Alfalfa Seeds, Poppy Seeds, Desiccated Coconut, etc

Roll out puff pastry (ready made or your own) and cut strips 2 cm wide. Wrap around conical cream horns (available from cake shops), brush with egg and bake. Allow two horns per person.

Defrost the sweetcorn and in a processor blend it to a cream. Add the cream cheese and curry paste and continue to blend until as smooth as possible.

When the horns are cool fill them with the cream and dip the open end in the mixed seeds and coconut

SCOTLAND

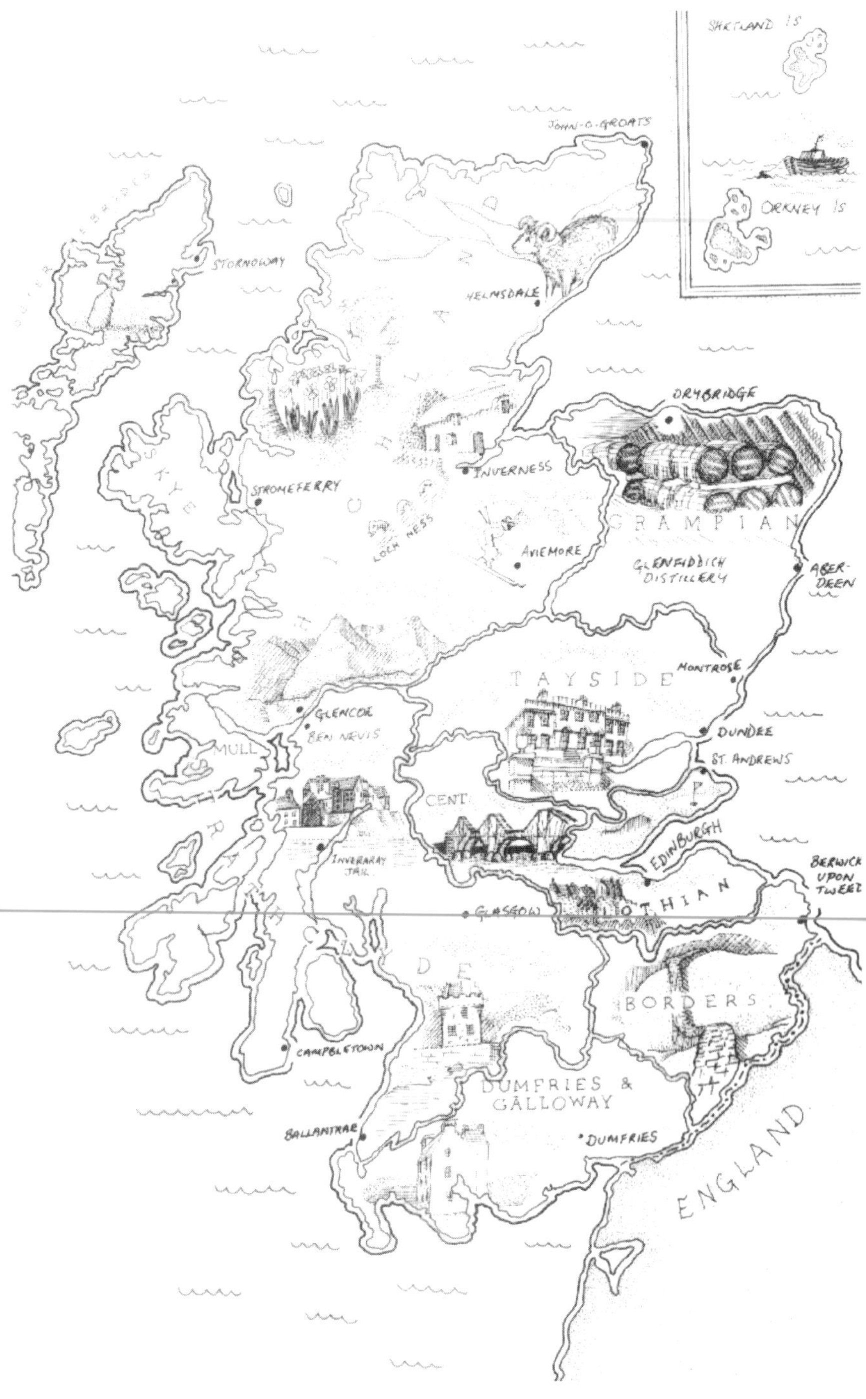
SHETLAND IS
ORKNEY IS
JOHN-O-GROATS
STORNOWAY
HELMSDALE
DRYBRIDGE
INVERNESS
STROMEFERRY
LOCH NESS
AVIEMORE
GRAMPIAN
GLENFIDDICH DISTILLERY
ABER-DEEN
TAYSIDE
MONTROSE
DUNDEE
ST. ANDREWS
GLENCOE
BEN NEVIS
MULL
CENT
INVERARAY JAIL
EDINBURGH
BERWICK UPON TWEED
GLASGOW
LOTHIAN
BORDERS
CAMPBLETOWN
DUMFRIES & GALLOWAY
BALLANTRAE
DUMFRIES
ENGLAND

SCOTLAND

Dumfries & Galloway, Borders, Lothian, Strathclyde, Central, Fife, Tayside, Grampian, Highlands & Islands

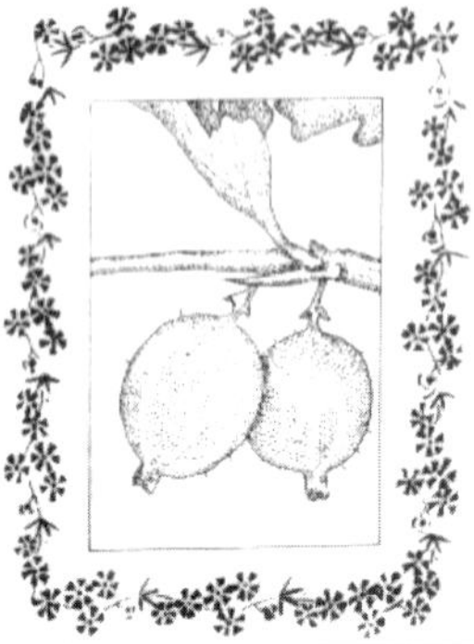

Scotland covers an area of approximately 30,000 square miles, surrounded on three sides by water, which strongly influences the climate of the country and has contributed to determining the character of the people.

The culture of Scotland has been formed by successive waves of settlers and invaders throughout the 8,000 or more years that the country has been inhabited. The name Scotland was derived from the Scoti, a Celtic tribe who arrived in Scotland around the 5th century from Ireland and settled in Argyll. Other Celts arrived from northwest Europe and a strong Celtic influence has remained ever since. When the Romans later invaded they called these early inhabitants Britons, and the peoples of the northern lands were named Picts. The Roman influence was minimal, and gradually these groups came together, a Scottish/Pictish Kingdom being formed late in the 1st century.

Since that time Scotland seems to have had more than its fair share of wars and uprisings, the border with England in frequent dispute, and it was not until the 1328 Treaty of Northampton that England accepted Scotland's independence, but this was then short lived as the death of King Robert I in 1329 led to another crisis of succession, a theme which is repeatedly found in Scotland's history.

Despite many aspects of it having at one time been banned, Gaelic culture remains very strong, and the Highlands still have their most potent symbols, the tartan and the bagpipes, not forgetting the famous Highland Games. The rest of Scotland including the Lowlands where the majority of the population live, has likewise retained its own vigorous personality.

Scotland is divided into three geographical areas, roughly in line with the diagonal border itself. The Highlands, about half the land area, lie north of a line known as the Highland Boundary Fault from **Helensburgh** in the west to **Stonehaven** in the east. This broad definition includes low-lying ground around the MORAY FIRTH. The Lowlands or 'Central Belt', with the highest population density, lie below the Highlands, the southern boundary being another line defined by geology, running from **Girvan** in the west to **Dunbar** in the east, and below this is the Southern Uplands, running to the Border.

Crofters cottages on the Isle of Skye

The fact that Scotland is on the same latitude as Moscow accounts for the sometimes Arctic weather conditions, but it is also warmed by the North Atlantic Drift, part of the Gulf Stream.

Because of the latitude, northern Scotland benefits from the 'Aurora Borealis', the scientific name for the night sky phenomenon otherwise known as the 'Northern Lights' and sometimes called the 'Merry Dancers' by local folk. The aurora occurs as a result of solar flares sending charged particles into space, affecting the upper layers of atmosphere. Though this is most noticeable in the winter it occurs all year round, seen most clearly in country areas because street lights can make the night sky difficult to see. A good display usually starts with a greenish light observed low down in the northern sky after sunset has faded, and is well worth the wait.

A straight line placed north to south on the west coast covering just 260 miles, stretches with the indented coastline to over 2,000 miles, which gives a good guide to the kind of coast to be found. The many islands have resulted from jagged areas of coastline cut off from land by the forces of nature.

The most prominent island groupings in the west are those off the Clyde estuary, **Arran** and **Bute**, the **Inner Hebrides**, where **Mull**, **Islay** and **Skye** are to be found, and the **Outer Hebrides** with the **Isle of Lewis**, also known as the Western Isles. The **Orkney Islands** are to the north, and further north still are the **Shetlands**.

In a recent study comparing vegetarians with carnivores, lifelong vegetarians made only 22% of the visits to hospital as outpatients and spent only a similar proportion of time in hospital.

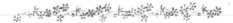

As you travel through Scotland, look out for the prominent NATIONAL TOURIST ROUTE signs (white lettering on a brown background). There are now ten separate routes and if you follow these signs you will discover areas of interest and beauty which could easily be overlooked travelling on the main motorways or trunk routes.

Single track roads are still found in some parts of Scotland, especially in the north west and on the many islands. Care and consideration are the order of the day and the passing places should never be used as parking spots or picnic areas. Many of these roads are not fenced so look out for straying sheep and deer.

For cycling holidays there is a network of rural roads and designated CYCLIST ROUTES, in many places making use of former railway tracks and Forestry Commission access roads. The GLASGOW-KILLIN CYCLEWAY is one of the most popular. Scotland is one of the last areas of Britain where you can pitch a tent away from recognised camp sites, although it is still necessary to obtain permission from the land owner.

Scotland's history lends itself to THEMED TRAILS and you can follow a car trail in Speyside which takes in eight malt whisky distilleries. The Gordon district has so many castles that they are now linked in a castle trail. You can follow a trail through the gardens of Argyll, or discover the Christian heritage of the Solway, or the wool trade of the Borders, and we must not forget Scotland's national poet, Robert Burns who lived in Ayrshire and Dumfries; you can follow his story from humble beginnings to his town house, to places which he made famous by association.

Much of Scotland's land mass being in the Highlands makes this a paradise for hill walkers and sightseers alike. Footpaths or rights of way are defined in Scotland as routes between 'Places of Public Resort', fortunately the difficulty that may arise in defining a 'Place of Public Resort' is avoided as most landowners show tolerance to walkers on their land.

At certain times of year, mainly May to August on humid evenings, the midges abound, particularly where there are damp mosses and marshy places, around lochs, burns and woodlands in the Highlands. They seem to prefer people in dark clothing! Spending the day being pursued and bitten by these natives enables one to understand something of what it feels like to be hunted and eaten alive.

On the subject of hunting, in much of the country the so-called civilised humans follow the philosophy of 'if it moves, shoot it'. The stalking and shooting season is around August to October. It is very important when walking in the Highlands at this time of year to check with local estates or farmers about your intended route, for your safety as well as theirs. The 170 Tourist Information Centres throughout Scotland are of great help on this subject.

Regular dosing of farm animals used in meat production can lead to bacteria becoming resistant to drugs which are also used in human medicine.

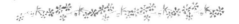

There are several LONG DISTANCE FOOTPATHS, all well signposted, but it should be remembered that the weather can change extremely quickly, particularly along the west coast in the path of fast-moving weather systems off the Atlantic Ocean, turning what was a pleasant afternoon stroll into a much more serious undertaking requiring a high degree of skill, endurance and map reading ability.

Not for the faint of heart is the SOUTHERN UPLAND WAY which runs from **Portpatrick** in Galloway in the west to **Cockburn** on the coast of the Scottish borders in the east. It crosses high ground in places and walkers should be well equipped, for it is 212 serious miles long.

Also not for the inexperienced walker is the 95 mile long WEST HIGHLAND WAY which starts on the outskirts of **Glasgow** and runs to **Fort William** via **Loch Lomond** and part of **Glencoe**. Some parts of the Way are remote and rough going.

The Vegetarian Society claims that around 4 million people in Britain now say they are vegetarian, with up to half the population cutting down on the amount of meat they eat.

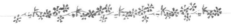

A somewhat easier walk is the SPEYSIDE WAY, 30 miles long, following the river Spey from **Tugnet** at the mouth of the river to **Ballindalloch**.

For the experienced climber 'Munro collecting' is a popular pastime. There are 279 peaks over 3,000 feet, called MUNROS after the mountaineer who first classified them. Only seven exceed 4,000 feet, with BEN NEVIS near **Fort William** at 4,406 feet being Britain's highest mountain. Most of these Munros and the larger hills are quite accessible and within a reasonable distance from a public road and car park. The visiting climber can in a short holiday experience the character of many mountains in several parts of the country.

Scotland is possibly more famous for its lochs than for its mountains. The largest Loch in capacity is LOCH NESS, the greatest surface area is LOCH LOMOND, the deepest is LOCH MORAR and the longest is LOCH AWE.

The longest river in Scotland is the RIVER TAY stretching for 118 miles, and the highest waterfall is the EAST COUL AULIN at 658 feet.

The CALEDONIAN CANAL is 60 miles long from coast to coast, and connects LOCH LOCHY, OICH and NESS with 22 miles of canal, altogether the longest short-cut in Britain. The area around the 9 mile CRINAN CANAL is a truly beautiful sight, and it was constructed in 1801 to shorten the sea journey round the **Mull of Kintyre**.

Water sports abound in Scotland, on the CALEDONIAN CANAL and many areas around the west coast, boats and yachts can be chartered, and there are many good areas of water for windsurfing, water-skiing, jet-skiing and canoeing, in particular at LOCH EARN, LOCH MORLICH and STRATHCLYDE PARK.

Diving is a well established sport in the **Orkneys** where there are many wrecks to be investigated, and the area around **St Abbs** in The Borders is especially popular because of the clarity of water and diversity of underwater species to be seen.

There are five ski resorts in Scotland, **Nevis Range** and **Glencoe** in the west, **Cairngorm** on Speyside, **Glenshee** and **The Lecht** further east in the Grampian mountains. The Lecht is especially good for beginners, but all five cater for all abilities right up to Black runs. Cross country skiing is available at **Glenmore Forest**, **Glenisla** and **Glenmulliach**. Skiing is usually possible from January until April or even May.

Golf, for those who like a little exercise with their walking, is well provided for with over 400 golf courses: MUIRFIELD, ROYAL TROON, CARNOUSTIE, TURNBERRY, ST ANDREWS AND GLENEAGLES, to name just a few. There are more golf courses per head of population in Scotland than anywhere else in the world.

The world's cattle consume a quantity of feed equal to the calorific needs of nearly double the human population of the planet. Yet millions starve.

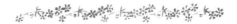

Another favourite occupation of visitors to Scotland is bird watching. Inland, golden eagles and ospreys are to be found in good numbers, whilst the coastal areas and islands throng with the clammer of sea birds. Of the 790 islands off the west and north coasts, only 130 are inhabited by man, many being simply too small and too wild, but they present ideal conditions for many birds, many of the islands being home to millions.

Copinsay, one of the Orkney Islands is administered as a bird sanctuary by the RSPB having been bought by the WWF as a memorial to a naturalist.

There are 70 islands in the **Orkneys**, but now fewer than 20 populated, and that number is diminishing despite the fact that the closest is only eight miles from the mainland. Most of them are low-lying, the exception being **Hoy** with some of the most spectacular cliffs anywhere, soaring to over 1,000 feet above sea level alongside the 'Old Man of Hoy', a splendid isolated stack of red sandstone. The islands have a wealth of prehistoric sites; at **Quoyness**, on **Sanday** chambered tombs date back to 2,900 BC, and at the unique site of SKARA BRAE, preserved beneath the sand for more than 4,000 years, is a real picture of neollithic life; at **Stenness** the RING OF BRODGAR is a stone circle to equal Stonehenge. The vast harbour of SCAPA FLOW between the islands was a strategic naval base during the 2nd World War. The capital **Kirkwall** is famous for the ST MAGNUS CATHEDRAL, and for the Orkney Festival under the auspices of the Orcadian composer Sir Peter Maxwell Davies.

On the **Shetland Islands**, at **Lerwick**, at the end of January each year they celebrate the ceremony of 'Up-Helly-Aa', when a Viking boat is burned. Many of the islands, and in particular **Jarlshof**, have many remarkable remnants of the Viking era. The island of **Fair Isle** is world famous for its unique knitwear and traditions here can be traced back for many centuries, although discovery of oil in the North Sea has vastly changed the islands. Shetland is home to the contemporary poet George Mackay Brown.

On the mainland, the region of THE HIGHLANDS, which covers the new administrative districts of Western Isles, Highland, Grampian, most of Tayside and parts of Central and Strathclyde, has much to commend it to visitors.

THE FINDHORN FOUNDATION on the **Moray Firth** is a remarkable working community which welcomes visitors. It was started in 1962, its aim to foster a common vision and help create a better world through spiritual and personal growth. Workshops are open to guests from all over the world. The 'Ecological Village' at Findhorn is aimed as a technical guide to building greener houses, using natural materials and saving as many of the earth's resources as possible, in an effort to assist those wishing to help stop global warming and heal the world.

To the west is **Inverness** the rapidly growing Highland capital and home, at BALNAIN HOUSE, to a traditional music museum in the town which is regarded as the capital of the bagpipe. Nearby at **Moniack**, the MONIACK WINERY has an exhibition of country wines and jams.

Whisky Barrel Houses at Findhorn

Up the river Ness from Inverness, is **Loch Ness**, created by a geological fault and so deep that a monster could well dwell there almost without detection. Loch Ness is not unique in its monster legends as there have been many other sightings in Scotland over the past centuries. **Drumnadrochi**t is the sightseeing centre for the monster, with an exhibition on this intriguing subject.

To the north, the former county of Sutherland was the 'southern land' of the Norsemen who came in the 9th century and were dominant in the 11th to 13th centuries. It has the best mountain scenery in Scotland. To the north again, in former **Caithness** pre-historic man left his mark with a wealth of brochs (round towers), cairns, forts and standing stones, as well as early Christian chapels. By the small village of **Lybster** the HILL O' MANY STANES comprises some 200 stones set in precise rows, an extraordinary ancient site.

On the north coast here many ships have been wrecked. The PENTLAND SKERRIES off **John o' Groats** are particularly dangerous due to the many vicious whirlpools with innocuous names like 'Merry Men o' May'.

Many of the inhabitants in these far north lands are still crofters although the land use was much changed by the' Clearances' in the 19th century.

South of the exceptionally beautiful **Spey Valley** with some of the finest Scottish castles alongside the wooded river banks, is the recreation centre of **Aviemore** in the CAIRNGORM MOUNTAINS, now home to imported reindeer. In the valley at **Kingussie** the HIGHLAND FOLK MUSEUM gives a lot of information on how life was lived and is lived in this region.

On the far side of the Cairngorms is BALMORAL CASTLE, the Royal Family's Scottish home.

Aberdeen is one of the richest of cities in Scotland, thanks to the North Sea Oil industry, although not every aspect of this association is a positive one and many locals resent the intrusion.

Aberdeen's HAZELHEAD PARK has an unusually large and complicated maze for a municipal park and the village of **Udny Green** east of **Oldmeldrum** contains a circular stone building called a Mort House, used to keep bodies safe from the resurrectionists!

On the opposite coast, the famous INVEREWE GARDENS stand at the head of Loch Ewe. Their superb collection of sub-tropical plants are a wonder to behold in this spectacular landscape.

The area around **Glen Torridon** in Wester Ross is a must for walkers, climbers and naturalists. Here is a 16,100 acre estate with some of the finest mountain scenery in Scotland.

A little to the south, by the village of **Dornie**, inland from the **Kyle of Lochalsh** at the junction of three lochs, stands the EILEAN DONAN CASTLE, once a Chieftan's castle and a Jacobite stronghold, and still a magnificent sight, as are the nearby FALLS OF GLOMACH with a 370 feet drop over spectacular black cliffs.

From the Kyle of Lochalsh the trip to **Skye**, one of the Inner Hebrides, is a short one. This island more than anywhere shows the dramatic contrast of moors and mountains, with working crofts and ancient castle ruins, and the phenomenal natural rock formations of the OLD MAN OF STORR and the ragged lava pinnacles of KILT and QUIRANG.

The awesome size and the blue hue of the CULLIN HILLS literally fill the sky, as best appreciated from **Glen Brittle** or **Elgol**.

Legend has it that the extraordinary CALLANISH STONE CIRCLE on **Lewis** in the Outer Hebrides was at one time giants who were turned to stone when they refused to be baptised, although there are other legends which add further to the mystery of this atmospheric place.

Eilean Donan Castle sits on the island in Loch Duich

The island of **Iona** off Mull has early Druid associations and has remained a sacred and magical place. The even smaller island of **Staffa** is St Columba's 'sacred isle', where, in calm weather, you can explore the basalt rocks which match those of Antrim's 'Giant's Causeway'. The cliffs on the south and west of the island are splendidly perpendicular and FINGAL'S CAVE is truly impressive with its grotesque formations which inspired Mendelssohn's 'The Hebrides' overture.

The small island of **Gigha**, west of Kintyre has very fertile soil, and is especially known for its gardens and valuable plants. At ACHAMORE HOUSE there is a fine collection of rhododendron hybrids.

The AUCHINDRAIN MUSEUM OF COUNTRY LIFE near **Inveraray**, Strathclyde, is a preserved crofting settlement in situ, with more than 20 buildings in various stages of restoration, some of them furnished, showing the way of life of a communal tenancy settlement.

The TREASURES OF THE EARTH exhibition at Corpach, **Fort William** includes a mineral and fossil exhibition, and just to the south is **Glencoe**, certainly one of Scotland's most beautiful glens, the magnificent scenery with its history and wildlife makes every step you take worth the effort.

The Central Lowlands, which include the busy cities of **Edinburgh** and **Glasgow** as well as other important towns such as **Dundee, Perth, Stirling** and **Kilmarnock**, is made up of the regions of Lothian, Fife and parts of Tayside, Central and Strathclyde.

The 'Fair Maide of Perth' was immortalised by Sir Walter Scott and has given readers a knowledge of this lovely area. The town has many museums and parks. One such, the BRANKLYN GARDEN is a truly outstanding collection of alpines, rhododendrons, herbaceous and peat garden plants gathered from all over the world.

The DOOCOT at **Finavon** north of Perth is the largest dovecot in Scotland and now houses an exhibition on similar buildings in **Angus**, a better occupation for the building than its intended one - which was to breed doves for the table. At **East Linton**, west of Dunbar, the PHANTASSIE DOOCOT is a part of the centre at PRESTON MILL with one of the oldest mechanically working water driven meal mills in Scotland.

In **Airth** at DUNMORE PARK is a building in the shape of a pineapple, which started out as a two storey summerhouse, built by the Earl of Dunmore in 1761 when the pineapple was an exotic novelty. It is now owned by the Landmark Trust.

In Fife **Anstruther** is worth a visit for those who like their houses decorated in shells.

COLINSBURGH BALCARRES CRAIG in Fife has a splendid castellated folly to the north of the town, and in **Edinburgh**, probably the most famous of all canine monuments is the one to GREYFRIARS BOBBY.

In Edinburgh THE SALISBURY CENTRE is a residential community based in a large Georgian house with an organic garden near Arthur's Seat. This centre organises classes for meditation, massage, self-healing, yoga and shiatsu, and welcomes anyone who wishes to meet for meditation or discussion.

Robert Burns and friends formed their debating club at the BACHELOR'S CLUB at **Tarbolton** near Ayr, a thatched house built in the 17th century.

The cities of Edinburgh and Glasgow are generally well documented, and include a vast array of important sites and worthwhile places to visit. Much of the interest is historical, but comparatively recent years have seen some exciting developments in the arts, **Glasgow** having been home to the art nouveau designer and architect Charles Rennie Mackintosh whose fine SCHOOL OF ART built at the turn of the century is a true masterpiece. Glasgow is also home to the very special BURRELL COLLECTION. **Edinburgh** is famous throughout the world for its EDINBURGH INTERNATIONAL FESTIVAL as well as the Fringe Festival.

The Pineapple House, a unique holiday cottage

The Southern Uplands cover the regions of Borders and Dumfries & Galloway along with some of the far southern fringes of Strathclyde. This is a region not of mountains but of gentle hills rising from ground that is for the most part already well above sea level. The land is well suited to sheep grazing which led to the successful woollen cloth industry which took its name from the river Tweed, around the town of Berwick-upon-Tweed, actually in England. The Border Collie was used here to help in the sheep farming.

The east coast above Berwick is a ragged one, **St Abb's Head** with its small sandy harbour nestled beneath 300 feet cliffs, is surrounded by caves at one time used for smuggling. The fine views of the rocky coast take in the ruins of FAST CASTLE, the 'Wolf's Crag' of Scott's 'Bride of Lammermoor'. It is a most spectacular promontory described as 'the most important locality for cliff-breeding sea birds in south east Scotland'. The four abbeys all dating from the early 12th century, which lie in a line east of **Selkirk**, have been much painted and much written about in prose and poetry. They are all in ruins, following many border skirmishes. MELROSE ABBEY is the most substantial of the ruins with some fine detail remaining, but JEDBURGH ABBEY and KELSO ABBEY are in a less complete state. The idyllic setting of DRYBURGH ABBEY is where Sir Walter Scott chose to be buried.

" *He who does not value life does not deserve it.* "

Leonardo Da Vinci

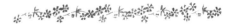

The magnificent ABBOTSFORD HOUSE was built by Sir Walter Scott in the early 19th century and he lived here until his death in 1832. It now acts as a museum to his life with artefacts still much as he left them.

The little toll house at **Gretna Green**, and later the town's Smithy were the first places in Scotland where elopers from England could make use of the Scottish marriage laws, but the law was changed in 1940 and running away to Gretna Green is no longer possible.

The red sandstone ruins of SWEETHEART ABBEY stand on the banks of the Solway Firth with views to the Lake District.

Famous for its 13th century moated castle, **Caerlaverock** in Dumfries can also boast a very important nature reserve. The CAERLAVEROCK NATURE RESERVE on the north shore of the Solway Firth consists of some 13,000 acres of saltmarsh, visited every winter by something like 10,000 barnacle geese. It is the most northerly area for the natterjack toad, a species so protected that it is even an offence to pick one up.

The DEVIL'S BEEF TUB, by the main route north near the spa town of **Moffat** is not a corrupted place name but is actually associated with beef, cattle raiders hiding their animals in the deep dell.

Ten years ago Scotland was a relative wasteland for vegetarians, but things have very much improved; there are now quite a number of solely vegetarian places to eat and stay, and even though the vast majority of places in Scotland still have no leaning towards vegetarianism, there is an increasing understanding of what is required.

Jamaican Bananas

A powerful dessert, impressive at a dinner party

Serves 4

6-8	Bananas, under ripe
2 oz	Butter or Margarine
4 Tbs	Lemon Juice
4 Tbs	Dark Rum
	Yoghurt Accompaniment
8oz	Natural Yoghurt, or Fromage Frais
2 Tbs	Lemon Juice
4 oz	Dark Muscovado Sugar

Make the accompanying yoghurt mixture first. Dissolve the Muscovado sugar in the lemon juice, then add to the yoghurt and mix well.

Peel the bananas and slice them in half lengthways. Using the butter or margarine, fry the bananas cut side downwards until browning, then turn over, add the lemon juice and continue cooking. Separately heat the rum and just before serving pour it over the bananas in a heat-proof dish and set it alight as you take it to the table.

Restaurant

THE VINE LEAF RESTAURANT

131 South Street, St Andrews, Fife, KY16 9UN.
Telephone: (0334) 77497, Facsimile: (0334) 77497

FOR the last seven years Ian and Morag Hamilton have been steadily building a first class reputation in the delightful restaurant they own and run at the end of a small passageway on the north side of South Street just behind the baked potato shop. The Vine Leaf has been awarded too many accolades to mention, deservedly. The building has stood for over 200 years and has seen many different uses but today it is charming, intimate and has a definite feel of the Mediterranean about it.

The Vine Leaf is only open in the evenings from Tuesday to Saturdays from 7-9.30pm and you will find yourself dining in delightful surroundings in a totally non-smoking environment. Everything about the restaurant has style and certainly that includes the menu. As well as specialising in gourmet vegetarian dishes there is a daily changing selection of seafood and game dishes. Imagine starting with fresh chestnut and orange soup, followed by a wild mushroom ravioli with fresh pasta, naturally, and accompanied by red peppers and sun dried tomatoes. The desserts are all tempting but gooseberry and sweet geranium fool is a great favourite. There is a set price for the three courses.

Few people can resist good wine. The Vine Leaf offers a choice of 140 from virtually all the wine producing countries in the world. There are four vegetarian wines and 12 organic. If you are driving or a teetotaller you will be rewarded by a fruity elderflower. As we go to print, new bedrooms are being added to the Vine Leaf and there can be no doubt that they will maintain the very high standard of the whole establishment.

Useful Information

OPEN: Tues-Sat: 7-9.30pm. Closed last two weeks in June and first two weeks in January
CREDIT CARDS: Visa/ Access
CHILDREN: Welcome
LICENSED: Yes
ON THE MENU: Gourmet vegetarian dishes / seafood & game
DISABLED ACCESS: Yes, but no special toilet facilties
GARDEN: Yes, large
ACCOMMODATION: From late1994

Hotel

BENLEVA HOTEL

Drumnadrochit, Invernesshire. IV3 6UH.
Telephone: (0456) 450288

BENLEVA is a former manse and a Listed Building which has stood firmly for 400 years. It is reputedly haunted by a former Minister. Outside is a superb Spanish Chestnut tree which is said to be the 2nd largest in Scotland. On the down side it is also said to have been a hanging tree! Hard to believe that such gruesome happenings occurred in what is now a wonderfully peaceful place.

For forty years it has been a hotel and has acquired a delightful atmopshere of its own during that time, none more so than under the present understanding ownership of Joy and Ian Skinner. The rooms are all attractively furnished and mainly en-suite whilst in the bar you will find a friendly face or two with whom to share a drink before dinner. Sometimes there is live entertainment with a duo or a disco and the gentle sound of Scottish music is played in the background in the bar. In the summer the patio is available for afternoon or evening drinks.

This area of Scotland is renowned for its beauty and hospitality which is why it attracts so many visitors, and for vegetarians there can be no better place than Benleva which is the only hotel in this part of Scotland to offer a full vegetarian menu. The food is imaginative and changes regularly with seasonal variations. You will come down to an excellent and very substantial breakfast in the morning which is more than enough to set you up for a day's exploration of the stunning countryside. Wherever possible fresh, local produce is used.

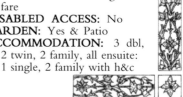

Useful Information

OPEN: All Year: Noon-11pm. Closed: Christmas Day, New Years Day & January 2nd
CREDIT CARDS: Access/ Visa/Mastercard/Eurocard
CHILDREN: Welcome
LICENSED: Yes
ON THE MENU: Wide choice of excellent vegetarian fare
DISABLED ACCESS: No
GARDEN: Yes & Patio
ACCOMMODATION: 3 dbl, 2 twin, 2 family, all ensuite: 1 single, 2 family with h&c

Guest House

TIGH-NA-MARA VEGETARIAN GUEST HOUSE

(House by the Sea)

The Shore, Ardindrean, Nr Ullapool, Loch Broom, Ross & Cromarty, IV23 2SE.
Telephone: (0854) 85 282, Facsimile: (0854) 85 282
From Autumn 1994 Tel & Fax: (0854 655) 282

THIS interesting building which is over 200 years old, was a lochside shop when locals travelled mainly by boat. It has been carefully and delightfully converted with what would be best described as a 'croft house decor' with lots of stone and the use of wood. A spiral staircase adds to the scene. It is very homely and when you sit down to dinner it is just like being at a dinner party at which you have been introduced to one or two new friends.

Tigh-Na-Mara is not the easiest place to find. Taking the A835 north from Inverness, nine miles south of Ullapool you turn west to Letters/Logie. Park at Ardindrean telephone box and then there is a 200 yard walk down through a steep, muddy croft to the shore. Sounds tough but it is more than worthwhile. Tigh-Na-Mara is a memorable experience.

Scottish gourmet vegetarian and vegan farmhouse cooking is how Tony and Shân Weston, the owners would describe their fare. They also cater for oat-tolerant cœliacs. In the five years that they have been running Tigh-Na-Mara they have been recognised by the 'Best B & B Guide', 'Off the Beaten Track', commended by the Scottish Tourist Board who awarded them 3 crowns and appeared in the BBC Vegetarian Good Food magazine. The menu changes every day and works on a 14 day cycle. The cheeseboard offers over a dozen Scottish vegetarian ewes', cow and goats' milk cheeses, even Scottish vegan cheeses.

There is always plenty to do at Tigh-Na-Mara, there are some wonderful walks close by. The area is ideal for those who enjoy active sports and equally for those who just want to forget the world for a while. Ullapool is just 12 miles away.

Useful Information

OPEN: All Year
CREDIT CARDS: None taken
CHILDREN: Welcome - must eat before seven and in bed by 8.30pm
LICENSED: No - bring your own
ON THE MENU: Scottish gourmet vegetarian and vegan farmhouse cooking
DISABLED ACCESS: No
GARDEN: Yes
ACCOMMODATION: For six people

Bed & Breakfast and Evening Meal

THE ROSSAN

Auchencairn, Castle Douglas, Kirkcudbrightshire, DG7 1QR.
Telephone: (055 664) 269 or (0556 640) 269

THE Rossan is an early Victorian ex manse on the eastern edge of Auchencairn, standing well back from the A711 in over one acre of grounds between the Screel Hills and the sea. The house overlooks the bay, and is a convenient centre for touring Galloway, bird watching, painting etc. There are two sandy beaches close by. It is the most relaxing household. The bedrooms are virtually large bed sitting rooms, each equipped with a kettle, biscuits and tea and coffee. Each is a family room. Although there are no en-suite facilities there are three bedrooms and two bathrooms so there are no queues.

Mrs Bardsley, the owner, has been catering for vegetarians since 1960. Nearly everything is home-made and no substitutes are used. Organic white flour is occasionally used in puddings. The Rossan is not licensed but you are very welcome to bring your own wine, beer etc. After you have been fed from a delicious mainly wholefood menu, the tables are cleared and there is plenty of space to write up notes if you are a birdwatcher - and many of The Rossan's guests are.

Useful Information

OPEN: All year except two weeks in January
CREDIT CARDS: None taken
ON THE MENU: Home-made vegetarian dishes, vegan options, plus Gluten-free & other medical diets
DISABLED ACCESS: Yes + toilets but no bedrooms on ground floor

Brasserie

OWLIES BRASSERIE

Little John Street, Aberdeen, Scotland, AB1 1FF.
Telephone: (0224) 649267, Facsimile: (0224) 626558

BUILT in the mid 1920's, Owlies was part of the Department of Engineering at Aberdeen University and is really a warehouse complete with chain pulleys, girders and a glass roof. The decor and the atmosphere are excitingly out of the ordinary. Secondhand wooden chairs and tables stand on a brilliantly painted cement floor.

There is absolutely nothing that matches but with candles in bottles, plenty of greenery from the plants and walls covered with artwork which is for sale, the whole ambience is special and great fun. Here you will be offered French country cooking to a very high standard and with a good choice of vegetarian dishes. You will be hard to please if you do not enjoy the delicious creations placed before you. Nothing is bought in and everything is freshly prepared. Owlies is somewhere that contends happily with a variety of tastes, diets and budget requirements. The brasserie is licensed.

Useful Information

OPEN: Tues-Thurs: 11.30-10pm, Fri-Sat: 11.30-10.30pm. Closed Dec 24 - Jan 6
CREDIT CARDS: Access/Visa/Switch
ON THE MENU: Delicious French country cooking. Vegetarian choices
DISABLED ACCESS: Not for wheelchairs, but disabled toilets

Hotel & Restaurant

AULD KIRK HOTEL

Braemar Road, Ballater, Grampian, Aberdeenshire, AB35 5RQ.
Telephone: (03397) 55762, Facsimile: (03397) 55707

AT the north end of the small Scottish town of Ballater is the Auld Kirk, a delightful, unusual hotel which formerly was the United Free Church built in 1870. With a great deal of care and attention it has been converted into an establishment of charm and character whilst still retaining many of its original striking features.

Auld Kirk is somewhere in which one can relax totally and enjoy well cooked Scottish fare which varies day by day. The menu is designed to please carnivores as well as vegetarians and each dish is prepared using ingredients and produce that is local wherever possible and always fresh. The hotel is licensed.

Each of the nine ensuite bedrooms is individually decorated and has a comforting beverage tray as well as TV, direct dial telephone and hairdryer.

Useful Information

OPEN: 11am until after dinner. Closed Dec 25th & Jan 1st & 2nd

CREDIT CARDS: Access/Visa/Mastercard

ON THE MENU: Fresh, Scottish fare with varied options for vegetarians & vegans

DISABLED ACCESS: Yes + toilets

Hotel & Restaurant

THE COACH HOUSE HOTEL

Netherley PLace, Ballater, Aberdeenshire, AB35 5QE.
Telephone: (03397) 55462 , Facsimile: (03397) 55462

BALLATER is probably the heart of Royal Deeside and is an ideal base from which to explore the many castles, stately homes and whisky distilleries in the area. In the centre of the village is The Coach House Hotel which stands beside the church green. This is one of those friendly establishments where the locals mix happily with the many visitors who come every year. The bar is cosy, the food excellent.

The restaurant offers good seasonal produce, carefully presented and served with courtesy. On the menu you will always find dishes especially prepared for vegetarians. These dishes can be augmented by others if the restaurant is informed. Much of the produce and the vegetables are locally grown. In addition to the main meals there are always good snacks available in the bar. For those who would like to stay awhile there are three double and three twin-bedded rooms, all en-suite.

Useful Information

OPEN: All year. Bar: 11am-midnight STB 3 Crown Commended, Taste of Scotland 1993 & 1994

CREDIT CARDS: Visa/Access/Mastercard/Amex/Diners/Switch

ON THE MENU: Scottish, Oriental & European

DISABLED ACCESS: No

Cafe

GLEN NEVIS CENTRE CAFE

Glen Nevis, Fort William, Inverness-shire, PH33 6SY.
Telephone: (0397) 703601

THE Glen Nevis Centre is three miles from Fort William town centre in Glen Nevis itself, and right next door to the Youth Hostel at the foot of Ben Nevis. It is a friendly cafe, in a timber building that fits well into its beautiful surroundings on the banks of the River Nevis with Ben Nevis across the river.

It is a relaxed place with an eating area, a general sitting about room and a games room. It is strictly non-smoking, unpretentious and inexpensive. The Glen Nevis Centre is open every day from 8am-9pm from the beginning of March until the end of October. The food is excellent, traditional home-cooking which one might describe as International in flavour with a Scottish bias. A large percentage of the dishes are suitable for vegetarians. As we write a licence has been applied for but in the meantime you are very welcome to bring your own wine.

Walking boots, rucksacks and child carriers are available for hire, and the shop on site sells maps, socks, laces and films.

Useful Information

OPEN: 8am-9pm 7 days. Closed end of October until end of February
CREDIT CARDS: Visa/Mastercard
ON THE MENU: Traditional home-cooked. Many dishes for vegetarians
DISABLED ACCESS: Yes + toilets

Bed & Breakfast

NEVIS VIEW

14 Farrow Drive, Corpach, Fort William, Inverness-shire, PH33 7JW.
Telephone: (0397) 772447

IF you appreciatewonderful views you will enjoy Nevis View with its south facing living rooms and bedrooms which soak up all the available sunlight. However that is just one ingredient of this interesting establishment. Built 30 years ago it was architect designed and is fascinating. Everyone who stays here is intrigued. Barbara Grieve runs this strictly non-smoking house, and looks after a husband and children at the same time. Her lively personality and her love and knowledge for this exciting part of Scotland, make her the ideal person with whom to discuss the places to visit.

For those who enjoy lazing about, the garden is inviting, and for everyone the beautifully cooked breakfast is something to look forward to when you wake in the morning after a good night's sleep in a comfortable bedroom. Evening meals are available on request but need to be ordered in advance. With a husband who is a vegetarian Barbara is well versed in catering for your needs. Nevis View is not licensed but you are invited to bring your own wine.

Useful Information

OPEN: All year
CREDIT CARDS: None taken
ON THE MENU: Well chosen dishes for vegetarians, vegans & meat eaters
DISABLED ACCESS: No. The path is too steep

Guest House

AVINGORMACK

Boat of Garten, Inverness-shire, PH24 3BT.
Telephone: (0479) 831614

FOUR miles north of Aviemore, Avingormack is a converted Croft over 100 years old, surrounded by hills and farmland with stunning views to the Cairngorm Mountains. The rooms, two of which are en-suite, are newly decorated, bright and spacious. In fact the house is charming throughout with antiques, paintings and crafts on view and for sale - a wonderful memento of a special holiday. Soak up the wonderful views from the large garden or just walk through the gate into the lovely Birch woods. The owners, Jan and Matthew Ferguson also run a ski-school with ski-hire, suitable for complete beginners to experts. You can hire mountain bikes at the house, play golf or try some water sports. There are plenty of walks, wildlife, birds and trips to see Dolphins and Seals in the Moray Firth.

The imaginative vegetarian cuisine uses fresh vegetables organically grown in the garden, fruits of the forest, home-baking and wholefoods. Sample menus are available on request. Avingormack also caters for meat-eaters.

Useful Information

OPEN: All year except for November
CREDIT CARDS: None taken
ON THE MENU: First class vegetarian fare and dishes for meat-eaters
DISABLED ACCESS: No

Small Guest House

SHALIMAR GUEST HOUSE

Woodside Avenue, Grantown-on-Spey, Morayshire, PH26 3JR.
Telephone: (0479) 873204

IN close proximity to the River Spey and beautiful woodland walks, this comfortable, homely, non-smoking guest house offers you a warm and friendly welcome.

Situated in a quiet residential area of the town, you are treated to the best in vegetarian cooking and home-baking provided by the resident proprietor, Lynne Metcalfe, who has been welcoming guests for the past few years.

Fresh local produce is used as well as organic wholefoods whenever possible. The menu is imaginative and changes daily. Breakfast is a substantial meal, packed lunches are available for those who want to venture afield exploring and every evening a tempting three course vegetarian meal awaits you. The house is not licensed but you are encouraged to bring your own refreshment. Booking is essential for the evening meal. Children and pets are also made most welcome. Bed and Breakfast is £14-16, full board is available. Further details on request.

Useful Information

OPEN: All Year
CREDIT CARDS: None taken
ON THE MENU: Totally vegetarian
DISABLED ACCESS: No

Cafe

WHOLEFOOD CAFE AND RESTAURANT

Plockton Road, Kyle of Lochalsh, Wester Ross, IV40 8DA.
Telephone: (0599) 4388

THIS attractive, 90 year old Victorian building, set in a large walled garden, was built as the village school. Now, instead of classrooms, it houses a Wholefood Cafe and Restaurant in large, bright spaces with the original timbered ceiling still in place in the restaurant. It is an informal, happy establishment which caters exclusively for vegetarians with vegan options. All food is cooked on the premises and the emphasis is on the use of organic and local produce. Such a thing as a microwave is taboo and you can look forward to very tasty dishes at affordable prices.

The Cafe and Restaurant are both licensed. The wine list is small but well chosen and at sensible prices. 25% of them are vegetarian and 20% organic. You will also find organic beers, lagers and cider.

Useful Information

OPEN: 10am-9pm, July-August. 11am until early evening Spring-Autumn.
CREDIT CARDS: Access/Visa/ Mastercard
ON THE MENU: Home-cooked, organic vegetables. Tasty food.
DISABLED ACCESS: Yes but no special toilet facilities

Guest House

BRUACH MHOR

Fionnphort, Isle of Mull, PA66 6BL.
Telephone: (06817) 276

BRUACH Mhor is an 80 year old croft house which has received sympathetic modernisation and is now blessed with the comfort of central heating in the colder months. It is a wonderful place in which to stay and take the opportunity of invigorating walks, brushing up on your knowledge of the bird world and using a camera to capture some of the most beautiful scenery anywhere. The croft is situated just half a mile from the ferries to Iona and Staffa. Bruach Mhor is open all the year round and all day long if you feel like staying in and enjoying the warmth of the house whilst you curl up with a book or write a postcard or two.

Whilst Bruach Mhor is not specifically for vegetarians the home-made, imaginative vegetarian and vegan food always available has become known to many non-meat eaters. Over 50% of the dishes on offer are for vegetarians and vegans and home grown organic vegetables are used most of the time.

Useful Information

OPEN: All day except Christmas Day & New Years Day
CREDIT CARDS: None taken
ON THE MENU: Home-made dishes. 50% vegetarian. organic vegetables
DISABLED ACCESS: No

Hotel & Restaurant

BURRASTOW

Walls, Shetland, ZE2 9PB.
Telephone: (059571) 307, Facsimile: (059571) 213

FOR many of us the Shetlands are a magical experience and this is heightened by the discovery of Burrastow at Walls, a hotel and restaurant of charm, comfort and distinction. From Lerwick you drive due north and west to Walls and then on, up hill over a cattle grid, turn left and keep going to the sea.

Burrastow is a 1759 Listed house which has been in the Foster and Anderton family for approximately 100 years. Old fashioned peat fires, four poster and half tester beds and a wonderful panelled dining room create a superb atmosphere.

The menu, which changes daily, has a good range of vegetarian with vegan options and everything from bread, croissants, etc is home-made. Frequently the vegetables are home grown or locally produced. Meat-eaters are also catered for. Burrastow has an interesting wine list from around the world which includes organic wines.

Useful Information

OPEN: 12-2.30pm, 3.30-5.30pm & 7.30pm. Open to non-residents. Closed 25/26 Dec. Jan & Feb

CREDIT CARDS: None taken

ON THE MENU: Delicious home-made vegetarian and vegan dishes. Non-resident's dinner by prior reservation only.

DISABLED ACCESS: Yes, toilets

Also from
Griffin Publishing Ltd

an invitation to
THE CATHEDRAL CITIES
of Southern England

" an unusual insight into the life of each Cathedral and City and some interesting places within easy reach "

" written by people with a love of Cathedrals and their Cities "

* 352 pages, hundreds of beautiful illustrations
* Available at most good book shops or directly from Griffin Publishing, 24-26 George Place, Stonehouse, Plymouth, PL1 3NY.
* Priced at £9.95 + £1.95 p&p

WITH THANKS

For assistance with the compilation of this guide we have been in contact with all the Branches, Groups and Information Centres affiliated to the Vegetarian Society. Some have been very helpful, and we would particularly like to thank the following:

Bradford Vegetarian Society
Brighton Vegetarian and Vegan Society
Colchester Vegetarian and Vegan Society
Horsham Vegetarian Group
Jersey Vegetarian Group
Ross-on-Wye Vegetarian Information Centre
Tamer Valley Vegetarian Group
Vegetarian Animal Concern, Inverness-shire

and we would also like to offer thanks to:

Amber Valley Vegetarians
Animal Rights Bureau, Bradford
Basingstoke Vegetarian Information Centre
Bristol Branch of the Vegetarian Society
Castle Donnington Vegetarian Information Centre
Chester & District Vegetarian Group
Cookhill Vegetarian Information Centre
Coventry Vegetarians
East Devon Animal Rights
Edinburgh & South East Scotland Branch of the Vegetarian Society
Glasgow & West of Scotland Branch of the Vegetarian Society
Grampian Open Vegetarian Group
Guildford and District Vegetarian Society
Gwent Vegetarian Society
Harrow Vegetarian Group
Havering Vegetarian Information Centre
Hull Veggies
Isle of Wight Vegetarians
Jersey Animal Rights
Keele University Vegetarian Society
Kingston Vegetarians
Lichfield Vegetarian Information Centre
Maidstone Vegetarian Group
Medway Vegetarian Group
Milton Keynes & District Vegetarians
Norfolk and Norwich Vegetarian Society
North Cornwall Vegetarian Information Centre
Oxford Vegetarians
Pembroke Vegetarian Information Centre
South Cheshire Vegetarian Group
Southampton & District Vegetarian Society
Stoke on Trent Vegetarian Group
Tigh Na Mara Vegetarian Information Centre
Upper Deeside Vegetarian Information Centre

USEFUL ADDRESSES

Action Against Allergy
24-26 High Street, Hampton Hill,
Middlesex, TW12 1TD
(postal communication only)
Aims to bring awareness of allergy to the medical community and the public at large.

Animal Aid
The Old Chapel, Bradford Street,
Tonbridge, Kent, TN9 1AW
Tel: 0732 364546
Pressure group working to end the abuse of all animals, particuarly in farming and vivisection, towards a cruelty-free lifestyle.

The Animal Welfare Trust
Tyler's Way, Watford Bypass,
Watford, Hertfordshire, WD2 8HQ
Tel: 081 950 8215
Rescue Centre for unwanted pets. Animals are rehoused or kept and not put to sleep. Special pet care schemes are offered to the elderly and disabled.

The Ark Environmental Foundation
8-10 Bourdon Street,
Mayfair, London, W1X 9HX
Tel: 071 409 2638
A registered charity, Ark provides practical ways (green products and information) for people to care for the environment in their daily lives.

Beauty Without Cruelty Charity
57 King Henry's Walk,
London, N1 4NH
Tel: 071 254 2929
Once connected with the cosmetics firm of the same name, the Charity is now separate. Promotes cruelty-free alternatives to vivisection and animal testing.

Bio-Dynamic Agricultural Association
Woodman Lane, Clent, Stourbridge,
West Midlands, DY9 9PX
Tel: 0562 884933
An approved organisation within the UK Register of Organic Food Standards, promoting bio-dynamic methods of production.

British Library Environmental Information Service
25 Southampton Buildings,
London, WC2A 1AW
Tel: 071 323 7955
Provides a range of information services, priced and free, on many aspects of the environment, from consumers through to technology.

British Organic Farmers/Organic Growers Association
86 Colston Street, Bristol, BS1 5BB
Tel: 0272 290661
Gives suppport and advice on organic production to farmers and the farming industry. Publishes 'New Farmer and Grower'.

British Trust for Conservation Volunteers
36 St Mary's Street, Wallingford,
Oxfordshire, OX10 0EU
Tel: 0491 839766
The UK's leading organisation providing opportunities for volunteers of all ages and backgrounds to protect and improve their local environment.

British Union for the Abolition of Vivisection
16a Crane Grove, Islington,
London, N7 8LB
Tel: 071 700 4888
BUAV campaigns peacefully for an end to animal experiments. Currently campaigning to stop the international trade in primates for research.

British Wind Energy Association
4 Hamilton Place,
London, W1V 0BQ
Tel: 0753 882447
Professional association of engineers and scientists involved in wind energy. Runs workshops and seminars, and lobbys parliament.

Campaign for the Protection of Rural Wales
Ty Gwyn, 31 High Street,
Welshpool, Powys, Wales, SY21 7JP
Tel: 0938 552525
Funded by donations, CPRW is a national environmental charity which organises concerted action to protect the beauty of Wales' coast and countryside.

Centre for Alternative Technology
Machynlleth, Powys,
Wales, SY20 9AZ
Tel: 0654 702400
The centre aims to inspire, inform and enable the general public, to rediscover that a greener way of life can lead to living within the limits of the planet. (additional information given in the chapter on Wales)

Compassion in World Farming
Charles House, 5a Charles Street,
Petersfield, Hampshire, GU32 3EH
Tel: 0730 264208
Leading group campaigning against factory farming as well as genetic engineering of farm animals.

The Food Commission
3rd Floor, Viking House,
5-11 Worship Street, London, EC2A 2BH
Tel: 071 628 7774
Britian's leading consumer watchdog on food, providing independently research information to ensure good quality food for all.

The Fox Project
11 Caistor Road, Tonbridge,
Kent, TN9 1UT
Tel: 0732 367397
A pro-fox information and resue organisation for those who do like to have foxes around as well as for those who do not.

Friends of Animals League
Foal Farm, Jail Lane,
Biggin Inn, Kent, TN16 3AX
Tel: 0959 572386
Have as an aim to take in as many sick, distraught and unwanted animals as possible, and return them to health.

Friends of the Earth
26-28 Underwood Street,
London, N1 7JQ
Tel: 071 490 1555
FoE is one of the UK's leading environmental pressure groups, fighting against environmental destruction locally, nationally and internationally.

Greenpeace
Canonbury Villas, Canonbury,
London, N1 2PN
Tel: 071 354 5100
A non-violent international independent environmental pressure group which acts against abuses to the natural world.

Hunt Saboteurs Association
PO Box 1, Carlton,
Nottingham, NG4 2JY
Tel: 0602 590357
Non-violent direct action group which aims to cause disruption to hunting, with the aim of ending all forms of hunting for sport in this country.

International Animal Welfare Alliance
163 Marsden Road, Blackpool,
Lancashire, FY4 3DT
Tel: 0253 765072
The Internatioanl AWA campaigns againt circuses using performing animals and promotes a better understanding of the rights of all captive animals.

Leauge Against Cruel Sports
Sparling House, 83-87 Union Street,
London, SE1 1SG
Tel: 071 403 6155
Campaigning for Parliamentary legislation to protect wildlife and abolish all hunting with hounds of live animals. Ownes over 2,000 acres of sanctuary land.

London Ecology Centre
45 Shelton Street, Covent Garden,
London, WC2H 9HJ
Tel: 071 379 4324
An information service on ecological and environmental issues, open to the general public, also providing services for schools. (Further information given in the London section).

National Anti-Vivisection Society
261 Goldhawk Road, London,
W12 9PE
Tel: 081 846 9777
Campaigns for an end to experiements on live animals, through public education, political lobbying and the issue of scientific reports.

Organic Farmers and Growers Ltd
Administration: 50 High Street,
Soham, Ely, Cambridgeshire, CB7 5HF
Administration: 0353 720250
Certification: 0449 781814
Advice: 0449 615858
Organic Fruits and Vegetables: 0647 24251
A national farmers cooperative, giving advice on all aspects of organic farming and product marketing, and offering inspection and certification.

Organic Food Federation
The Tithe House, Peaseland Green,
Elsing, East Dereham, Norfolk, NR20 3DY
Tel: 0362 637314
A trade federation concerned with the manufacturing and importing sectors, offering advice, providing certification, and lobbying on behalf of the industry.

Parents for Safe Food
5-11 Worship Street,
London, EC2A 2BH
Tel: 071 628 2442
Runs campaigns and projects to promote public health and a good environment through education on all food matters.

Royal Society for Nature Conservation
The Green, Witham Park, Waterside South,
Lincoln, LN5 7JR
Tel: 0522 544400
The RSNC is the coordinating body for the 49 Wildlife Trusts, mostly county based, throughout England, Scotland and Wales.

Schumacher Society
Ford House, Hartland,
Bideford, Devon, EX39 6EF
Tel: 0237 441621
Engaged in the advancement of education in the use and preservation of the natural environment, promoting the philosophies of Dr E.F. Schumacher.

Scottish Orgainc Producers Association
Milton of Cambus Farm, Doune,
Perthshire, FK16 6HG
Tel: 0786 841657
A central focus for organic producers in Scotland, aimed at increasing demand, providing marketing, lobbying Government, and acting as an advisory body.

The Soil Association
86 Colston Street,
Bristol, BS1 5BB
Tel: 0272 290661
An educational membership charity which aims to promote to everyone the benefits of organic food and farming.

Sustainable Agriculture, Food and Environment Alliance
38 Ebury Street,
London, SW1W OLU
Tel: 071 823 5660
A coalition of organisations in Britain and Europe, researching and promoting sustainable methods, and highlighting the problems of intensive agriculture.

The Tree Council
35 Belgrave Square,
London, SW1X 8QN
Tel: 071 235 8854
The aims are to improve the environment in town and country by planting and conservation of trees and to act as a forum for interested organisations.

UK Register of Organic Food Standards
MAFF, 3rd Floor, Whitehall Place,
West Block, London, SW1A 2HH
Tel: 071 270 3000
Sets production standards and operates a certification system for organically produced foods, and maintains a register of all approved producers.

The Vegan Society
7 Battle Road, St Leonards-On-Sea,
East Sussex, TN37 7AA
Tel: 0424 427393
Promotes a way of life entirely free of animal products for the benefit of humans, animals and the environment. A membership and promotion organisation.

Vegetarain Matchmakers
Westside Chambers, 13 Weston Park,
London, N8 9SY
Tel: 081 348 5229
A dating and friendship agency for vegetarians, vegans and like-minded people.

The Vegetarian Socciety
Parkdale, Dunham Road,
Altricham, Cheshire, WA14 4QG
Tel: 061 928 0793
The membership organisation for vegetarins which campaigns for and promotes a vegetarian lifestyle.

Whale and Dolphin Conservation Society
Alexander House, James Street West,
Bath, Avon, BA1 2BT
Tel: 0225 334511
Concerned with the conservation, protection and welfare of whales, dolphins and porpoises, campaigning against whaling, captivity, pollution and other threats.

Working Weekends on Organic Farms
19 Bradford Road, Lewes,
East Sussex, BN7 1RB
Tel: 0273 476286
The WWOOF provides accommodation, food and the opportunity to learn, in exhange for work on organic farms, gardens and smallholdings.

World Wide Fund for Nature
Panda House, Weyside Park, Godalming,
Surrey, GU7 1XR
Tel: 0483 426444
The WWF is concerned with wildlife, wild sites and the wise use of nature at home and abroad.

INDEX

READERS COMMENTS

In order that we can sustain the high standard of facilities listed in this guide, we would welcome your comments about venues you have visited. We will of course pass on to the venue concerned your approval or any complaints.

Venue visited: ....

Town: ....Date: ....

In the space below please give your overall opinion of the venue

eg. menu, food & drink consumed, service, atmosphere, etc

....

....

....

★ How was the standard of vegetarian fare? ....

★ Did the venue provide you with a good choice of dishes? YES NO

★ Did the write-up give you a true representation of the venue? YES NO

Was there any information other than that in the guide which would have helped you select a venue?

....

....

....

★ Are there any other comments you would like to make?

....

....

....

....

....

I declare that am not connected in any way with the proprietors or management of the above establishment

Name: ....

Address: ....

....

Griffin Publishing, 24-26 George Place, Stonehouse, Plymouth, PL1 3NY